Taxes, Jobs AND Inflation

Timely Reports to Keep
Journalists, Scholars and the Public
Abreast of Developing Issues, Events and Trends

August 1978

CONGRESSIONAL QUARTERLY INC.
1414 22ND STREET, N.W., WASHINGTON, D.C. 20037

Congressional Quarterly Inc.

Congressional Quarterly Inc., an editorial research service and publishing company, serves clients in the fields of news, education, business and government. It combines specific coverage of Congress, government and politics by Congressional Quarterly with the more general subject range of an affiliated service, Editorial Research Reports.

Congressional Quarterly was founded in 1945 by Henrietta and Nelson Poynter. Its basic periodical publication was and still is the CQ *Weekly Report,* mailed to clients every Saturday. A cumulative index is published quarterly.

The CQ *Almanac,* a compendium of legislation for one session of Congress, is .published every spring. *Congress and the Nation* is published every four years as a record of government for one presidential term.

Congressional Quarterly also publishes paperback books on public affairs. These include the twice-yearly *Guide to Current American Government* and such recent titles as *The Middle East: U.S. Policy, Israel, Oil and the Arabs, Third Edition; U.S. Defense Policy: Weapons, Strategy and Commitments;* and *Electing Congress.*

CQ Direct Research is a consulting service which performs contract research and maintains a reference library and query desk for the convenience of clients.

Editorial Research Reports covers subjects beyond the specialized scope of Congressional Quarterly. It publishes reference material on foreign affairs, business, education, cultural affairs, national security, science and other topics of news interest. Service to clients includes a 6,000-word report four times a month bound and indexed semiannually. Editorial Research Reports publishes paperback books in its fields of coverage. Founded in 1923, the service merged with Congressional Quarterly in 1956.

Editor: Margaret Thompson
Major Contributor: Christopher R. Conte. **Contributors:** Irwin B. Arieff, Linda Cumbo, Harrison H. Donnelly, Martin Donsky, Bob Livernash, Kennedy P. Maize, Bob Rankin, Barbara L. Risk, William V. Thomas, Elizabeth Wehr.
Editorial Coordinator/Indexer: Mary Neumann.
Art Director: Richard Pottern. **Staff Artists:** Terry Atkinson, Gwendolyn Hammond.
Production Manager: I.D. Fuller. **Assistant Production Manager:** Maceo Mayo.

Book Department Editor: Patricia Ann O' Connor.

Library of Congress Cataloging in Publication Data

Congressional Quarterly, Inc.
   Taxes, jobs, and inflation.

   Bibliography: p.
   Includes index.
   1. United States — Economic policy — 1971-
2. Taxation — United States. I. Title.
HC106.7.C673 1978   330.9'73'0926   78-13735
ISBN 0-87187-139-4

Table of Contents

Editor's Note

Taxes, Jobs and Inflation surveys the major economic issues facing the President, Congress and the American people, including tax reform and reduction, rising inflation and the prospect of a slow-down of economic expansion.

The book discusses Carter's general economic policy, his proposals to fight inflation and his fiscal 1979 federal budget, as well as his tax reduction and reform package as compared to alternative measures sponsored by members of Congress. In particular, the book focuses on the debate on reducing the capital gains tax, the idea of utilizing tax incentives to stem inflation, and the so-called "middle-class tax-payers' revolt," as evidenced by the approval in California of "Proposition 13" to reduce property taxes and by moves in Congress to roll back scheduled Social Security tax increases and to provide tax credits for tuition costs.

Also examined are farm policy issues and the inflation of food prices; the President's urban and energy policies; and his proposals to curb soaring hospital costs and to deregulate the airline industry. Other chapters discuss changing methods of compiling and computing unemployment statistics; trade policy and international monetary issues; and congressional action to extend federal aid to New York City.

An appendix contains important background material summarizing major legislation in the field of economics for the period 1973-1977. There is also a selected bibliography.

Introduction

"Government cannot solve all our problems, it can't set our goals, it cannot define our vision. Government cannot eliminate poverty, or provide a bountiful economy or reduce inflation or save our cities or cure illiteracy or provide energy, and government cannot mandate goodness. Only a true partnership between government and the people can ever hope to reach these goals."

—President Jimmy Carter
State of the Union Message
January 19, 1978

Jimmy Carter's election in 1976 returned the White House to the Democratic Party after eight years of Republican rule.

But even with a heavy Democratic majority in Congress, the recapture of the presidency failed fully to restore the earlier Democratic confidence that an expansive government could devise solutions to all social ills, steer the economy toward greater and greater prosperity, and still defend the "free world."

Vietnam and Watergate had seriously shaken faith in that view of government. The Arab oil embargo and the ensuing rise in world oil prices had jolted the economy and created a new sense of international vulnerability. Inflation, a growing problem since the late 1960s, had spawned a sense of economic insecurity, leaving voters skeptical of ambitious government programs and making business reluctant to invest in the future.

By the time Carter became president, conservatives spoke with renewed fervor against "big government" and its interference with individual initiative. Even many liberals came to view the 1970s as the beginning of an era of "limits" — limits to resources and to the ability of government to solve complex social problems.

The new president tried to walk a narrow path between the old and new attitudes. He promised welfare and tax reform, national health insurance, and aid to the cities. But he also reminded voters that government could not solve all problems, and he pledged to slow the growth of the public sector.

Mixed Economic Performance

A mixed performance by the economy contributed to Carter's blend of old liberalism and new conservatism.

In some respects, the economy had been running very well. By August 1978, it entered its 41st consecutive month of advance, thus surpassing the longest previous peacetime expansion since World War II.

Since the end of the worst post-war recession, in March 1975, real output of goods and services had climbed by more than 16 percent. Utilization of the country's manufacturing capacity had climbed to about 84 percent from 75 percent. More than 10 million new jobs had been created, boosting civilian employment to a record 59 percent of the adult population.

But those achievements were clouded by continuing high rates of unemployment and inflation. Joblessness had dropped from a peak of 9.1 percent in May 1975, but it still hovered around 6 percent and threatened to edge higher again. At the same time, inflation appeared to be stuck at about 6 percent.

To make matters worse, a dramatic rise in food prices helped send the inflation rate back to double-digit levels in early 1978. In addition, there were signs that the recovery was about to run out of steam, even though unemployment was still unusually high.

Differing Analyses

There were three basic interpretations of these developments in 1978.

The most orthodox view held that the economy needed further stimulus — probably in the form of a tax cut that would increase consumer buying power and thus encourage more production and employment — to help it complete its recovery from the recession.

The orthodox analysis depicted inflation as the result of past "shocks" — such as the sudden rise in oil prices in the early 1970s — that had become deeply engrained in the economy through the "wage-price spiral."

A second view, which shared many of the theoretical underpinnings of the orthodox theory, held that the economy was actually near full capacity. Noting that more people were employed in mid-1978 than ever, proponents argued that unemployment statistics had lost their previous meaning. The higher rates resulted not from a scarcity of jobs, the second theory suggested, but from the fact that generous unemployment and welfare benefits encouraged more people to stay unemployed.

Proponents of the second view concluded that everyone who wanted a job — except for minorities and people with special employment problems — could find one. They argued that further stimulus for an economy already near its full capacity would only bid up prices and wages, and thus foster more inflation.

A third group of economists, much smaller than the first two groups but large enough to receive considerable attention, held that the more conventional theories missed the point. The nation's economic ills, the third group argued, were due to high taxes and big government. According to the third theory, taxes sapped incentives to work and invest, thus holding down production. Inflation, under the third theory, was fostered by the resulting unnecessary limitation on the supply of goods and services, which raised prices.

Under the third view, the best economic policy would be to cut taxes where they would most encourage new investment.

President Carter subscribed to the first theory, proposing to stimulate the economy with a major tax cut. He stuck to traditional Democratic ideals by tilting the cut to the lower and middle income groups. At the same time, he half-heartedly kept alive a commitment to public service employment, and he came up with a new strategy for helping the nation's cities.

But Carter also bowed to the new "era of limits" philosophy by trying to hold down federal spending, and by promising to reduce the relative size of the federal government.

As 1978 went on and concerns about inflation mounted, Carter made some concessions to the second economic analysis, paring back the size of his tax cut. He also sought business and labor cooperation in a voluntary effort to slow inflation.

But he encountered several unexpected obstacles to his blend of old Democratic ideals and 1970s realities.

Middle Class "Revolt"

Perhaps most serious, 1978 produced a "taxpayers revolt" led by the politically powerful middle class.

Tired of government programs aimed to help mainly the poor, and discouraged by continuing inflation, middle income taxpayers first flexed their muscles by lending surprisingly strong support to proposals to provide federal college tuition aid.

Then came Proposition 13, the referendum in California that resulted in a dramatic cut in property taxes. While the meaning of the California vote was ambiguous, Proposition 13 was interpreted generally as an expression of frustration with both high taxes and big government.

That attitude combined with the third economic theory to produce a surprisingly strong attack in Congress on the Carter tax package. The administration was caught off guard by a move to reduce taxes on capital gains — profits from the sale of property and stock — which apparently gained support because of the claim that it would encourage private initiative and help the economy by restoring incentives to invest.

Carter found it very difficult, even in a Democratic Congress, to persuade lawmakers that the capital gains reduction should be defeated because it would help the well-to-do rather than the needy.

Carter's promise to diminish the size of government won more support. Some efforts were made to cut spending back even more dramatically than he proposed, but powerful interest groups — especially farmers and state and local governments — were a major countervailing force.

Dealing with powerful interest groups in the era of limits proved a special problem. Some felt that Carter's new plan to help the cities, for instance, was crippled by the political decision to divide the limited funds available among almost all cities, possibly leaving too little for those with the most severe problems.

Similarly, Carter found himself in a difficult position on health care. He faced stiff opposition from doctors and hospitals in his efforts to control soaring costs. But he earned the ire of some liberals for suggesting that the nation couldn't afford as comprehensive a health insurance system as they wanted.

Winding down the role of government in the economy proved difficult in other areas as well. Deregulating some industries — such as transportation — was questioned by "free enterprise" itself — namely, businesses afraid to go without the steadying hand of government. In other cases — such as energy — deregulation ran afoul of consumer groups concerned about what business would do with new found freedom.

Long-term Uncertainties

As those battles raged, some fundamental questions presented themselves. Could a reduced government still fulfill the old "Great Society" promise to end poverty and inequality? Or did the middle class taxpayers revolt — especially as revealed in the capital gains tax dispute — suggest that society would accept no further equalization of income and that inequality would be the price we would have to pay for further economic progress?

Finally, given the long-term directions of the economy, would the problems of the 1970s become more or less acute? Economists noted with concern that businesses weren't investing rapidly enough to assure sufficient growth to keep unemployment from rising in the future. And even more distressing, few people believed that the limited government strategies to fight inflation — relying essentially on voluntary cooperation of business and labor — would be adequate to slow the unsettling rise of prices and wages to which many of the political and social ills of the day could be traced.

Christopher R. Conte
August 1978

Carter Sets Agenda for the Nation's Economy

In a flurry of activity between Jan. 19 and Jan. 23, 1978, President Carter delivered to Congress his State of the Union address and also sent to Capitol Hill his economic message, tax proposals and recommended fiscal 1979 budget — setting a policy agenda for the nation's economy for 1978.

The economic package was unveiled in the wake of revised Labor Department statistics showing the unemployment rate to have dropped to a three-year low of 6.4 percent (by June the rate had dropped to 5.7 percent). But while that was encouraging news, policymakers also had to contend with forecasts which suggested the nation's three-year economic recovery could falter by the end of the year and that a high-inflation rate would persist.

Carter's economic package was greeted with particular interest, since it included the first budget and fiscal plan that was truly the president's. The fiscal 1978 budget was basically written by Carter's predecessor, Gerald R. Ford, and the new president was able to make only some revisions during the first months of his presidency.

Carter's 1978 economic plan reflected a president walking a narrow path laid out by budget decisions of earlier presidents and Congresses, the uncertain state of the economy in 1978, and several self-imposed — and many thought contradictory — goals embodied in Carter's own promises.

Budget Constraints

Specifically, the fiscal 1979 budget was prepared by the administration — and was reviewed by Congress — in the context of several limiting factors, including:

● The economy, which while improving slowly but steadily since the 1974-1975 recession, was still performing far below peak capacity, and was expected to slow down during the latter part of 1978 and 1979 unless provided new stimulus.

● Inflation, and laws already approved by past Congresses, which would push spending levels from almost $460 billion for fiscal 1978 to $495 billion or more for the new fiscal year — even before any new policy decisions were made.

● Taxes, which would increase substantially as a result of new laws and inflation, virtually necessitating a new tax cut in order to avoid dragging down the economy.

● Carter's promise to hold down the growth of federal spending, and his goal of balancing the budget by 1981 — a promise he had repeated despite the below par performance of the economy and growing skepticism about the chances of achieving a balanced budget by that date.

● Considerable pressure for more federal support from powerful groups, including a coalition of advocates of more aid to urban areas, and also economically frustrated farmers.

The State of the Economy

What Congress did with Carter's proposals depended in part on whether it accepted his view of the economy.

By most analyses, the U.S. economy was recovering from the staggering 1974-1975 recession at a dogged pace, but the recovery was too slow to increase utilization of the nation's industrial plant to anywhere near full capacity.

Most economists predicted that, rather than grow substantially, as would be necessary to reduce joblessness, the economy could slacken in late 1978. Most thought 1979 would be worse.

That outlook led to a general consensus among policymakers that the economy would need some new priming in late 1978 and 1979. Other factors prompted them to focus on a tax cut rather than substantial spending increases.

Rising Tax Burden

For one thing, the tax burden on most Americans was expected to rise just when the economy started to fall, as a result of congressional enactment of a major tax boost to restore the Social Security system to solvency. If Congress approved President Carter's proposed energy legislation, taxes would rise even more.

Estimates of the impact of the policy changes on revenues varied. The Congressional Budget Office (CBO) pegged the Social Security tax rise at $6-$8 billion in fiscal 1979, $8-$10 billion in 1980, $17 billion in 1981, $21-$23 billion in 1982, and $23-$26 billion in 1983.

The House Budget Committee predicted that the House-passed energy package would hike taxes another $3 billion in fiscal 1979, $12 billion in 1980, $15 billion in 1981 and so on, amounting to a total increase of almost $33 billion by 1985.

If the Senate version of the energy program were approved, however, taxes would decline annually by a cumulative total of $25 billion by 1985.

While the final form of the energy program was uncertain in mid-1978 because the legislation was still stalled in conference committee, policymakers could be relatively certain that a tax cut between $20 billion and $30 billion would be necessary just to offset rising Social Security and personal income taxes.

Offsetting 'Fiscal Drag'

The CBO tried to assess how much economic stimulus would be necessary to offset the "fiscal drag" caused by inflation and known policy changes such as the increase in Social Security taxes.

In budget projections released in December 1977, it suggested that Congress would have to cut taxes in fiscal 1979, or increase expenditures, by $33 billion just to keep the economy on target toward the goals spelled out in the second budget resolution for fiscal 1978. That estimate took into consideration the new Social Security taxes, but not a change in tax burden that would result from an energy compromise.

The budget office analysis assumed a fiscal policy goal, adopted by Congress in 1977, of cutting unemployment steadily from 6.5 percent in calendar 1978, to 6.2 percent in 1979, and so on down to 4.5 percent in 1983.

It also forecast "moderate" growth by the private sector. Specifically, it assumed GNP would grow 4.8 percent in 1978 and approximately 4.7 percent each year from 1979 through 1982. One other assumption was that the inflation rate would continue steadily between 5.5 percent and 6 percent per year through 1983.

Under those assumptions, taxes would increase from CBO's estimate of $401 billion in fiscal 1978 to $460 billion in fiscal 1979, $528 billion in 1980, $606 billion in 1981, $692 billion in 1982 and $777 billion in 1983.

Expenditures, assuming no change in policy, would rise because of inflation to $494 billion in 1979, $528 billion in 1980, $563 billion in 1981, $603 billion in 1982 and $651 billion in 1983.

That analysis would suggest that the budget would be balanced by fiscal 1980. The only problem was that, with the forecast growth in taxes, the economy would be slowed and would be unable to reach the levels assumed in the analysis.

The Congressional Budget Office thus performed one additional computation — a complex one — to show what additional stimulus, or "fiscal drag offset," would be needed to keep the economy on the path assumed.

The results were that, in fiscal 1979, there would have to be $33 billion in tax cuts or spending increases to meet the desired targets.

In fiscal 1980, the offset would have to be $61 billion; in 1981 it would have to be $92 billion; in 1982, $127 billion; and in 1983, $145 billion.

The implications of that analysis were several. First, it suggested that the chances of balancing the budget were very slim if Congress agreed to stimulate the economy enough to keep unemployment down and maintain a level tax burden.

"Without a lot of luck — namely, a very strong private sector — the government couldn't achieve full employment and a balanced budget," concluded William Beeman, assistant director of CBO for fiscal analysis.

In addition, the analysis suggested that Congress would probably be cutting taxes continually over the next few years just to keep the tax burden on citizens fairly uniform. That implied in turn, that tax reductions might be the favored form of economic stimulus for the foreseeable future.

Limits to Stimulus

The year 1978 has sometimes been compared to 1964 and 1965, when Congress approved substantial tax cuts to stimulate a laggard economy. By most estimates, a tax reduction of $40-$50 billion would be necessary in 1978 to have the same stimulative impact of the $13 billion Kennedy-Johnson reductions.

But 1978 was different in one very important respect. In 1964 and 1965, inflation was at pre-Vietnam War levels below 3 percent. In 1978, the rate was more than twice that.

Concern about inflation made policymakers considerably more hesitant about approving tax reductions. Conservatives argued that continued high deficits would drive up interest rates as the federal government enters capital markets to finance its debt. They also warned of the danger that federal borrowing would "crowd out" private borrowers, dampening economic growth in sectors that were especially important — such as housing.

Jitters about inflation also came from the equities markets, where there was fear that a new round of inflation would drive away foreign investment, worsening the already bad U.S. balance of trade and sparking further dollar devaluation. That would lead, in turn, to yet more inflation.

Other economists dismissed the "crowding out" theory on the grounds that present industrial facilities were so underutilized that there was relatively little demand for capital for new expansion. They concluded that considerable federal borrowing wouldn't be seriously inflationary.

Still, the fear of inflation persisted, and it was a powerful force working for lower federal spending and reduced deficits.

Carter's 1977 Statement

The president himself, in a televised interview in late December 1977, depicted his fiscal policies as being designed to achieve competing goals simultaneously. Promising to bring federal spending down from 22 to 21 percent of GNP by the end of his term through "careful management and wise spending," the president hedged slightly in his promise to balance the budget by the end of his first term in office.

"Well, obviously, I can't guarantee that," he said. "We've always known that balancing the budget would be difficult."

Carter continued: "If there was an absolutely rigid fixation on a balanced budget, then there would be no chance for tax cuts. But I think when you take into consideration that we have $25 billion tax reductions for the people next year with about $6 billion tax reductions this year — that's $31 billion — that's a major benefit to the people. I just can't give a firm commitment on how we will balance tax cuts versus a balanced budget by 1981."

The president, later in the interview, said he still believed the unemployment rate could be reduced "below" 6 percent.

"We want to cut the unemployment rate down considerably, and of course, we want to deal with the problems of the cities," he said. "We want to meet the legitimate needs of our people and at the same time not let inflation get out of hand."

The Spending Equation

While inflation made tax reductions a likely prospect, it posed a less pleasant task for budget writers on the spending side of the equation. The growth of existing programs due to inflation and policy changes already approved by Congress would increase total spending almost to the $500 billion level.

By some estimates, about 50 percent of the federal budget is indexed, either directly or indirectly, to rise automatically with inflation. Openly indexed are programs such as Social Security and federal retirement. Indirectly indexed are a wide variety of programs, such as Medicare and Medicaid which, because the government pays medical bills after they are incurred, reflect inflation in health care costs regularly.

The CBO estimated that current policy expenditures in fiscal 1979 would reach $495 billion. That figure assumed that Congress would enact health care cost control measures designed to save $3 billion, even though the prospects for enacting the anti-inflation proposals were considered slim in 1978.

The largest expected growth area was Social Security, which the CBO said would require $10 billion in new expenditures in 1979 as a result of previously mandated benefit increases. Federal pay increases would cost an extra $4 billion, interest costs would rise $3 billion and so on.

In addition, the CBO expected special inflationary pressures to require adjustments of $3 billion to maintain the 1978 level of grants and other purchases, and $2 billion to maintain the 1978 level of defense purchases.

The conclusion that emerged was that there would be relatively little room for new programs or enrichment of existing programs — especially if Carter and Congress held the budget to $500 billion.

"Whoever's economic assumptions you use, it's going to take very nearly $500 billion to carry on existing programs without any new initiatives at all," said Senate Budget Committee senior counsel Sidney L. Brown.

New Pressures

But there were considerable pressures on the administration and Congress to increase spending in several areas. In some, Carter had committed himself to new spending.

Defense spending rose in Carter's fiscal 1979 budget, despite the president's campaign promise to decrease it by $7 billion in the first year of his term.

As in recent years past, the defense budget was a major source of controversy in 1978. Defense outlays declined steadily in real terms from the peak of the Vietnam War in the late 1960s until 1975, and they have climbed since then.

Among the factors that increased defense spending in fiscal 1979 were concerns in the administration that conventional forces in Europe needed to be strengthened to avert the non-nuclear Soviet threat there. Carter committed himself to a 3 percent real increase in U.S. contributions to the North Atlantic Treaty Organization (NATO).

The other major new initiative in Carter's budget was the president's urban policy, which was sent to Congress on March 27, 1978. *(See p. 117)*

Other new policy areas that were raised by the budget included:

● Welfare reform. Carter said that his proposal would cost an additional $2 billion, but other estimates ranged as high as $15 billion.

● National health insurance. The administration planned to submit a proposal late in 1978, although it did not expect action on it that year. The fiscal implications would be a major issue.

● Jobs programs. The Comprehensive Employment and Training Act (CETA) was up for renewal in 1978, and budget considerations focused on its future and its relationship to welfare reform. *(See p. 71)*

● Transportation. Highway and mass transit programs were due for reauthorization as well, and Congress was expected to debate financing mechanisms for both programs.

Carter's Economic Message

Outlining an overall strategy that attempted to balance the conflicting pressures of reducing inflation, unemployment and taxes, President Carter on Jan. 20, 1978, sent to Congress his economic message. The president proposed reducing taxes by $25 billion, while allowing only a slight increase in federal spending during the coming year.

The message, which contained no real surprises, included proposals to attack structural unemployment among groups particularly hard-hit by joblessness, and several suggestions for reducing the rate of inflation through voluntary efforts by government, business and labor.

In general, the message suggested only a cautious departure from existing economic policies while maintaining the administration's previous goals of reducing unemployment and at the same time decreasing the federal share of gross national product (GNP). It did mark a retreat from earlier, quite ambitious, hopes of reducing the inflation rate substantially, though.

"I have begun from the premise that our economy is basically healthy, but that well-chosen government policies will assure continued progress toward our economic goals," the president said.

Carter said his economic policies were guided by four basic objectives: reducing unemployment, especially among the disadvantaged; relying principally on private sector expansion to bring down joblessness; reducing the rate of inflation; and contributing to the health of the world economy.

To meet those objectives, Carter listed eight principal elements in his economic strategy.

Adoption of a National Energy Policy

The president reiterated his call on Congress to enact a national energy policy that would reduce energy consumption while encouraging production. He said the policy should be designed so that no segment of the population bears a disproportionate share of the cost, and so that no industry reaps "unnecessary and undeserved windfall gains."

Careful Management of Expenditures

Carter said he would propose increasing total federal expenditures by less than 2 percent, adjusted for inflation. That would reduce the federal share of GNP from 22.5 percent to 22 percent, moving toward his goal of 21 percent.

The president suggested that careful management, including techniques such as zero-base budgeting and multiyear budgeting, would help achieve that goal.

Tax Reductions

Carter said tax reductions would be the principal method by which the federal government would promote growth. Specifically, he recommended tax cuts totaling $34 billion and "reforms" that would increase revenues by $9 billion — for a net reduction of $25 billion. All changes would take effect at the beginning of the new fiscal year on Oct. 1.

The package included personal tax reductions of $24 billion, offset by $7 billion in tax "reforms." The principal recommendations included an across-the-board reduction in personal tax rates "with special emphasis on low- and middle-income taxpayers."

In addition, Carter recommended "simplifying" personal taxes by replacing the existing personal exemption and credit with a $240 tax credit for each person in a taxpayer's family.

Carter said the proposal would make the tax system more progressive. For a typical four-person family with $15,000 in income, the reduction would amount to $258, or 19 percent, he said.

The president proposed business tax reductions totaling $8 billion, offset by $2 billion in reforms.

Carter's Council of Economic Advisers Warns of...

While fiscal policy can be used to help sustain the nation's slow economic recovery, it cannot provide for full employment without sparking an unacceptable new round of inflation, according to President Carter's economic advisers.

That conclusion, which shed new light on how the administration would interpret its responsibilities under the Humphrey-Hawkins full employment bill, was contained in the annual report of the President's Council of Economic Advisers. The report, released Jan. 31, 1978, was prepared by the three council members, Charles L. Schultze, Lyle E. Gramley and William Nordhaus.

In general, the report reflected the administration's confidence that the economy was basically healthy, and that fairly modest government stimulus would keep it growing.

But beyond that, the report suggested that the administration was deeply concerned about the sluggish pace of business investment, and about continuingly high rates of inflation.

The report argued that the unusually low level of investment was a major cause of the slowness of the economic recovery, and that it could be a worsening problem in the future.

It also suggested that inflation was a major constraint on fiscal — tax and spending — policy, making the 4 percent unemployment goal established in the Humphrey-Hawkins bill (HR 50) unachievable by traditional government pump-priming techniques.

That, in turn, led the economic advisers to shift their emphasis in the report away from fiscal policy as a means of achieving full employment toward other policies which they suggested can "reduce the conflict between low unemployment and inflation."

The Economy in 1977

The economic advisers described the performance of the economy in 1977 with considerable satisfaction.

They concluded that at the end of the year, the economy was healthy, although still operating below its capacity.

"Prospects for a continued expansion were favorable as 1977 came to a close," the report said. "The sectors of the economy were in good balance, inventories were relatively lean, and the balance sheets of businesses and financial institutions were strong."

Business Investment Problem

The economic advisers singled out business investment as a particular problem, however. At the end of 1977, they reported business investment was still 2 percent below its previous peak level, which had been reached four years earlier. At a comparable stage in the four major previous recoveries, investment was 14 percent higher than its previous peak, the advisers noted.

"At a time when strong growth in capital stock is needed to meet future goals, investment appears to be drifting below normal trends," the report said. "This drift must be reversed."

The economic advisers were hard-pressed to explain the low level of business investment. They said it was lower than traditional indicators — such as the growth in output, capacity utilization and cash flow — would suggest. They concluded that business had been exceptionally cautious about investing in light of the severity of the last recession and continued uncertainty about inflation, energy costs, government regulation, and the excess capacity and slow rate of growth in other industrialized nations.

The uncertainty argument was amplified by a finding that, while investment in plant and equipment continued at about the levels that would be expected, investment in structures accounted for much of the overall shortfall in 1977. In testimony before the House Ways and Means Committee Jan. 31, Schultze argued that businesses were still wary about investing in structures because of the long period of time it takes to recover such funds in the form of increased sales. The relatively smaller investments in plant and equipment can be recovered much more quickly, and hence are seen as being safer, he said.

The economic advisers' concern about investment explained a major part of Carter's economic strategy, including especially his proposals to cut corporate tax rates and to liberalize the investment tax credit. In particular, the Carter recommendation that the investment tax credit be extended to investments in structures was explained by the economic advisers' analysis.

The report repeated a number of familiar arguments in support of the general contention that economic stimulus would be needed to keep the recovery going in fiscal 1979. It observed that the rapid rate of consumer spending and housing construction, which have fueled much of the recovery, were unlikely to continue, and that the government would have to step in to keep up the economic pace. It also described a number of fiscal "drags" — including scheduled increases in Social Security taxes and the increases in taxes resulting from inflation — that would slow down the economy without some government "offset."

But a major emphasis of the council's report was that, while government stimulus was needed in the coming year, there were limits to how much the government could boost the economy without causing unacceptable inflation. The economic advisers said they do not consider accelerating inflation a serious danger in fiscal 1979 — even though the budget deficit resulting from Carter's proposals would be $60.6 billion. But they warned that inflation poses a real threat thereafter. "At the present time there are still ample supplies of idle labor and capital resources available. In the period immediately ahead, growth in real output can therefore proceed at a rate above its longterm trend without risking a resurgence of demand-induced inflation," the report said.

In testimony before the congressional Joint Economic Committee, Schultze argued that the proposed deficit would not be inflationary because of unusual slack in the economy resulting from a very substantial surplus in state and local government budgets. He estimated that surplus — much of it in pension funds — to be about $30 billion.

. . .Inflation Risk In Efforts to Cut Unemployment

The administration's concern about inflation was carried over into the report's discussion of the Humphrey-Hawkins bill, which Carter endorsed. While the main feature of the bill was a provision setting a federal goal of reducing the unemployment rate to 4 percent within five years, the economic advisers emphasized provisions in the compromise version that strengthened the president's hand to reject full employment policies that would be inflationary.

The report went on to call the 4 percent unemployment goal "very ambitious," and it suggested that traditional fiscal policy would not be able to achieve it without setting off inflation.

"Given the present structure [of labor and product markets], it is unlikely that a 4 percent unemployment rate could be achieved through aggregate demand policies alone without at the same time causing a significant increase in the rate of inflation," the report said. "Responsible policy, however, requires not that we abandon efforts to reach the 1983 unemployment goal, but that we work steadily to reduce the conflict between unemployment and inflation by developing structural measures to improve the functioning of markets."

Structural Unemployment

The economic report argued specifically that the overall unemployment rate was no longer a good measure of the "tightness" of labor markets, and hence of the danger that economic stimulus would be inflationary.

It has traditionally been believed that, during periods of high unemployment, government policies stimulating demand prompt employers to hire more workers in order to increase output. Inflation is considered no danger in such conditions, because the supply of labor is sufficient to keep the demand for additional workers from bidding wages up. But during periods of low unemployment, stimulating demand is more likely to increase wages and prices, because the economy at such times is already producing near its total capacity.

The economic advisers suggested that the overall unemployment rate was no longer a good measure of when labor markets are so tight that increasing demand would result in higher prices rather than increased output. That is because the 1978 labor force included more groups with traditionally high joblessness rates—including teen-agers and the disadvantaged — who were not actually available to be called on to increase output during periods of high demand.

That theory, foreshadowed in the president's budget, suggested that policies to stimulate aggregate demand may be more inflationary than they were once considered. The administration budget suggested that an unemployment rate of 4.9 percent in 1978 would reflect the same degree of labor market "tightness" as a 4 percent rate reflected in the 1950s.

The conclusion that flowed from that argument was that efforts to stimulate the economy to grow enough to reduce unemployment to below 4.9 percent would be inflationary, and possibly would not succeed anyway.

The economic advisers argued in their report that the "conflict" between unemployment and inflation could be reduced by attacking "structural unemployment," which is the joblessness among groups that are unable to work even when jobs are available.

Ending structural unemployment would do more than fiscal policy to reduce the overall joblessness rate, since it would make it easier for teen-agers and the disadvantaged to move into jobs as the economy grows. At the same time, it would ease inflationary pressures by making more workers available for jobs, thus bidding wages down.

The economic advisers suggested that training and employment programs have been "fairly successful" in reducing structural unemployment. But they were more critical of public service jobs. "Until recently...regular public service employment programs for adults have not focused significantly on the structurally unemployed to the extent that they should," they said. "As the overall unemployment rate declines, employment and training programs should be carefully directed demographically and geographically toward this goal."

The Anti-Inflation Effort

While concluding that traditional approaches to bringing down unemployment were unlikely to succeed without setting off renewed inflation, the economic advisers also argued that the traditional means of controlling inflation — by cutting national output and increasing unemployment — would not work either.

They suggested that the 1978 6 percent rate of inflation was a result not of excess demand, but rather of an "inflationary momentum" that sustained the steady rise in prices from previous periods.

Carter's anti-inflation policy was based on a request for voluntary commitments from business and labor to hold price and wage increases to less than the percentage increase of the year before. Carter said that government would do its part by trying to control the cost-raising impact of various regulations.

The 1978 Outlook

The Council of Economic Advisers predicted that inflation would continue at about the 6 percent pace through 1978 without any "deceleration" effort. Schultze has said the administration hoped to shave about a half a percentage point off that rate through its voluntary "arduous task of unwinding." If Congress approved Carter's stimulus package, the council predicted that GNP would rise by 4.5 to 5 percent, adding about 2.75 million new jobs to the labor force. The labor force was expected to increase by 2.25 to 2.5 million, so the net result would be a decrease in the unemployment rate to about 6 or 6.25 percent.

One fairly encouraging prediction was that the nation's massive balance of trade deficit — $26.7 billion in 1977 — would not grow worse, although it was unlikely to improve much. The council predicted little change in the amount of oil imports during the year, and it expressed hope that foreign economies would improve, thus strengthening U.S. exports.

Specifically, he recommended reducing the overall corporate tax rate from 48 to 45 percent in fiscal year 1979, and to 44 percent in fiscal year 1980. In addition, he proposed making the 10 percent investment tax credit permanent, and extending it to cover investment in industrial and utility structures. He also proposed liberalizing the credit so that it could be used to offset up to 90 percent of a corporation's federal tax liability, as opposed to the existing 50 percent limit.

Carter mentioned in his economic message that his business tax "reform" proposals would include recommendations to "reduce the deductibility of a large class of business entertainment expenses," and to change the tax status of international business transactions (presumably by phasing out tax advantages given to export earnings of domestic international sales corporations, or DISCs).

Other Carter proposals would eliminate the federal telephone excise tax and reduce the unemployment insurance tax rate, for a $2 billion revenue loss.

The president's total $25 billion tax reduction would help offset a $15 billion increase in unemployment insurance and Social Security taxes previously approved by Congress, and a roughly $15 billion increase in personal taxes resulting from inflation pushing taxpayers into higher tax brackets, according to the chairman of the president's Council of Economic Advisers, Charles L. Schultze.

Schultze said the net effect for individual taxpayers would be a tax reduction, and he argued that the president's proposals would provide enough new economic stimulus to keep the nation on a path toward growth and diminished unemployment.

Carter said that, without the proposed tax cut, the economic growth rate would slow from about 6 percent in 1977 to 3.5 percent in 1979. Unemployment would stop going down and might start rising, and new business investment would grow much less than expected, he said.

With the reduction, Carter predicted economic growth of between 4.5 and 5 percent in 1978 and 1979. He said that one million new jobs would be created, and that unemployment would decline as a result to around 5.5 or 6 percent by late 1979. The joblessness rate was 6.4 percent at the end of 1977.

The president noted that additional tax reductions might well be needed in fiscal year 1980, but he refused to commit himself to proposing any in 1978.

Reducing the Federal Deficit

Carter, who promised repeatedly to try to balance the federal budget by the end of his first term, suggested in his economic message that his success would depend largely on the strength of the private economy. He also said that two other factors would have particular importance: the financial condition of state and local governments, whose $30 billion surplus had "set a drag on the economy," and the extent to which the American foreign trade deficit could be reduced.

Schultze suggested the trade deficit in 1978 "will be in the same ballpark" as 1977's enormous imbalance. *(Trade problems, p. 111)*

Recognizing that chances for a balanced budget by fiscal year 1981 were growing slim, Carter hinted that goal might have to be deferred.

"With unusually strong growth in the private economy, we would need a balanced federal budget. In an economy growing less strongly, however, balancing the budget by 1981 would be possible only by forgoing tax reductions needed to reach our goal of high employment," he said. "In those circumstances, the date for reaching the goal of budget balance would have to be deferred."

Attacking Structural Unemployment

Carter argued in his message that the best way to bring down the joblessness rate, especially among disadvantaged black and Spanish-speaking people, while avoiding excess spending that might be inflationary, would be with programs aimed at the particular problem groups.

He recommended several approaches to the problem of structural unemployment, including:

• Continuing public service employment at the 725,000-job level it would reach in March through fiscal 1979. He said the number of jobs could be reduced gradually in subsequent years as unemployment declines. *(Public Service Jobs, p. 71)*

• Expanding the Youth Employment and Demonstration Projects Act to $1.2 billion, enough to provide 166,000 job slots.

• Providing money in the budget for 50,000 jobs as part of a demonstration project to launch Carter's welfare reform proposals. The program, as recommended by the president in 1977, would ultimately provide 1.4 million jobs to help welfare recipents get off the welfare roles.

• A $400 million new initiative for private sector hiring of the disadvantaged.

• Expansion of the Job Corps to add 13,000 new employment and training positions.

Carter also emphasized in his economic message his support for the Humphrey-Hawkins full-employment bill.

Promoting Capital Formation

Carter acknowledged that the rate of new business investment had been inadequate to assure enough future economic growth to keep unemployment down. He said that his tax and other economic proposals should assure business an expanding market for new output by promoting a "sustainable rate of economic recovery." He also suggested that investment opportunities should increase since his business tax reductions would increase after-tax profits.

Reducing the Rate of Inflation

Carter's anti-inflation package included a promise to create a "high level interagency committee" to work with various regulatory agencies in an attempt to consider the inflationary impact of various government regulations.

In addition, Carter proposed that business and labor work voluntarily to "decelerate" the rate of wage and price increases.

"This program does not establish a uniform set of numerical standards against which each price or wage action is to be measured. The past inflation has introduced too many distortions in the economy to make that possible or desirable," Carter said. "But it does establish a standard of behavior to reduce the rate of wage and price increase in 1978 to below the average rate of the past two years."

Schultze said the administration would focus its efforts to "consult" over wage and price increases in industries where there are particular problems or where there is a good chance of slowing inflation.

He said each industry would be judged according to its own particular circumstances, and that the discussions over appropriate increases would take place largely in private. But he said the administration would take its case to the public "from time to time when there is something that doesn't conform to the kind of standard of behavior" proposed by the administration.

Schultze said the administration hoped its anti-inflation efforts would be able to bring down the rise in wages and prices by half a percentage point a year. The rate was 6 percent in 1977, and most economists predicted about the same rate would continue through 1978.

The president's economic adviser said that wage-price controls had been ruled out, but that other "novel" approaches to reducing inflation by tax reductions or tax incentives might be considered in the future.

Carter did recommend, however, that state governments planning tax reductions should "consider the advantages to the national economy of reducing sales taxes, thereby helping to slow inflation."

International Economic Policies

Carter pledged in his economic message to continue promoting economic recovery and to help reduce widespread imbalances in international payments. The United States would focus its efforts on devising a national energy plan, he said.

Beyond that, the president called on nations whose economies have "slack" to stimulate growth. And in a comment aimed especially at Japan, he said that "lifting restraints on imports from abroad and reducing excessive government efforts to promote exports would be useful." Carter said that the Japanese said they would take steps toward reducing their trade surplus.

Concerning the unsteady state of the dollar in international markets, Carter said the United States "will not permit speculative activities in currency markets to disrupt our economy or those of our trading partners." But he said the system of flexible exchange rates has operated well since its inception in 1973.

The president also pledged to support a proposal to strengthen the International Monetary Fund by establishing a new Supplementary Financing Facility to "encourage countries with severe payments problems to adopt orderly and responsible corrective measures."

Carter ended his message with a reiteration of the United States' support for a "free and open trading system."

"The United States will firmly resist the demands for protection that inevitably develop when the world economy suffers from high unemployment," he said. "But international competition must be fair. We have already taken and we will, when necessary, continue to take steps to ensure that our businesses and workers do not suffer from unfair trade practices."

Reaction: Few Rave Reviews

Carter's economic proposals had something to please — and something to displease — almost everyone. But, because of the apparent absence of any dramatic new ideas in the budget, the tax program and the economic message, reactions generally ranged only from faint praise to mild condemnation.

The overall fiscal plan — relatively slow spending growth and a moderate tax reduction — was thought to be within the range of stimulus judged necessary to achieve the 4.75 percent growth rate set as a goal by the administration.

A preliminary analysis by the Congressional Budget Office (CBO) concluded that the administration was optimistic about the economic impact of its fiscal policies, but that its forecasts were within the realm of possibility.

The president won high marks from Senate Budget Committee Chairman Edmund S. Muskie, D-Maine, who said Carter had used "sound economic reasoning" in developing the overall strategy. Muskie predicted that the $500.2 billion spending total and the $24.5 billion tax reduction were "about right, subject to further examination as we...get further evidence on the state of the economy."

Similarly, House Budget Committee Chairman Robert N. Giaimo, D-Conn., said Carter's budget "moves in the right direction on two counts — first, by working to maintain our economic growth, and second, by calling for restraints on the growth in federal spending."

The reactions of business and labor to the president's policies were mixed. The size of the proposed tax cut was equal to the minimum reduction for two years proposed by the Chamber of Commerce's vice president and chief economist, Jack Carlson.

But while business took some cheer in proposed reductions in corporate taxes and a liberalization of the investment tax credit, it was discouraged by Carter's assault on some prized business prerogatives — including deductible entertainment expenses and special tax breaks for foreign operations.

AFL-CIO President George Meany also praised Carter's decision to stimulate the economy. But while chamber officials said more of the tax reduction should go to encourage business investment, Meany denounced the business tax cuts and said the president should have expanded job-creating programs.

Both business and labor were very critical of Carter's mild proposal to try to slow the rate of inflation through voluntary action by business, labor and government.

Lawmakers generally ignored the anti-inflation part of the program, turning their attention more to specifics of the budget and tax program sure to take up a considerable part of the congressional agenda through the year.

A number of Republicans challenged Carter's claim that the proposed budget was "restrained." They suggested that spending would actually exceed the $500.2 billion figure set by the president, and that the resulting deficit would be greater than the $60.6 billion he predicted.

House Minority Leader John J. Rhodes, R-Ariz., accused Carter of including a number of "phony cuts" to "understate" the likely growth in spending during the coming fiscal year. He cited as an example an assumption in the new budget that farm disaster payments would be considerably lower than in 1978 due to a return to "normal" weather in the farm belt.

Rep. Bill Frenzel, R-Minn., said the budget limited spending in areas that Congress would inevitably increase, such as the Small Business Administration and veterans' benefits.

"In my judgment, those items will be increased by the Congress, and I think the president's budget people know that and expect them to be increased," Frenzel said.

Rep. Barber B. Conable Jr., R-N.Y., also accused the president of assuming a lower interest rate than would be likely, in an attempt to understate the actual interest costs for the federal government in the coming year.

In all, Conable estimated that the deficit in Carter's budget would be $7 billion larger than was predicted.

The CBO did not address itself to most of the Republican complaints in its preliminary analysis of the budget, but it did find one possible underestimate that could fan a budget brushfire.

Defense an Issue

In its analysis, the CBO concluded that the president's budget underestimated the growth in defense spending by about $2 billion. It suggested that the administration's budget failed to make appropriate adjustments for the usually rapid inflation in military purchases costs, and that the budget assumed a lower-than-likely pay raise.

"To buy what they propose to buy could add $2 billion to the defense budget," said James Blum, assistant director for budget analysis.

Rep. Parren J. Mitchell, D-Md., chairman of the Congressional Black Caucus, said Carter was "dead wrong" in proposing an increase as large as he did.

"If $10 billion is to be added, it should be for economic stimulus," Mitchell said. "And the Department of Defense does not stimulate the economy."

Mitchell vowed to fight for an increase in jobs programs, an area he said Carter had neglected in the budget.

That promise had a large constituency in the nation's mayors and governors. The mayors, meeting in Washington during the week, expressed "alarm" at what they described as relatively low spending proposed for urban programs. They called for additional spending of $11.3 billion for cities.

The nation's governors, even though they were a heavily Democratic group, were also less than enthusiastic about Carter's recommendations.

Govs. William G. Milliken, R-Mich., and Milton J. Shapp, D-Pa., the chairman of the National Governors' Association and the chairman of the association's Committee on Executive Management and Fiscal Affairs respectively, praised the budget for "reflecting many priorities that the governors have communicated to the White House," but they said it would do little to ease fiscal pressures on state governments.

"On the whole, the budget does not cut growth in programs where state and local governments would be forced to make up the difference out of their own funds," they said. "But it does not provide any new dollars that could be used to meet needs deferred during the recession."

Support for Limiting Growth

Despite those pressures for increased spending, there was a strong sense in Congress that 1979 would not be a good year for much growth in federal outlays. Lawmakers expressed growing concern that it has become very difficult to justify a large budget deficit during the fourth year of a recovery. Fears of inflation weighed heavy, and even liberals noted strong constituent pressure to bring down the deficit.

"The spending total [in Carter's budget] leaves some chores on the economic agenda undone, but realistically there is no way they could be done," sighed Rep. Abner J. Mikva, D-Ill., one of the House's more liberal members. "This year is almost a test of our capacity to run government. The people sense that a government that keeps running a deficit year after year doesn't know how to run its own ship."

Republican Critique

While the Carter proposals were being criticized by liberals for underemphasizing the needs of cities and overemphasizing other programs, such as defense, Republicans expanded on their own critique.

Rhodes and Reps. Barber B. Conable Jr., R-N.Y., and Delbert L. Latta, R-Ohio, lambasted the Carter budget at a Jan. 31 press conference, accusing the administration of deliberately "understating" the deficit that would result from its proposals. They said the "real" deficit would be about $100 billion.

To get the higher figure from Carter's estimated $60.6 billion deficit, the Republican lawmakers:

● Added $6 billion to make up for what they termed "cost underestimates" for a number of automatic entitlement programs, including farm price supports and farm disaster loans.

● Predicted that $3 billion in proposed Carter "cuts" would be restored, and they said the administration made the cuts knowing Congress would make the changes. The cuts included money for water resources, dams, power projects, conservation and land management, the Small Business Administration and veterans' benefits.

● Added $9 billion, predicting that Congress would not approve the revenue-raising tax reforms.

● Added $20 billion, which they said represented the extent to which Carter underestimated outlays. That adjustment was based on the argument that the Carter budget assumed a lower-than-justified ratio of outlays to budget authority.

"He's set us up," said Conable of the president. "Hidden in this thing is a time bomb that's going to blow up in the Congress' face."

Democrats did not share in that criticism. Rep. Richard Bolling, D-Mo., chairman of the Joint Economic Committee, said the administration had "set realistic goals for 1978 and set policies on the right path."

Rep. George Mahon, D-Texas, chairman of the House Appropriations Committee, responded favorably to McIntyre's argument that the Carter budget was "lean and tight," saying: "If there's any revolutionary statement that has been made this morning it's that there are limits to what government can do. That's very refreshing."

Revised Economic Forecast

Although the President had said in January 1978 that his policies were based on "the premise that our economy is basically healthy," by mid-year both administration and congressional economists were in substantial agreement on a sobering new forecast for the nation's economy. They foresaw slower real growth and higher inflation — but also less unemployment — during 1978 and 1979 than they had predicted in January.

In testimony before the House Budget Committee July 11-13, 1978, both administration and congressional experts expressed confidence that the economy would not fall into recession in 1979. They warned, however, that the risks of recession were increasing — partly because inflation appeared likely to accelerate.

That cautious optimism was subject to important conditions. Most notably, the economists assumed in their revised forecasts that Congress would approve a substantial tax cut — about $15 billion during the fiscal year beginning

Oct. 1, 1978 — and that the Federal Reserve Board would not further tighten up on interest rates.

The renewed discussion about the economic outlook was prompted by the release July 6, 1978, of the Office of Management and Budget (OMB) mid-session budget review.

Besides revising its economic predictions, the agency modified its budget estimates. It reported that federal spending in fiscal 1978 would fall far short of original estimates, resulting in a deficit of about $51 billion rather than the $62 billion figure predicted in January.

Moreover, because of President Carter's decision to scale back the size of the tax cut he proposed in January, the fiscal 1979 deficit would be about $48 billion, not almost $61 billion as predicted in January, OMB reported. *(Tax proposal revision, p. 21)*

Still, the agency predicted that the fiscal 1980 deficit would be about $42 billion — a level it said would have to be substantially reduced.

New Outlook

In its new economic predictions, OMB suggested that gross national product (GNP) would grow only 4.1 percent in real terms in 1978. In January, it had predicted a 4.7 percent growth rate for the year.

For 1979, the agency predicted a 4.3 percent growth rate, as compared to its January forecast of 4.8 percent growth.

The agency said the lower growth rate was a result partly of the effects of higher inflation on consumer purchasing power and spending. It also attributed the lower rate to a "less stimulative" fiscal policy — lower spending and a smaller tax cut — than was envisioned at the time of the January forecast.

Economists were somewhat baffled by new forecasts suggesting that unemployment would drop more than predicted in January. OMB's new forecast suggested a joblessness rate of 5.9 percent at the end of 1978 and 5.6 percent at the end of 1979, as compared to its January estimates of 6.2 percent and 5.8 percent respectively.

But the good unemployment news was offset by worsening predictions about inflation. Citing an unexpectedly rapid rise in food prices during the first part of 1978 and an increase in import prices resulting from the devaluation of the dollar, OMB predicted that prices would rise 7.2 percent in 1978 and 6.5 percent in 1979. That compared to the January inflation forecast of 6.1 percent in 1978 and 6 percent in 1979.

The OMB estimates were generally confirmed by Alice M. Rivlin, director of the Congressional Budget Office (CBO). In testimony before the House Budget Committee July 11, she predicted economic growth would be between 3.5 percent and 4.5 percent during 1978, slowing by about one-half percentage point in 1979. Unemployment should fall to between 5.5 percent and 6.1 percent by the end of 1978, and to between 5.2 percent and 6 percent at the end of 1979, she said.

The CBO director predicted that prices would rise between 6.8 percent and 7.8 percent in 1978, and at a slightly less rapid rate in 1979.

Policy Implications

The new economic forecast posed a serious policy dilemma for Congress. Rivlin told the House Budget Committee that it faced "the most difficult moment for economic policymakers since the beginning of the budget process" in 1974.

"Inflation is accelerating just at the moment that the economic recovery is showing signs of running out of steam," she noted.

She said predicting whether the economy would fall into recession was a "close call," but concluded that economic trends did not point to a recession. That was based on several assumptions, including the following:

● The tax cut envisioned in the first budget resolution — reducing revenues by $15 billion in fiscal 1979 — would be enacted, offsetting the effects of rising payroll taxes and inflation on disposable personal income.

● The Federal Reserve Board would not move further to tighten credit markets.

● The tax cut would stimulate business investment.

● The depreciation of the dollar would boost exports.

The CBO director laid special emphasis on the assumption that monetary policy would not be tightened. She noted that many forecasters anticipated a recession in 1979, brought on by a credit crunch caused by Fed decisions to increase interest rates to slow inflation.

That danger, Rivlin said, pointed to the need for more coordination between fiscal policy set by the administration and Congress, and monetary policy set by the Federal Reserve Board.

"Past experience suggests that some incidences of poor performance by the economy have resulted from excessive shifts of monetary and fiscal policies in the same direction," Rivlin noted. "The fiscal and monetary authorities each assumed that the other would not take appropriate action in response to current economic trends; together they overreacted."

To help coordinate fiscal and monetary policy, Rivlin recommended that the Federal Reserve be required to specify its money and credit targets for present and coming fiscal years before Congress enacts its budget resolutions, to reveal its estimates of the levels of unemployment, production and prices for the end of fiscal years, and to explain periodic revisions of its objectives and plans.

Administration Analysis

Administration spokesmen were even more forceful in asserting that, with their proposed economic policy, a recession could be avoided.

"Admittedly, it is unusual to anticipate growth to continue into the fifth year of an economic recovery," Treasury Secretary W. Michael Blumenthal told the House Budget Committee July 12. "But we have been fortunate in avoiding some of the excesses that in past recoveries have forced the economy to pause and often to reverse direction."

Blumenthal and Charles L. Schultze, chairman of the Council of Economic Advisers, noted that businesses have kept their inventories lean, avoiding excesses that in the past have led to sharp production cutbacks.

But Blumenthal conceded that there were "significant risks" to continued economic growth.

"We will not be able to achieve or maintain a satisfactory rate of growth unless we encourage a faster rate of investment in new productive facilities, unless we restrain inflation and unless we redress the serious imbalance in our foreign trade," he said.

Striving to strike a balance between a tax cut that would stimulate the economy enough to maintain a "moderate" growth rate, and the desire to reduce the federal

Carter Urges Broad Attack on Inflation

Asserting that government alone cannot halt inflation, President Carter on April 11, 1978, said he would set an example for the private sector by proposing a 5.5 percent ceiling on federal pay raises and by vetoing congressional actions that would increase the budget deficit.

The president, speaking to the American Society of Newspaper Editors, again rejected wage-price controls. He also refused to support fiscal policies that would slow inflation by increasing unemployment.

Carter concluded that the future direction of inflation will depend in large part on voluntary decisions by business and labor.

"It is a myth that the government itself can stop inflation," Carter said. "Success or failure in this overall effort will largely be determined by the actions of the private sector of the economy."

Renewed Concern

Concerns about inflation heightened in the first three months of 1978 because of indications that the climb in wages and prices could be accelerating.

In his economic report released in January, the president predicted a continuation of inflation at about 6 percent through 1978. But the annual rate of increase in January, February and March was 7.4 percent. *(Economic report p. 3)*

Still, the president's April 11 address suggested no dramatic departure from past anti-inflation policies, which have included a call for some fiscal restraint, for enactment of an energy program and other Carter legislative proposals, and for voluntary agreements by business and labor to keep price and wage increases below the average rate for the last two years.

Carter announced that Robert S. Strauss, his special trade representative, would assume a principal role in the "deceleration" effort in the private sector. Strauss, Carter said, "will have specific authority to speak for me in the public interest."

Specific Proposals

The speech was probably the most comprehensive description by the president of his anti-inflation strategy. Its main elements included:

• The energy program, which Carter said was essential to improve the nation's balance of trade and thus halt the decline in value of the dollar. The president threatened to take "administrative actions" — probably the imposition of a tariff on imported oil — to slow oil imports if Congress failed to enact his energy proposals.

• Formation of a Cabinet-level task force, chaired by the secretary of commerce, to report within 60 days on additional measures to increase exports.

• A vow to veto congressional actions that would increase the budget deficit beyond the level projected in Carter's budget — $60.6 billion. The president said he was "especially concerned" about tuition tax credits, highway and urban transit programs, postal service financing, farm legislation and defense spending. *(Tuition tax credit, p. 53)*

• A freeze on pay for all executive appointees and members of the president's senior staff, and a 5.5 percent ceiling on pay for federal white-collar workers. Carter said he had written to the nation's governors and many mayors urging similar limits on pay increases.

• Efforts to reduce the inflationary impact of government regulation.

• Airline regulatory reform, which he said should be passed "despite the opposition of private interests." Carter said he was "re-examining excessive federal regulation of the trucking industry" as well. *(Airline deregulation, p. 79)*

• A pledge to veto any farm legislation, beyond what he had already recommended, that would lead to higher food prices or budget expenditures. *(Farm policy, p.127)*

• Instructions to the departments of Agriculture and Interior, the Council on Environmental Quality and the President's Council of Economic Advisers to determine within 30 days the best ways to increase timber harvests on federal, state and private lands. Carter said the increased lumber production could slow the rise in housing construction costs.

• Hospital cost controls, which, along with airline deregulation, Carter called "the two most important measures the Congress can pass to prevent inflation." *(Hospital costs, p. 95)*

• A directive to executive agencies to avoid or reduce, if possible, purchases of goods and services whose prices are rising rapidly. Carter also said that federal contracts which contain price escalator clauses should reflect the principle of deceleration.

Private Effort

Still, the president emphasized that his efforts to control inflation would have little impact unless the private sector agrees to voluntary wage and price restraints.

"Let me be blunt about this point," he said. "I am asking American workers to follow the example of federal workers and accept a lower rate of wage increase. In return, they have a right to expect a comparable restraint in price increases for the goods and services they buy."

To help in the deceleration program, Carter said he had asked Strauss, an experienced negotiator, to take on additional duties as "special counselor on inflation."

The president added that he expected in the long run to devise additional programs to deal with sectors of the economy where government can have the greatest impact on inflation — including housing, medical care, food, transportation, energy and the primary metals industries.

But for the short run, he returned repeatedly to the need for voluntary cooperation.

"No act of Congress, no program of our government, no order of my own can bring out the quality we need: to change from the preoccupation with self that can cripple our national will, to a willingness to acknowledge and to sacrifice for the common good."

deficit in order to ease inflationary pressures, the administration spokesmen rejected proposals to increase the size of the tax cut and they promised stringent budget controls in the future.

The Republican Roth-Kemp tax bill (HR 8333, S 1860), which would reduce individual income tax rates by about one-third over three years, would be a "sure-fire recipe for inflation," Schultze said. *(Roth-Kemp proposal, p. 26)*

Blumenthal joined in the attack, estimating that the proposal would increase the federal deficit by $12 billion in the first year and by $38 billion by the time it is fully implemented.

"Massive tax reduction in an economy already suffering from inflationary pressures is sheer waste," Blumenthal said. "We do not have the financial or physical resources to absorb such stimulus without adding to inflationary pressures, and whatever benefits might be envisioned would be quickly negated by the rise in prices and in interest rates."

On the spending side, Blumenthal reiterated the president's determination "to use the full powers of his office, including the veto, to ensure that spending increases and tax cuts stay within the limits of his budget proposals."

According to the mid-session budget review, Congress had tentatively agreed in its budget resolution to spending policy increases $3.6 billion above those recommended by Carter. That figure excluded $1.4 billion in energy tax rebates proposed by Carter but considered dead in 1978.

In its mid-session budget review, the administration promised to recommend to Congress spending below the $549.4 billion "current planning base" for fiscal 1980.

"A 1980 budget below the current planning base will be extremely constrained," the review said. "Achieving this result...will require a common recognition that the time has come for a 'pause' in the rate of increase in the federal budget."

Inflation Fight Criticized

While not proposing any major changes in its anti-inflation campaign, administration officials confessed to being disappointed in the acceleration in prices and wages.

Schultze and Barry P. Bosworth, director of the Council on Wage and Price Stability, told the House Budget Committee that winning support for the voluntary deceleration program from organized labor had proved to be a problem.

The problem could become exacerbated, they said, if wage and fringe benefit demands from small union and non-union workers continued to accelerate very rapidly in an effort to catch up with more substantial settlements won by large unions.

The only solution, both officials said, would be a significant decline in the rate of increase in major union contracts. House Budget Committee members expressed skepticism about the administration's anti-inflation program. Butler Derrick, D-S.C., questioned how the program differed from the Ford administration's "Whip Inflation Now" effort, which was considered unsuccessful.

Norman Y. Mineta, D-Calif., raised the possibility that the administration might want to "dust off" the idea of imposing wage-price controls. Administration spokesmen dismissed that suggestion, but Budget Committee Chairman Robert N. Giaimo, D-Conn., said they might sing a different tune if inflation continued at the double-digit levels it hit during the first part of 1978. ∎

Carter Asks $500.2 Billion in Spending

President Carter on Jan. 23, 1978, provided Congress the final details of his proposed economic strategy by recommending a fiscal year 1979 budget totaling $500.2 billion. Combined with a $24.5 billion net tax reduction, it anticipated a deficit of $60.6 billion.

Characterized by the President as "the administration's first full statement of its priorities, policies and proposals for meeting our national needs," the budget recommended a markedly slowed rate of growth in federal spending, coupled with a middle-of-the-road tax reduction.

It presented no major shift in federal priorities, continuing most programs at levels just sufficient to keep pace with inflation. The few new initiatives had relatively minor fiscal impact during the budget year.

By Carter's analysis—judged to be overly optimistic by some critics—the overall spending and tax proposals would spur solid, but not spectacular economic growth, and thus achieve a modest drop in unemployment. *(Carter economic message, p. 3)*

In general, the budget appeared to underscore Carter's philosophy that government should be limited—a view reflected in his proud assertions that he held real spending growth to less than 2 per cent, actually diminishing the relative size of the federal government in the economy.

"In formulating this budget, I have been made acutely aware once more of the overwhelming number of demands upon the budget and the finite nature of our resources," Carter said in the message accompanying the budget. "Public needs are critically important; but private needs are equally valid, and the only resources the government has are those it collects from the taxpayer.... The span of government is not infinite."

Carter estimated that receipts for fiscal year 1979 would amount to $439.6 billion, assuming congressional approval of the proposed tax reductions. The resulting deficit, given $500.2 billion in proposed outlays, was projected to be $60.6 billion.

Besides proposing policies for fiscal 1979, the President's budget contained estimates for fiscal 1978, which ended Sept. 30, 1978. It predicted that outlays would reach $462.2 billion, and that revenues would total $400.4 billion, resulting in a deficit of $61.8 billion.

The revised figures differed from the administration's previous estimates in November 1977, which predicted outlays of $459.8 billion and revenues of $401.4 billion, for a deficit of $58.5 billion.

The estimated deficit for fiscal 1978 was very nearly the same as predicted by Congress in September 1977 in its second budget resolution, although it envisioned reaching that bottom line with lower outlays and receipts. Congress set a ceiling on outlays of $458.25 billion and a $397 billion floor on receipts, resulting in a deficit of $61.25 billion.

Most of the proposed $38 billion increase resulted from continuing existing policies through fiscal 1979 with adjustments for inflation and demographic changes. The ad-

The Budget Totals

(In billions of dollars)

	Budget Authority	Outlays	Revenues	Deficit
Administration January Budget	$568.2	$500.2	$439.6	$60.6
Administration July Revision	$571.4	$496.6	$448.2	$48.5
Congressional First Budget Resolution	$568.85	$498.8	$447.9	$50.9

ministration estimated that only $7.8 billion of the spending increase resulted from new spending initiatives. That represented a growth rate of only 1.6 per cent.

New Budget Estimates

On July 6, 1978, the Office of Management and Budget (OMB) released its mid-session budget review containing revised budget estimates. The administration estimated that fiscal year 1978 would end Sept. 30, 1978, with revenues totaling $401.2 billion and outlays of $452.3 billion, for a resulting deficit of $51.1 billion. The reduction of the estimated deficit from the January forecast of $61.8 billion reflected almost entirely a "shortfall" in spending by federal agencies. Moreover, because of Carter's decision to scale back the size of the tax cut he proposed in January, the fiscal 1979 deficit would be about $48 billion, not almost $61 billion as predicted in January 1978, OMB reported.

For fiscal 1980, the administration predicted that outlays would total $549.4 billion, and that revenues would be $507.3 billion, resulting in a deficit of $42.1 billion.

"I want to stress, and stress strongly, that the estimates for fiscal 1980 and beyond do not represent the actual totals to be published in the president's 1980 budget," said OMB director James T. McIntyre Jr.

Declaring the projected spending and deficit totals for 1980 "unacceptably high," McIntyre pledged the administration to bring both figures down.

Administration Priorities

Carter listed several "new priorities" in his January 1978 budget message, including:

● Energy, with special emphasis on conservation and non-nuclear research development, accelerated acquisition of a strategic petroleum reserve, resolution of problems of nuclear waste management, and research into alternatives to the plutonium-fueled liquid metal fast breeder reactor.

● Human needs, especially a beginning to Carter's welfare reform program, health care for low-income mothers

Budget Terminology

The federal budget is a plan of expected receipts and expenditures, a statement of priorities, an accounting of how funds have been and will be spent and a request for authority to spend public money.

The 1979 budget covers the government's fiscal year beginning Oct. 1, 1978, and ending Sept. 30, 1979.

The federal expenditures reported are most frequently outlays: amounts actually paid out by the government in cash or checks during the year. Examples are funds spent to buy equipment or property, to meet the government's liability under a contract or to pay the salary of an employee. Outlays also include net lending—the difference between disbursements and repayments under government lending programs.

The administration's request to Congress, presented in the form of the budget, is for authority to obligate or lend funds.

Budget authority determines the scope of operations of the government. Congress confers budget authority on a federal agency in general in the form of appropriations.

Appropriations may be for a single year, a specified period of years, or an indefinite number of years, according to the restrictions Congress wishes to place on spending for particular purposes.

Congress also restricts itself in the appropriation process by requiring that an appropriation be preceded by an authorization to appropriate a certain or an indefinite amount of money for a certain purpose over a period of time.

Usually an authorization establishes the scope of a particular program, and Congress appropriates funds within the limits it has previously approved. In the case of authority to enter contract obligations, however, Congress authorizes the administration to make firm commitments for which funds must be appropriated later. Congress also occasionally includes mandatory spending requirements in an authorization, designed to ensure spending at a certain level.

Budget authority often differs from actual outlays. This is because, in practice, funds actually spent or obligated during a year may be drawn partly from the budget authority conferred in the year in question and partly from budget authority conferred in previous years.

---

and children, major increases in education assistance at all levels, jobs programs (especially for low-income youths), and the start of a program to prevent unwanted adolescent pregnancies.

- National defense, especially an increase in spending for the North Atlantic Treaty Organization (NATO).
- Research and development, earmarked for a 5 per cent real growth in spending.

Carter also suggested that the budget reflected a substantial commitment to urban revitalization, declaring that it attempted "to improve delivery and target existing programs better." He offered no spending total for essentially urban programs, but estimated that they had increased by about $11 billion since 1977.

Carter was expected to announce a new urban program in 1978. McIntyre, at that time the director-designate of the Office of Management and Budget, said the new program could be financed partly from a $1.7 billion allowance for contingencies in the budget, but he said the administration might submit to Congress a supplemental budget request.

McIntyre hinted, however, that an urban aid program might require changes in budget authority rather than outlays, suggesting that the administration proposals might emphasize loan guarantees and similar policies rather than direct spending. *(Carter's urban policy proposals, p. 117)*

The Carter budget proposed an increase in budget authority to $568.1 billion from $502.9 billion. That represented a 13 per cent increase, possibly indicating that the rate of growth in federal spending might speed up again in the future.

Legislative Proposals

The major new legislative proposals in the budget included:

- Expansion of the special supplemental food (WIC) program for women and children, $530 million.
- "A new initiative to provide employment opportunities in the private sector for youth and the disadvantaged," $400 million.
- Expansion of Title I of the Elementary and Secondary Education Act to provide special assistance to disadvantaged areas, $644 million.
- Expanded coverage under the Medicaid program for low-income mothers and children, $381 million; Medicaid cost controls expected to save $399 million.
- Demonstration projects to create 50,000 public sector jobs as part of the 1.4 million jobs eventually envisioned under proposed welfare reform, $200 million.
- A new program to help prevent unwanted teenage pregnancies, $20 million.
- A program to provide federal interest subsidies to local governments that choose to issue taxable bonds, $99 million (proposed budget authority, $7 billion).
- An expanded foster child care program, $64 million.
- A new home ownership assistance program for very low-income families, $6 million.

The Tax Program

One of the administration's top priorities was its detailed proposal for a series of tax reductions totaling $33.9 billion, along with "reforms" that would raise $9.4 billion in revenues. The details were spelled out in the President's tax message Jan. 21. *(Story, p. 21)*

The proposed reforms, while less ambitious than those promised by Carter during his presidential campaign, were still expected to stir plenty of controversy in Congress.

The administration acknowledged the possibility that lawmakers might approve the reductions without endorsing the full package of reforms, but it insisted that Congress enact a total tax package that would reduce revenues by roughly the same $24.5 billion proposed.

"If we cannot get the reforms, we would be $9 billion short," declared Treasury Secretary W. Michael Blumenthal. "That means we would have to cut back somewhere."

Outlays

The largest increases in the fiscal 1979 budget were proposed in the areas of income security ($12.4 billion, or 8.3

per cent), national defense ($10.1 billion, or 9.4 per cent), health ($5.4 billion, or 12.2 per cent), interest ($5.1 billion, or 11.7 per cent), education ($2.9 billion, or 10.7 per cent), energy ($1.8 billion, or 23 per cent), and international affairs ($944 million, or 14 per cent).

The income security increase included a $9.8 billion, or 10.1 per cent, rise in Social Security.

The most substantial decline in projected outlays was in agriculture, for which the administration projected a $3.6 billion, or 40 per cent, spending decline. That was based on the assumption that "normal weather" during the fiscal year would spare the government the need to make substantial payments to farmers for crop losses. If that assumption were to prove incorrect, expenditures would automatically increase.

Other budget functions that increased less than the overall average, or actually declined, included: community and regional development (down $1 billion, or 10.6 per cent), commerce and housing credit (down $555 million, or 15.8 per cent), general purpose fiscal assistance to states and localities (down $224 million, or 23 per cent), transportation (up $1 billion, or 23 per cent), transportation (up $1 billion, or 6.7 per cent), veterans' benefits and services (up $341 million, or 1.9 per cent), general science, space and technology (up $320 million, or 6.7 per cent), administration of justice (up $192 million, or 4.8 per cent), and natural resources and environment (up $97 million, or 0.8 per cent).

Carter estimated that between 75 and 80 per cent of the budget was "relatively uncontrollable," a situation he predicted will continue for the foreseeable future.

Uncontrollable expenditures included "open-ended programs" and fixed costs, which have risen from 36 per cent of the budget in 1967 to about 57 per cent in the 1979 budget. Carter estimated they will comprise 59 per cent of total spending by 1983.

"Prior year contracts and obligations" accounted for an additional 15 or 20 per cent of the budget considered relatively uncontrollable in the short run.

Current Services Increases

To give a better indication of actual policy changes in the budget, the administration submits each year its "current services estimates." They predict outlays and receipts for the coming year, assuming no change in policies, but only adjustments for inflation in indexed programs and demographic changes.

The current services estimates for fiscal 1979 indicated a spending total of $492.4 billion, and receipts of $463.8

The Budget Dollar
Where it comes from...

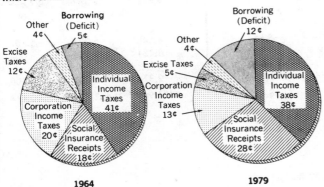

1964   1979

The Budget Dollar
Where it goes...

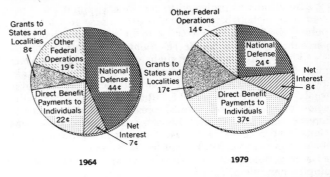

1964   1979

billion, for a deficit of $28.5 billion. Current services budget authority was estimated to be $538.3 billion.

Carter's proposed increase over current services outlays of $7.8 billion represented a growth in the budget resulting from newly proposed policies of only 1.6 per cent. His recommended budget authority total was $29.9 billion, or 5.6 per cent, above the current services estimate.

That means that new spending accounted for only $7.8 billion of the $32.1 billion addition to the likely 1979 deficit, compared to $24.5 billion in tax cuts. Seen from another perspective, the current services estimates suggest that, for every dollar Carter chose to spend on new policy initiatives, he decided to return $3.14 to the taxpayers in the form of tax reduction.

The current services estimates for 1979 suggested that Carter's top priorities for new policies were energy, defense and education, training, employment and social services programs.

The administration estimated its proposed increases over current services estimates as follows: energy, $2.1 billion; a proposed tax refund for purchasers of fuel efficient cars, $1.3 billion; defense, $1 billion; education, training, employment and social service programs, $1 billion; international affairs, $300 million; transportation, $300 million; an allowance for contingencies, $1.7 billion; and other increases, $1.8 billion.

The administration proposed reducing expenditures below current service estimates by $1.8 billion, including Medicare and Medicaid savings resulting from hospital cost containment, $700 million; Social Security changes, $600 million; and other actions cutting costs, $400 million.

The prospects for the fuel efficiency tax refund are considered very slim in Congress, but the chances of hospital cost containment are slight, too, suggesting that the actual increase over current services estimates might be more on the order of $8.4 billion.

The administration also estimated that, assuming adoption of Carter's proposals for fiscal 1979 and their extension into the future without further policy changes, federal spending would reach $650 billion by 1983.

Economic Impact

The administration asserted that its proposed combination of tax reduction and spending increases would stimulate the economy enough to grow at a respectable 4.75 per cent rate in 1979. It predicted that the unemployment rate would drop as a result to about 6.2 per cent by the end of 1978, and to 5.8 per cent by the end of 1979. It suggested that the tax package alone would add one million jobs that otherwise would not exist in 1979.

Inflation was projected to continue at about the 6 per cent rate, although the administration's new anti-inflation policy was hoped to cut the rate by about one-half of a percentage point each year. *(Economic assumptions, p. 20)*

Those estimates were slightly more optimistic than most. The Congressional Budget Office (CBO) concluded in a study in December 1977 that the combined stimulus would have to be about $2.5 billion higher to achieve the same effect. Michael Evans, president of the economic forecasting firm Chase Econometrics, estimated that Carter's economic strategy would result in a growth rate of about 4 per cent in 1979. That would be enough to prevent economic deterioration, but not enough to reduce unemployment significantly.

For the years 1980-1983, the administration set an objective of real growth of about 4.75 per cent per year, with unemployment declining to 4.9 per cent by the end of 1981 and to 4 per cent by the end of 1983.

But it also hinted that the 4 per cent goal, contained in the Humphrey-Hawkins full employment bill endorsed by Carter, might be impossible to achieve.

In estimating its "high employment budget"—a measure of government outlays and receipts during periods of high employment—the Carter administration assumed a joblessness rate of 4.9 per cent, rather than the 4 per cent rate traditionally considered full employment.

"These rates are consistent with a 4 per cent rate in 1955, adjusted for changes in the composition of the labor force toward groups that typically experience higher rates of unemployment," the budget document said.

Budget Authority and Outlays by Agency

(in millions of dollars)†

	BUDGET AUTHORITY			OUTLAYS		
DEPARTMENT OR OTHER UNIT	1977 actual	1978 estimate	1979 estimate	1977 actual	1978 estimate	1979 estimate
Legislative branch	$ 1,043	$ 1,076	$ 1,161	$ 976	$ 1,057	$ 1,175
The Judiciary	430	469	492	392	458	489
Executive Office of the President	78	76	79	73	78	78
Funds appropriated to the President	4,639	8,964	10,974	2,487	4,916	5,089
Agriculture	15,467	17,209	20,026	16,738	22,625	17,727
Commerce	8,204	2,370	2,722	2,606	4,524	4,385
Defense—Military[1]	108,425	115,264	125,567	95,650	105,300	115,200
Defense—Civil	2,495	2,744	2,457	2,280	2,536	2,547
Energy[2]	6,620	10,632	11,642	5,217	8,152	10,087
Health, Education, and Welfare	147,628	162,281	185,007	147,455	164,595	181,265
Housing and Urban Development	33,900	38,143	33,112	5,838	8,411	9,529
Interior	3,708	4,257	4,452	3,194	3,904	4,002
Justice	2,334	2,365	2,457	2,350	2,527	2,533
Labor	31,203	20,676	29,861	22,374	23,742	25,134
State	1,240	1,443	1,465	1,076	1,247	1,355
Transportation	9,298	13,560	17,355	12,514	14,395	15,798
Treasury	49,391	56,571	69,648	49,560	56,688	62,612
Environmental Protection Agency	2,763	5,503	5,627	4,365	5,063	5,679
General Services Administration	304	224	300	−31	289	306
National Aeronautics and Space Administration	3,818	4,063	4,370	3,944	3,982	4,269
Veterans Administration	19,042	19,042	19,048	18,019	18,898	19,238
Other independent agencies	28,253	31,596	32,220	19,878	24,467	24,899
Allowances[3]	—	—	4,150	—	—	2,800
Undistributed offsetting receipts:						
Employer share, employee retirement	−4,548	−5,024	−5,157	−4,548	−5,024	−5,157
Interest received by trust funds	−8,131	−8,595	−9,064	−8,131	−8,595	−9,064
Rents and royalties on the Outer Continental Shelf lands	−2,374	−2,000	−1,800	−2,374	−2,000	−1,800
Total budget authority and outlays	**$465,231**	**$502,907**	**$568,172**	**$401,902**	**$462,234**	**$500,174**

† Figures may not add to totals due to rounding.
1. Includes allowances for civilian and military pay raises for Department of Defense.
2. This agency assumes the energy activities previously performed by the Energy Research and Development Administration, the Federal Energy Administration, and several other agencies.
3. Includes allowances for civilian agency pay raises and contingencies.

SOURCE: Fiscal 1979 Budget

Some economists have argued that a 4 per cent unemployment rate may no longer be the best measure of full employment, but the administration has not endorsed that suggestion. The "high unemployment" estimates in the new Carter budget possibly reflected a shift toward that line of reasoning, however. *(Employment statistics, p. 67)*

Finally, the budget restated Carter's commitment to reduce the size of the federal sector to 21 per cent of gross national product (GNP). The Carter fiscal 1979 budget would bring that percentage down from a 1978 level of 22.6 per cent to 22 per cent.

The budget acknowledged the fading chances of achieving Carter's goal of balancing the budget by 1981, and it stated flatly that that goal might have to be "deferred" if the President decides the economy needs additional stimulus to achieve his economic goals.

The administration stressed that tax reduction would continue to be the favored form of stimulus, in keeping with the President's determination to keep outlays down to 21 per cent of GNP.

Administration Defenses

The President and his top advisers defended the fiscal package from both conservative and liberal attack. Carter called the spending total "restrained," and he pointed with pride to the relatively slow growth rate and the diminished relative size of the budget in the economy. At the same time, he said it included provisions to meet critical national needs.

Treasury Secretary Blumenthal defended the tax portion of the package, saying the reductions were substantial enough to offset the economically chilling impact of scheduled increases in Social Security taxes and inflation, but that the resulting deficit would not set off renewed inflation.

Blumenthal specifically dismissed the "crowding out" theory, which suggests that increased federal borrowing to finance the deficit would create a squeeze in capital markets, increasing interest rates and setting off renewed inflation.

"I suspect there is a persistent tendency to underestimate the depth and resiliency of this country's magnificent financial system," he said.

Budget Director McIntyre reasserted the administration's hopes of balancing the budget by 1981, even though the prospects were conceded to depend on an extraordinarily good performance of the private economy over the next few years.

At the same time, the budget director made clear that, given a choice between a stagnant economy with high un-

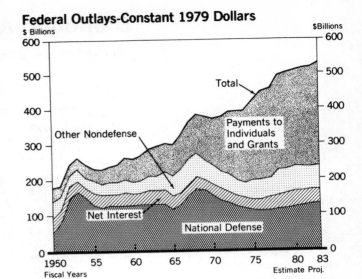

Federal Outlays-Constant 1979 Dollars

employment and a balanced budget, the President would "defer" his goal of eliminating the deficit.

Charles L. Schultze, chairman of Carter's Council of Economic Advisers, described the entire economic package as one "not designed to rescue an economy about to fall into recession," but rather as one to keep a "basically healthy economy" on track.

McIntyre summed up the administration's view of its fiscal plan, calling it "realistic, responsible and responsive to the nation's most critical needs."

Federal Debt and Borrowing

The federal debt was projected to rise in fiscal 1979 by $88 billion, to $873.6 billion, according to the administration budget. The share held by the public was estimated likely to rise from $617.8 billion to $690.8 billion. The rest of the debt was expected to be held by federal agencies or by government trust funds.

Most of the increase in debt was attributed to the federal deficit, although increased federal loan activities also contributed.

The administration estimated that outlays for off-budget agencies—essentially the difference between their new loans and repayments of old ones—would amount to $12.5 billion during the year. Almost all of that sum was attributed to the Federal Financing Bank, which raises money for other federal agencies.

Other off-budget agencies include the Rural Electrification and Telephone Revolving Fund, the Rural Telephone Bank, the Pension Benefit Guaranty Corp., the Exchange Stabilization Fund, the Postal Service Fund and the U.S. Railway Assn.

The administration estimated that new direct loans by on-budget agencies would exceed repayments by $4.3 billion, contributing to the total federal debt.

The administration estimated that total new lending by on-budget agencies would amount to $26.6 billion, and total new lending by off-budget agencies would be $16.8 billion.

In addition, it estimated that the federal government would guarantee or insure net loans totaling $23.2 billion. That sum would not require additional federal outlays, except in cases of default.

BUDGET RECEIPTS BY SOURCE

(In billions of dollars)

Source	1977 actual	1978 estimate	1979 estimate	1980 estimate
Individual income taxes	$156.7	$178.8	$190.1	$223.9
Corporation income taxes	54.9	58.9	62.5	69.1
Social insurance taxes and contributions	108.7	124.1	141.9	160.1
Excise taxes	17.5	20.2	25.5	31.1
Estate and gift taxes	7.3	5.6	6.1	6.5
Customs duties	5.2	5.8	6.4	7.0
Miscellaneous receipts	6.5	6.9	7.2	7.5
Total, budget receipts	$356.9	$400.4	$439.6	$505.4

Economic Assumptions

(Calendar years; dollar amounts in billions)

Item	Actual 1976	FORECAST			ASSUMPTIONS			
		1977	1978	1979	1980	1981	1982	1983
Gross national product:								
Current dollars:								
Amount	$1,706	$1,890	$2,099	$2,335	$2,587	$2,858	$3,133	$3,400
Per cent change	11.6	10.8	11.0	11.2	10.8	10.5	9.6	8.5
Constant (1972) dollars:								
Amount	$1,275	$1,337	$1,400	$1,467	$1,537	$1,614	$1,690	$1,761
Per cent change	6.0	4.9	4.7	4.8	4.8	5.0	4.7	4.2
Incomes (current dollars):								
Personal income	$1,383	$1,536	$1,704	$1,892	$2,095	$2,315	$2,538	$2,754
Wages and salaries	892	989	1,099	1,219	1,363	1,521	1,670	1,812
Corporate profits	157	172	192	217	245	274	301	326
Price level (per cent change):								
GNP deflator:								
Year over year	5.3	5.6	6.1	6.2	5.7	5.2	4.7	4.2
Fourth quarter over fourth quarter	4.7	5.9	6.3	6.0	5.5	5.0	4.5	4.0
Consumer Price Index:								
Year over year	5.7	6.5	5.9	6.1	5.7	5.2	4.7	4.2
December over December	4.8	6.9	6.1	6.0	5.7	5.2	4.7	4.0
Unemployment rates (per cent):								
Total:								
Yearly average	7.7	7.0	6.3	5.9	5.4	5.0	4.5	4.1
Fourth quarter	7.9	6.6	6.2	5.8	5.3	4.9	4.4	4.0
Insured[1]	6.4	4.6	4.1	3.6	3.3	2.9	2.6	2.3
Federal pay raise, October (per cent)[2]	4.8	7.0	6.0	6.0	6.0	6.0	5.7	5.4
Interest rate, 91-day Treasury bills (per cent)[3]	5.0	5.2	6.1	6.1	6.1	6.1	5.8	5.3

1. Insured unemployment as a percentage of covered employment.
2. These are the rates used in determining the dollar allowances for additional funds needed to cover pay increases. Agencies will be required to absorb any pay increase in excess of the allowances.
3. Average rate on new issues within period. The forecast assumes continuation of market rates at the time the estimates were made.

SOURCE: Fiscal 1979 Budget

Control Over Lending

The administration of former President Ford recommended reforming the government's lending activities by returning the off-budget agencies to the budget. Dismissing the argument that off-budget lending has little fiscal impact since it theoretically requires no net outlays, Ford argued that unifying the separate agencies with the entire budget would lead to greater control.

President Carter made no mention of the Ford proposal, but he agreed that the government needs a "systematic way to consider the resource allocation implied" by the various lending activities and "whether the share of credit transactions being made or guaranteed by the federal government is reasonable."

Specifically, Carter said he would recommend a new set of control procedures, providing that the President and Congress include in their budget processes decisions setting overall ceilings on authority to make direct loans and to guarantee loans, and that annual appropriations acts include limitations on the amounts of direct loans and loan guarantees by individual agencies.

For 1979, Blumenthal estimated that the government would have to borrow about $70 billion, give or take $5 billion, to finance the debt. The rest of the money would be raised from government agencies. That was about the same level of borrowing as in 1978.

Interest on the debt was estimated likely to cost about $48.9 billion.

While that was a substantial sum, the actual size of the federal debt in the economy in 1979 was estimated to be 37.4 per cent of GNP, up from 36 per cent in 1974 but substantially lower than in years before that. In 1958, for instance, the federal debt comprised 63.3 per cent of GNP.

Congress Challenges Carter Tax Proposals

The most innovative and controversial part of President Carter's 1978 economic package — and also its centerpiece — was his proposal for a $33.9 billion reduction in revenues, partially offset by $9.4 billion in revenue-raising recommendations. The President's tax program, released Jan. 21, 1978, included provisions to reduce personal taxes by $23.5 billion while implementing "reforms" in the personal tax system that would raise $8.4 billion; to reduce business taxes by $8.4 billion while introducing changes to raise $1.1 billion; and to reduce individual and business taxes by an additional $2 billion by eliminating the excise tax on telephone service and reducing the federal unemployment compensation payroll tax.

"Fundamental reform of our tax laws is essential and should begin now," said the President in outlining his tax package. "The enactment of these proposals will constitute a major step towards sustaining our economic recovery and making our tax system fairer and simpler."

But despite Carter's statement, the administration's tax package encountered obstacles on several fronts almost immediately. By midyear, the administration had been forced to scale down its proposed reductions to $19.4 billion — and later even to $15 billion — and to abandon many of its proposed "reforms." One of the reasons for the resistance to the Carter tax package on Capitol Hill was that many members of Congress were troubled that so large a tax reduction would contribute to an unacceptable increase in the budget deficit and would also spur the already high rate of inflation. Moreover, many lawmakers did not see eye to eye with Carter on the kind of tax reforms that were needed. They were pressing for "middle class" tax relief measures such as a roll-back of the scheduled increases in Social Security taxes, a proposed tax credit for education expenses and a reduction in capital gains taxes — all of which Carter opposed. In agreeing to scale down the tax reduction, Charles L. Schultze, chairman of the Council of Economic Advisers, said in May, "There was wide recognition that economic and financial conditions had changed substantially since the budget and tax messages were prepared late last year and submitted to the Congress early this year."

The administration's tax proposals suffered a major defeat in Congress, when the House Aug. 10, 1978, voted 362-49 to pass a $16.3 billion tax cut bill that was markedly different from Carter's initial package. The bill approved by the House, in sharp contrast to Carter's proposal and most tax measures of the recent past, would not increase the progressivity of the income tax. Rather than provide disproportionate relief to lower income people, it would direct most of the benefits to middle and upper income groups.

Initial Carter Proposals

In announcing his tax program, Carter claimed the net $24.5 billion tax reduction would stimulate the economy to grow at a rate between 4.5 and 5 per cent through 1979, as compared to a relatively poor 3.5 per cent growth rate

without it. He said the reduction would add one million jobs to the national economy, decreasing the unemployment rate to between 5.5 and 6 per cent by the end of 1979.

Carter also said the tax changes were designed to fulfill his promise to make the tax system more progressive. While the reductions would benefit all typical taxpayers with incomes of $100,000 or less, most of the relief — 94 per cent of it—would go to individuals and families earning less than $30,000 per year, he said.

For a typical family of four earning $15,000 a year, the tax proposals would reduce income taxes by $258, a 19 per cent reduction, Carter said. Families with income less than $15,000 would benefit even more, while families with more income would benefit less.

Tables released by the Treasury Department suggested that a typical four-person family earning $10,000 would have its income tax liability reduced to $134 from $446, a reduction of 70 per cent. A four-person family earning $40,000, however, would have income taxes drop to $6,630 from $6,848, a decrease of only 3 per cent.

Treasury Secretary W. Michael Blumenthal estimated that the program would eliminate about six million taxpayers with income at or below the poverty line from the tax roles. The poverty line in early 1978 was $3,252. It would rise to $3,449 in 1979.

The actual change in taxes paid between 1977 and 1979 under Carter's proposals would differ from those figures, however, because of increases in Social Security taxes already approved by Congress.

The Treasury Department estimated that typical families with one wage earner and four dependents and income less than $20,000 would still experience a net tax reduction, while such families with income above $25,000 would have a net tax increase.

The actual impact would vary depending on the number of wage earners and the number of dependents in a family.

Details of the President's major tax proposals as initially formulated follow.

Tax Reductions

Individual Income Tax Rates

The rates for the individual income tax would be reduced across-the-board by 2 per cent, so that they would range from 12 per cent for the lowest bracket to 68 per cent for the highest bracket, as compared to the current range of 14 to 70 per cent.

Carter observed that the rate reduction would benefit people in low income brackets more than people in the upper brackets, since it would mean a larger proportionate tax reduction in lower brackets.

Tax Credit

Instead of allowing a $750 per person tax exemption and a $35 credit, families would be allowed a $240 credit per person. An exemption is a sum of money removed from a taxpayer's taxable income, while a credit is a sum subtracted from his actual tax liability. Exemptions generally benefit taxpayers in upper income brackets more, because of the high effective tax rates for such brackets. A $750 exemption is worth $375 to a taxpayer in the 50 per cent tax bracket, for instance. A $240 credit, on the other hand, is worth the same to taxpayers in different brackets.

The combined effect of the change in personal tax rates and the switch to the $240 credit would be a decrease in federal revenues of $6.1 billion in 1978 (the change would take effect on Oct. 1). In 1979, revenues would be cut by $23.5 billion.

Corporate Income Tax Rates

The tax rate on corporate income above $50,000 would be reduced from 48 per cent to 45 per cent effective Oct. 1, 1978, and to 44 per cent effective Jan. 1, 1980. The rate on corporate income below $25,000 would be reduced from 20 per cent to 18 per cent, and the rate on corporate income between $20,000 and $25,000 would be reduced from 22 per cent to 20 per cent. Both reductions for the lower brackets would take effect Oct. 1, 1978.

The change would decrease revenues by $6 billion in 1979.

Investment Credit

The existing 10 per cent investment tax credit, which was scheduled to drop to 7 per cent in 1981, would be continued permanently at 10 per cent. In addition, it would be liberalized so that it could be used to offset up to 90 per cent of a corporation's tax liability, as compared to the present 50 per cent ceiling. It also would be extended to investments in industrial and utility structures, in addition to applying to machinery and equipment. Carter also proposed allowing pollution control equipment to qualify for the full 10 per cent credit, even if it qualifies currently for five-year amortization.

Carter estimated that the changes would encourage new business investment by reducing taxes by $2.4 billion in 1979.

Telephone Excise Tax, Unemployment Tax

The 4 per cent levy on telephone and telegraph service would be repealed Oct. 1, 1978, rather than being phased out gradually as provided in existing law. The federal unemployment compensation tax would be reduced to .5 per cent from .7 per cent on Jan. 1, 1979. It was scheduled to drop in the 1980s.

Carter said those two changes, which would decrease revenues by $2 billion in 1979, were part of his anti-inflation program.

Tax Revision

Itemized Deduction Changes

Carter proposed several changes in itemized deduction provisions in the tax code. He said the changes would prompt six million taxpayers to switch from itemizing deductions to using the standard deduction, increasing the number of taxpayers using the simpler approach from 77 per cent to 84 per cent of all taxpayers. The changes would raise $7.8 billion in revenues in 1979.

The President specifically recommended eliminating special deductions for general sales taxes, taxes on personal property (except for real estate), gasoline taxes and other miscellaneous taxes. He said the itemized deduction system was unduly complicating the tax system. In addition, he argued that many of the deductions—such as the gasoline tax deduction, which has actually served to make gasoline cheaper—could not be justified on public policy grounds.

Carter also proposed eliminating provisions allowing for an itemized deduction of up to $200 for political contributions, while keeping the provision allowing taxpayers to claim a credit of up to $50 against their tax liability for one-half of the amount of a political contribution. The President said the deduction was unfair because it provided a larger subsidy for taxpayers in higher income brackets, while the credit provided an equal subsidy regardless of income.

The tax program also proposed combining medical expenses and casualty losses into a single "extraordinary expense" deduction, which would be allowed only when such expenses exceeded 10 per cent of income. A variety of provisions tightening up on the allowance of such expenses were also included in the proposals.

Carter said the existing, more liberal allowances for medical and casualty deductions were no longer adequate in limiting such deductions to expenses that are "unusually large and have a significant impact on the taxpayer's ability to pay."

Crackdown on Business Entertainment

Some of the most controversial of Carter's tax revision proposals were designed, in his words, "to curtail inappropriate subsidies, special privileges, inequities and abuses in the tax system." The estimated increase in revenues that would result from reforming them was $1.5 billion in 1979.

Carter proposed eliminating tax code provisions allowing deductions for purchases of tickets to theater and sporting events, for maintaining yachts, hunting lodges and swimming pools, and for fees paid to social, athletic or sporting clubs.

"The overwhelming majority of our citizens pay for their theater and sports tickets out of their own after-tax dollars," Carter said.

"No taxpayer should be asked to help subsidize someone else's personal entertainment," he added.

The President also recommended allowing deductions for only 50 per cent of the currently deductible cost of business meals and beverages. This proposal, frequently referred to as Carter's attack on the "three-martini lunch," came under criticism from representatives of the restaurant industry. Treasury Secretary Blumenthal conceded that it might reduce employment in that industry by about 1 per cent, but he said that it could lead to a "better allocation of resources" and actually increase overall employment.

A related provision would limit deductions for the cost of business-related air travel to the cost of coach, as opposed to first class, fare.

The tax proposals also included a provision that taxpayers would only be allowed to claim deductions for expenses relating to foreign conventions if it could be demonstrated that factors such as purpose and membership made it "reasonable" to hold the convention outside the United States.

Foreign Business Operations

The President's tax package included two provisions reducing tax benefits to corporations for overseas activities. First, Carter recommended phasing out over three years provisions allowing U.S. corporations to defer taxes on their export earnings funneled through domestic international sales corporations (or DISCs).

The President argued that the DISC tax break was "a very inefficient and wasteful export subsidy." He estimated that it probably contributed only $1-$3 billion to U.S. exports in 1974, at a cost of about $1.2 billion. It may have had no beneficial impact on the nation's balance of trade, he said.

Carter also recommended a three-year phase-out of the provision allowing U.S. corporations to defer taxes on incomes of foreign subsidiaries until the money is repatriated.

"By providing a preference for foreign source income, the current deferral provision provides an incentive for investing abroad rather than in the United States, thereby having the effect of reducing job opportunities of Americans," he said.

Ending the deferral would increase revenues by $800 million annually once fully implemented.

Tax Shelters

The President's proposals included three provisions to crack down on tax shelters used by some upper income taxpayers to limit their tax liabilities. Carter complained that shelters "attract investment dollars away from profit-seeking businesses and into ventures designed only for tax write-offs."

Carter proposed several specific changes, which would raise about $500 million in revenues annually:

Minimum Tax. Taxpayers have been required to pay a minimum tax on income from certain activities that otherwise would be shielded from taxation. The aim is to keep them from escaping taxation entirely. The 15 per cent minimum levy applies to all preference income that exceeds the greater of $10,000 or one-half of an individual's regular tax liability. Carter proposed keeping the $10,000 reduction, but eliminating the provision allowing one half of a taxpayer's regular income tax liability to be subtracted from the minimum tax. He argued that the change "will make the minimum tax more progressive and a more sharply focused deterrent to the use of tax shelters."

'At Risk' Rule. The tax package would extend to all tax shelters except real estate the provision limiting deductibility of a shelter investor's paper losses to losses for which he actually has a personal liability. The existing provision, designed to prevent deductions for losses that the investors do not actually have to pay, only covered some tax shelters.

Other proposed restrictions on the use of tax shelters included recommendations tightening up on depreciation of most real estate investments for tax purposes; preventing deferral of tax on interest on annuities, except for annuities of a certain size judged to be *bona fide* retirement funds; a classification of some limited partnerships that currently qualify for sheltered treatment, as corporations for tax purposes; and facilitating Internal Revenue Service audits of tax shelter partnerships.

Other Provisions

Discrimination in Fringe Benefits. The tax program had several provisions tightening up on tax preferences for fringe benefits that are applied discriminatorily. The

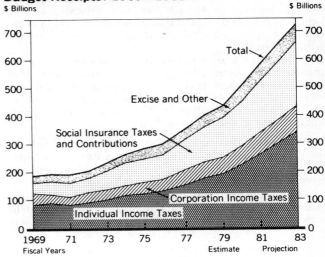

Budget Receipts: 1969 - 1983
$ Billions

changes would increase revenues by less than $100 million annually.

Specifically, Carter recommended denying tax exemption to employer-established medical, disability and group life insurance plans that discriminate in favor of officers, shareholders and higher paid employees. He also proposed eliminating the tax exclusion for the first $5,000 of payments made by an employer on account of the death of an employee, arguing that such death benefits frequently are in the nature of deferred wages and that adequate tax relief for the employee's heirs is provided through a complete tax exemption for insurance proceeds.

In addition, the President recommended revising the law so that pension plans "qualified" for a preferred tax status cannot provide benefits to supplement Social Security payments for highly paid employees unless all employees receive some coverage.

Unemployment Compensation. Carter proposed phasing out the existing tax exemption for unemployment compensation benefits for individuals with income above $20,000, and for married couples with income above $25,000.

"In some cases...the unemployment compensation system discourages work for taxable income," Carter said. "Since unemployment benefits are tax-free, they are more valuable than an equivalent amount of wages.... There can be no justification for conferring this tax-free benefit upon middle and upper income workers."

Taxable Bond Option and Industrial Bonds. Carter proposed several tax law revisions designed to tighten up on opportunities to avoid taxes by investing in tax-exempt bonds. He said the proposals would not limit the ability of state and local governments to obtain low-cost financing.

Specifically, the President recommended giving state and local governments the option of issuing fully taxable bonds and receiving federal interest subsidies, or continuing to issue tax-exempt bonds. Carter said governments exercising the option would benefit by receiving interest subsidies, and those not exercising it would benefit because the market for their bonds would improve and thus allow them to issue bonds at lower interest rates.

Carter proposed eliminating the tax exemption for interest on pollution control bonds, bonds for the development of industrial parks, and private hospital bonds unless state certification is given that the hospital construction is needed. He said those activities were primarily for the benefit of private users and that, in some cases (such as excessive hospital construction) they ran counter to the public interest.

The tax program also included a provision limiting the present tax exemptions for "small issue" industrial bonds—those valued at less than $1 million or for projects with total capital investment of less than $5 million—to economically distressed areas. The small-issue exemption would be increased to $10 million.

Financial Institutions. Carter proposed several tax law changes cutting back on "favored tax status" for financial institutions. He took aim particularly at tax-exempt "reserves" they are allowed to set up for bad debts.

Carter proposed speeding up the scheduled elimination of a tax law allowing commercial banks to claim bad debt deductions greater than their actual losses. The law was

---

"These reforms will make our tax system both fairer and simpler."

—President Carter

---

due for extinction in 1987. Carter proposed repealing it in 1979, and requiring banks to base their bad debt deductions on actual loss experience after that.

Mutual savings banks and savings and loan associations would have their bad-debt deduction reduced to 30 per cent of taxable income over five years, from a 1979 level of 40 per cent.

Also under Carter's tax program, credit unions would have their tax-exempt status phased out over five years.

Capital Gains. Carter, as expected, backed down from his earlier promises to propose elimination of the special tax treatment on capital gains. But he did propose tightening up on the tax treatment of capital gains for upper-income individuals.

Under existing law, taxpayers were required to include only 50 per cent of income from capital gains in their tax base. But another provision set a 25 per cent tax ceiling on the first $50,000 of capital gains.

That means that taxpayers in the 50 per cent tax bracket and higher receive an extra tax break on the first $50,000 of capital gains.

Carter proposed eliminating the 25 per cent ceiling, known as the "alternative tax."

Reaction

As expected, Carter's tax proposals stirred considerable controversy. Republicans appeared to be rallying behind an alternative proposal (S 1860, HR 8333) sponsored by Sen. William V. Roth Jr., R-Del., and Rep. Jack F. Kemp, R-N.Y.

Their proposal would reduce individual income tax rates across-the-board by about 33 per cent over three years. When fully implemented, rates would range from 8 per cent for the lowest income bracket to 50 per cent for the highest one, as opposed to the present range of 14 to 70 per cent.

Roth dubbed Carter's tax proposals "a tax fraud on the American people." He claimed it would be insufficient to offset the higher tax burden created by inflation, Social Security tax increases, and possible new energy taxes.

"The President's tax package is neither big, bold nor beneficial," said Roth. "And besides being too small, the President's tax cut does not provide enough relief to middle-income taxpayers."

Some Republicans hit Carter for proposing an Oct. 1, 1978, effective date for the tax reduction. The President reportedly chose that date for two reasons: Economic forecasts suggested that stimulus would be needed toward the end of the year, and both Muskie and Giaimo had urged him in a meeting in December to make the cut take effect in the new fiscal year so that Congress would not have to pass a third budget resolution in fiscal 1978, which ends Sept. 30, 1978.

Still, some critics of the President hinted that the Oct. 1 date was set with the November elections in mind. Others argued that October would be too late to spare taxpayers the burden of higher Social Security taxes through nine months of 1978. Roth suggested making the reduction retroactive to Jan. 1. Rhodes proposed a March 1 date.

Tax Reform

The House Republican leader suggested that early deadline could be reached by separating Carter's proposed "reforms" from the reduction and expediting the tax cut.

While the idea of an early effective date had a supporter in House Ways and Means Committee Chairman Al Ullman, D-Ore., the chairman was adamantly against dividing the package. Ullman set a May target for getting the tax package through the House, but he conceded that it was not likely to win final enactment until September.

As usual, Ullman's Senate counterpart, Finance Committee Chairman Russell B. Long, D-La., had no comment.

Even if the proposed cuts and reforms remained linked, most observers gave the reform proposals fairly slim chances. House Speaker Thomas P. O'Neill Jr., D-Mass., said on CBS' "Face the Nation" on Jan. 22 that Carter would be lucky if half of the proposals were approved.

Even strong advocates of tax reform agreed with that. "The climate is not good for getting the kind of reform the President wants," said Mikva. "There's just not a constituency for it."

Ullman, whose committee began hearings on the tax proposals on Jan. 30, said he thought the reductions proposed by Carter were too large. Besides recommending an overall cut of $15 or $20 billion, Ullman said that many of the proposed reforms would have to wait.

The Ways and Means chairman said that proposals to remove special tax treatment for foreign corporate income and to tighten up on tax breaks for business expenses were "too comprehensive and controversial to consider this year."

But the chairman did say he hoped to accomplish some tax simplification, to eliminate the gasoline tax deduction, to approve Carter's proposal for taxable local bonds, and to "tighten up" on some tax deductions and shelters.

Ullman also expressed an interest in ending the so-called double taxation on corporate profits—a proposal considered, but not proposed, by Carter.

Finally, a number of reform proposals appeared sure to run into firm opposition from lawmakers arguing that the middle-income taxpayer needs a break. Some of Carter's proposals to eliminate itemized deductions for expenses such as medical bills, appeared to be in trouble on that front. Similarly, his proposal to replace the $750 personal exemption with a tax credit was scored as an attack on the middle-income taxpayer—an attack that even Mikva admitted gave him problems.

Advocates of middle-income tax relief had their own counterattack planned—the controversial tax credit for education costs. *(Tuition credits, p. 53)*

The administration repeated its opposition to the tax credit idea, but Sen. Bob Packwood, R-Ore., said he would attach his tax credit proposal to the tax bill. The Packwood bill (S 2142), cosponsored by Sen. Daniel Patrick Moynihan, D-N.Y., would provide tax credits to help offset education expenses for parents of college, elementary and secondary school children, whether the children attend public or private schools.

Budget Committees Action

In May 1978, Carter and Congress agreed to scale back the administration's proposed $24.5 billion tax cut to $19.4 billion and to delay its effective date three months, to Jan. 1, 1979.

That decision helped pave the way for final congressional approval of the first concurrent budget resolution (S Con Res 80), setting non-binding spending and tax goals for the fiscal year beginning Oct. 1, 1978. Binding figures would be set in a second resolution in September.

By reducing the size of the expected tax cut — its impact during fiscal year 1979 would be to reduce revenues by only $15 billion — lawmakers were able to project a significantly smaller deficit than was forecast in earlier budget proposals by the administration or either branch of Congress. *(Budget proposals, p. 15)*

The budget compromise drafted by a Senate-House conference committee May 11, 12 and 15 won strong bipartisan support in the Senate, even though the revenue figure allowed for a tax cut significantly smaller than recommended by either the Finance or Budget Committees. In part, that reflected a growing consensus that, in view of falling unemployment and accelerating inflation, the economy should not be stimulated as much as many policymakers had previously believed.

"Inflation has increased and unemployment has fallen more than expected," noted Budget Committee Chairmen Sen. Edmund S. Muskie, D-Maine, and Rep. Robert N. Giaimo, D-Conn., in announcing the compromise with the White House on taxes. "Monetary policy has become more restrictive, and interest rates have risen, in response to the fears of higher inflation and weakness of the dollar.

"This reduced deficit will signal Congress' determination to maintain fiscal discipline, reduce inflationary pressures, ease the pressures on capital markets, and maintain the integrity of the American dollar as a reserve asset."

The scaled back tax proposal was immediately hailed by Federal Reserve Board Chairman G. William Miller, who had been calling for just such a shift.

Miller said the decision was "very properly made," and he suggested that it might enable the Federal Reserve Board to ease up on interest rates, which had risen about a half percentage point since Miller took office in March.

"The more discipline we have in fiscal policy, the more pressure we take off monetary policy," Miller said.

House Republican Opposition

The plan didn't draw such a favorable response from House Republicans. House Minority Leader John J. Rhodes, R-Ariz., described the conference committee's budget as "completely inadequate" and "inflationary."

During floor debate May 17, Rhodes and other Republicans complained that the conference committee had reduced the deficit almost entirely by cutting the size of the expected tax cut, rather than by limiting federal spending.

They argued that the smaller tax cut would be inadequate to offset the increase in tax burden resulting from inflation and rising Social Security taxes. Rhodes said inflation would increase taxes $14 billion by pushing taxpayers into higher tax brackets. He said Social Security taxes would rise another $9 billion.

"If you vote for this conference report, you're voting for a tax increase on the American people, and for a $51 billion deficit," Rhodes said.

Comparison with Jones Proposal

When the House Ways and Means Committee met July 20 to resume consideration of a tax bill — after a three-month lapse — it had before it not only the Carter tax package but an alternative proposal introduced by Chairman Ullman, ranking Republican Barber B. Conable Jr., N.Y., and James R. Jones, D-Okla.

The "Jones compromise" would provide net tax cuts for individuals and business of $15.4 billion in 1979. The tax cut for individuals would be $11.5 billion, including $1.2 billion in capital gains reduction, while business taxes would be cut by $3.9 billion, including a $100 million reduction in capital gains taxes. *(Capital gains tax issue, p. 29)*

In addition to capital gains cuts, the Jones plan would widen the tax brackets by about 6 per cent. For example, under existing law, a married couple with taxable income, after deductions, of $23,200 to $27,200 paid taxes at a rate of 32 per cent within that bracket. Under the Jones plan, the 32 per cent bracket would be raised to include taxable income of $24,600 to $28,840.

In addition, the Jones plan included modest rate cuts in certain middle-income brackets, primarily designed to offset the pending rise in Social Security taxes. *(Social Security taxes, p. 59)*

For individuals, the existing $750 personal exemption for each taxpayer and dependent would be raised to $1,000.

For businesses, the Jones plan would reduce the top corporate tax rate to 46 per cent from 48 per cent. But the level at which a corporation would pay the top rate would increase from $50,000 to $100,000 of taxable income. On the first $25,000 of taxable income, a corporation would pay 17 per cent as compared to the existing 20 per cent rate. On the next $25,000 the rate would drop to 20 per cent from 22 per cent. A corporation's third $25,000 of taxable income would be taxed at 30 per cent, and its fourth $25,000 would be subject to a 40 per cent rate.

Like the Carter proposal, the Jones plan would liberalize the investment tax credit, but would not extend the credit to utility and industrial buildings. And, like the Carter plan, the Jones compromise would eliminate individual deductions for state and local sales, gasoline and personal property taxes.

Although the Jones compromise did not contain many of Carter's revenue-raising "reform" proposals, it did include repeal of the existing deduction for political contributions and some tightening of the deduction for medical expenses.

Republicans Push Their Bill

Meanwhile, with divisions within the Democratic ranks over the various tax proposals, Republicans launched a drive to win support for their own bill, the so-called Kemp-Roth proposal, providing for a 33 per cent tax cut over a three-year period. In a speech at the National Press Club June 29, House Minority Leader John J. Rhodes, R-Ariz., said, "Starting here and now, Republicans intend to make sure that the American voter knows which party seeks a real tax cut and which party...really wants to continue a policy of high taxes."

"I think after Proposition 13, a lot of Democrats will support Roth-Kemp because they are concerned about their political futures," said Republican National Committee Chairman Bill Brock. *(Proposition 13, p. 45; Middle class taxpayers revolt, p. 39)*

Under the Roth-Kemp proposal, a family of four with an $8,000 income would pay $12 instead of $120 in taxes; one earning $15,000 would pay $811 instead of $1,330; one earning $25,000 would pay $2,047 instead of $3,150; and one earning $40,000 would pay $4,512 instead of $6,848. The bill would lower the corporate tax rate to 45 per cent from 48 per cent and increase the floor for the maximum corporate rate to $100,000 from $50,000.

Ways and Means Reports Bill

In an almost total defeat for President Carter, the House Ways and Means Committee July 27 approved a $16 billion tax cut that included a substantial reduction in capital gains taxes.

The committee's 12 Republicans were joined by 13 Democrats on the 25-12 vote endorsing the bill (HR 13511) in essentially the "compromise" form proposed by Jones.

One major addition to the Jones proposal, designed in part to mute liberal criticisms of the capital gains reductions, provided homeowners a one-time complete exemption from capital gains taxes on profits up to $100,000 from the sale of personal residences.

In another effort to assuage liberal members, the committee approved a new "alternative minimum tax" to ensure that the new capital gains tax reductions don't make it possible for some very wealthy taxpayers to avoid paying taxes completely.

In addition, an unlikely coalition of committee members approved a provision "indexing" the capital gains tax beginning in 1980, sheltering taxpayers from paying taxes on inflation-induced appreciation of their assets.

The bill bore almost no resemblance to the tax program Carter sent to Congress in January. It excluded almost all of the President's proposed tax "reforms," aimed the benefits of the tax cut primarily toward people in the middle- and upper-income brackets rather than lower down the income scale as suggested by Carter, and included capital gains tax reductions that the President threatened to veto.

"This obviously is not a tax reform bill," said Ways and Means Chairman Ullman. "It is an economic tax package. We have voted here a substantial reduction in the deficit. It is very counter-inflationary."

"This helps the middle class taxpayer in a manner much more substantial than the traditional tax reform bill."

—Barber B. Conable Jr., R-N.Y.

The tax cuts wouldn't take effect until Jan. 1, 1979, so they would only reduce revenues in the fiscal year beginning Oct. 1 by $9.3 billion.

Congress had agreed as part of its first budget resolution to a $15 billion tax cut during the fiscal year. President Carter endorsed that figure.

Ullman drove the committee hard during three days of markup to complete action on the bill, and he described the final version as the "best compromise" possible.

The compromise left the committee's 12 liberal Democrats out in the cold. One of their most outspoken members, Abner J. Mikva, D-Ill., called the bill "outrageous." He threatened to go to the House Democratic Caucus to rally support for a floor fight against the committee action.

Committee Republicans, on the other hand, were quite pleased by the product wrought by them and the 13 more conservative Democrats.

"This reflects the American people's view of tax reform because it is a tax reduction," said the committee's ranking Republican, Barber B. Conable Jr., R-N.Y. "And it helps the middle-class taxpayer in a manner much more substantial than the traditional tax reform bill."

Also pleased was William A. Steiger, R-Wis., who set off the capital gains controversy by proposing a reduction in the maximum possible capital gains rate to 25 per cent from 49 per cent.

"This is a very significant first step in the reduction of taxes on capital gains," Steiger said. He predicted that the Senate would reduce capital gains taxes even further, paving the way for a "more acceptable" final compromise.

Liberals, who opposed the capital gains tax cut and hoped to skew individual tax reductions toward lower income people, were outgunned throughout the markup.

Their strategy, which was only loosely developed, appeared to include two elements. The first was a substitute amendment prepared by Joseph L. Fisher, D-Va. The second was the idea of loading the Jones proposal down with so many unattractive amendments that it would eventually sink, leaving the Fisher proposal floating alone.

Instead, the liberals lost most of the amendments they sought, and watched helplessly as the committee approved a number of amendments that undercut the Fisher proposal.

Social Security

The first liberal defeat came on a proposal by Richard A. Gephardt, D-Mo., to provide employers and employees an income tax credit equal to 5 per cent of their Social Security taxes during 1979 and 1980. The proposal, which would have cost about $6 billion annually, was designed to offset scheduled increases in Social Security taxes. It was

Summary of House-Passed Tax Bill

The "Revenue Act of 1978," approved by the House Ways and Means Committee July 27 and passed by the House Aug. 10, would provide $10.4 billion in tax cuts to individuals, and $3.8 billion to businesses during 1979. It would reduce capital gains taxes by $1.9 billion, of which $1.7 billion would go to individuals and about $200 million would go to businesses.

Individual Cuts

About 64.4 million tax returns would receive a tax decrease, averaging $163 per return. The size of the decrease would rise with income, from an average of about $19 for persons with expanded income below $5,000 to an average of $219 in the $20,000-$30,000 income class, to $1,740 in the $100,000-$200,000 class and $9,940 in the over $200,000 income class.

About 2.6 million returns would receive a tax increase averaging $24. The increase, which would fall mostly on single people, would range from $14 in the lowest income class to $1,611 in the highest.

Highlights of the individual tax cuts included:

● A 6 per cent widening of income tax brackets designed to prevent taxpayers from being pushed into higher tax brackets as their incomes rise.

● An increase in the zero bracket amount — formerly called the standard deduction — to $2,300 from $2,200 for single persons and to $3,400 from $3,200 for married couples.

● An increase in the personal exemption for each taxpayer and dependent to $1,000 from $750, and elimination of the existing general tax credit. That change accounts for most of the tax increases on single taxpayers.

● Elimination of itemized deductions for state and local motor fuel taxes and political contributions (the existing tax credit for political contributions would be retained).

● A somewhat tightened medical expense deduction, although not as much as Carter had proposed.

● A provision that unemployment compensation benefits equal to one half the income in excess of $20,000 for single persons and $25,000 for married persons be taxed.

Corporate Cuts

The bill would establish a graduated corporate income tax as follows:

● For corporate income up to $25,000, the tax rate would be reduced to 17 per cent from 20 per cent.

● For income between $25,000 and $50,000, the rate would be reduced to 20 per cent from 22 per cent.

● For income between $50,000 and $75,000, the rate would be 30 per cent.

● For income between $75,000 and $100,000, the rate would be 40 per cent.

● For income above $100,000, the rate would be reduced reduced to 46 per cent from 48 per cent.

Other changes in corporate taxation include:

● An increase in the amount of regular tax liability that can be offset in a single year by investment tax credits to 90 per cent from 50 per cent, to be phased in at a rate of 10 per cent per year.

● Replacement of the existing general jobs tax credit with a targeted jobs credit for employers who hire welfare recipients, supplemental security income (SSI) recipients, unemployed Vietnam veterans and youths who participate in high school or vocational school work-study programs.

Capital Gains Tax Changes

Changes in capital gains taxation include:

● Elimination of the "alternative" 25 per cent maximum tax rate on capital gains up to $50,000.

● Elimination of capital gains as preference items subject to the minimum tax and to the "poison" of the maximum tax on earned income. The effect of the two provisions would be to make the maximum possible tax rate on capital gains 35 per cent, instead of 49.1 per cent. *(Capital gains, p. 29)*

● Indexation of the basis of capital gains beginning Jan. 1, 1980, so that the amount of gains subject to taxation will be reduced by the amount of the increase of the consumer price index each year.

● Repeal of the capital gains and minimum tax on up to $100,000 in profits on the sale of a principal residence occupied by the owner for at least two years. The provision would be available only once in the life of a taxpayer. It would apply to any sale after July 26, 1978.

● A new "alternative minimum tax" on capital gains that a taxpayer would have to pay if his regular tax liability was less than the new tax. The levy would be equal to 10 per cent of the portion of his capital gains exempt from regular taxation, with a $10,000 exemption.

---

rejected, 11-24, in the first major display of the support for the Jones package. The vote also reflected that rolling back Social Security taxes, a popular issue early in the session, had lost support. *(Social Security taxes, p. 59)*

Indexing

The liberals appeared to score a partial victory when some of them helped approve an amendment by Bill Archer, R-Texas, to index the capital gains tax.

Archer's amendment provided that the base value of an asset subject to the capital gains tax would be increased by the same percentage as the rise in the consumer price index each year — effectively reducing by the rate of inflation the amount of capital gains subject to taxation.

While the proposal would have a negligible effect during its first few years, experts estimated that it could eventually cut revenues from the capital gains tax in half. The amendment was approved on a 21-16 vote.

Later, Bill Gradison, R-Ohio, offered an amendment to index the personal income tax, but it was rejected 13-23.

Capital Gains

The biggest blow to the Fisher proposal came when the committee approved on a voice vote an amendment by

Sam Gibbons, D-Fla., providing a once-in-a-lifetime complete exemption from capital gains and minimum taxes on profits up to $100,000 from the sale of personal residences.

The Gibbons amendment added about $745 million to the capital gains tax breaks previously included in the Jones bill. But more important, it strengthened the package politically by neutralizing one of the main advantages of Fisher's proposal — namely a proposed capital gains tax break for homeowners.

Referring to the Archer and Gibbons amendments, Jones later said: "I'm not sure I can justify them economically, but politically they strengthen the bill."

Strengthening Amendment

The Oklahoma congressman later added one further strengthening amendment to his capital gains proposals. Answering complaints by the administration that the bill would free a small number of millionaires completely from taxes by removing capital gains from the present minimum tax, he won committee support, 33-3, for a new "alternative minimum tax."

The new tax would be computed quite differently than the existing tax. While the current minimum tax is added on to taxpayers' regular capital gains tax liability, the new tax would only be paid if it exceeded a taxpayer's regular liability.

Conable described it as a "true minimum tax," as opposed to the existing levy, which he called an "add-on tax."

The alternative minimum tax would pick up $120 million in revenues, mostly from very wealthy taxpayers. That compares to $1.2 billion that would be returned, also mostly to wealthy people, through the Jones proposal to remove capital gains from the present minimum tax.

Fisher Substitute

Fisher tried to outflank Jones' supporters by expanding his original substitute to embrace the proposed Social Security tax credit and other proposals. In its final version, it would have allowed a $23.4 billion tax cut.

Fisher said his proposal would preserve a "meaningful" minimum tax on capital gains, more directly encourage capital investment, focus more relief on middle- and lower-income taxpayers, and provide direct relief for rising Social Security taxes.

Jones complained that the Fisher substitute would add $7.5 billion more to the federal deficit, provide less relief to taxpayers in the "middle" $20,000-$50,000 brackets, and preserve disproportionately high tax rates for married people.

The Fisher proposal was rejected, 13-24.

Other Substitutes

The committee also turned down, 11-24, a substitute by James C. Corman, D-Calif. that would:

• Increase the existing general tax credit to $150 for the first exemption and $110 for all other exemptions, and keep the alternative credit of 2 per cent of the first $9,000 of income.

• Retain the existing earned income credit and investment tax credit.

• Reduce corporate tax rates to 18 per cent for the first $25,000 of income, 20 per cent for income between $25,000 and $50,000 and 46 per cent for income above $50,000.

• Include the Gibbons amendment on the capital gains tax exemption for personal residences.

• Provide a targeted jobs credit.

Finally, the committee rejected, 11-26, a proposal by Charles A. Vanik, D-Ohio, and J. J. Pickle, D-Texas, to enact no new tax cut.

Business Entertainment Deductions

While a wide variety of other amendments were considered, the largest number involved a completely unsuccessful attempt by committee liberals to tighten up somewhat on business entertainment deductions.

From the outset, the liberals set their sights much lower than Carter had during his campaign assaults on the "three martini lunch," but even their more modest proposals were consistently rejected.

The most ambitious proposal, by William M. Brodhead, D-Mich., would have limited business entertainment deductions to $44 per person per day. It was rejected, 14-23.

After that, proposals were scaled down progressively until Andy Jacobs Jr., D-Ind., suggested merely disallowing business entertainment deductions for entertaining members of Congress. It was rejected on a voice vote.

In one surprise vote, the committee rejected, 15-22, an amendment by Fisher and Conable to allow taxpayers who take the standard deduction to make a special additional deduction for charitable contributions. The proposal had been tentatively approved by the committee in April 1978.

The Rule

Aware that attempts probably would be made to amend the bill on the House floor, the committee agreed to seek from the Rules Committee a rule allowing floor votes only on complete substitutes to the bill it approved.

Specifically, the Ways and Means panel agreed to allow votes on the Corman, Fisher and Vanik-Pickle substitutes, and also on the Roth-Kemp bill (S 1860, HR 8333) providing a one-third, across-the-board reduction in income tax rates over three years.

In early August, following an administration lobbying blitz, Ways and Means Committee liberals agreed to support a two-part proposal that would shift the tax cuts toward low- and middle-income taxpayers and trim a cut in capital gains taxes. The plan, sponsored jointly by Reps. Corman and Fisher, was drafted with Treasury help. *(Details, p. 33, 52)*

Long's Plans

In the meantime, Senate Finance Committee Chairman Russell B. Long, D-La., told the National Press Club July 26 that his committee would take a different approach to the tax bill. Long said his committee would approve a proposal to reduce the portion of capital gains subject to taxation to 30 per cent from the existing 50 per cent.

Long said his proposal would have the advantage of helping capital gains taxpayers in all income ranges, and he noted that it would leave the present minimum tax intact. Under the proposal, the maximum possible capital gains tax rate would be 28.5 per cent. The change would cost the treasury $3 billion in revenues annually.

When the Senate Finance Committee opened up hearings Aug. 17 on tax cut legislation, Long repeated his hope to reduce capital gains tax rates. Long's idea was similar to a 1963 proposal by then-President Kennedy.

(Continued on p. 52)

Capital Gains Tax Issue: Carter *vs.* Congress

When Jimmy Carter promised during his presidential campaign in 1976 to seek to end the preferential tax treatment afforded capital gains, many thought he was merely continuing a tax reform tradition that had begun in 1969.

Two years later, Carter dropped the proposal, bowing to political realities and a perceived need to win business confidence.

But he did try to keep alive the trend toward limiting the special tax break by proposing a relatively mild further restriction.

Even that proved to be an overly ambitious proposal. By the spring of 1978, the administration was forced into a headlong retreat on its tax ideas, devoting much of its energy to fighting a surprisingly strong movement to unravel "reforms" of the recent past and actually ease up on the tax treatment of capital gains.

Probably more than any tax issue in 1978, the capital gains battle has revealed the extent to which Congress has become more interested in reconsidering the tax "reforms" of 1969 and 1976 than in extending them.

In addition, the debate has uncovered a deep division among the nation's economic policy makers — one that has stymied politicians and set off a strenuous debate among economists.

On one side are politicians and economists who argue that a reduction in capital gains taxes would spur the economy to grow significantly, in the process spinning off new jobs, increasing government revenues, shrinking the federal deficit and slowing inflation.

Against them are arrayed other politicians and economists who claim that the change would have minimal economic impact while providing a whopping tax break to some of the wealthiest people in the country.

By mid-1978, there was substantial bipartisan support in Congress for a rollback of the tax on capital gains. At the same time, the administration launched an intense lobbying campaign against legislative proposals to cut the tax.

Despite the administration's efforts, the House Aug. 10 passed a tax bill that included a substantial reduction in the capital gains tax, and it appeared likely that the Senate Finance Committee would approve even further reductions. At a news conference June 26, Carter indicated he might veto any tax bill that contained such legislation. *(House action, p. 52)*

Background

Capital gains are profits realized from investments in stock, real estate and other capital assets held for at least a year. They have long been taxed at lower rates than "earned income," such as wages and salaries, and other forms of "unearned income," such as interest and dividends.

In general, taxpayers are allowed to deduct half of their capital gains from their taxable income. Since income tax rates range from 14 percent to 70 percent, that means the rate on capital gains in effect runs from 7 percent to 35 percent.

Prior to 1969, however, there was a 25 percent ceiling on the capital gains tax rate, even for taxpayers whose total income put them in the 50 percent tax bracket and higher.

In the Tax Reform Act of 1969, Congress made several changes to tighten up on the tax breaks allowed on capital gains. First, it limited the 25 percent maximum to only the first $50,000 of capital gains. For corporations, it moved the maximum rate up to 30 percent.

Concerned that some wealthy taxpayers were largely avoiding taxes, Congress also established in the 1969 act a 10 percent minimum tax on "preference" items such as capital gains. But it exempted the first $30,000 of preference income from the minimum tax.

In 1976, Congress further restricted the capital gains preference. It increased the minimum tax rate to 15 percent, and it reduced the exemption to the greater of $10,000 of preference income or half of a taxpayer's regular taxes.

The 1976 act also diminished the special treatment given capital gains by increasing taxes on wages and salaries for taxpayers benefiting from the preferential gains rate. Under existing law, the maximum tax on earned income is 50 percent. But the 1976 act provided that the amount of earned income qualifying for that maximum be reduced dollar-for-dollar by the amount of capital gains excluded from regular taxation.

The combined effect of the minimum tax, the maximum tax and the "preference poison" that capital gains deals to earned income is to increase the maximum possible tax rate for capital gains to 49.125 percent.

It is fairly unusual, however, for a taxpayer to incur the maximum possible rate. The Treasury Department estimated that the actual capital gains tax rate for most people at all levels of income is substantially lower than the theoretical maximum. Even for taxpayers earning more than $200,000, the department estimated that the average effective rate would be 37.1 percent in 1978.

Carter Proposal

Although he originally had hoped to end entirely the special tax treatment of capital gains, President Carter in January 1978 recommended only that Congress eliminate the 25 percent tax ceiling on the first $50,000 of capital gains.

Carter argued that the maximum (also called the "alternative" tax) benefits only very wealthy taxpayers. Individual taxpayers have to be in the 50 percent tax bracket — earning $34,200 — or higher to benefit.

The proposal never caught on. Beginning with House Ways and Means Committee hearings in March 1978, it became apparent that the president's capital gains recommendation would serve not as a rallying point but as a target for a backlash against the 1969 and 1976 restrictions on capital gains taxes.

The movement was led by three groups — the American Electronics Association, the National Venture

Capital Association and the American Council for Capital Formation.

All carried a similar message to the Ways and Means Committee. They said that the increase in capital gains taxes had sapped the incentive for investors to put their money in new risky ventures. If the capital gains tax were lowered, they said, investors would return to the stock market and spur new economic growth.

They found a responsive listener in Ways and Means Committee member William A. Steiger, R-Wis. Steiger enlisted another committee Republican — Bill Frenzel, Minn. — and two Democrats — Ed Jenkins, Ga., and James R. Jones, Okla. — to push for a capital gains tax reduction.

Steiger Proposal

Steiger proposed (HR 12111) rolling back the maximum capital gains tax rate to the pre-1969 level, 25 percent. Specifically, he recommended eliminating capital gains from the preference items subject to the minimum tax, and imposing the 25 percent maximum for all gains rather than just those less than $50,000. He also recommended rolling back the corporate rate to 25 percent from 30 percent.

A companion bill (S 3065) was introduced in the Senate by Clifford P. Hansen, R-Wyo. It had 61 cosponsors by the end of May. Finance Committee Chairman Russell B. Long, D-La., also endorsed a capital gains cut.

While Steiger was generally recognized to have a solid majority of the 37-member Ways and Means Committee supporting his amendment, the committee became deadlocked when a number of liberals who were adamantly opposed to the capital gains revision threatened to join opponents of any tax cut if the Steiger proposal were adopted.

It was generally believed that the coalition might be large enough to prevent any bill from emerging from the committee.

Jones Compromise

Committee Chairman Al Ullman, D-Ore., designated Jones to search for a compromise. Jones suggested exempting capital gains from the minimum tax and setting a ceiling on all gains — including those below $50,000 — of 35 percent. He also recommended reducing the capital gains tax for corporations to 28 percent from 30 percent.

That capital gains recommendation was part of a general tax proposal pushed by the Oklahoma congressman. Other elements included:

● Cutting individual income tax rates by 6 percent across-the-board. The proposal would involve increasing the personal tax exemption to $1,000 from $750 and eliminating the present $35 per person tax credit.

● Rejecting all of Carter's proposed tax reforms except for the proposed repeal of deductions for state and local gasoline taxes and personal property taxes.

● Reducing corporate taxes to 46 percent from 48 percent, and increasing to $75,000 from $50,000 the amount of corporate income taxed at reduced rates.

Word went out after a meeting June 6 of Ways and Means Committee leaders that the Jones compromise would win support by the full committee, enabling the suspended markup to resume after a five-week hiatus.

The committee resumed markup on July 20, and on July 27 approved the Jones "compromise" (HR 13511) by a vote of 25-12.

A Capital Shortage?

Support for the capital gains tax rollback is rooted in growing concern that the rate of business investment in the United States has slowed to the point that future economic growth may be insufficient to keep unemployment from increasing as the work force grows.

That concern was acknowledged by the administration in the annual report of the president's Council of Economic Advisers in January 1978, and it was repeated by Treasury Secretary W. Michael Blumenthal in a speech on May 8 citing the need to encourage investment by increasing the "profitability of American enterprise."

"This means cutting business taxes — to boost the real rate of return, to provide an increased cash flow, and to improve the ratio of equity to debt on corporate balance sheets," he said.

The secretary said the administration had considered a variety of methods of achieving that goal — including looking at the special rate on capital gains, the "double taxation" of corporate dividends and others.

"But the advice we received, uniformly, was to stay away from any such tinkering this year, to keep our

package simple, and thereby minimize delay and uncertainty," Blumenthal concluded.

Steiger and his allies on the Ways and Means Committee had no such qualms. Capitalizing on the attention Carter's "reform" proposals directed at the capital gains tax, and arguing that restoring the tax to its pre-1969 levels would be fairly easy to accomplish, they quickly found a substantial number of lawmakers who believed that the time had come to stimulate business investment directly.

The rapidity with which the Steiger proposal gained support in the Ways and Means Committee caught most observers by surprise. Some explained the phenomenon by noting that proposals to spur investment by eliminating the double taxation of corporate dividends were too complex for the committee to consider in 1978.

Proposals to liberalize investment tax credits raised suspicions among lawmakers representing economically declining regions who feared that a government prod to investment in plant and equipment might accelerate the flight of industry to growing areas in the South and West.

At the same time, the Steiger amendment picked up some support because, while seen as an incentive to investment, it would benefit individuals.

Growth Scenario

"The proposal is as close to a free lunch bill as you could get," boasted Dr. Richard Rahn, executive director of the American Council for Capital Formation.

Rahn, echoing arguments used by most Steiger amendment proponents, claimed the proposal would prompt a large number of investors to return to the stock market. Those investors, he said, had been using their money for consumption, putting it into less risky investments (such as municipal bonds), or simply holding onto their capital assets in order to avoid realizing gains that have to be taxed at current high rates.

Reducing the gains tax, Rahn continued, would thus encourage economic growth, especially among technologically innovative industries which are most reliant on the stock market.

At the same time, the change would reduce the extent to which business has relied on debt financing, in turn lowering interest rates and thus further encouraging growth while also slowing inflation, Rahn said.

The end result, he concluded, would be more jobs and, in turn, more government revenues, a lower deficit and less inflation.

Critics of the Steiger amendment question the validity of the entire scenario. They note, first, that less than 30 percent of all capital gains occur on corporate stock. The lion's share of capital gains — 50 percent by one estimate — occur on real estate.

Reducing the tax, far from encouraging new investment, would merely reward real estate "speculators," some critics conclude.

The opponents argue further that the Steiger amendment proponents have no proof of how much capital gains are currently "locked in" as a result of the existing high tax rates. They argue that there is still sufficient incentive for investors to sell capital assets, and they question whether a reduction in capital gains taxes would significantly accelerate such sales.

They also argue that there is no proof that the proposed reduction would increase investment or shift it from areas such as real estate to the stock market.

Finally, the opponents challenge claims that a reduction in the capital gains tax would so accelerate economic activity that it would actually increase government revenues. In a letter to the Ways and Means Committee May 11, Blumenthal estimated that the Steiger proposal would decrease federal revenues by $2.2 billion. (The cost of the Jones compromise was estimated to be $1.36 billion.)

Supporters of the capital gains tax cut dispute Blumenthal's assertion. They describe it as a "static" analysis that assumes a reduction in the tax rate would have no effect on the amount of capital assets sold. In fact, they argue, a reduction in the rate would greatly increase sales, thus actually increasing revenues.

It is virtually impossible to find an accepted technique for predicting such "second order" effects of a capital gains tax reduction, however. A staff member for the Joint Committee on Taxation, which performs technical analyses for both the House Ways and Means Committee and the Senate Finance Committee, said the joint committee refuses to attempt such analyses because "there is no accepted theory on how to go about it, and to try to do so would lay the joint com-

mittee open to charges of playing politics in making technical estimates."

Equity Issue

The biggest objection to the proposed capital gains tax cut, however, is that it would benefit very wealthy people.

In his May 11 letter, Blumenthal said that over 80 percent of the benefits of the Steiger proposal would go to people earning more than $100,000.

The joint committee estimated that the benefits would be divided as follows:

Income (thousands)	Share of Benefits (percent)
$0-20	4.1
$20-30	4.2
$30-50	8.0
$50-100	15.0
$100-200	12.7
$200 and over	56.1

The joint committee estimated that the proposal would benefit about 370,000 tax-paying households out of a total of 88.5 million.

Steiger amendment supporters have not challenged the basic argument that the proposal would reduce the progressivity of the tax system. But they have argued that it would be worth it because it would create jobs and increase government revenues, thus lowering overall taxes for middle and lower income people.

"There is a basic conflict between the rate of economic growth and egalitarianism," noted Rahn. "Countries with the most egalitarian tax systems tend to have lower rates of economic growth. Any society has to find a balance.

"We've swung too far toward egalitarianism," he continued. "It's time to swing back and increase economic growth because we'll all be better off if we do."

Steiger opponents were unconvinced. "If [the amendment] would do what they say it would do, I'd be all for it — even though it would help a tiny number of people with tremendous incomes," said Ralph B. Bristol Jr., chief of econometric analysis for the Treasury Department. "But there is not a shred of evidence it will provide any economic stimulus."

Econometric Debate

Bristol was at the center of a raging debate among experts over the

effect of the proposed capital gains tax reduction.

The debate began when Michael K. Evans of Chase Econometrics Associates Inc. released a report April 17, 1978, claiming that the Steiger proposal would increase the average growth rate of the economy, adding 440,000 jobs to the workforce and reducing the federal deficit by $16 billion.

The report was given a large share of the credit for the very substantial support for the Steiger amendment.

Evans' analysis was based on the claim that the Steiger amendment would increase stock prices by 40 percent. The rest of his analysis — the higher rate of capital spending, resulting in economic growth, and ensuing decline in the deficit — all flowed from that argument.

In support of his claim, Evans suggested that sharp declines in stock prices since 1969 have resulted from previous congressional actions to tighten up on capital gains taxes.

Bristol strenuously challenged that assertion. He said the increase in stock prices predicted by Evans couldn't be scientifically supported, but was, rather, an assumption external to the mathematical model used by Chase Econometrics.

In fact, Bristol argued, econometricians haven't yet been able to develop a model that can predict the ups and downs of stock prices.

"People have been forecasting the stock market for years," Bristol said in an interview with Congressional Quarterly. "The only ones who have made money from it are the ones who sold books telling people how to invest."

A preliminary analysis of the Chase study by the Congressional Research Service for Rep. Charles A. Vanik, D-Ohio, also suggested that the Evans argument should be taken with a grain of salt.

That study noted the inadequacy of econometric models in predicting the stock market. It compared the Chase assumptions about the effect of capital gains taxes on stock prices with other economic analyses, concluding that the Evans assumptions "appear to be quite generous."

Battle Heats Up

The Carter administration and the Democratic House leadership mounted a new effort June 26, 1978, to head off proposals to relax the capital gains tax, signaling the beginning of what most observers expected to be the biggest donnybrook of the second session of the 95th Congress.

The drive followed a series of meetings the previous week, during which the administration and Democratic leaders agreed to drop all of President Carter's tax "reforms" — at least for a while — and to push for a straight $15 billion tax cut as an alternative to proposals to reduce capital gains taxes. *(Carter "reform" proposals, p. 21)*

Even before the new drive began, though, there were signs of disunity between the administration and the Democratic leadership.

House Speaker Thomas P. O'Neill Jr., D-Mass., told reporters June 22 that the administration was pushing for a simple $15 billion tax cut — $10 billion for individuals and $5 billion for businesses — and that it had dropped all efforts to enact tax "reforms."

"The attempt is to draw a line so we have this $15 billion straight proposal versus Steiger," a knowledgeable congressional staffer explained.

A White House statement the same day, however, said that any change in Carter's proposals — including reducing the tax cut from the proposed $19.4 billion beginning Jan. 1 or dropping the recommended "reforms" — was designed only to get a bill out of the stalled Ways and Means Committee. Administration officials said they hoped to restore some "reforms" by amending the bill on the House floor.

While the administration and its Democratic allies in the House were divided on what tax package they would like to see ultimately, they were united in their opposition to any capital gains tax reduction.

Carter himself launched the new campaign at a press conference June 26 with an all-but-outright threat to veto any tax bill containing a capital gains tax cut.

In an opening statement accompanied by a four-page "fact sheet" on the Steiger proposal, Carter argued that the capital gains reduction would add more than $2 billion to the federal deficit while benefiting the very wealthy.

The next day, the House Democratic leadership fired a salvo of its own at the Steiger proposal. A "whip issue paper" by Majority Whip John Brademas, D-Ind., lambasted the

Steiger proposal as "regressive, ineffective in terms of capital formation, and unwarranted in terms of expanding already generous tax treatment for capital gains."

The paper called the proposal "tax favoritism at its most regressive."

Questioning whether Carter or the Democratic Congress would be willing to kill a tax bill in an election year, even if it contained a capital gains tax cut, Steiger said the veto threat was a "bluff."

He continued his drive to enact the capital gains proposal in testimony June 28 before the Senate Finance Subcommittee on Taxation and Debt Management Generally.

"Our president has been given misleading statistics . . . he's been given some poor advice about economic growth and . . . he himself miscounts what it is that encourages private individuals to buy their homes and to take investment risks that ultimately create jobs and enhance the productivity of a free enterprise system," he said.

Steiger suggested that increases in capital gains taxes since 1969 were largely responsible for the decline in business investment in recent years, and he concluded:

"If we lower this tax, economic activity will accelerate. Stock market values will increase. The portfolios of private pension plans — the main source of savings of the American worker — will recover from the disaster of the 1970s. New equity capital will be available, companies can expand, employment can increase and everyone benefits."

Just how much the administration's new drive had aroused congressional passions became clear when Treasury Secretary Blumenthal spoke against the Steiger proposals, also before the Senate Finance subcommittee.

Blumenthal called the proposal "a millionaire's relief bill," and he argued that it would increase the federal deficit and reduce money available for other business tax cuts that would more efficiently encourage new capital investment.

Blumenthal also said there was "no basis" for econometric studies that have claimed the Steiger proposal would result in substantial economic growth.

His entire testimony was branded as "demagoguery" by Sen. Bob Packwood, R-Ore., a charge that Blumen-

thal denied, saying he was just presenting "facts."

"This is going to go down all the way," said one congressional staffer. "This fight will continue until one minute before adjournment."

Liberal Alternative

Liberal Democrats finally came up with an alternative July 20 to the Republican-inspired plan to reduce capital gains taxes. But, coming late and receiving only lukewarm support from the Carter administration, its chances of enactment were dim.

The alternative, prepared by Rep. Joseph L. Fisher, D-Va., in consultation with House Ways and Means Committee liberals and administration officials, would ease capital gains taxes somewhat — especially for homeowners.

But the plan would leave almost completely intact the minimum tax on capital gains, a recent tax "reform" which, though prized by liberals, has become the main target for capital gains tax critics. By keeping the minimum tax, liberals argued, their proposal would avoid providing enormous tax breaks to very wealthy taxpayers, whom the liberals say would benefit from other capital gains tax reduction proposals.

Fisher unveiled his proposal as the Ways and Means Committee held its first markup session on major tax cut legislation since it became deadlocked over the capital gains issue April 24. *(Fisher substitute, p. 28)*

Ways and Means Chairman Al Ullman, had hoped that the markup session would proceed fairly smoothly to endorse the Jones compromise. But the session fell into disarray after several hours. The confusion at the markup was heightened as a number of members signaled their intention to load the bill with a number of pet amendments — tax breaks for charitable contributions, adjustments to the tax code to offset the effects of inflation, a Social Security tax rollback, tax credits for investments in solar energy and others.

Appearing to have little success in his pleas that members show restraint, Ullman abruptly adjourned the committee until July 24.

Fisher Proposal

The three-day weekend recess did provide time for Fisher and the administration to prepare more arguments in support of the alternative.

While it overlapped with the Jones proposal in some respects, it included important differences, especially on capital gains.

Specifically, the Fisher bill would modify capital gains taxes by:

● Increasing the exemption for all tax preferences (including capital gains) under the minimum tax to the greater of $10,000 or *all* of a taxpayer's regular taxes. Existing law exempts only the greater of $10,000 or *one-half* of a taxpayer's regular taxes.

● Repealing a provision in the tax code whereby the amount of earned income qualifying for the 50 percent maximum tax rate on earned income is reduced by the amount of capital gains excluded from regular taxation.

● Removing from the minimum tax capital gains realized from the sale of a principal residence.

● Excluding from income all gain realized from the sale of a personal residence by a person 59 years of age or older.

The Treasury Department estimated the cost of those changes to be $688 million, as opposed to the $1.2 billion that the Jones capital gains proposal would cost. (The maximum possible capital gains tax rate under Fisher's proposal would be 37.1 percent, as opposed to 35 percent under Jones and 49 percent presently.)

Also in response to the Jones bill, Fisher recommended establishing a new "equity credit" for venture capital. Under that proposal, investors would receive a tax credit equal to 10 percent of the capital gain realized from the sale of stock. The credit would be limited to the original purchaser of the stock.

Fisher recommended that the credit expire after three years unless extended by Congress. "This 'sunset' provision will enable us to judge whether the tax incentive is effective in spurring new equity issues," Fisher said, testing one of the major arguments made by proponents of the capital gains tax roll back.

The Treasury Department had no estimate of the cost of the credit during the Ways and Means Committee meeting July 20.

Administration Position

Although the Carter administration helped draft the Fisher proposal, it was only partially helpful in promoting it before the Ways and Means Committee. While saying the proposal was "preferable" to the Jones

bill, the administration refused to endorse it.

Assistant Treasury Secretary Donald C. Lubick did tell the committee that the Fisher plan went a long way in meeting four standards set by Treasury Secretary Blumenthal for any capital gains tax reduction: that the revenue loss be less than would result from the Jones proposal, that the benefits be available to a "wider spectrum" of taxpayers, that homeowners benefit, and that the breaks be better "targeted" to encourage desirable forms of investment.

"There is no doubt whatsoever that the Fisher proposals make a very substantial improvement," Lubick said. "[But] they are not the administration's."

Carter, in the meantime, weakened the prospects for the Fisher proposal by softening his earlier threat to veto the Jones approach. At a press conference after the committee session July 20 Carter said he would "have to wait until the final tax package is placed on my desk.... At that time, I will decide whether or not the tax bill is in the best interests of our country. If it's not, I will veto it."

Ways and Means Bill

After wrestling with the capital gains issue for months, the Ways and Means Committee July 27 finally approved a tax reduction/reform bill (HR 13511) that essentially was the Jones compromise, with an additional provision allowing homeowners a one-time complete exemption from capital gains taxes on profits up to $100,000 from the sale of personal residences. *(Details of committee bill, p. 27)*

The bill was approved despite the warning of House Speaker O'Neill that "we can write a far more democratic bill" and that "it goes too far as far as capital gains is concerned."

In addition to the prospects of a floor flight in the House over the bill, Senate Finance Committee Chairman Russell B. Long, D-La., July 26 predicted that his committee would "recommend a large cut in the tax rates on capital gains." Long said he personally favored reducing to 30 percent from the existing 50 percent the portion of capital gains subject to taxes. *(Long proposal, p. 28)*

Meanwhile, the administration launched a counterattack on the tax reform measure as reported by the Ways and Means Committee.

Administration Efforts

In a meeting with Treasury Secretary Blumenthal on August 3, House Ways and Means Committee liberals agreed to back a new amendment to the bill reported by the panel.

The major element in the new package, sponsored by Fisher and James C. Corman, D-Calif., was a proposal to change the method of figuring capital gains taxes. The main thrust of the amendment would be to prevent very high-income investors who had accrued "paper losses" from tax shelters from using those writeoffs to escape payment of all but a small minimum tax. The committee bill would impose a 10 percent tax on some shelter income (down from the existing 15 percent minimum), but would allow taxpayers to reduce this with "paper losses." The administration proposal would replace this with a graduated alternative tax that would require taxpayers to offset their capital gains with tax-shelter "losses" before excluding 50 percent of their profits from taxation, rather than after. The administration plan would retain the provisions of the committee bill that eliminated the 15 percent minimum tax and the 50 percent maximum tax on earned income, as well as retaining the committee bill's provision allowing a one-time exemption from capital gains taxes on profits up to $100,000 from the sale of personal residences. *(Homeowners' exemption, p. 28)*

Under existing law, according to the Treasury Department, many persons with tax shelters pay tax on millions of dollars of capital gains at the rate of 7.5 percent or less. Under the Ways and Means bill, a person who was able to shelter all his income from regular tax would not pay more than 5 percent on his gains through the alternative minimum tax. Under the administration-backed amendment, that person would pay between five percent and 17.5 percent on his gains. According to Treasury, the plan would raise about $300 million in revenues.

The other major feature of the administration's package was the proposal to shift more of the bill's tax breaks away from upper-income tax brackets in favor of taxpayers with incomes of $30,000 or less. The Ways and Means proposal had cut individual taxes through a different adjustment in tax brackets, a higher standard deduction, selected rate cuts and an increase in the personal exemption to $1,000 from the existing $750. The administration plan, in addition to a different adjustment in tax rates, would retain the $750 personal exemption and raise the existing $35-per-person general credit to $100. Treasury Secretary Blumenthal said the amendment would provide more tax relief than the Ways and Means bill for all income classes through $50,000.

The administration opposed a provision in the Ways and Means bill that would allow for the first time an "inflation adjustment" for capital gains. *(See p. 27)*

The Corman-Fisher-administration proposal omitted another possible floor amendment that would relieve some of the burden of the scheduled Social Security tax increase. *(Social Security amendment, p. 26, 52; Social Security Tax issues, p. 59)*

In early August, Blumenthal predicted that the administration had

"perhaps a 50-50 chance" of success when the House took up the bill.

But the administration's hopes were dashed on Aug. 10, when the House voted 362-49 to pass the Ways and Means Committee version of the tax bill. The final vote came after the House rejected, 193-225, the administration-backed Corman-Fisher substitute. Also rejected was an effort by liberals to create a new income tax credit equal to five percent of Social Security taxes during 1979 and 1980, as well as the Republican Roth-Kemp proposal for a 33 percent reduction in income tax rates over three years.

Before passing the bill, the House approved, by a vote of 249-167, a committee amendment that would index the capital gains tax for inflation beginning in 1980.

As passed by the House and sent to the Senate, the capital gains tax

reductions would be especially beneficial to wealthy people. More than 70 percent of the benefits of the special one time capital gains tax exclusion for the sale of a personal residence would go to people earning between $20,000 and $50,000, while only 12.7 percent would go to people earning less than $20,000.

Of the other capital gains tax changes, 60 percent of the benefits would go to people earning more than $200,000, and 96 percent would go to people earning more than $50,000.

Those features of the bill won strong Republican support. Noting that the bill would break with a tradition of "redistributing" income through the tax code, Barber B. Conable Jr., N.Y., ranking Republican on the Ways and Means Committee, called the measure "revolutionary." *(Floor action, p. 52)* ∎

Using Tax Incentives to Stem Inflation

By 1978, inflation had displaced unemployment as the predominant concern of economic policy makers.

If there was any doubt about that, it was probably erased by hearings May 22-23, 1978, by the Senate Banking, Housing and Urban Affairs Committee. During those hearings, a number of economists warned of a danger of accelerating inflation and expressed skepticism that the Carter administration's program to combat it would succeed. *(Carter program, p. 12)*

While doubtful that Carter's policies would slow inflation, the experts did not entirely agree on an alternative strategy. They did discuss, though, one novel approach to the problem — the idea of using tax incentives to encourage business and labor to modify price and wage hikes.

That idea — called "tax-based incomes policy," or TIP — sparked enough interest on the part of the committee's chairman, William Proxmire, D-Wis., that he asked proponents to prepare a TIP bill for congressional consideration.

Growing Support for Plan

The interest in TIP was prompted by a convergence of several beliefs: that general fiscal and monetary policies would not solve the inflation problem without sending the economy into a recession; that wage-price controls, an anathema to politicians and economists of almost every stripe, cannot control inflation without severely disrupting the economy; and that a purely voluntary wage-price restraint program such as proposed by President Carter lacks sufficient incentives to convince the private sector to ease activities that contribute to inflation.

A March 1978 Harris poll found 56 percent of respondents favoring the proposition that companies which limited price and wage increases to under six percent would be taxed less as an incentive to control inflation, while those which increased prices and wages over 6 percent would be taxed more.

Proxmire, according to an aide, hoped to sustain public discussion about TIP through 1978, and to have a TIP bill ready for serious consideration

in 1979 if inflation persisted as expected.

The Senate hearings reflected the extent to which the focus of economic policy discussions had shifted in early 1978.

In January, most of the talk emphasized the danger of an economic downturn by year's end. President Carter's budget thus called for a major tax cut to head off the feared slackening of growth. It acknowledged the threat of inflation secondarily, with a relatively mild limitation on the growth of federal spending and a pledge to seek ways of combating joblessness in the future with less federal spending.

Several months into the year, the major concern had become inflation. The Federal Reserve Board, traditionally the first to sound inflation warnings, signaled the shift by letting interest rates move upward. Carter acknowledged it with a major anti-inflation speech April 11. *(p. 12)*

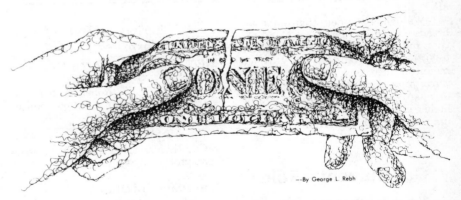

—By George L. Rebh

Then, on May 12, the president bowed to pressure from the inflation-worried Federal Reserve Board and Congress by scaling back his proposed tax cut to $19.4 billion effective Jan. 1, 1979, from $24.5 billion effective Oct. 1.

How Serious?

While the first few months of 1978 clearly sent a wave of concern about inflation through the economy, there was little agreement about how serious the problem was.

In January 1978, the administration predicted that the inflation rate for the year would be about the same as the year before — 6 percent.

Trade Ambassador Robert S. Strauss, Carter's special counsel on inflation, told the Senate committee May 22 that the problem had been worse than expected for the first quarter of 1978.

Strauss reported that hourly earnings during the period climbed at an annual rate of 9.2 percent — a rate 30 percent faster than in 1976 and 1977. Total compensation (hourly earnings plus benefits) rose at a record 13.2 percent annual rate.

Combined with a 3.3 percent decline in productivity (output per unit of labor cost), the climb in compensation resulted in a 17 percent annual rate of increase in labor costs during the first three months of the year, Strauss said.

Prices also rose more rapidly than expected, he added. The consumer price index (CPI) climbed at an annual rate of 9.3 percent during the first quarter, compared to the 5.8 percent average annual increases in 1976 and 1977.

Strauss said that some of the speed-up in inflation could be attributed to one-time causes, including mandated increases in Social Security taxes and the minimum wage, both of which took effect in January. Similarly, much of the increase in prices reflected a rise in food prices that might not continue, he said.

"There is no cause for an all-out alarm, but an all-out alert is surely warranted," Strauss concluded.

Dr. Barry P. Bosworth, director of the Council on Wage and Price Stability, drew roughly the same conclusion when he told the committee that the annual inflation rate for 1978 should be about 7 percent.

"If we look at the underlying industrial rate of inflation, which excludes volatile items like food, mortgage interest rates, energy and used car prices, the rate of inflation is inching up only a little," he said.

"Essentially we are bogged down in an inflation rut," Bosworth continued. "We are not really sinking much deeper."

Bosworth took only slight comfort from the thought that inflation was not seriously accelerating, however. Noting that inflationary pressures tend to increase as the economy nears full employment, he suggested that it would become more and more difficult to deal with the problem if the economy continued growing rapidly.

Even less comforted was Henry C. Wallich, a member of the board of governors of the Federal Reserve System.

"We do not have the choice between doing something about inflation and leaving it alone," he told the committee. "Left alone, it will accelerate."

Wallich explained that inflation breeds uncertainty and fears about future inflation. That prompts labor, business and lenders to "inject mounting insurance premia into their wage, price and interest rate behavior to guard against the contingency of higher inflation," in the process causing the higher inflation that was feared.

Government's Role

Virtually all of the economists testifying before the Senate committee described inflation as a multifaceted phenomenon with a variety of causes.

Most agreed that government is a major contributor, thanks to a variety of policies that increase prices. They include Social Security and unemployment insurance taxes, which add to labor costs; various import controls and regulatory policies, which limit or prevent competition that might otherwise drive prices down; and regulatory policies, such as environmental con-

trols, that add to the cost of producing goods.

Bosworth estimated that government policies would contribute 1.5 points of the expected 7 percent inflation rate.

While insisting that government policies should be more aware of the inflationary impact of its policies, the experts did not agree on which federal policies should be modified, delayed or canceled in the war against inflation.

Former Federal Reserve Board Chairman Arthur F. Burns suggested in written testimony sent to the committee that the government should drop or relax restrictions on agricultural production, ease legal requirements on minimum wages, suspend or abolish the Davis-Bacon Act (which requires construction firms doing work financed by federal funds to pay "prevailing" wages to their workers), and postpone the target dates for compliance with environmental regulations.

Others, such as Bosworth, argued that the government need not desert the social goals embodied in such policies for the battle against inflation. He said government should become more aware of the inflation costs of regulations, and that it should seek more efficient methods of regulation

---

"There is no cause for an all-out alarm, but an all-out alert is surely warranted."

—Robert S. Strauss,
Carter inflation counsel

---

rather than simply giving up the goals that prompted regulation.

Importance of Deficit

The experts were divided on the importance of the federal deficit in contributing to inflation.

Traditional economic theory suggests that a large deficit causes inflation during periods of low unemployment by driving up wages and prices in competition with the private sector for scarce productive resources.

Under the theory, inflation and unemployment are opposite ends of a see-saw: When the economy is operating near full capacity so that unemployment is low, inflation is seen as a danger; when the economy is operat-

ing below full capacity and unemployment is high, then prices should tend to move downward to adjust to the lower demand.

The traditional theory suggests that during times of high unemployment the economy should be stimulated to produce more — either by government spending to increase the demand for goods and services, or by an increase in the money supply to make it easier for people to purchase goods.

By the same token, the traditional theory holds that the cure to inflation is federal action to reduce excess demand, either by cutting federal spending or restricting the supply of money.

Some economists — such as David Lilly, a former member of the Federal Reserve Board — argued that, with unemployment expected to drop below 6 percent by the end of 1978, the federal deficit was inflationary.

"The first order of business for a government intent on stopping inflation should be to cut the budget deficit," he said. "Only by slowing the growth of federal debt can we slow the growth of the price level in a fundamental non-distorting way."

Wallich also subscribed to that theory. He said the proposed tax cut should be scaled back to $5 billion or $10 billion in order further to reduce the projected deficit.

The applicability of traditional fiscal and monetary restraints was disputed by other experts, including Brookings Institution economist Arthur M. Okun, a former chairman of the Council of Economic Advisers in the Johnson administration. He said the economy was well below full capacity, and that no change in fiscal or monetary policy was necessary to curb inflation.

"Fighting inflation by curbing demand at a time when it is not being caused by excess demand is absurdly inefficient," Okun said. "It is like burning down the house to roast the pig."

University of Pennsylvania economist Sidney Weintraub agreed. He called the argument that unemployment is a necessary cure to inflation a "destroy-to-revive-fantasy."

Okun told the committee that a 1 percent reduction in nominal gross national product (GNP) would cost between .85 and .95 of a percentage point in production while saving only between .05 and .15 of a percentage point in inflation.

That would mean a substantial increase in unemployment for a fairly small reduction in the inflation rate. Bosworth estimated that one million people would have to be unemployed for two years to achieve a 1 percent reduction in inflation. The administration spokesmen basically agreed.

"In dealing with inflation, this administration will not fall back on remedies that seek to solve the inflation puzzle through increased joblessness," Strauss said. "Too much fiscal stimulus is clearly inflationary, but too little stimulus threatens the continuation of the expansion. We are not going to throw people out of work in the hope that this will moderate wage demands."

Still, Strauss pledged the administration to a "responsible fiscal policy." He said it would "gradually . . . reduce the federal deficit by controlling federal expenditures and sustaining the economic expansion."

Consumer Prices

INDEX (1967 = 100; Ratio Scale)

SOURCE: Department of Labor

Collision Course?

Okun added a special note of urgency to the hearings by observing that the decisions by the Federal Reserve Board to tighten up interest rates in an effort to combat inflation could lead to a credit crunch in the housing industry — an eventuality that some believe could tip the economy into a recession.

"In their discussions on fiscal policy, the administration and Congress show that they are not willing to pay that price; while in its decisions on monetary policy, the Federal Reserve apparently considers it essential to pay that price," Okun said.

"Hence, the nation is facing the serious risk that fiscal and monetary policy may be on a collision course," he continued. "In light of all these unfavorable circumstances, I simply cannot see a realistic happy ending to the present scenario of policy."

'Momentum' Inflation

Okun and others argued that the 1978 inflation was not caused by excess demand, but rather was "embedded" in the process by which wages and prices are set.

Okun described the 1978 inflation as a "momentum" inflation, set off by excess demand in the 1960s and now perpetuated by the spiraling process whereby wages try to keep pace with prices, in turn raising prices and creating new pressures for still higher wages.

Weintraub elaborated on that theory. He said the basic cause of the 1978 inflation was that wages were increasing more rapidly than productivity. As a result, the cost of labor had increased, pushing up prices with it.

The cure to momentum inflation is to break the wage-price spiral, Okun said. Weintraub agreed, adding that the way to break into the cycle is to focus on wage increases.

One method of breaking the spiral would be wage-price controls, but that strategy — tried with limited success in 1971-74 — has been rejected almost universally. In his April 11 speech on inflation, Carter rejected wage-price controls and urged voluntary restraints instead.

"They [wage-price controls] are bureaucratic, dilatory, harassing, costly to administer, apt to be politicized, requiring a legion of snoopers and enforcers, and too anxious to make criminal offenses out of consensual agreements involving transactions as simple as purchases of a quart of milk or loaf of bread," Weintraub declared. "Controls would clog court calendars, providing mainly a forum for histrionic performances by lawyers, and full employment for them, and a retinue of court attendants and jailers."

Beyond those concerns, many economists have argued that wage-price controls interrupt the elaborate mechanism whereby prices help match supply and demand. With con-

trols, there is a considerable danger of shortages, the argument goes.

TIP Concept

In 1978 another policy was being pursued by the administration, which was asking business and labor voluntarily to moderate their price and wage demands.

That strategy was attacked during the Senate hearings as inadequate. Burns suggested that government would have to do more to set an example for voluntary wage restraint. He proposed that top federal officials take a 10 percent pay cut, and that other pay raises be limited to half the amount necessary to achieve comparability with private sector wages.

He also suggested that the president should call on top corporate executives to refrain entirely from pay raises over the next two years.

Okun and others argued that business and labor needed other stronger incentives to hold down price and wage increases. TIP, he said, could provide that incentive.

'Stick' vs. 'Carrot'

Under one version of TIP, proposed by Wallich and Weintraub, employers would have to pay a tax penalty if their wage increases went above a predetermined "non-inflationary" guidepost.

To that "stick" approach, Okun suggested a "carrot" alternative, whereby firms holding down wage increases would qualify their employees for a tax credit.

The stick approach would have the advantage that it would not cost the federal government money. In addition, it would be much easier to administer because, being mandatory, it could be designed only to apply to a relatively few, large firms.

The carrot approach, on the other hand, would be voluntary and thus probably more popular. But it would probably have to be universal, so it would entail much greater administrative problems. In addition, it would be more costly.

Program Details

The carrot approach recommended by Okun has received more attention than other TIP proposals.

Okun suggested an initial three-year program, and he said a possible wage guidepost for the first year could be to aim for wage increases averaging no more than 6 percent.

Firms that keep the growth of wages below that level, under the plan, would qualify their employees for a tax credit equal to 1.5 percent of their wages up to a certain level — say, $20,000. The credit could be included in their withholding.

The 1.5 percent credit would be the equivalent of a more than 2 percent pay raise before taxes, Okun noted. That means employees would be better off with a 6 percent raise and the credit than with an 8 percent raise and no credit.

Firms that pledge to hold down their wage increases but fail would have to pay back to the government an amount equal to the withheld credit, Okun noted. To provide them an incentive for taking the risk of making a pledge, he suggested that firms that promise in advance to meet the wage guidepost should receive an extra tax award — possibly in the form of a tax credit equal to one-quarter the amount withheld for employees.

Firms that meet the guidepost without pledging to do so in advance would still qualify their workers for the credit, but they wouldn't receive the corporate tax bonus.

The obvious incentive for firms to enroll in the program, however, is that it would help them hold down their labor costs, Okun said. Employees would probably agree to participate because the tax credit would be the

equivalent of higher wages to them, he said.

Okun predicted that an "overwhelming majority" of non-union employers would enroll in the program, and that a "significant fraction, though probably only a minority" of union employers would participate as well.

He estimated that probably two-thirds of all workers would be enrolled.

Possible Problems

Critics of the TIP concept included Lilly and Princeton University economist Albert E. Rees, former director of the Council on Wage and Price Stability.

"TIP is presented as a mild form of wage-price controls," Lilly said. "I agree that, as such, it will probably deliver less of the good effects of controls, and I fear it will deliver as much or more of the bad effects of more general controls."

Lilly warned that TIP could lead to economic distortions by tipping the balance between capital-intensive and labor-intensive firms. He also argued that it would prove very costly to administer.

Finally, he complained that the TIP idea would serve to distract attention from the true cause of inflation, which he said is government regulation and spending.

Rees elaborated on the administrative problems of a TIP program. He said the "carrot" approach especially would involve "administrative nightmares," and that a "carrot" TIP would prove very costly in terms of reduced tax collections.

But the "stick" TIP based on wages could make wage negotiations more difficult by strengthening the resolve of management to hold wages down, Rees said. That could result in more strikes, possibly contributing to inflation by creating shortages, he argued.

Beyond that, Rees said, TIPs would raise other problems — including how to compute wages to determine whether a firm should qualify for a credit (an especially thorny problem since firms would be tempted to increase non-monetary compensation in order to qualify for the credit). Also, setting a fair wage guidepost itself would be very difficult, he argued. In some cases, the guidepost would probably be too high, and it would actually be inflationary by serving as a mini-

mum, rather than a maximum, for wage increases.

TIP as Insurance

The administration has shown an interest in the TIP concept, but as of mid-1978 had not endorsed it.

Noting all the possible problems, Bosworth suggested that a modified TIP could be used effectively as a supplement to a voluntary wage-price restraint program.

One problem with the administration's program, Bosworth noted, was that it is very difficult for workers to commit themselves to wage restraint given the fact that most labor contracts last for several years.

While business can always increase its prices on relatively short notice if a voluntary restraint program proves untenable, labor does not have that option, Bosworth noted.

Unions might be more willing to accept wage restraint if the government agreed to insure them against price increases in excess of the government's target.

For instance, if a union agreed to limit its average wage increase to 7 percent, the government could commit itself to pay workers an amount equal to the excess of the rise in consumer prices above 7 percent.

That would make a voluntary restraint program much more palatable to unions, he argued.

Further Study Planned

Okun conceded that the TIP concept "is not tried and true." But, he said, "the present scenario has been tried and found sadly wanting.

"Clearly, the basic current controversy is not among alternative forms of TIP," he said. "Rather it is between slowing the wage-price spiral by some form of TIP or other innovative cost-reducing strategy, on the one hand, and the hideous alternatives of letting inflation rip, fighting it by recession, or suppressing it by wage-price controls on the other."

Proxmire found that argument persuasive. Arguing that TIP might be "one of the very few options we have to fight inflation," he asked Okun and his colleagues to assist in drawing up a bill to implement TIP. That work was expected to be completed in 1978. Proxmire said he hoped the matter could be more thoroughly discussed in 1978, so that TIP would be ready in the nation's economic policy arsenal for use in 1979, if necessary. ∎

Steps Urged To Ease Middle Class Tax Burden

In 1978, support was growing in Congress for the notion that, after years of striving to help the poor and the disadvantaged, government should turn its attention to middle income people.

That could be seen in the groundswell of support for tuition tax credits, in many of the criticisms of President Carter's tax program, and in the rush to roll back scheduled increases in Social Security taxes.

And it could be heard in rhetoric almost daily — in warnings by lawmakers such as Sen. William V. Roth Jr., R-Del., that middle income families can no longer afford college educations for their children; and in declarations such as one by Sen. John H. Chafee, R-R.I., that the middle class has been "mauled" by past federal policies.

Indeed, the rhetoric has run full circle, so that many lawmakers, besides worrying about the impact of various policies on the middle class, actually define that class as the group of people who would suffer from the policies.

Even as the debate raged, though, there was considerable confusion as to how to define the middle income group in society. There was also a great deal of uncertainty about how that group really has fared.

Several studies of census and tax return data have shed some light on the matter.

They show that people who are in the middle of the income spectrum in the United States actually are poorer than many of the definitions of middle income used in Congress.

The studies do lend some credence to the belief that middle and upper income people have been forced to bear a relatively heavier burden in federal taxes over the last few years.

But surprisingly, they suggest that all but the very wealthy actually have a lighter federal income tax burden now than they have had during all but a few of the preceding 25 years. Still, the drop in income tax burdens has been less substantial for well-to-do families, so they pay more relative to other groups than they used to.

At the same time, the studies show that Social Security taxes have risen steadily, with the largest increases going to middle and upper income wage earners.

Finally, the studies show that, even as the federal income tax has been declining in importance, state and local taxes have increased dramatically.

Those taxes put the heaviest burden on lower income families. As a result, the overall tax system continues, as it has for a number of years, to be basically proportional — meaning that the vast majority of taxpayers pay the same percentage of their income in taxes — although everyone pays more now than they used to.

Who Is Middle Class?

While many members of Congress don't try to define the middle class very specifically, most descriptions put it between income levels as low as $10,000 or $15,000 and as high as $30,000, $40,000 or even $50,000.

In fact, the majority of Americans have incomes at the low end of that range and below.

According to Bureau of the Census estimates, the median income for families and individuals — the income level which half of the people are below and half are above — was $11,137 in 1975.

The Census Bureau estimates that 65.2 percent of all people in 1975 had incomes below $15,000; 80.3 percent had incomes below $20,000; 89.2 percent had incomes below $25,000; and 98.9 percent had incomes below $50,000.

If middle income is defined as the middle one-third of all Americans, it would include people with incomes in 1975 between $7,300 and $15,400. If it is defined more broadly as the middle one-half of all Americans, it would include people with incomes in 1975 between $5,500 and $18,000.

Census figures have been criticized on the grounds that they don't count all people at the low end of the income scale. An alternative measure of income used to escape that problem are figures compiled by the Internal Revenue Service from tax returns.

Information provided the House Ways and Means Committee by Treasury Secretary W. Michael Blumenthal in support of President Carter's tax program suggested that the median adjusted gross income for taxpayers in 1975 was $9,600.

Using the definition that the middle class includes the middle one-third of all taxpayers, Blumenthal's statistics suggest a range between $6,000 and $14,000. Using the broader definition that the middle class includes the middle one-half of all taxpayers, his figures indicate a range between $3,500 and $17,000.

Adjusted gross income is total income less a variety of business and personal deductions. It is generally estimated that adjusted gross income is 80 percent of total income.

In that case, the range of total income suggested by Blumenthal's tax figures would be from $7,500 to $17,500 by the narrow definition of middle income. By the broader definition, it would be from $4,400 to $21,200.

Tax statistics are biased downward, however, because a substantial number of returns are filed by part-time casual wage-earners, such as teenagers holding summer jobs. To correct for that problem, some tax experts have suggested using only joint returns. While joint returns represent only about one-half of all income tax returns, they make up about three-quarters of the income reported on income tax forms.

Using joint returns for 1975, the last year available, the median adjusted gross income was $14,000. By the narrow definition of middle income, the range for middle income taxpayers filing joint returns in 1975 was $10,500 to $18,000. By the broader definition, the range was $9,500 to $20,100.

Making the adjustment for total income, those figures suggest that the actual income for middle income families filing joint returns in 1975 ranged between $13,100 and $22,500 by the narrow definition, and between $11,900 and $25,100 by the broader definition.

Finally, those figures can be corrected somewhat to reflect inflation. Assuming that the incomes kept pace with inflation in 1976 and 1977, during which the consumer price index measured inflation respectively at 5.7 and 6.5 percent annually, the narrow range definition middle income families would be $14,700 to $25,300. The broad range would be from $13,-400 to $28,200.

Income Tax Burdens

Many of the complaints that the middle class has suffered disproportionately from government policies are directed at the income tax. The income tax is progressive, meaning that it takes a larger portion of the income of wealthier families than it takes from poorer ones.

But the 1975 joint tax returns suggest that the 80 percent of all taxpayers at the lower end of the income scale actually paid less than their share of income in income taxes. The figures are as follows:

● The poorest 20 percent of all taxpayers, with adjusted gross incomes up to $7,300, earned 4.7 percent of the income and paid .65 percent of the income tax.

● The second 20 percent, with incomes between $7,300 and $12,000, earned 12 percent of the income and paid 5.8 percent of the income tax.

● The middle 20 percent, with incomes between $12,000 and $16,300,

earned 17.9 percent of the income and paid 13.1 percent of the income tax.

● The fourth 20 percent, with incomes ranging from $16,300 to $22,300, earned 23 percent of the income and paid 20.1 percent of the income tax.

● The richest 20 percent, with incomes above $22,300, earned 42.3 percent of the income and paid 60.3 percent of the income tax.

If income and the income tax burden were divided evenly, each class would earn 20 percent of the income and pay 20 percent of the tax. The figures indicate that income is distributed quite unevenly — the richest 40 percent of the joint return filers made 65.3 percent of the income; the poorest 40 percent made 16.7 percent.

But they also show that only the richest 20 percent of the taxpayers actually had to pay proportionately more in income taxes than they earned.

Shifts in Burden

Evaluating how different income groups have done over time is difficult, because it involves assessing the impact of inflation. Inflation increases income tax burdens by pushing taxpayers into higher tax brackets. Because the income tax is progressive, the tax bite in higher brackets is greater. To the extent that taxpayers find themselves in the higher brackets because of inflation, they have to pay higher taxes even though their income is unchanged in real terms.

Congress has recognized the impact of inflation on tax burdens by periodically reducing income tax rates. But at the same time, it has tinkered with the structure of the income tax, shifting relative burdens.

In late 1977, the Joint Committee on Taxation conducted a study to determine how different income groups have fared under the income

tax in light of inflation and congressional actions. It took typical taxpayers with incomes of $8,000, $15,000, $25,000 and $50,000 in 1977, determined what the equivalent incomes in previous years would have been before inflation, and then calculated income tax rates for every year back to 1950.

The study showed that single people at all the income levels paid a smaller portion of their income in income taxes in 1977 than they did in 1967 or any year before that.

For people who earned $8,000 in 1977, the decline in rates had been a steady one, hitting 10.1 percent in 1977. For people earning $15,000, the rate climbed in 1977 to 16.1 percent from 15.7 percent the year before, but it was still lower than it was in 1973 or earlier. For people earning $25,000 or $50,000, the rate in 1977 was 20.6 percent and 29.8 percent respectively — higher than the rates for equivalent incomes had been since 1973, but still lower than in years before that.

The joint committee's study showed similar results for families of four that filed joint returns. Families that earned $8,000 in 1977 paid income taxes totaling 1.5 percent of their income, while families earning $15,000 paid 9.2 percent. Both rates were lower than comparable families paid in any year back to 1950. Families that earned $25,000 and $50,000 paid taxes worth 14.6 percent and 23 percent of their income respectively — higher than they paid in 1974-1976, but still lower than in any other year since 1951.

Those figures suggest that the income tax burden has declined over the long run for all income groups — even taking inflation into consideration.

The decline has been most dramatic at the lower ends of the income scale, however. For families earn-

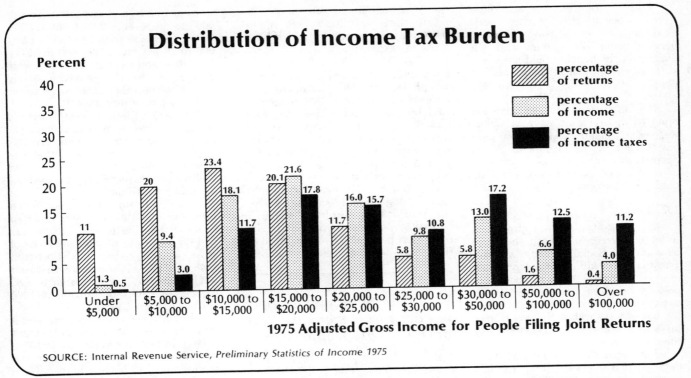

Distribution of Income Tax Burden

Percent

Legend:
- percentage of returns
- percentage of income
- percentage of income taxes

Income Category	% of returns	% of income	% of income taxes
Under $5,000	11	1.3	0.5
$5,000 to $10,000	20	9.4	3.0
$10,000 to $15,000	23.4	18.1	11.7
$15,000 to $20,000	20.1	21.6	17.8
$20,000 to $25,000	11.7	16.0	15.7
$25,000 to $30,000	5.8	9.8	10.8
$30,000 to $50,000	5.8	13.0	17.2
$50,000 to $100,000	1.6	6.6	12.5
Over $100,000	0.4	4.0	11.2

1975 Adjusted Gross Income for People Filing Joint Returns

SOURCE: Internal Revenue Service, *Preliminary Statistics of Income 1975*

ing $8,000 in 1977, the drop was to 9.2 percent from 12.4 percent 10 years earlier, while families earning $50,000 experienced a drop to only 23 percent from 23.6 percent in 1967.

Finally, the figures show that since 1974 there has been a slight increase in income tax burdens for single people earning $15,000, $25,000 and $50,000, and for families earning $25,000 and $50,000.

The Effect of Indexing

The joint committee's findings were generally confirmed in a 1976 study by Emil M. Sunley Jr. and Joseph A. Pechman of the Brookings Institution. Sunley in 1978 was deputy assistant secretary of the treasury for tax policy.

Their study was designed to compare actual tax rates established by Congress to what the rates would have been if the tax system had been indexed. Indexing means making automatic adjustments in the tax system to correct for inflation. *(Indexing argument, box, p. 43)*

The Sunley-Pechman study compared 1975 taxes to the tax rates that would have resulted if the income tax system had been indexed beginning in 1960, in 1965 or in 1972.

The study concluded that Congress had actually reduced the overall income tax more than enough to compensate for inflation since 1960.

It also showed that effective tax rates in 1975 were lower than indexed rates for all incomes under $25,000, higher between $25,000 and $200,000, and lower again above $200,000.

That was due primarily to the **Revenue Act of 1964,** which reduced individual and corporate income tax rates substantially.

If indexing had been started after that law took effect, in 1965 for instance, it would have resulted in larger tax reductions than were actually allowed by Congress for all income classes above $10,000, according to the study. In other words, starting from a base in 1965, changes in the tax structure have been inadequate to offset the effects of inflation for people earning more than $10,000.

If indexing began in 1972, every income group would have been better off in 1975 than they actually were, the study showed.

Again, the study showed that if indexing had begun in 1965 or 1972, the most substantial benefits would have gone to people in income classes between $25,000 and $200,000.

The Sunley-Pechman study suggested, in short, that Congress has offset the effects of inflation for all but the $25,000-$200,000 income class since 1960, but that most of the credit for that goes to the 1964 law. Since then, inflation has outstripped tax reductions for most income groups.

The Payroll Tax

Besides the income tax, the payroll tax has come under criticism by those who complain that the middle income groups in society have suffered disproportionately from tax policies.

The payroll tax, used to raise funds for the Social Security system, is proportional up to a certain income level, after which it is regressive.

A proportional tax imposes the same percentage burden on people in different income classes. A regressive tax puts a greater burden on lower income people relative to their total income.

The payroll tax is a flat percentage of wages on a certain wage base. Wages above the base are not taxed at all.

In 1978, the payroll tax rate was 6.05 percent and the wage base was $17,700. People with wages up to $17,700 paid the same portion of their income in payroll taxes, while the portion declined for people earning wages higher than that.

Increases in the wage base affect wage earners whose income was previously above the base. When the rate and the wage base are both increased, such people are hit twice — and thus they suffer the largest relative increase in payroll taxes.

Both the rate and the wage base have climbed steadily for many years, as the number of old people drawing benefits from the system and the amount of the benefits paid have outstripped the growth in the number of people contributing taxes to the system.

The Joint Committee on Taxation reported in 1977 that a typical single wage earner making $8,000 a year paid 5.9 percent of his income in Social Security taxes that year, while a person with equivalent income in 1950 paid only 1 percent.

1977 Law

In 1977, Congress approved a series of increases in both the wage base and the Social Security tax rate. Those changes will pose the largest tax increase for wage earners above the present wage base, since they will have to pay the higher rates on wages below the old base as well as having to pay taxes for the first time on wages above the old base.

For wages equal to the 1976 wage base — $15,300 — payroll taxes didn't increase at all in 1977. They rose 3.4 percent in 1978, and they will rise another 1.3 percent in 1979.

But for wages above the base for each of the years between 1976 and 1979 — $22,900 — the payroll tax increases are dramatic. For that wage level, the tax rose 7.8 percent in 1977, and 10.9 percent in 1978. In 1979, they will rise another 31.1 percent.

While the payroll tax rate is flat for all wage earners above the wage base, the impact relative to total income is greatest for wage earners closest to the base. They include a substantial number of middle income taxpayers.

"The middle and upper middle income groups have borne a disproportionate share of making the Social Security tax less regressive," concluded Rudolph G. Penner, American Enterprise Institute economist.

Total Tax Burdens

While there is thus some evidence that relative income tax and payroll tax burdens have increased most for middle income taxpayers, a different picture emerges when one considers the total tax burden — including state and local taxes.

One attempt to consider the impact of a variety of state and local taxes has suggested that they neutralize the effect of federal taxes, with the result that total taxes are almost perfectly proportional for the vast majority of taxpayers.

The study, performed by Brookings Institution economist Joseph J. Minarik, considered tax burdens imposed in 1966 and again in 1977 by the federal income tax, state and local income taxes, personal Social Security contributions (employers also pay a share of the payroll tax), property taxes, personal property taxes, federal sales and excise taxes, state and local sales and excise taxes and state and local auto taxes.

While the numbers were, of necessity, estimates because the information in some cases was hard to find and because there are con-

---

"The middle and upper middle income groups have borne a disproportionate share of making the Social Security tax less regressive."

—Rudolph G. Penner, American Enterprise Institute economist

---

siderable variations from state to state, the conclusions of the Minarik study are the best available estimates of overall tax burdens.

Basically, they indicate that the overall tax burden increased between 1966 and 1977, but that the tax system itself remained essentially proportional for people with income between $5,000 and $50,000.

In 1966, total tax rates varied only between 26 and 29 percent throughout that range of incomes. In 1977, they were between 30 and 32 percent over the same range.

Only for taxpayers earning more than $50,000 did the progressive income tax impose a significantly heavier burden.

In 1966, the average total tax burden for people earning $50,000-$100,000 was 28.1 percent; for people earning more than $100,000, it was 40 percent. In 1977, people in the $50,000-$100,000 range paid 38 percent of their income in taxes, while people earning more than $100,000 paid 54 percent.

The Minarik study demonstrates, as expected, that the federal income tax is progressive, though not as much so as is often thought to be the case. Its

rates ranged from 7 percent at the $5,000 income level to 20 percent at $50,000 in 1966, and from 2 percent at $5,000 to 16 percent at $50,000 in 1977.

State and local income taxes were also progressive, though only modestly so, while the other taxes were either proportional or regressive.

A major reason why the overall tax system has remained proportional even as the federal income tax has become more progressive is that the federal income tax is declining in relative importance in the tax system, according to Minarik.

The Advisory Commission on Intergovernmental Relations reported in 1976 that the federal income tax had taken up a fairly constant share of gross national product (GNP) between 1948 and 1975. It equaled 8.5 percent of GNP in 1975, as compared to 7.85 percent in 1948, 8.17 percent in 1960 and 9.42 percent in 1970.

But at the same time, state and local taxes increased from 5.43 percent of GNP in 1948 to 9.84 percent in 1975.

While federal revenues represented 60.7 percent of all government revenues in 1942, they amounted to only 55.3 percent in 1975. Over the same period, state and local revenues rose to 44.7 percent of all government income, from 39.3 percent.

The advisory commission reported that state and local governments have made some efforts to broaden their tax systems to be more progressive, but that they still are less progressive than the federal tax system.

That would explain why, even as the federal income tax has shifted burdens toward those more able to pay, the overall distribution of the tax burden has remained about the same.

Future Trends?

The future of tax burdens is a subject for considerable conjecture. One good possibility, according to Minarik, is that the overall tax burden will continue to be proportional, despite the dramatic changes scheduled in Social Security taxes.

Minarik suggested that, at the same time Social Security taxes are rising to cover the costs of a relatively larger population of retired people, regressive taxes such as the property tax may decrease in relative importance as the school age population shrinks.

If the population growth rate continues to slow as it has in recent years, and if school districts hold teacher salaries and the level of school services constant in real terms, then property tax burdens may decline. That could offset the heavier payroll tax burdens scheduled for the future, Minarik hypothesized.

Options

Long before the long-term trends are known, Congress would have to make a number of decisions on the 1978 tax bill. The House Ways and Means and the Senate Finance Committees had signaled their intentions to approve tax cuts totaling between $27 and $36 billion.

While the overall impact of the tax cuts they approve would depend on how they decided a large number of smaller issues, they had at least four comprehensive proposals before them: President Carter's plan, a proposed reduction in Social Security taxes, a Republican income tax reduction plan, and a liberal Republican alternative program.

President Carter's Proposals

The most substantial relief in President Carter's proposed individual income tax cuts would go to low income people. *(Carter tax proposals, p. 21)*

Since people with incomes below $20,000 would be net beneficiaries of the president's program in 1979, even after inflation and the increase in Social Security taxes, it appeared that part of the middle class would be better off and part would suffer a net increase in overall tax burdens.

Using Blumenthal's 1976 tax return statistics, 83.5 percent of the people who filed tax returns would have a net tax reduction, although the reduction would be fairly small for the 31.7 percent with incomes between $10,000 and $20,000.

Cutting the Payroll Tax

While a variety of payroll tax reduction proposals have been floated in Congress, the one that had gained the most attention (HR 10754) would remove health insurance and disability insurance from payroll tax financing. That would reduce tax rates to 4.33 percent in 1979, at a net cost of $28.4 billion.

It is difficult to compare the effect on different people of the payroll tax cut as opposed to income tax reductions, because their impact varies.

Index the Tax System?

In 1978, a number of bills were before Congress to index the tax system — to make automatic adjustments in taxes to offset inflation.

Arguments for indexing are that it would provide taxpayers some extra protection from inflation and the whims of Congress.

pro

"I believe strongly that the federal government should not be the beneficiary of tax hikes that Congress does not levy," said Rep. Bill Gradison, R-Ohio, who has introduced several indexing bills.

"The indexation of our tax system is an important step towards insulating all taxpayers against the effects of inflation."

Besides negating the effects of inflation on individual income tax burdens, an indexing system would slow the tendency of Congress to shift tax burdens, according to some conservatives.

Rudolph G. Penner, a budget expert under former President Ford and now an economist for the American Enterprise Institute, argued that Congress has been able to mask its decisions to ease relative tax burdens for lower income people while increasing them for middle and upper income people because the changes were done under the guise of tax cuts to offset inflation.

"In general, Congress has in the aggregate offset the effects of inflation and real growth pushing people into higher tax brackets," he said. "But while they have been doing that they have been acting particularly favorably to the lower income groups. To the extent that has been conscious, it hasn't been a big matter of debate."

Arguments against indexing are that it would preclude any opportunity for shifting tax burdens between groups, or for changing the overall real revenue raised by the income tax.

"Whether you support indexing depends on whether you think the tax system is equitable," said Brookings Institution economist Joseph A. Pechman. He explained that indexing would make sense to a person who believes that the relative impact of the income tax on different income classes is what it should be. A person who believes that burdens should be shifted further would probably prefer discretionary changes by Congress over automatic indexed adjustments that leave relative burdens unchanged.

One other argument against indexing has been voiced by the chairman of the President's Council of Economic Advisers, Charles L. Schultze. Appearing before several committees to argue for Carter's tax and economic program, Schultze said that Congress should keep its flexibility to change tax policy from year to year in accordance with changing fiscal conditions.

con

There might be some years, he said, when the economy would need a larger tax cut than would be provided through indexing, while there might be other years when indexing would result in a tax cut that would be more than needed for the overall economy. Congress should keep the freedom to act accordingly, Schultze concluded.

The Senate rejected an indexing plan in 1976.

The payroll tax is a tax on wages of individuals, while the income tax is a tax on income of families. Thus, families deriving a lot of income from sources other than wages obviously would benefit more from an income tax cut. By the same token, families with more than one wage earner would most likely benefit more from a cut in payroll taxes.

In general, the Congressional Budget Office (CBO) concluded that the overall distribution of the payroll tax cut between different income groups would be about the same as President Carter's program.

But it said certain groups would benefit more from the payroll tax reduction. They include single people with incomes between $10,000 and $25,000, whose tax savings from the Carter proposal would be fairly small; families with incomes above $30,000 — especially those with two wage earners; and people with incomes below $5,000, who wouldn't benefit much from an income tax cut because they have little or no income tax liability.

CBO Director Alice M. Rivlin elaborated on the CBO study in testimony before a Senate subcommittee April 5, 1978.

Roth-Kemp Proposal

Sponsored by Sen. Roth and Rep. Jack F. Kemp, R-N.Y., the Roth-Kemp bill (S 1860, HR 8333) would reduce income tax rates across-the-board by about one-third over three years. While that would result in the largest proportional cuts for lower income taxpayers, the reductions in absolute dollars would be more substantial for higher income people.

In general, a spokesman for Roth said, the bill would provide substantial tax relief to taxpayers earning more than $10,000, while Carter's program would concentrate most relief on people below that income level.

In addition, the bill would not provide some of the most important low income relief provisions of Carter's program — including the president's proposal to replace the $750 personal exemption with a $250 tax credit, which would benefit most taxpayers earning less than $20,000; and several of the president's proposals to restrict itemized deductions, which would actually increase taxes on some middle income taxpayers.

Danforth-Javits Plan

On March 23, 1978, a comprehensive tax plan was introduced by Sens. John C. Danforth, R-Mo., Jacob K. Javits, R-N.Y., Charles H. Percy, R-Ill., John H. Chafee, R-R.I., Richard G. Lugar, R-Ind., and Ted Stevens, R-Alaska.

For individuals, the Javits-Danforth proposal would index the tax system for the next three years. In addition, it would offset the increase in

Social Security taxes by allowing a 10 percent income tax credit for personal Social Security taxes.

The proposal would completely offset the increase in tax burdens resulting from inflation, while it would offset the Social Security tax rise for wage earners earning up to $18,000. Above that wage level, the plan would offset part, but not all, of the increase in Social Security taxes.

A spokesman for Danforth said the plan was designed essentially to leave all taxpayers in roughly the same condition as they were in 1977 before inflation and the increase in Social Security taxes. The plan would not provide a tax reduction for any income group in real terms.

The spokesman estimated that Carter's proposals, in contrast, would provide real tax reductions, after inflation and Social Security tax rises, for people earning between $7,400 and $12,500. ∎

Congress Reacts to California "Tax Revolt"

The approval June 6, 1978, by California voters of Proposition 13, a state constitutional amendment sharply reducing property taxes, rekindled a debate in Congress over federal spending and tax policies in 1978.

"The mood of Washington these days can be summed up in two words — Proposition 13," observed Senate Budget Committee Chairman Edmund S. Muskie, D-Maine, summarizing the way the California decision had become woven into the fabric of politics in Washington, denounced by some, and praised by many — although for very different reasons.

Few observers expected the California vote to lead to changes as dramatic in other states, or in Washington, as they were in California, where the voters slashed real estate taxes by almost 60 percent — about $7 billion — in one stroke. *(Provisions, p. 50)*

That was partly because the Proposition 13 movement had some characteristics peculiar to California. But it was also because lawmakers in Washington did not fully agree on what the national implications of the vote were.

In general, Proposition 13 was considered likely to reinforce a trend toward some restraint in spending. But beyond that, there was considerable disagreement over the best way to address the frustrations expressed in the 2-to-1 vote in support of the tax limitation initiative.

Some viewed the vote as an attack on the size of government itself. They insisted on substantial spending reductions, regardless of the effect on government services. But others predicting a backlash in California when voters there realized the extent to which Proposition 13 would reduce services, argued that the real message of the vote was that government must find ways to provide services more efficiently so that taxpayers would get more for their tax dollar.

Congress was even more divided over the federal tax implications of the Proposition 13 vote. Some have depicted it as a demand for lower federal taxes. But others believed it was mainly a reaction to inflation, which they argued could be worsened by large tax cuts that would swell the federal deficit.

Moreover, some viewed the vote as part of a broad-based tax revolt, while others saw it mainly as a reaction to California's unusually high property taxes. Behind that difference in interpretation lay a sharp disagreement in Congress on which federal taxes, if any, should be reduced.

"The reaction to Proposition 13 is in the eyes of the beholder," concluded John Shannon, assistant director of the Advisory Commission on Intergovernmental Relations (ACIR), an organization that monitors federal, state and local fiscal affairs.

Long-Term Trends

To the extent that Proposition 13 reflects a national reaction against rising government spending and taxes, there was some justification for it.

Federal spending has climbed steadily from about 18.7 percent of gross national product (GNP) in 1958 to an estimated 22.6 percent in 1978. Federal taxes have climbed as well. While they only surpassed 20 percent of GNP twice since 1958 — in 1969 and 1970 — they have been rising rapidly since 1976. In 1976, they comprised 18.4 percent of GNP, climbing to 19.4 percent in 1977 and to an estimated 19.6 percent in 1978.

State and local spending and taxes also have jumped significantly. Spending rose from 8.2 percent of GNP in 1959 (excluding federal aid) to 11.5 percent in 1974, although it dropped to an estimated 10.6 percent in 1977.

State and local taxes, in the meantime, have risen from 7.25 percent of GNP in 1960 to 9.66 percent in 1976, according to the ACIR.

There were some signs that trend could be slowing. President Carter, for instance, pledged to bring federal expenditures down to about 21 percent of GNP.

There also were signs of moderation on the state and local level, according to Shannon. He attributed the change to the fact that some of the pressures that rapidly increased expenditures there have eased somewhat. Education costs, for instance, were expected to decline as the school age population falls relative to the rest of the population.

A Harbinger?

The Proposition 13 vote has been depicted as the harbinger of tax limitation proposals in other states. *(Survey of state action, p. 50)*

To a certain extent, Shannon said, that could be true. But there were five major factors that contributed to the California vote that were unlikely to combine to produce so dramatic an outcome elsewhere, he said.

The first factor peculiar to California is that the state government there had accumulated a $5 billion surplus. That, according to Shannon, angered some voters who thought the money was being hoarded in Sacramento, and it also encouraged voters to support the property tax limitation scheme on the grounds that the state surplus could help cushion the impact.

Second, Shannon said, the Proposition 13 vote was prompted at least in part by the fact that California had an unusually high property tax burden, which had been rising at an exceptionally rapid rate. In 1943, the property tax in California was below the national average, consuming about 3.3 percent of residents' income. In 1976, however, it had climbed to 6.4 percent of income, a level 42 percent above the national average.

Third, the state and local tax burden in California was exceptionally high. Shannon estimated that it was about 20 percent above the national average.

Fourth, California had one of the easiest systems for initiative proposals in the country. In most states it would be much more difficult to enact constitutional amendments limiting taxes.

Finally, Shannon noted, residential property values had been climbing at very rapid rates in California. To make the resulting climb in taxes even

House Reaction to Taxpayer Revolt Pressures . . .

Just in case Carter administration officials missed the big news about the California taxpayer revolt, the House of Representatives relayed its version of the message to them in May 1978.

In a series of votes on appropriations bills, the House went on record in favor of forcing administration spending cuts in the fiscal 1979 budgets of dozens of federal programs. The tax revolt in California was one justification scalpel-wielding members gave for their support of the cuts.

Those votes let House members take credit for opposing big spending. But since the votes approved across-the-board cuts in the agencies' controllable spending, they left it up to the administration to answer the tough questions of exactly how the cuts would be made.

Thus House members avoided taking the heat from the numerous special interest groups that would be hurt when — and if — the administration must decide what to cut. By mid-1978, the Senate had not acted on the appropriations bills the House voted to cut.

"It's a chicken way to do things," said Edward W. Pattison, D-N.Y., an opponent of the sweeping cuts approved by the House. Pattison said the headlines about the California revolt created a "firestorm" in the House that showed its members were "much too responsive" to what was essentially a local issue.

Proposition 13

The California revolt involved the state's overwhelming vote June 6 in favor of Proposition 13, a plan to reduce the state's property tax rates. It also forced reductions in spending by state government, but did not address federal taxes or how they are spent.

However, Proposition 13 quickly became the number one topic of conversation in Washington after its almost 2-to-1 passage on the West Coast. Many felt the vote had a symbolic message for all politicians — not just those in California. Members of the House, anxious not to appear unresponsive in this election year, immediately began responding to the "message" that had been aimed at California officials.

The House "response" — some called it Proposition 13 fever — concentrated on the annual appropriations bills for fiscal 1979, which set in law the amount of money federal agencies will get to fund each of their programs. In the week following the California vote, the House approved amendments to four appropriations bills calling for across-the-board cuts totaling about $803 million in spending for dozens of federal programs.

The bills and amounts cut by the across-the-board amendments were: Labor-Health, Education and Welfare ($380 million); State, Justice and Commerce ($172 million); public works ($206 million) and legislative appropriations ($45 million).

Several members said the House had shown signs of a developing anti-spending mood prior to Proposition 13. For instance, the Democratic leadership had to struggle in early May to narrowly prevent House adoption of several cuts in fiscal 1979 budget targets.

But many members agreed that the mood grew stronger after passage of Proposition 13. Most of the across-the-board cuts approved by the House were proposed by Clarence E. Miller, R-Ohio, who drew little support when he offered similar proposals in previous years.

One opponent of the cuts, Parren J. Mitchell, D-Md., attributed the mood to political fear. "The House has reacted almost blindly to Proposition 13," he said.

Just after the House passed the third of the four across-the-board cuts, Mitchell facetiously suggested some of his colleagues might need psychiatric care. "The situation in California has been a traumatic experience for many of us," he told the House. Mitchell prescribed "psychiatric services" for House members "to sort of cushion the psychological impact."

Meat Ax

Critics of Miller's across-the-board amendments call them the "meat ax approach" because they do not try to pick out specific programs that are the most wasteful or poorly run. "They penalize everyone for the sins of a few programs," said Bob Carr, D-Mich.

Carr described voting for across-the-board cuts as "what a politician does when he's chicken and doesn't want to go on record as opposing a particular cut."

Carr voted for some of the across-the-board cuts. But he described his action as a "last resort" attempt to reduce federal spending, after he had voted to cut specific programs he found wasteful. When those specific cuts were rejected by the House, those who wanted to register their "cost consciousness" were "left with no alternative" to the across-the-board cuts, Carr said.

One of the specific cuts Carr supported was an amendment offered by Robert W. Edgar, D-Pa., to kill funding for eight water projects in the public works bill. While Carr supported both Edgar's specific cut proposal and an across-the-board cut proposed for public works spending, more than a dozen of his colleagues opposed Edgar but supported the across-the-board cut.

---

more painful, the state had a better-than-average assessment system.

"I just can't see all those things playing out in other states," he concluded.

Shannon did predict, however, that other states would enact limitations on spending and taxes. But he said a more common pattern would be to limit spending or tax growth to the

rate of growth of the state economy — much as Tennessee has done. That would slow growth, but it wouldn't have the same sharp impact that Proposition 13 is expected to have in California.

Federal Reaction

Confirming Shannon's observations, both Democrats and Republi-

cans claimed to be in step with Proposition 13.

Some liberals, such as Sen. George McGovern, D-S.D., expressed sympathy with the "frustrated" voters of California. But McGovern denounced a "degrading hedonism" implicit in the Proposition 13 vote, and he criticized politicians for becoming "instant economizers and flailing

...Leaves Tough Choices to the Administration

Avoiding specific cuts in favor of the across-the-board approach misleads the public, Pattison said. The 2 percent cut the House approved in the public works bill could force the administration to reduce fiscal 1979 spending on the eight water projects Edgar failed to kill and other items. But it would not save any money in the long run, Pattison said, because the House eventually would appropriate money to finish all projects in the bill.

Liberal Support

Several young, liberal Democrats who supported across-the-board cuts against the wishes of their party leaders echoed Carr's judgment that the amendments were a "last resort."

Phil Sharp, D-Ind., said congressional attempts to cut specific programs are usually unsuccessful because the special interest groups who benefit from them put pressure on members to keep up — or increase — the spending. "It's so hard for us to say 'no' . . . to individual programs," said Sharp, a consistent supporter of the across-the-board cuts.

Leon E. Panetta, D-Calif., a former director of HEW's Office of Civil Rights, said most federal agencies would sustain a 2 percent budget cut with minimal damage. Although he said cuts ideally should be made in specific programs after study by congressional committees, he defended his support of several floor amendments to cut across-the-board as "the only way you're going to get [spending] reductions."

Miller, chief sponsor of all but one of the across-the-board cuts approved by the House, agreed with his Democratic colleagues that scrutinizing individual programs for waste and inefficiency was the ideal way to cut spending.

But since Congress often funds federal programs for political reasons that have little to do with their merit or efficiency, Miller said he resorted to the across-the-board proposals. His amendments would not affect "fixed" programs, such as Social Security benefits established by law, but they would require federal agencies to come up with overall reductions in their flexible programs.

In the first 11 years he offered across-the-board cut amendments to appropriations bills, Miller succeeded only once. The amendments, which drew little support, were regarded as more symbolic than serious. "People never took Miller seriously in the past," said Carr.

But by mid-1978, Miller had succeeded in getting House approval of cuts in three bills, come close on several others, and lost a vote on the legislative appropriations bill when the House decided it wanted a bigger cut than Miller had proposed.

Inflation Worries

Miller credited Proposition 13 with his success in 1978. But he agreed with others that the House had already begun to move in the direction of fiscal conservatism. He said the move — speeded up by what House members thought was the "message" of the California vote — had been prompted by increasing public unhappiness with high inflation and federal spending.

Miller also gained support in 1978 by scaling down his amendments. In previous years, his proposals called for 5 percent across-the-board cuts. In 1978, they all called for 2 percent cuts.

"It would be pretty hard to find any program, good or bad, that doesn't have at least 2 percent waste in it," said Carr, who acknowledged that he had been persuaded to vote for some of Miller's amendments in 1978 in part because they were scaled down.

After three successes, Miller's amendments began to lose. Miller credited the Democratic leadership with the defeat of four across-the-board cut proposals. Democratic leaders noticeably stepped up efforts to oppose Miller after the Republican's initial victories. For instance, when Miller appeared to have won on an amendment to cut the agriculture appropriations bill by 2 percent, the leadership went to work twisting arms until enough members had switched their votes to defeat Miller, 189-201.

Other factors both helped and hindered Miller. For instance, bad publicity about fraud and abuse in HEW programs increased sympathy for cutting that department's huge budget, several members said.

On the other hand, the House voted down a Miller amendment to cut the Housing and Urban Development Department appropriations bill partly because it also contained funding for veterans' programs, agreed some members. "That's a sacred cow in Congress," Sharp said.

Miller planned to offer his 2 percent across-the-board cut amendments to the remaining fiscal 1979 appropriations bills for foreign aid, defense and the District of Columbia. Some members were skeptical that any House-approved cuts would survive in the Senate, which is traditionally more sympathetic to many of the programs the House votes would affect.

But with California taxpayers still fresh in many minds, no one was willing to predict whether the Senate will uphold its traditions or succumb to the House's Proposition 13 fever.

---

taxcutters" in response to the vote, rather than calling for "dynamic government" unafraid to set important goals and to persist in their achievement.

"Today the fault for the heavy burden of unfair taxes rests not on liberal programs, but on needless war, a reckless arms race and an unjust tax system designed and continued by selfish special interests," McGovern said.

But for every liberal who argued that the answer to Proposition 13 was not to turn back on liberal programs, there was at least one conservative arguing just that.

Rep. Charles Thone, R-Neb., for instance, declared: "The taxpayer mutiny now arising across America is most of all a revolt against the nation's welfare mess."

Referring to President Carter's welfare reform proposal, Thone added: "If the president wants to get in tune with the voters, he'd better withdraw that disaster and come back with a plan to make deep cuts both in the number of those on welfare and the billions it costs."

Limits to Government

One of the attitudes most criticized by activists such as McGovern was the belief, accentuated by the Proposition 13 vote, that government is limited in what it can do.

Muskie agreed that such a "negative" response was the predominant reaction to the California vote.

"Fiscal conservatives cry gleefully that the battle lines have been drawn — that the public oracle has spoken, and free-spending politicians are on the run," Muskie said. "At the other end of the spectrum, some liberals are saying that the California vote has ominous overtones — that it signals a retreat from our long-standing promise to help those at the bottom of the economic ladder."

The Senate budget leader said the two interpretations were essentially the same, the only difference being that one side was "pleased," and the other "dismayed."

Muskie offered an alternative, "positive" interpretation. "People know government has a job to do, and they want it done well — with as little waste as possible, and with the maximum result," he said. "In effect, they told their elected leaders they want the fat in government eliminated before they agree to pay any more."

The answer, Muskie said, is not to enact "willy-nilly cuts in spending across the board — cuts which erode not just the fat but the muscle of government as well."

Instead, he argued, a complete re-examination of government programs was needed, one that would result in the ineffective programs being weeded out.

"So far [in mid-1978], neither Washington nor the public has come to grips with this sobering choice," Muskie concluded. "For that choice runs directly against the grain of a bad habit we've developed over the years — a habit of trying to please everybody, by spreading federal dollars around."

The Spending Debate

Looking at more immediate congressional issues, Senate Majority Leader Robert C. Byrd, D-W.Va., said the budget resolution setting spending targets for the fiscal year beginning in October 1978 proved that Congress was showing fiscal restraint.

The resolution, adopted before the Proposition 13 vote, called for federal outlays totaling $498.8 billion and revenues totaling $447.9 billion — enough to allow a $19.4 billion tax cut beginning Jan. 1, 1979. The $50.9 billion deficit envisioned in that 1979 fiscal year plan was almost $10 billion less than proposed by President Carter in January 1978.

That represented an increase of 10 percent over the estimated spending level for the fiscal year, as opposed to a 15 percent rise in fiscal 1978, 9.9 percent in 1977, 12.1 percent in 1976, 20.9 percent in 1975, 9.1 percent in 1974 and 6.5 percent in 1973.

The growth rate would have been even less, except that federal agencies were unable to spend all the money that Congress appropriated for fiscal year 1978. If spending had been up to the allowed level, the budget target for fiscal 1979 would be only a 7.9 percent increase.

"I think Congress has been ahead of Proposition 13," Byrd said. He interpreted the California vote as "not so much a protest against taxes as against paying more and getting less. The message they're sending is: 'We want greater efficiency. We want a dollar's worth of services for a dollar's worth of taxes.' "

Republicans disagreed. House Minority Leader John J. Rhodes, R-Ariz., criticized the Democratic-controlled Congress for rejecting a Republican amendment to the budget resolution that would have cut spending to $488.3 billion. The budget resolution, Rhodes said, was "the same old Democratic medicine — spend and spend, tax and tax."

A Federal Spending Limit?

Some proposals have been made, partly in response to the Proposition 13 vote, to place a clamp on the growth of federal spending. A variety of proposals were thrown in the 1978 legislative hopper, for instance, to require a balanced federal budget. Some were sent to the House Judiciary Committee because they would provide for a constitutional amendment requiring balanced budgets.

Despite efforts by supporters — most notably Bill Archer, R-Texas — to force hearings on the issue, the balanced budget proposals were given little chance of being enacted in 1978.

Besides the difficulty Congress would have in cutting spending or raising taxes enough to erase a federal deficit in the $50 billion range, the balanced budget proposals could have such a dramatic economic impact that they could cause a recession, many economists warn.

Finally, there was little consensus even among proponents of a balanced budget about the level of spending and taxing at which balance should be achieved.

In mid-1978, Rep. Philip M. Crane, R-Ill., introduced an alternative proposal (H J Res 985) to put a lid on federal spending. He would limit spending to 33.3 percent of the average national income of the previous three years. With national spending estimated in 1979 to be 34.5 percent of the national income, the Crane proposal would require a budget of about $482.4 billion — about $17 billion below the level tentatively approved by Congress in May 1978.

Short of those proposals, Congress was likely to consider more recommendations for across-the-board cuts in appropriations bills, much like four measures already approved by mid-1978 by the House.

Proponents argued that the across-the-board cuts reflected a desire by Congress to reduce the size of government. But others suggested that they demonstrate a lack of determination.

If Congress really has the will to reduce federal spending, they argued, it would specify where the cuts should be made, rather than leaving it to the administration to implement the cuts and take the political heat. They also suggested that across-the-board cuts were less likely to be permanent than cuts that resulted from actual policy changes ordered by Congress.

Still, the across-the-board cut method had some respected advocates in Congress. One such cut, proposed during consideration of the first fiscal 1979 budget resolution, fell only eight votes short of being approved.

But the across-the-board cutting approach was far from universally accepted, even among Republicans.

"I don't like across-the-board cuts," said Rep. Barber B. Conable Jr., R-N.Y. "They are not a very artistic way of exercising legislative discretion. They actually leave discretion to the president."

Conable also noted that across-the-board cuts fail to take into consideration the fact that some programs, such as entitlement programs, cannot be cut — a fact that means an across-the-board cut will actually result in larger cuts in controllable spending programs.

Tax Implications

The tax implications of Proposition 13 were even more obscure than the spending implications.

Probably the most enthusiastic of reactions to the California vote came from Sen. William V. Roth Jr., R-Del. He was the sponsor, along with Rep. Jack F. Kemp, R-N.Y., of a bill (S 1860, HR 8333) to reduce individual income tax rates to 45 percent from 48 percent, and to increase the floor for the maximum corporate rate to $100,-000 from $50,000.

"The results from California prove beyond doubt that we are no longer on the verge of a taxpayers' revolt — we are in the midst of one," Roth said. "With California, an entire state has gone on record as recognizing taxpayers as an endangered species."

At least one liberal California legislator disagreed. Rep. Fortney H. "Pete" Stark, D-Calif., said the Proposition 13 vote resulted from a situation peculiar to California.

"Very clearly, the vote in California signified a frustration by the voters with the governor and the legislature for failing to deal with the property tax problem," Stark said.

Roth and Kemp argued that their bill was needed to provide relief to beleaguered taxpayers — especially those in the middle income ranges. While some estimated that the bill would reduce federal revenues by as much as $80 billion, they also contended that it would encourage people to work harder, firms to invest more and the economy to grow more so that it would actually increase federal revenues.

Democrats were unimpressed with those claims. House Speaker Thomas P. O'Neill Jr., D-Mass., called the bill "a fraud," referring to Kemp as "a pretty boy with a lousy bill."

In the meantime, while Roth and Kemp argued for a larger tax reduction, there was considerable pressure from the business community for a smaller one in order to fight inflation. In response, President Carter scaled back his original request for a $25 billion tax cut effective Oct. 1 to $19.4 billion effective Jan. 1, 1979. Carter and the Democratic House leaders discussed a further reduction — to $15 billion — as a possible compromise with Ways and Means Committee members.

Negotiations over the size of the tax cut were inextricably bound up with the debate over tax reform. Carter hoped to be able to implement a larger tax cut by convincing Congress to pass revenue-raising reforms. But, by mid-1978, the reforms appeared all but dead.

"Most people don't view tax reform as the president does, as the closing of loopholes, but as tax relief," Conable said.

Finally, in addition to the debate over the fiscal 1979 budget and tax policies, the Proposition 13 vote sparked renewed discussion about the process by which Congress sets fiscal policies. Some lawmakers, agreeing with Muskie's assertion that ways must be found to cut the "fat" but not the "muscle" out of government programs, argued that Congress needed to strengthen procedures by which it sets spending priorities and monitors the effectiveness of government programs.

To that end, Rep. Leon E. Panetta, D-Calif., proposed that Congress begin adopting biennial budgets. Under his plan (HR 9077), Congress would spend one year adopting the budget, and the next year it would work in "oversight."

On a somewhat more partisan level, Reps. Clair W. Burgener, R-Calif., and Marjorie S. Holt, R-Md., introduced legislation (HR 12345) that would require Congress to adopt overall spending and tax goals, or "aggregates," before approving totals for specific subsections.

Proponents of that approach argued that it would force Congress to consider overall economic policies, rather than just adding up spending totals to adopt an overall budget. Critics of the proposal claimed that it was an essentially political move designed to force lawmakers to take the politically embarrassing move of going on record voting for deficits that were inevitable in any case. ∎

Initial Reaction to Proposition 13:

States Vie to Curb Taxes, Spending

Call it a "taxpayers' revolt." Or the string of events "in the wake of Proposition 13." Whatever one labeled it, there was a growing tax-relief movement in the states which seemed to have gained impetus from California voters' approval June 6 of a state constitutional amendment that cut property taxes drastically.

Proposition 13, or the Jarvis-Gann initiative — named for its authors and chief proponents Howard Jarvis and Paul Gann — took effect July 1, 1978. Its provisions:

● Limited property tax collections by local governments to 1 percent of "full cash value" — 1975-76 assessments.

● Limited increases in assessments to 2 percent each year; allowed reassessments only when property is sold.

● Required a two-thirds vote of both houses of the legislature to levy any new taxes aimed at increasing revenue.

● Prohibited local governments from imposing any new property taxes, and required two-thirds voter approval for other new local taxes.

The effect was an estimated 57 percent decrease in property tax rates statewide, and a tax savings of between $5 and $7 billion for California residents. Governor Edmund G. Brown Jr., D, who opposed the proposition, agreed to work with the legislature to implement it. But the state was considering using a bail-out plan for the first year of Proposition 13's effect, returning part of the state's $5 billion budget surplus to localities to ease their adjustment to suddenly decreased revenues.

Meanwhile, in other states many legislatures were considering or had approved measures to limit state spending, cut taxes, or shift the tax burden by creating new levies or increasing old ones.

Change on the federal level also could be brought about by the 1978 "revolt." By mid-year, at least 22 states had called for a constitutional convention to adopt a constitutional amendment requiring a balanced federal budget.

Following is a summary of what was happening in the states in mid-1978. Those marked by an asterisk (*) have petitioned Congress to call a constitutional convention.

*Alabama: Governor's proposals for property tax relief and repeal of the state utility tax did not pass the legislature in the 1978 session. A special session might be called to consider a constitutional amendment putting a 20 percent lid on county tax increases. If passed, it would be put before voters in November 1978.

Alaska: Three tax-reduction petition drives were gathering support, and a state legislator predicted a "tax revolution." But there were not enough signatures for a vote in 1978 to amend statutes.

*Arizona: The legislature passed a constitutional amendment limiting tax revenue to 7 percent of personal income in the state. The proposal will be on the November ballot. Consideration was given to calling a special session to freeze property assessments. Two proposed amendments similar to Proposition 13 were pending.

Arkansas: A constitutional amendment sponsored by an initiative drive was expected on the November ballot. The proposal would eliminate sales taxes on food and drugs. The state legislature, which meets biennially, also might consider a comprehensive tax reform proposed by a citizens' advisory group when it convenes in January 1979.

California: The Jarvis-Gann initiative, Proposition 13, received overwhelming voter approval in June.

*Colorado: Two petition drives seek constitutional amendments. One that seemed near success proposes state and local government spending limits equal to statewide cost-of-living increases. If qualified, the proposal would be on a November ballot. The other, which would limit property taxes, appeared unlikely to succeed. Colorado's legislature in 1977 voted a 7 percent hold on spending increases, and several tax relief proposals have been introduced.

Connecticut: A Connecticut taxpayers' association was working to influence the legislature to pass constitutional amendments that would provide for the initiative and referendum, create state and local spending ceilings, and prohibit passage of a broad-based personal income tax.

*Delaware: A bill to limit state spending to 98 percent of anticipated

revenue passed the legislature. The governor has proposed an amendment to the state constitution to require a three-fifths vote of the legislature to raise any taxes.

*Florida: A proposal similar to the Jarvis-Gann amendment was being advanced by three state senators who hoped to put it to a November public vote. Plans were reportedly being made to circulate petitions for a limitation initiative to be placed on a 1979 ballot. Several groups were urging the legislature to vote tax relief in the 1978 session.

*Georgia: A spending limitation amendment was introduced in the legislature, and a local group was seeking representatives' support for the measure.

Hawaii: A state constitutional convention might consider a spending limitation amendment when it convened in July 1978.

Idaho: A group seeking to limit property taxes to 1 percent of assessed value had by mid-1978 collected nearly enough signatures to place a tax cut initiative on the November ballot. The governor began planning for anticipated state revenue cutbacks.

Illinois: A spending limitation amendment was blocked by the state Senate. Supporters planned to reintroduce it. Residents of one county staged a massive property tax "strike" leading to a $60 million tax reduction. Other counties could follow suit. A measure that would rebate to taxpayers a percentage of annual income from property taxes passed the legislature, but the governor decided to veto it.

Indiana: Several bills providing property and sales tax relief, particularly for the elderly, were passed and signed into state law. Most of the legislation expands tax exemptions. One bill allows a larger tax base for financing schools.

Iowa: Tax reform measures introduced in the legislature died in committee. Supporters planned to reintroduce proposals.

*Kansas: A homestead property tax exemption measure and exemptions for agricultural equipment were enacted. Another new law allows rebates on sales tax to offset food tax burdens. The legislature on adjourning appointed an interim tax committee of legislators and representatives of citizens' groups and private interests to look into other proposals.

Kentucky: A gubernatorial candidate has commissioned research on tax and spending limitations.

*Louisiana: Legislators were said to be eyeing several tax reform proposals.

Maine: A referendum passed in December 1977 repealed uniform property taxes for education funding. A new law provides $20 million in tax relief.

*Maryland: A constitutional amendment (Maryland Resolution 13) to impose a ceiling on state spending was gathering signatures for consideration by the legislature.

Massachusetts: A constitutional amendment to limit state spending was passed by the 1978 legislature, but the 1979 session must concur to put the proposal on the 1979 ballot. The legislature voted to freeze property taxes at 1977 levels, with only a 5 percent increase for inflation.

Michigan: A group supporting a constitutional state taxation lid filed 410,000 signatures to put the proposition on the ballot. Required are 266,000 valid ones. The plan would limit taxes to 8.3 percent of personal income. A vote was expected in 1978.

Minnesota: Spending limitation legislation was being drafted in 1978 for the next legislative session. Minnesota already limits property tax increases.

*Mississippi: Two tax relief measures passed the legislature in 1978. One removes the sales tax on utility payments, the other doubles the standard income tax exemption on homes.

Missouri: At least one local group (in Springfield) was sponsoring a petition drive aimed at encouraging state lawmakers to enact expenditure limitations. The legislature passed no major tax relief measures in its 1978 session.

Montana: A state senator's proposed referendum was gathering signatures with a qualifying deadline of July 24 for placement on the November ballot. The plan would shift property tax burdens to income tax and local governments facing significant losses would be reimbursed by the state. A new law provides increased exemptions on owner-occupied homes.

*Nebraska: A special session of the legislature in late June approved two

bills to limit local government property tax increases and to allow spending lids imposed by local voters on themselves. The governor, who said he will let the bills become law without his signature, has urged voters to support an initiative petition drive to make spending limits constitutional.

*Nevada: Near qualifying for a November vote was an initiative styled after California's Jarvis-Gann proposal. It would limit tax assessments to purchase value. In the legislature, tax cut and tax shift measures were being discussed, but no legislative action is expected before 1979.

New Hampshire: The governor reportedly was seeking a referendum to limit property taxes and prohibit sales and income taxes.

New Jersey: The first state to enact a tax expenditure ceiling, New Jersey in 1976 shifted its tax burden by simultaneously instituting a statewide income tax. The law limits spending by linking increases to personal income growth.

*New Mexico: Cuts totaling $55 million in taxes were enacted in 1978. They took the form of a permanent reduction in state income tax, a sales tax decrease and expansion of low-income tax credits.

New York: A state senator, member of a tax limitation task force, introduced a state constitutional amendment to cap state spending at 8 percent of total statewide personal income.

North Carolina: Several tax relief measures were defeated in 1978.

*North Dakota: Petitions were being circulated to put to the public an initiative that would make a one-third cut in state income tax.

Ohio: Facing a 1977 court decision that put school financing into jeopardy, the state has been considering measures to shift the tax burden to personal and corporate income. At least two citizens' groups were pushing for initiatives — one to limit property taxes, the other to limit taxes generally.

*Oklahoma: No proposals had been filed by mid-1978, but voters were said to be organizing tax reform efforts.

*Oregon: Supporters of an initiative similar to Proposition 13 have enlisted the help of California's Paul Gann to get approval for limiting property taxes to 1.5 percent of market value.

*Pennsylvania: Two measures setting spending ceilings tied to the rate of inflation and personal income growth have been introduced in the legislature. One would amend statutes, the other the state constitution.

Rhode Island: A pressure group was said to be forming to move for a Jarvis-Gann type amendment, Rhode Island's "Proposition 14," to be enacted by the legislature.

*South Carolina: Pending in the legislature was a constitutional amendment to provide uniform taxation and assessments. A bill already signed into law gives constitutional tax relief to the elderly.

South Dakota: A bill to limit state spending to a percentage of personal income, prohibit decreases in state funding of local governments, and require a balanced budget failed by one vote in 1978 but plans were to reintroduce it next session.

*Tennessee: Many groups in other states have been patterning tax reform efforts after Tennessee's constitutional amendment linking state spending with growth in personal income. The measure was passed in March 1978.

*Texas: The governor was considering calling a special legislative session in July 1978 to consider a constitutional spending cap.

Utah: Groups have been circulating petitions to introduce a spending limitation proposal in the next legislative session. They hope for a 1980 ballot.

Vermont: Tax reform supporters in the state faced a time-consuming process if they want to change the constitution. One requirement is that all towns hold meetings to decide on the amendment.

*Virginia: A group started by a businessman was trying to gather support for a proposed constitutional change limiting all state taxes to 6.34 percent of personal income.

Washington: A petition drive was under way to get the legislature to consider a spending limitation statute.

West Virginia: The legislature was considering an amendment to increase tax exemption categories. Another proposal would require a balanced state budget.

Wisconsin: A spending limitation amendment was blocked by the legislature in 1978.

*Wyoming: A committee in the legislature began hearings the end of June 1978 on proposals for limiting state taxes constitutionally. ∎

House Passage

A $16.3 billion tax cut that sharply divided Democrats but won general support from Republicans was approved by the House Aug. 10, 1978, after a last-ditch attempt by the Carter administration to amend it fell 32 votes short.

The final 362-49 vote came after an all-day debate in which Republicans derided the administration as "irrelevant" to the decision, and even Democrats who supported the Carter position sought to keep their distance from the president.

Before approving the bill, the House rejected a final liberal effort to ease the burden of rising Social Security taxes. And, in a vote with strong partisan overtones, it rejected the Republican Roth-Kemp proposal for a 33 percent reduction in income tax rates over three years.

An effort to kill the tax cut entirely was defeated easily, so the bill (HR 13511 — H Rept 95-1445) was sent to the Senate in exactly the form it emerged from the Ways and Means Committee.

The total size of the cut was $4.6 billion less than envisioned by the first budget resolution approved by the House in May. However, it fell about $7 billion short of the amount that would be needed to offset scheduled Social Security tax increases and inflation-induced income tax increases expected in 1979. As a result, many taxpayers would pay more in taxes in 1979 despite the House-passed bill.

Ways and Means Committee Chairman Ullman and James R. Jones, D-Okla., were credited with finding the tax bill compromise despite what some veteran observers described as the greatest Democratic Party divisions on a tax bill in memory. Ullman received some criticism from liberal Democrats for failing to develop a package that could better unite their party. But most liberals directed their public complaints about the final bill more toward Carter.

"The president and his advisers were totally naive about the legislative process, and [they] gave the chairman no help," said Vanik.

New Administration Proposal

Treasury Secretary Blumenthal, working with disgruntled liberals on the Ways and Means Committee, made one last effort to win support for a more progressive tax cut. The new proposal was disclosed by Corman and Fisher, on Aug. 4, more than a week after the Ways and Means Committee completed action on the long-delayed bill.

Corman and Fisher, both of whom had previously prepared detailed complete substitutes for the committee bill, agreed to drop their separate proposals and push instead for two amendments to the bill, which would:

● Increase the general tax credit to the greater of $100 per exemption or 2 percent of the first $9,000 of income, and make some rate reductions. The proposal would increase the size of the personal tax reductions by $2.3 billion, to $12.7 billion. Most of the benefits would go to people earning less than $15,000.

● Keep provisions in the committee bill reducing the maximum possible tax rate on capital gains to 35 percent, but replace the committee's "alternative minimum tax" on capital gains with a provision designed to establish a graduated minimum tax.

Rules Committee Action

The Rules Committee took up the tax bill Aug. 8-9, in a situation considerably changed since July 27, when the Ways and Means Committee had agreed to seek a rule allowing House votes on the earlier Fisher and Corman substitutes, a no-new-tax-cut proposal by Vanik and Pickle and the Roth-Kemp proposal.

A new fight was brewing over Social Security taxes. First, 105 mostly liberal House members petitioned the Rules Committee to allow a floor vote on a proposal by Gephardt to create a new income tax credit equal to 5 percent of Social Security taxes during 1979 and 1980.

The Social Security issue proved to be the most difficult for the Rules Committee to resolve. In the end, three Democrats joined the committee's five Republicans for an 8-7 vote disallowing a vote on the Gephardt proposal.

The Rules Committee concluded by allowing floor votes on Ways and Means Committee amendments, the Vanik-Pickle proposal, and the new Corman-Fisher proposal. Republicans eager to force a vote on Roth-Kemp were forced to do so by moving to recommit the bill to the Ways and Means Committee with instructions to amend it by adding the Roth-Kemp individual tax reductions.

Floor Action

Debate on the rule provided the only chance for floor consideration of the Social Security issue, but the liberal effort to amend the proposed rule so as to allow a vote on the Gephardt amendment was blocked on a procedural motion, 284-130.

The House next approved, 249-167, a committee amendment originally offered by Archer to index the capital gains tax for inflation beginning in 1980.

The House then overwhelmingly rejected, 57-356, the Vanik-Pickle proposal to enact no new tax cut.

The major tax bill showdown came over the Corman-Fisher proposal. "Here is the big vote," declared Bill Frenzel, R-Minn. "The Corman amendment will decide whether we will really choose new directions.... The Corman amendment redistributes income. The committee bill cuts taxes evenly." The Corman-Fisher proposal aroused opposition from conservative Democrats who had been instrumental in forming the coalition on the Ways and Means Committee that produced the committee bill.

"This is nothing but a disruptive practice," declared Joe D. Waggonner Jr., D-La., of the proposal.

Directing his fire at the administration, he added: "They will change their mind as they have for months been changing their mind. But we hear it said that the rate cuts are larger. Absolutely they are larger. If you want to increase the deficit, you can make them still larger. If you add the same deficit back to the committee bill, you can have the same rate reduction."

Even House Speaker O'Neill, in a rare floor speech in support of the amendment, faulted the administration for being slow in developing the alternative.

"The administration has been tardy in bringing tax legislation to this body," O'Neill said. "I truly feel, though, if the amendment...had been brought up here five months ago, it would have been the product of the committee by now, and it would have sailed through this Congress."

Even that was inadequate to win the day for the amendment, which was defeated on a 193-225 vote.

Only the vote on the Roth-Kemp proposal fell along party lines.

On the 177-240 vote defeating the proposal, only three Republicans voted "no." A total of 37 Democrats defected party ranks to vote in favor of the Republican-backed measure. ∎

Controversy Surrounds Tuition Tax Credit

The proposed tax credit for education expenses, which nearly stalled passage of major Social Security legislation in the first session of the 95th Congress, sparked renewed controversy in 1978.

The credit, and other proposals to grant special tax breaks to help parents offset the costs of their children's education, has been debated for years.

Many favor the idea of tax relief for the middle class. They see education costs as typical of the burdens faced by middle-income families who are in a worse economic position than the very wealthy, who can afford the costs, and the poor, who qualify for federal aid programs.

Other advocates of tuition tax credits take the traditional Republican position that it is better to put education money directly in the pockets of consumers than to send it to institutions or provide it in the form of grants that have "red tape" and federal regulation attached.

Finally, some see tuition tax credits as a way to provide government support to parochial schools while avoiding constitutional prohibitions. They support bills such as one (S 2142) sponsored by Sens. Bob Packwood, R-Ore., and Daniel Patrick Moynihan, D-N.Y., which would make families with dependents in public or private elementary and secondary schools eligible for tax breaks.

Riding on what many have called a growing wave of middle-class tax revolt, the concept of tuition tax credits enjoyed broad popular support in election year 1978. Responding to this pressure, the House June 1 voted to give federal income tax relief to help pay the costs of college as well as private elementary and secondary education.

The Senate followed suit on Aug. 15, but only after approving an amendment that would cut out any aid to elementary and secondary school students. And, complicating the situation still further, the Senate the next day passed a rival Carter-backed plan that would expand existing federal grant programs.

Opponents of the education tax break have conceded that support for the idea was very substantial, but they vowed to fight it because of what they considered serious policy implications.

Many critics question the need for a major new education aid program, and they warn that it could become a significant drain on the federal budget.

Others doubt the arguments that middle-income families have a special need for help. They suggest that the proposed tax break would be bad tax policy since it would be regressive, and since it would be less efficient in channeling aid to families actually in need than existing aid programs.

Some critics argue that the tax credit would merely encourage colleges to increase tuition, so that the money provided to individuals would end up very quickly in institutions. They also suggest that the break could put private institutions, with higher tuition, at a greater competitive disadvantage with public schools.

President Carter on April 11, 1978, said he opposed tuition tax credits as costly and unconstitutional.

Some proposals provided for tax deductions rather than credits for educational expenses. Credits were the generally favored approach, however, since deductions were recognized to be more valuable to the wealthy.

One alternative to the deduction and credit proposals was the idea of allowing families with dependents in school to defer their taxes until after the dependents graduate. Rep. Abner J. Mikva, D-Ill., has argued that the deferral approach would do more to help families through the serious cash-flow problems faced when their children are in school, while posing less of a burden for the government in the long run. One problem with Mikva's proposal, however, was that its initial cost to the Treasury would be greater than the various tax credit plans, since it would allow taxpayers to defer more in taxes than most proposed credits.

The proposal which won most attention in 1978 was sponsored by Sen. William V. Roth Jr., R-Del. In its original form (S 311), it would have provided for tax credits increasing annually up to $500 in 1980 for each

---

"We are rapidly approaching a situation in this country where only the very affluent and the very poor will be able to attend college."

—Sen. William V. Roth Jr., R-Del.

Alternative Approaches

The 95th Congress had before it a variety of alternative approaches to the idea of providing tax breaks for education costs.

Most provided a tax credit — a straight reduction in taxes owed by a specified amount—for school expenses. Some included provisions making the credit refundable, so that families too poor to have tax liabilities equal to the proposed credit could receive the same aid as wealthier families. Others had income eligibility ceilings, limiting the tax relief available to very wealthy families.

dependent attending college or post-secondary vocational school full-time.

When that proposal failed to emerge from the Senate Finance Committee in 1977, Roth attached an amendment calling for a $250 tuition tax credit to Social Security legislation. It was approved by a lopsided 61-11 vote.

That was the sixth time the Senate had approved some form of education expense tax break since 1967. Most observers agree that a similar proposal could sail through that chamber in 1978.

The matter never came to a direct vote in the House in 1977, largely due to the opposition of Ways and Means

Committee Chairman Al Ullman, D-Ore., and his predecessor, Wilbur D. Mills, D-Ark., 1939-77. Still, support was strong in the House, where more than 80 education tax relief bills were introduced in the 95th Congress.

In a test vote on Sept. 8, 1977, the House endorsed the concept by a 311-76 margin, lowering its fiscal 1978 revenue floor $175 million to permit enactment of a tuition tax credit. The Senate followed suit the next day on a voice vote.

The Roth proposal generated considerable interest during deliberations by the conference committee on Social Security legislation in December 1977, but it was ultimately dropped from the bill due to opposition from House conferees.

Rising Education Costs

On one point, there is no debate. The increase in education costs is well documented. According to the College Entrance Examination Board, the average annual cost of a public university education increased more than 40 per cent in the last five years, from $1,-782 to $2,906. For a private university, the cost climbed more than 35 per cent, from $2,793 to $4,811.

But opponents of education tax breaks argue that family income has been more than keeping pace with the rise in schooling costs. The Congressional Budget Office reported in July 1977 that median family income rose 72.9 percent between 1967 and 1975, compared to an increase in college charges during that period of about 65 percent. College costs took up a smaller portion of family income in 1975 than in 1967, it said.

Existing Aid Programs

The office also noted that appropriations for major student aid programs grew 281 per cent during the same period. In fiscal 1977, the federal budget included $9.7 billion in spending and tax expenditures to provide financial aid to students, out of a total higher education budget of $14.4 billion.

The financial aid included tax allowances (such as the rule that parents can list students as dependents even if they are over 19 years of age, and the deduction for charitable contributions), grants, loans and loan guarantees.

Most of the programs were designed to aid low-income students. The largest direct aid program provides "basic educational opportunity grants" to families with adjusted incomes of less than $6,000 per year.

But guaranteed loans are available to middle-income students. Under the major loan program, families with income up to $25,000—representing 85 per cent of total student enrollment—can borrow up to $15,000 and qualify for federal interest subsidies while their dependents are in school.

Middle-Income Relief

Advocates of tuition tax breaks argue that these programs have failed to ease the special burden on many middle-income families. They say the programs are underutilized, and that the squeeze on middle-income families is growing worse as tuition rises.

"We are rapidly approaching a situation in this country where only the very affluent and the very poor will be able to attend college, and I am convinced that action must be taken to ease the financial plight of middle-income families," declared Roth.

The House Budget Committee has confirmed Roth's argument that middle-income college enrollment has declined. It reported in November 1977 that enrollment of children from families with earnings between $10,000 and $15,000 had declined 16 per cent since 1969, compared to a 15 per cent decline for families earning less than $10,000, and a 9 per cent drop for families with income above $15,000.

Opponents of the tuition tax break have not challenged those figures, but some suggest that the enrollment decline may reflect a growing feeling among middle-income families that education is not considered as valuable as it used to be, rather than proving that rising costs have put education out of the reach of some middle-income families.

The prestigious American Council on Education, while noting that economists have had difficulty documenting the alleged squeeze on the middle class, suggested in an analysis in October 1977 that many middle-income families may feel themselves "relatively worse off" because much of the education cost

Many critics argue that a broad tax break would merely encourage colleges to increase their tuitions, so that the money provided to individuals would end up in institutions.

burden has been lifted from lower-income students through public and private financial aid programs.

"We're cognizant of the need for middle-income relief, but we don't know if tax credits are the right mechanism," concluded Sheldon Steinbach, the organization's counsel.

Tax Implications

Advocates of the various tax break proposals suggest that the tax system is the best mechanism because it reaches large numbers of people at relatively low administrative costs. They complain that participation rates in existing programs have been low, and that eligibility standards are arbitrary.

Critics of the tax break concept counter that it would complicate the tax system and force the Internal Revenue Service to become involved in evaluating educational expenditures to determine which qualify for relief—a situation at least as bureaucratic as the existing aid programs.

The critics also argue that tax breaks are inefficient because they provide relief without reference to actual need. Under Roth's original proposal, they note, a millionaire sending his child to a $4,000 private college could claim the full credit, while a laborer sending his child to a $200 community college could only claim $200. If the laborer was too poor to pay taxes, he could claim no credit at all.

Although part of that problem could be corrected by making credits refundable and imposing income eligibility ceilings, the tax break critics suggest that existing programs can be more finely targeted to the people who need help. If educational aid is the goal, they say, grant and loan programs are the best methods; if general tax relief is the goal, it would be easier and more efficient to change tax rates than to establish a new tax credit that bases the amount of relief on the number of dependents in school.

Califano Criticisms

"Two factors presently determine the amount of aid a student receives from Office of Education programs: the family's ability to pay, and the cost of the chosen college," said Health, Education and Welfare Secretary Joseph A. Califano Jr. in a letter sharply critical of the tuition tax credit.

"When ability to pay is subtracted from cost, we have need, and in this sense all the Office of Education programs are need based," he continued. "Perhaps, as some argue, different ways of determining need should be considered, or assignment of responsibility for meeting need among different programs could be improved. I cannot, however, imagine endorsing a student grant program which would completely discard need as a relevant factor in the manner of some tuition tax credit proposals."

How Regressive?

It is generally agreed that a tuition tax credit would be regressive, but estimates vary as to the extent.

Califano suggested in early 1977 that 60 per cent of the benefits of a tax

---

"I cannot...imagine endorsing a student grant program which would completely disregard need as a relevant factor in the manner of some tuition tax credit proposals."

—Health, Education and Welfare Secretary Joseph A. Califano Jr.

---

credit would go to families with incomes of $18,000 or more. The American Council on Education estimated that only 11.4 per cent of the benefits would go to families earning more than $25,000. But the Congressional Budget Office said that families with incomes over $20,000 would receive 78 per cent of the benefits, and that only 6 per cent would go to families with incomes below $9,000.

Assistant Secretary of the Treasury Laurence N. Woodworth estimated during hearings before the House Budget Committee in May 1977 that the median income of families with 18-to-24-year-old dependents in college is $4,000 higher than the median income for all families with dependents that age, and $6,000 higher than the median income for all families.

One other factor could contribute to the regressiveness of the credit, according to critics of the idea. Approval of a major tax expenditure to help middle-income families finance their education costs could lead to pressure to reduce appropriations for the existing programs—an eventuality that

would probably cut back on financial aid to low-income families.

Institutional Impact

Apart from the debates about whether a special education tax break is necessary or equitable are some serious disagreements in Congress about the impact a new tax expenditure would have on institutional arrangements in the field of education.

Many critics argue that a broad tax break would merely encourage colleges to increase their tuitions, so that the credit would flow through directly to institutions. They say the danger of such an eventuality is less with a more narrowly aimed aid program, since colleges would know that a tuition increase designed to absorb the aid would hurt the relatively larger number of students receiving no help under the narrower program.

Critics also argue that a credit program could create an ever-growing demand on the federal Treasury. A $250 credit doesn't amount to much when tuition can be as high as $7,000, they argue, concluding that Congress would be under continuous pressure to increase the size of the credit.

The possibility of an escalating demand for higher and higher credits could, in turn, absorb all additional money for higher education, according to some. The cost of proposals before Congress in 1978 ranged from $1 billion to $8 billion annually. Roth's $250 credit was estimated likely to cost $1.2 billion. If Congress were to include elementary and secondary school costs in the bill, the price tag would climb to $4.7 billion.

Parochial School Issue

The controversy over aid to parochial schools has been viewed as a time bomb that could blast the tuition tax credit debate into an entirely different world. Although such aid has been ruled unconstitutional in the past, it has remained politically a hot issue. President Carter himself pledged during his campaign to seek some constitutional way for the government to support parochial schools.

Packwood and Moynihan argue that the tax credit, if extended to all taxpayers with dependents in school could be the answer. At the very least, Moynihan said in May 1977, the Supreme Court should be given a chance to rule on the matter again. "We have more than once seen minorities on the court become majorities," he said.

Legislative Battle

The 1978 battle over tuition tax breaks centered initially in the Senate. On Feb. 22, the Senate Human Resources Education Subcommittee approved a bill (S 2539) to expand existing student aid programs to assist middle-income families. The bill, sponsored by Claiborne Pell, D-R.I., was similar, but not identical, to a proposal by the Carter administration. In essence, it expanded the Basic Educational Opportunity Grant program so that more middle-income families could qualify for aid. Both the president's proposal and the bill approved by the subcommittee were advanced "as alternatives to the tax credit proposals.

Advocates of the tuition tax credit approach responded quickly to the Education Subcommittee action. Patching together the two most prominent tax credit proposals — the Roth bill and the Packwood-Moynihan measure — the Senate Finance Committee Feb. 23 approved a bill allowing a college tax credit of up to $250, increasing the credit to a maximum of $500 in 1980 and extending it to cover elementary and secondary education costs.

The Joint Committee on Taxation estimated that the combined Roth-Packwood-Moynihan plan would cost $5.3 billion annually by the time it would be fully implemented in fiscal year 1983. The joint committee analysis suggested that 75 percent of the tax credits would go to parents with children in college and vocational schools.

By contrast, the staff of the Education Subcommittee estimated that the expanded grant and loan program approved by that panel would cost about $1.5 billion per year when fully implemented. Carter's proposals were estimated to cost about $1.2 billion — the price tag of the Roth proposal.

Attention then focused on the House, where supporters of increased federal aid to middle-income college students March 8 gained a step over backers of the tuition tax credit in their race to the House floor. On that day, the House Education and Labor Committee approved a bill (HR 11274) adding $1.2 billion to existing federal student assistance. The bill was supported by the Carter administration

and by public education organizations. Tuition tax credit legislation was still in the House Ways and Means Committee. Ullman had blocked similar legislation in the past. Despite Ullman's opposition, however, the committee April 11 approved legislation (HR 11776) granting federal income tax credits for college expenses. At the same time, it rejected an attempt to extend credits for elementary and secondary school tuition.

Despite the urgings of the Carter administration and the Democratic leadership, the House March 20 voted not to consider the direct federal grants bill (HR 11274) without having a chance to vote on tuition credits as well. The showdown on the issue in the House came on June 1, when the House voted 237-158 to approve the tuition tax credit bill. Before passing the bill, the House by a narrow 209-194 vote adopted a controversial amendment by Charles A. Vanik, D-Ohio, to extend eligibility to elementary and secondary school students.

As passed by the House, the bill provided a reduction of income taxes equal to 25 percent of tuition expenses for each student in private elementary and secondary schools, and public or private colleges, universities and postsecondary vocational schools. The credit for higher education tuition would be limited to $100 per student in 1978, rising to $250 by 1980. For lower-school tuition credit the limit would be $50, going up to $100 by 1979. The bill would expire after 1980. (*Provisions, below*)

The Joint Committee on Taxation estimated that the bill would cost $25 million in lost revenues in fiscal 1978, $635 million in 1979, $1.1 billion in 1980, and $1.2 billion in 1981. About 70 percent of the loss would be due to college credits, 30 percent to the elementary and secondary credit.

The threatened veto by Carter may have helped to generate more votes for the bill than it might otherwise have secured. Staff aides observed before the vote that some members intended to vote for the politically popular measure in the firm belief that it would never become law. Paul Simon, D-Ill., said the veto threat meant "you can do two things: You can know the bill's going to be vetoed, and you can tell the folks back home you voted for it."

The intensive lobbying campaign against the private school credits by public school groups, organized as the National Coalition to Save Public

Education, was effective, but started a little too late to carry the day. Private and parochial school forces apparently had already gained the upper hand before their opponents even began.

Catholic and other private school groups conducted a strong grass-roots campaign for the credits early in 1978. Public school groups did not mobilize until spring. By then the private school groups had built up such a strong lead that the public educators couldn't quite catch up. William D. Ford, D-Mich., said many members had already committed themselves publicly in favor of the credits before opponents could even present their case effectively.

Nevertheless, the public school lobbying did convert a runaway into a cliffhanger, reducing what some had thought was a 60-vote margin to 15 votes by the time of the vote. Barber B. Conable Jr., R-N.Y., said the close vote was "a tribute to the effective lobbying of the National Education Association," a leading member of the coalition.

The elementary and secondary credits occupied most of the lobbying on the bill. Neither the coalition nor the college and university groups spent much time working against the college credits.

Opponents predicted that adoption of the elementary and secondary credits would make a presidential veto all the more certain. "The surest way of making certain that there is no bill that ever becomes law is to include in it elementary and secondary education," said Mikva. But supporters of the bill were hopeful that Carter might change his mind and sign it.

House Speaker Thomas P. O'Neill Jr., D-Mass., said June 1 that the House was unlikely to override a veto.

House Provisions

As passed by the House, major provisions of HR 12050:

● Allowed as a credit against federal income taxes an amount equal to 25 percent of the tuition paid to eligible institutions of higher learning, postsecondary vocational schools, or private, non-profit elementary or secondary schools, up to a specified amount.

● Set the maximum credit for postsecondary school tuition at $100 per student in calendar 1978, $150 in 1979 and $250 in 1980; set the maximum for elementary and secondary school tuition at $50 per student in 1978 and $100 in 1979 and 1980.

● Provided that the credit go into effect Aug. 1, 1978, and end after Dec. 31, 1980.

● Made eligible for the credit tuition payments for students enrolled in qualified elementary or secondary schools or in courses leading to a baccalaureate or associate degree or a certificate of course-work from a vocational school; excluded tuition for graduate students, kindergarten or nursery school students.

● Defined as eligible elementary and secondary schools those schools which are privately operated, are accredited or approved under state law or meet the requirements of state compulsory school attendance laws, and qualify as tax-exempt organizations; also included facilities offering education to physically or mentally handicapped persons.

● Made eligible for the credit tuition payments for persons enrolled as full-time students at least four months of the year, or who took at least half the normal course load for eight months a year.

● Made tuition payments and course fees eligible for the credit, but excluded costs for books, supplies and living and travel expenses.

● Prohibited dependent students from claiming the tuition credit on their own tax returns.

● Required that any reduction in a person's taxes under the bill not be taken into account when determining eligibility for any other educational assistance program.

● Stipulated that the bill would not grant additional authority to the Internal Revenue Service to inspect the records of church-controlled schools except to the extent necessary to determine eligibility; also stipulated that schools enrolling students who benefited from the credit not be considered as recipients of federal aid under the bill.

● Provided for an expedited court review of the bill's constitutionality.

Senate Action

More than four months after the House passed its version of the legislation, the principal Senate sponsors of tuition tax credit legislation proposed sharp cutbacks in the amount of tax assistance that their bill would give to students and their parents.

The unveiling of the new tuition credit package in early August fol-

lowed rejection of the original bill by two Senate committees and what some observers called a slow erosion of support for the measure.

On Aug. 3, Moynihan, Packwood and Roth announced new amendments that would cut the projected $5.2 billion cost of the original bill (HR 3946) in 1982 to $2.9 billion.

The Senate Finance Committee gave its approval to the compromise by a 12-1 vote the same day, reporting it as HR 12050, the number of the House-passed bill.

In addition to reducing the cost of the credits, the revised plan was designed to circumvent the negative recommendations on the bill voted by the Appropriations and Budget Committees Aug. 1 and 2. Sponsors took out the parts of the bill which had resulted in the referral to the two committees.

Key Changes

As reported by the Finance Committee, HR 12050 made the following key changes in HR 3946:

● Reduced the maximum credit for elementary and secondary school students to $250, from $500.

● Eliminated eligibility for graduate students and students who took less than half the normal course load.

● Deleted the "refundable" credits, which would result in cash outlays to parents or students whose tax obligations were less than the amount of credit.

● Provided that the credit be reduced by the amount of any other need-based federal educational assistance, such as Basic Educational Opportunity Grants, received by the student.

● Required a Cabinet-level report on the effectiveness of efforts by the Internal Revenue Service to prevent students at racially segregated schools from getting the credit.

● Eliminated eligibility of tuition paid for students at public elementary and secondary schools.

● Delayed to Oct. 1, 1980, from Aug. 1, 1980, the effective date of the elementary and secondary credit and the increase in the college credit to $500 from $250 per student.

Sponsors said they planned to offer the refundability provision on the floor as an amendment.

Appropriations Committee

The Finance Committee-reported bill had been referred to the Appropri-

ations Committee because the provision for a "refundable" tax credit for tuition would require a $117 million appropriation in fiscal 1979.

Ernest F. Hollings, D-S.C., moved that the committee report HR 3946 with a negative recommendation. Hollings had been a leader in Senate opposition to credits for elementary and secondary school students. He reportedly had been working to block quick floor consideration of the bill.

The Hollings motion was adopted 13-4. Opposition to the bill reflected a variety of factors, including opposition to the refundable credits and concern over the effect on public schools. "It was obviously not a clear-cut thing," said an aide.

Budget Committee

The Budget Committee action against the tuition credits underscored the growing problems facing the bill shown by the Appropriations vote. Robert Dole, R-Kan., observed that "some of us are having second thoughts" about credits for elementary and secondary students. "There's been a lot of erosion of support," he said.

Because the spending in HR 3946 had not all been provided for in the first budget resolution, sponsors of the bill had to get a waiver from the Budget Committee. By a 5-8 vote the committee rejected a Dole motion to report the waiver resolution (S Res 524) favorably. Then by a 9-4 vote the committee reported the resolution unfavorably.

Committee disapproval of the waiver would not have blocked floor consideration of HR 3946, since the Senate could have adopted S Res 524 by majority vote before considering the bill. But the waiver itself was made unnecessary by the new version of the bill reported by the Finance Committee, because it did not contain any spending that required a waiver of the 1979 budget resolution.

Budget Committee Chairman Edmund S. Muskie, D-Maine, argued that the committee's responsibility was not to block the bill but to point out its future budgetary implications. Estimating that the bill could cost $14 billion in the next five years, he warned, "once we put this on the books, we'll never get it off. We can't block it, but we sure can raise a big red flag."

Muskie's emphasis on the cost of the bill raised new problems for the college student credit part of the bill. Most of the opposition to tuition credits had focused on the parochial and private school issue, leaving the higher education credits relatively untouched. But the college credits would cost far more than the private school credits — three-quarters of the aid would go to families with students in higher education.

Floor Action

After three days of often heated debate, the Senate Aug. 15 voted 65-27 to pass the tuition tax credit bill, but only after voting 56-41 in favor of an amendment offered by Hollings to strike out all benefits for elementary and secondary school pupils. As passed by the Senate, the bill was a scaled-down version of the legislation reported by the Finance Committee in

February. The Senate bill would allow parents to claim a tax credit of 50 percent of tuition and fees for each student in college or post-secondary vocational school, up to a maximum of $250 a student. The credit would become effective as of Aug. 1, 1978. On Oct. 1, 1980, it would be increased to a maximum of $500 a student.

The vote to strike the tax credits for elementary and secondary school students was a tactical victory for the Carter administration, which had opposed the measure as unconstitutional. However, approval of the Senate version was expected to give the tuition credit legislation a boost over the alternative measure (S 2539) supported by the Carter administration that would aid middle-income students by expanding existing federal college scholarship programs.

That measure passed the Senate barely 14 hours after it had approved the college tuition credit measure. The vote on the Carter-approved bill, sponsored by Pell and reported by the Human Resources Committee in February, was 68-28. The major provision of the Pell bill would expand the existing grant program by allowing grants to students from families with incomes exceeding $16,000 a year. The program was tailored to aid the middle class, with 89 percent of the benefits intended for families with incomes of $25,000 or less and 64 percent expected to go to families earning $15,000 to $25,000. The estimated cost of the Pell plan was $1.46 billion for 1979, as compared to $1.7 billion for the measure approved by the Senate Aug. 15 and $1.2 billion for the House-passed version.

Social Security Financing Debated Anew

Efforts to hold down Social Security taxes exploded as a major legislative issue in 1978, but the prospects for passage of such proposals continued to be shaky in light of opposition from key congressional leaders and the Carter administration.

The payroll tax, which finances the three trust funds that make up the Social Security system, rose in 1978 under a law enacted six years earlier. The resulting public outcry created new doubts among some lawmakers about the wisdom of a series of large hikes scheduled to begin in 1979 under a law approved in 1977.

Some have suggested that general revenues should pay part of the cost of the Social Security system in order to relieve the rise in payroll taxes. That has been resisted in the past on the grounds that the system should be self-supporting.

To meet that objection, a group of lawmakers led by Sen. Gaylord Nelson, D-Wis., and Rep. Abner J. Mikva, D-Ill., proposed an alternative approach to general revenue financing. Under their plan, two elements of the system — disability insurance and health insurance — would be opened to general revenue financing while the old age and survivors trust fund would continue to be supported by the payroll tax.

Background: 1977 Action

Congress Dec. 15, 1977, gave final approval to Social Security tax increases totaling $227 billion over the next 10 years.

Intended to counteract short-term and longer run problems with the system, the Social Security measure (HR 9346) was the country's largest peacetime tax increase ever. Aware of probable economic side effects, President Carter quickly pledged to design income tax cuts and other stimulative proposals with the Social Security taxes in mind. Carter signed HR 9346 into law (PL 95-216) on Dec. 20.

Conferees on the bill removed the last hurdle Dec. 14 by agreeing to drop an unrelated Senate provision establishing a $250 tax credit for college tuition expenses. Faced with resistance from House leaders and veto threats from the administration, Senate proponents of the credit backed down, determined to revive the idea in 1978. Once in place, the tuition subsidy would cost the Treasury $1.2 billion a year. *(Tuition credit, p. 53)*

The Carter administration, while not prepared to give in on the tax credit issue, repeatedly prodded Congress to finish action on Social Security before adjournment. Frustrated perhaps by the lack of progress on energy legislation, House and Senate leaders echoed these appeals.

Though it sailed through the Senate 56-21, the final version of HR 9346 encountered stiff opposition from Republicans in the House. Appalled by the size of the tax increases, Barber B. Conable Jr., R-N.Y., ranking minority member of the Ways and Means Committee, claimed more

reasonable alternatives were available. "A vote against this bill will not end Social Security," he argued. "It will give us a chance to reconsider a major mistake."

But House Speaker Thomas P. O'Neill Jr., D-Mass., in a rousing speech, made a final pitch for the bill. Recalling a vote to recommit the original Social Security legislation in 1935, O'Neill said Republicans had voted 97-1 to kill the program. "The interesting fact about it is that the philosophy has not changed on the Republican side since 1935," thundered the Speaker. "If I've ever seen an issue that's a Democratic issue, it's this." The House then cleared the bill by a vote of 189-163. Earlier the House agreed to consider the conference report by only three votes, 178-175.

Though inspired in part by administration proposals, the final package relied exclusively on traditional payroll tax financing for Social Security. The new schedules, featuring steady increases in both tax rates and the amounts of wages on which the tax is paid, meant higher Social Security contributions for all covered workers, beginning in 1979. Over the course of the decade, the bill more than tripled the maximum tax payment, borne by middle- and upper-income workers and their employers. By 1987, for example, workers and employers would each pay a tax of 7.15 per cent on earnings up to $42,600, for a maximum payment of more than $3,000 apiece. In 1977, with Social Security taxes of 5.85 per cent each on earnings up to $16,500, the maximum contribution was $965. *(Tax increases compared, box, p. 62)*

Some of these increases would have occurred anyway, because of inflation adjustments required by existing law. But the program's dwindling balances prompted calls for additional funding; each year since 1975 the Social Security system had paid out more to beneficiaries than it collected from taxes. Government actuaries forecast continuing deficits, capable of draining trust fund reserves completely within a few years.

Though other factors contributed, the main cause of these shortfalls was the recent combination of inflation and recession, which together raised Social Security benefit costs and reduced tax receipts. Because of this, some experts saw little reason to rush ahead with new Social Security taxes, suggesting that improved economic performance might sufficiently replenish the trust funds.

But few denied that the program faced grave strains in the future. Projections showed demographic factors—such as low birth rates, longer life spans and the aging of the "baby boom" generation—eventually undermining the system, as a shrinking work force became responsible for the support of a growing number of retirees.

Carter Proposal

The Carter administration in May 1977 outlined a Social Security rescue plan that would have channeled an additional $83-billion to the trust funds over the next five years. Because it proposed to supplement payroll tax receipts with income tax revenues in times of high unemployment, the administration plan involved lower Social Security tax increases than ultimately enacted.

Both houses, in addition to rejecting any large-scale use of general revenues for Social Security, reworked the Carter package in other ways. The final bill did include administration-backed procedures for correcting a defective inflation adjustment formula, which had threatened to drive up benefits sharply over the next several decades. But Congress also decided to ease the "retirement test," allowing elderly persons to earn more without losing a portion of their benefits, and liberalize the treatment of divorced and widowed beneficiaries. The administration had criticized all of these changes as costly.

Alternatives involving fundamental revisions of the program generally made little headway in either chamber. The House voted overwhelmingly against requiring Social Security coverage of government workers and summarily dismissed proposals to finance Medicare from Treasury revenues, freeing substantial hospital insurance taxes for Social Security. An administration proposal requiring a higher taxable wage base for employers than for employees only narrowly survived in the Senate, and conferees later discarded it.

The final version of the bill included several welfare proposals attached by the Senate Finance Committee in hopes of expediting them. The main provisions gave additional money to state and local governments to meet welfare costs, created financial incentives for state programs to reduce their error rates and authorized special work projects—a pet idea of Finance Committee Chairman Russell B. Long, D-La. — on an experimental basis.

Final Provisions

As signed into law, HR 9346 (PL 95-216):

● **Short-Term Funding.** Raised the Social Security wage base for employers and employees above levels provided automatically under existing law in each of the years 1979 to 1982. Under this schedule, the base would increase from the 1978 level of $17,700 to $22,900 in 1979, and in stages to $31,800 in 1982; after that, to keep pace with inflation, automatic adjustments would occur annually, for a projected base of $42,600 by 1987.

● Raised payroll tax rates, starting in 1979. Coupled with increases already scheduled under existing law, Social Security tax rates would climb from the 1978 level of 6.05 per cent each for employees and employers to 6.13 per cent in 1979, 6.65 per cent in 1981, 6.70 per cent in 1982, 7.05 per cent in 1985, 7.15 per cent in 1986, and 7.65 per cent in 1990. *(Box, this page)*

● Set the Social Security tax rate paid by self-employed individuals at 1½ times the employee rate, beginning in 1981.

● Shifted revenues from the retirement and survivors programs to the disability insurance trust fund, beginning in 1978.

● Stipulated that the financing changes did not affect certain tax base computations of either the railroad retirement program or the Pension Benefit Guaranty Corporation that had been tied to the Social Security wage base.

● **Inflation Adjustment.** Adopted "decoupling" procedures to correct a flaw in the existing benefit formula that overadjusted for inflation. The new techniques, which changed only the starting benefit levels of future retirees, guaranteed the average worker initial benefits equal to 43 per cent of pre-retirement wages.

Social Security Tax Levels

PAYROLL TAX

Year	Existing Tax Rate[1]	Final Bill Tax Rate[1]
1977	5.85%	5.85%
1978	6.05	6.05
1979	6.05	6.13
1980	6.05	6.13
1981	6.30	6.65
1982	6.30	6.70
1983	6.30	6.70
1984	6.30	6.70
1985	6.30	7.05
1986	6.45	7.15
1987	6.45	7.15
1990	6.45	7.65

1 Both the employee and the employer are taxed at this rate. The tax is computed on all of an employee's wages up to a specified level, which is shown below. Wages above those levels are not taxed.

TAXABLE WAGE BASE

The table below shows the maximum wage levels that are taxed for Social Security. Both employees and their employers pay tax on the same amounts. The figures with no asterisk (*) are specified by statute; figures marked with an asterisk are estimates based on an automatic adjustment mechanism in law that increases the wage base as incomes increase.

Year	Existing Law	Final Bill
1977	$16,500	$16,500
1978	17,700	17,700
1979	18,900*	22,900
1980	20,400*	25,900
1981	21,900*	29,700
1982	23,400*	31,800
1983	24,900*	33,900*
1984	26,400*	36,000*
1985	27,900*	38,100*
1986	29,400*	40,200*
1987	31,200*	42,600*

● Arranged for a five-year transition period, to allow individuals retiring between 1979 and 1983 to receive benefits based on the 1978 formula if higher than under the new one.

● **Earnings Test.** Eased restrictions on outside earnings by Social Security recipients over age 65, setting new limits of $4,000 in 1978, $4,500 in 1979, $5,000 in 1980, $5,500 in 1981 and $6,000 in 1982. (Over those amounts, individuals would continue to lose 50 cents in benefits for each dollar earned.)

● Required subsequent yearly increases in the limits to reflect general wage trends.

● Dropped the test entirely, beginning in 1982, for Social Security recipients aged 70 and 71. Existing law already exempted persons aged 72 and over.

● **Marital Status.** Guaranteed pre-existing levels of benefits to persons over age 60 who marry or remarry, effective January 1979; permitted reapplications after that date by persons whose dependents' benefits were cut off because of changes in marital status.

● Permitted persons to qualify for Social Security benefits based on their spouses' earnings after 10, rather than 20, years of marriage.

● Reduced Social Security benefits to a dependent spouse by the amount of any federal, state or local civil service pension received by the spouse; established a five-year transition period, to protect women who retired early from government service, or had been planning to, in expectation of collecting spouses' benefits under Social Security according to the old rules.

● **Other Benefit Adjustments.** Froze the initial level of the "minimum benefit," currently claimed by persons with minimal coverage under Social Security, at the 1978 level of $121 a month; made adjustments for inflation each year for individuals actually drawing the benefit.

● Raised the "special minimum" benefit, available to persons with lengthy covered work experience at low wage levels, to allow as much as $230 a month for an individual and $345 a month for a couple, beginning in January 1979; provided for cost-of-living adjustments.

● Increased a bonus added to the entitlements of workers who delay their retirement beyond age 65, from the level of 1 per cent to 3 per cent per year; assured the same benefit bonus to widows or widowers of workers who postpone their retirement.

● **Coverage.** Excluded certain income of limited partnerships from Social Security coverage, beginning in 1978.

● Raised Social Security contributions for employers of tipped workers, requiring payments based on the full level of the minimum wage. (In practice, employers often pay wages below the minimum to tipped employees, because of a special "tip credit" allowed under the minimum wage law.)

● Authorized the President to work with foreign countries on ways of coordinating Social Security with counterpart programs abroad, to eliminate duplicative contributions and coverage; provided for a one-house veto of any such agreements with foreign countries within 90 days.

● **Studies.** Directed an interagency study, involving the Departments of Health, Education and Welfare (HEW) and Treasury, the Civil Service Commission, and the Office of Management and Budget, of proposed coverage of federal, state and local government workers under Social Security; required a report to Congress within two years of enactment.

● Directed HEW, in conjunction with a special Justice Department Task Force on Sex Discrimination, to examine differences in the treatment of men and women under Social Security, analyzing a variety of proposals affecting widowers and divorced husbands, illegitimate children, spouses of disabled workers and other special categories as well as general problems of inequality; required a report to Congress within six months of enactment.

● Established a nine-member National Study Commission on Social Security to study the financial condition of the retirement, disability and health insurance programs, as well as program coverage, benefit levels, inequities, coordination with related government programs and other issues; required a final report within two years.

● **Miscellaneous.** Eliminated an option for retroactive Social Security payments, effective January 1978.

● Required early mailing of Social Security checks if delivery falls on a weekend or legal holiday.

● Limited the employer share of Social Security taxes in cases of groups of related companies simultaneously employing the same individual to the amount owed by a single employer, effective January 1979.

● Broadened options for nonprofit organizations that paid Social Security taxes without taking formal action to cover employees under Social Security.

● Modified eligibility requirements for blind persons claiming disability insurance, setting the same limits on outside earnings applied to persons over age 65.

● Permitted, with certain safeguards and limits on cost, purchases of self-propelled "AMIGO wheelchairs" to be reimbursed by Medicare.

● **Welfare Provisions.** Provided state and local governments with an additional $187-million in fiscal 1978 to help them pay welfare costs; allocated half of these funds on the basis of states' relative expenditures for Aid to Families with Dependent Children (AFDC) and half according to the general revenue sharing formula.

● Established financial incentives for states to reduce welfare payment error rates, allowing states to retain 10 per cent of any federal savings if their error rates fell to between 3.5 per cent and 4 per cent, and 50 per cent of such savings if the rate fell below 2 per cent; required the error rate computations to count underpayments and unjust denials of public assistance as well as overpayments.

● Gave states access to wage record information maintained by the Social Security Administration and employment security agencies for potential or actual AFDC recipients.

● Authorized states to use AFDC program funds to experiment with special work projects for welfare recipients; permitted each state up to three such projects, which could last for up to two years; allowed states to implement one of their projects on a statewide basis; required the projects to pay participants prevailing wages, up to the total amount of their welfare benefits; gave HEW 30 days to disapprove state project proposals, with 30 days for public comment.

New Financing Proposals

Warning that scheduled increases in payroll taxes to finance the Social Security system were a "series of time bombs" that would intensify taxpayer discontent as they took effect, a group of lawmakers early in 1978 proposed a new approach to paying for part of the existing system with general revenues.

The group introduced a bill (HR 10754) that would separate disability insurance and hospital insurance (Medicare) from the present system of payroll tax financing. Those programs would be supported with general federal revenues. That would reduce the payroll tax by about one-third, leaving that levy to pay only for the old age and survivors components of the Social Security system.

The plan's sponsors were Sens. Gaylord Nelson, D-Wis., and John C. Danforth, R-Mo., and Reps. Abner J. Mikva, D-Ill., William M. Brodhead, D-Mich., Richard A. Gephardt, D-Mo., Timothy E. Wirth, D-Colo., and Jim Guy Tucker, D-Ark.

Idea Not New

The idea of using general funds to pay part of the cost of Social Security is not new. Rep. James A. Burke, D-Mass., chairman of the House Ways and Means Social Security Subcommittee, introduced four bills (HR 10668, 10719, 10720, 10794) to accomplish that. They would provide, basically, that one-third of Social Security costs be paid by federal general revenues, leaving the remaining two-thirds for equal contributions by employers and employees.

The idea of general fund financing has been resisted in the past, however, on the grounds that it would remove an important cost control. Once general funds are made available for Social Security financing, some lawmakers argue, it would become very difficult for Congress to resist proposals to increase benefits and thus drive costs up.

Cost Controls

Nelson said the new proposal would meet the cost control concern, since it would open to the general fund only those portions of the Social Security program that were already the focus of cost-control efforts. Basic retirement benefits, which are the portions of Social Security "most susceptible to political avarice," would remain in a separate fund financed through the payroll tax, he said.

Nelson estimated that disability insurance would require $15.3 billion in revenues in fiscal 1979, and that health insurance would cost another $22 billion.

Tax Impact

Mikva noted that the payroll tax, since it is levied at a flat rate on only the lower and middle ranges of income, is much less progressive than the income tax, which would pay a major share of the general fund financing proposed by the lawmakers.

He concluded that reducing the payroll tax as proposed in the new Social Security bill would be a more progressive tax cut than the reductions recommended by Carter.

"Which tax do you want to cut — the income tax, which is progressive or the Social Security tax, which is regressive?" he asked.

The progressiveness issue was addressed in other proposals for general funding of the Social Security system. A bill introduced by Burke would reduce the payroll tax rate while increasing the earnings base on which it is levied.

Economic Impact

Wirth argued that the payroll tax would be more effective in stimulating the economy than Carter's tax proposal, and he said it would shave one percentage point off the inflation rate by directly lowering the cost of goods and services. That would be a reduction in inflation twice what the Carter administration set as its 1979 goal.

Finally, Gephardt argued that the proposal would put the Social Security system on more sound actuarial footing by removing from the system the two programs for which benefits bear little relationship to contributions.

Probably the biggest obstacle to changing the system in 1978 was the fact that Congress completed a complicated and controversial revision in the system in 1977.

Social Security Tax Increases Compared

The table below shows the Social Security tax increases that different categories of workers were to pay in the next decade under the final version of HR 9346, compared with the amounts already scheduled under existing law. Under existing law and HR 9346, both the employee and employer paid equal amounts.

Table Explanation. Column (a) shows the amount of tax in dollars that employees and employers in different income categories would pay in 1977. For the later years, column 1 shows the amount of tax that would be paid under existing law and the final version of HR 9346. Column 2 shows the percentage increase that new tax liability was over 1977 tax liability. It should be noted that some of this increase would have occurred even if a new bill had not been passed, because of tax hikes provided in existing law.

Income		(a)	1979 (1)	1979 (2)	1982 (1)	1982 (2)	1985 (1)	1985 (2)	1987 (1)	1987 (2)
$10,000	Existing Law	$585	$ 605	3%	$ 630	8%	$ 630	8%	$ 645	10%
	Final Bill	585	613	5	670	15	705	21	715	22
$15,000	Existing Law	878	908	3	945	8	945	8	968	10
	Final Bill	878	920	5	1,005	14	1,058	21	1,073	22
$20,000	Existing Law	965	1,143	18	1,260	31	1,260	31	1,290	34
	Final Bill	965	1,226	27	1,340	39	1,410	46	1,430	48
$25,000	Existing Law	965	1,143	18	1,474	53	1,575	63	1,613	67
	Final Bill	965	1,404	45	1,675	74	1,763	83	1,788	85
$30,000	Existing Law	965	1,143	18	1,474	53	1,758	82	1,935	101
	Final Bill	965	1,404	45	2,010	108	2,115	119	2,145	122
$40,000	Existing Law	965	1,143	18	1,474	53	1,758	82	2,012	108
	Final Bill	965	1,404	45	2,131	121	2,686	178	2,860	196

Still, the idea of revising the system in an atmosphere not clouded by a sense of crisis had considerable support. House Ways and Means Committee Chairman Al Ullman, D-Ore., was one lawmaker very sympathetic to the idea. He has said that the committee should rethink the entire matter — but not until 1979. Treasury Secretary W. Michael Blumenthal also called for reconsideration of Social Security financing in testimony before the Joint Economic Committee Feb. 9, 1978.

Pressure to Cut Tax

Pressures to roll back the planned Social Security tax increases continued to mount on Capitol Hill in 1978, particularly in the House. In April, the House Budget Committee and the House Democratic Caucus went on record in support of a cutback in the projected increase. At the same time, Senate Finance Committee Chairman Russell B. Long, D-La., and President Carter both repeated their opposition to a change in the Social Security law.

Budget Committee Action

The Budget Committee, beginning markup of the first fiscal 1979 budget resolution, approved on April 4 a proposal by its chairman, Robert N. Giaimo, D-Conn., calling for a $7.5 billion reduction in payroll taxes in fiscal 1979.

It further proposed that general revenues in that amount be injected into the Social Security system to make up the loss.

Under the chairman's proposal, the Social Security tax rate could drop back to its 1977 level — 5.85 percent — while the wage base would return to what it would have been before Congress approved increases in 1977. That would mean a wage base of $18,900 in 1979.

That compared to a scheduled tax of 6.13 percent on wages up to $22,900 under the existing law.

Before acting on the chairman's recommendation, the committee rejected a more modest Republican proposal pushed by Conable. He suggested using $3.2 billion in general revenues to offset Social Security tax increases scheduled under the 1977 law. That proposal would allow increases planned under previous law to take effect.

Conable's proposal would have resulted in a tax rate in 1979 of 6.05 percent on wages up to $18,900.

Democratic Caucus

After trying unsuccessfully to put the party on record favoring a rollback March 15, House Democrats finally managed to get a quorum for a caucus April 5. The result was a 150-57 vote in favor of a resolution urging the Ways and Means Committee to propose the use of general revenues to forestall Social Security tax increases.

The caucus took that action despite the opposition of House Speaker O'Neill and Ways and Means Committee Chairman Ullman.

"You are making not only a mistake, but a very disastrous mistake," Ullman said. "You're building into the [Social Security] system the seeds of its destruction."

Ullman warned that allowing the use of general revenues to pay Social Security benefits would enable Congress to increase benefits and pay for them through federal deficit spending.

Noting that middle and upper income families will pay the bulk of the scheduled Social Security tax increases, he

also accused the caucus of playing "the worst kind of politics."

The middle class executive group and the commentators and columnists are the only ones who are giving you heat," he said in response to assertions that Congress is under considerable public pressure to roll back Social Security tax hikes.

"We're suggesting that a piece of the [1978 tax] cut be in the most regressive, inflationary tax there is," countered Ways and Means member Mikva, in arguing for a rollback.

Senate Hearings

In the meantime, the Social Security Subcommittee of the Senate Finance Committee received testimony April 5, 1978, from Treasury Secretary Blumenthal reiterating the administration's opposition to a rollback.

He was supported by Long, who urged the administration not to give in on the issue. If Carter were to approve "irresponsible" policies, Long warned, conservatives and moderates in Congress might protest by refusing to increase the federal debt limit.

Congressional Budget Office (CBO) Director Alice M. Rivlin also testified April 5. Assessing alternative tax programs, she said a proposal that general revenues pay one-third of all Social Security costs would be most progressive, followed by Carter's tax program. The proposal for general revenue financing of health and disability insurance would be least progressive, she said.

Under the one-third general revenue financing plan, 20.5 percent of all benefits would go to people earning less than $10,000, compared to 19.3 percent under Carter's program and 18.8 percent under the other approach.

People earning between $10,000 and $20,000 would receive 44.2 percent of the benefits under a one-third general revenue financing, 47.7 percent under Carter's program and 48.4 percent under the proposed general revenue financing of health and disability insurance.

People earning more than $20,000 would receive 31.1 percent of the benefits under a one-third general revenue financing plan; 33 percent under Carter's program; and 37 percent under the health-and-disability insurance general revenue financing scheme.

If the proposal to pay for health and disability insurance with general revenues were substituted for Carter's program, all families except those with earned incomes between $10,000 and $20,000 with two or more dependents would be better off. Single persons with earned income below $35,000 would be better off, according to Rivlin.

If the one-third general revenue financing idea were substituted for Carter's program, gainers would include: all two-earner families except those with earned incomes between $10,000 and $15,000 with two or more dependents; all one-earner families except those with incomes over $30,-000 and those with two dependents and earned incomes between $9,000 and $14,000; and single persons with earned incomes below $30,000.

Inflation Link

The groundswell of support for reducing Social Security taxes was encouraged by growing concerns about inflation. A surprising 1.1 percent increase in the February 1978 wholesale price index added to concerns that rising food prices, the deadline of the dollar and the four-month coal strike all could push the "underlying" rate of inflation above the expected 6 percent level.

Different Plans for Revising Social Security

While support for reducing payroll taxes grew in Congress, there was little indication which of the variety of proposals to accomplish that goal would win the most support.

Under the 1977 Social Security law, the Social Security tax rate would climb to 7.65 percent on wages up to an estimated $42,600 in 1990. The 1978 tax rate was 6.05 percent on wages up to $17,700.

Using General Revenues

One alternative, sponsored by Rep. James A. Burke, D-Mass., would divert general revenues to the Social Security system. His bill would provide that one-third of the system's costs be met with general revenues. Employers and employees would share equally the remainder of the costs.

It was estimated that Burke's bill would cost $30 billion in fiscal 1979. It would cut the payroll tax rate to 3.9 percent from 6.1 percent — resulting in a rate lower than the tax has been since 1965.

Burke would increase the wage base to which that tax rate applies from the scheduled $22,900 for 1979 to $100,000. The base would increase thereafter under an automatic formula linked to the growth in real wages. It is estimated that the formula would boost the wage base to $108,000 in 1980.

Separating Disability and Health Insurance

An alternative approach to general revenue financing that captured much attention in Congress in 1978 was to remove some components of the Social Security system from payroll tax financing.

While such approaches still open the system to general revenues, they are designed to overcome concerns that general revenue financing would reduce fiscal discipline in the program. Rather than injecting general revenues into the trust funds that pay Social Security benefits, the proposals provide that the funds continue to be financed solely by payroll taxes. That, theoretically, would prevent Congress from increasing retirement benefits without having to raise payroll taxes.

The proposal that has gained most attention was sponsored in the Senate (S 2503) by Gaylord Nelson, D-Wis., and in the House (HR 10754) by a group led by Abner J. Mikva, D-Ill.

The bill would provide for general revenue financing of disability and health insurance. It would reduce payroll tax revenues by about $34.3 billion in fiscal 1979, but its overall cost would be only about $28.4 billion since corporate taxes would rise because businesses would no longer be able to deduct health insurance and disability insurance as a business cost from their taxable income.

The Nelson-Mikva bills would reduce the payroll tax rate to 4.33 percent in 1979. It would keep the wage base provided under present law.

A similar bill (HR 11306) was introduced in the House by James A. Mattox, D-Texas. It would separate just health insurance from the Social Security system. That would reduce payroll taxes by $22.4 billion.

Under Mattox's bill, the payroll tax rate would be reduced to 5.05 percent 30 days after passage. In fiscal 1979 the rate would be 5.08 percent. It would apply to the wage base established by a 1972 formula — estimated to result in a base of $18,900 in 1979, $20,400 in 1980 and $21,900 in 1981.

Tax Credits, Other Proposals

A number of proposals have been made to use income tax credits to help offset the cost of rising payroll taxes. They have not gained as much support as other approaches, however.

The main argument for the tax credit approach is that it would provide relief to employees hurt by the rise in payroll taxes without undoing the 1977 law.

President Carter has argued that his recommended income tax cuts would offset the burden of rising Social Security taxes. Proponents of Social Security tax credits argue that their approach would be more effective, since it would direct relief specifically to people facing higher Social Security taxes, while Carter's tax cuts would provide relief also to people, such as federal employees, who are not hit by payroll tax hikes.

Sen. Thomas F. Eagleton, D-Mo., has proposed that taxpayers be allowed to claim an income tax credit equal to 15 percent of their annual contributions to the Social Security system. Under that proposal (S 2459), the federal government would provide $9.75 billion in annual tax relief.

A worker earning $10,000 a year in 1979 would receive a credit of $91 for his $613 payroll tax bill. That would be the same relief he would receive if his payroll tax rate were reduced to 5.23 percent.

Sen. Pete V. Domenici, R-N.M., introduced a similar Social Security tax bill (S 2741) that would allow taxpayers to claim a dollar-for-dollar income tax credit for all increases in the Social Security tax rate above 5.85 percent.

There have been suggestions to use new revenue sources for Social Security financing.

House Ways and Means Committee Chairman Al Ullman, D-Ore, has said that the burden for meeting rising Social Security taxes shouldn't be shifted to the income tax. "I am dedicated to a new revenue component in the Social Security system, but not out of general revenues," he said. "The income tax is already overloaded." Ullman suggested that a new "transaction tax," a form of sales tax, might bolster the Social Security system.

Also circulating in Congress was the idea of earmarking the revenues from President Carter's proposed crude oil equalization tax — $5.2 billion in the energy bill approved in 1977 by the House — for the Social Security system.

Ullman argued March 15, 1978, that it would be wrong to try to resolve the "complex" problem in an "emotional context." And ranking Republican on Ways and Means, Barber B. Conable Jr., N.Y., by the same token, warned Congress "not to panic . . . and do irreparable damage to the Social Security system in the process."

Concerns about inflation were voiced March 13 by Barry P. Bosworth, director of the Council on Wage and Price Stability. He proposed a number of actions the administration could take to hold down the inflation rate, including lending its support to a $6 billion reduction in Social Security taxes.

Cutting the payroll tax would reduce the cost to employers of producing goods, thus directly affecting prices, Bosworth argued. Federal Reserve Chairman G. William Miller agreed in testimony before the Senate Budget Committee March 15.

Some lawmakers argued that a payroll tax might even have a more beneficial impact on the unemployment rate, although the CBO concluded that the overall stimulative impact of the two types of cuts would be about the same.

The argument that a payroll tax cut would help reduce unemployment was based on the principle that, in addition to stimulating the economy by increasing buying power, the payroll tax reduction would make it less expensive for employers to hire workers.

House Ways and Means Action

After having approved, by a one-vote margin, a plan to roll back Social Security taxes, the House Ways and Means Committee reversed itself on May 17, rejecting the proposal by a vote of 16-21.

The proposal (HR 12736) would have cut the planned tax hikes and shifted $14.5 billion in general revenues to the system to make up the loss over a two-year period. It was tentatively approved by the committee May 11 on a 19-18 vote.

Two committee Democrats — including Chairman Ullman — and two Republicans switched from supporting to opposing the proposal, while one Republican reversed his previous opposition and voted in favor of the idea.

Besides Ullman, Ken Holland, D-S.C., Bill Frenzel, R-Minn., and L. A. "Skip" Bafalis, R-Fla., voted against the rollback after supporting it at the May 11 session. John J. Duncan, R-Tenn., who had voted against the proposal at the earlier meeting, supported it on the May 17 vote.

The dramatic reversal was seen by some committee Democrats who had favored the rollback as a direct rebuke to the House Democratic Caucus, which had voted to instruct the Ways and Means Committee to prepare a plan to use general revenues to forestall the scheduled Social Security tax increases.

House Speaker O'Neill told reporters even before the committee vote that the issue was dead for 1978. O'Neill said he doubted there would be further Democratic caucus action, and he reported that President Carter would veto a rollback proposal if it ever cleared Congress.

Later, Senate Majority Leader Robert C. Byrd, D-W.Va., said he would oppose a rollback proposal.

Ullman left the door open to further committee action on the issue in 1978, saying he would allow consideration of further compromise proposals.

The chairman, who had cast the deciding vote for the rollback on May 11, explained that he had to oppose it as a matter of "conscience" despite his responsibility to the caucus. He said he was unhappy with the precedent of using general revenues for Social Security.

"In any event, Social Security financing will be the first order of business in the next Congress," Ullman said. ∎

Unemployment: It's Not What It Used to Be

Unemployment just isn't what it used to be.

Once the most compelling economic statistic, the unemployment rate had taken a back seat to inflation in the minds of policymakers and the public by mid-1978.

While congressional supporters of the Humphrey-Hawkins full employment bill (S 50), named for its sponsors, the late Sen. Hubert H. Humphrey, D-Minn., and Rep. Augustus F. Hawkins, D-Calif., struggled to enact its national goal of a reduction of unemployment to 4 percent of the work force by 1983, a slow but fundamental change in the meaning of the unemployment rate for society seemed to be taking place.

Moreover, inflation had become the overriding issue in 1978. "The political climate has shifted, so we're swimming upstream," said one supporter of S 50.

Unemployment fell sharply in June 1978, to 5.7 percent from 6.1 percent in May. But in July, it climbed up to 6.2 percent, more than erasing its encouraging June drop.

Changing social habits and government policies, population shifts and human nature have combined, however, to make unemployment politically less important than it once was. Unemployment statistics may themselves undergo major changes as well. A national commission was looking at new definitions of employment and unemployment that could substantially alter national and local jobless rates.

Who Are the Unemployed?

The Labor Department estimated that in June 1978, 5,754,000 persons looked for work but could not find any. Together with the 94,819,000 persons who had worked at least an hour during the month, the total work force was 100,573,000.

The 5.8 million unemployed thus accounted for 5.7 percent of the work force — 1.4 percentage points below the level of June 1977. But because 3 million more people entered the work force during the year, the economy had to provide over 4 million more jobs in order to improve the unemployment rate by 1.4 percent.

The ratio of employment to the total non-institutional population over age 16, sometimes cited as an alternative to existing methods for measuring the employment situation, reached an all-time high of 58.9 percent — 1.5 percentage points higher than in June 1977.

Differing Rates

As examination of the June figures made clear, the unemployment rate, which was a national average, concealed vast differences among subgroups of the population.

The unemployment rate for blacks and other minorities was 11.9 percent in mid-1978, more than double the 4.9 percent level for all whites. Adult black males experienced a 7.8 percent unemployment rate; 11.3 percent of adult black women were out of work.

Women had a harder time finding work than men did. The adult female unemployment rate was 6.1 percent, compared with 3.9 percent for men.

Teenagers faced the worst unemployment problems of all. The unemployment rate for those aged 16-19 was 14.2 percent, as against a 4.8 percent rate for everyone 20 and over. The 14.2 percent rate did, however, represent a substantial improvement from the situation in May 1978, when 16.5 percent of youths were jobless.

Much of the teenage unemployment decline could be attributed to above-average success in providing temporary summer jobs. Almost all of the drop was concentrated among white teenagers, who went from 13.8 percent unemployment in May to 11.6 percent in June.

Comparing the extremes among population groups, the unemployment rate for minority teenagers, 37.1 percent, was more than 10 times as high as the 3.4 percent rate for adult white men.

Workers in low-paying and unskilled jobs generally had the worst unemployment problems. Managers (1.8 percent) and professionals (2.4 percent) experienced very low rates. But factory workers (7.9 percent) and non-farm laborers (9.9 percent) faced severe difficulties finding work. Construction workers were 9.3 percent unemployed.

Almost half (46.4 percent) of the unemployed were out of work for less than five weeks — in part representing the inevitable "frictional" unemployment caused when people look for new jobs in even the healthiest of economies. People who suffered through more than 15 weeks of joblessness made up 21 percent of all unemployed. The average period of unemployment was 12 weeks.

The largest single cause for being unemployed was from losing a previous job. Workers who had been laid off accounted for 10.5 percent of the unemployed, while 30.1

> *"The discomfort of being unemployed — that's clearly less than it was before."*
>
> —Assistant Secretary of Labor
> Arnold H. Packer

percent lost their jobs for other reasons. People who quit their last jobs were 14.7 percent of the unemployed. The rest of the jobless were coming back into the labor market after being out for a while (30.6 percent) and looking for a job for the first time (14.1 percent).

Hardship Measure

One factor in the decline in the central importance of the unemployment rate is that unemployment just doesn't hurt as much as it used to. Whatever the real human pain of being out of work, unemployment's broad impact on society has been lessened by changing social habits and government policies.

In the past, noted Sar A. Levitan, chairman of the National Commission on Employment and Unemployment Statistics, "unemployment was more or less equivalent to economic deprivation." Although some people could get help from relatives or charity, Levitan said, "basically people either worked or starved."

For one thing, most families depended on the support of one wage earner. "The man was the breadwinner," Levitan said, and if he was thrown out of work, the family's income was often immediately reduced to zero.

But by the mid-1970s, owing to a variety of changes in social norms, almost three-fifths of families benefit from the earnings of more than one worker. "There are many more families where both parents are working," observed Arnold H. Packer, assistant secretary of labor for research. Obviously a second income provides a buffer against economic catastrophe caused by loss of work.

Less Discomfort

Social programs enacted since the New Deal provided an even more important protection against the consequences of unemployment. "The discomfort of being unemployed — that's clearly less than it was before," said Packer.

Unemployment insurance offers help to the short-term jobless; welfare and other forms of public assistance aid the long-term unemployed. Together with food stamps, these programs provide much greater benefits than were avail-

---

Some economists think that the increasing numbers of women and young people in the labor force have brought about an unavoidable increase in the unemployment rate.

---

able even in the early 1960s. Social Security payments go to the aged and disabled, who otherwise might be forced to seek work.

These changes have had an important effect on the motivations and expectations of those looking for work. As the "cost" of being unemployed — the difference between the amount of public assistance available and the wages of a potential job — has gone down, so too has the incentive to find work as quickly as possible. Where in the past a breadwinner with a family to feed would likely jump at the first job that came along, now he or she has a chance to hold on for a while in the hope of finding the best paying or most satisfying employment.

Demographic Changes

Changes in the age and sex composition of the work force also can have a substantial effect on the unemployment rate and its validity as an overall indicator of economic well-being. Some economists think that the increasing numbers of women and young people in the labor force have brought about an unavoidable increase in the unemployment rate, regardless of particular economic conditions.

Women have greatly increased their participation in the world of work. Since 1950 the percentage of women

over age 16 who have looked or are looking for jobs has gone from 33.9 percent to 46.8 percent in 1976. The sharpest increases have been among young women. The percentage of women aged 20-24 who are in the labor force, for example, rose from 46.1 percent in 1950 to 65.0 percent in 1976, with the greatest part of the increase coming during the period 1965-70.

The explosive growth in the number of young people caused by the "baby boom" of the 1950s has also skewed the composition of the work force. The number of persons aged 16-19 who were part of the work force grew from 4.5 million in 1950 to 9.4 million in 1976 — a far greater proportionate increase than found in the total population.

These social and demographic changes have sharply reduced the former predominance of adult males in the work force. In 1950 males over age 24 accounted for 59.0 percent of the total civilian work force. But by 1975 their share of the labor market had fallen to 46.9 percent. Women went from 29.6 percent of the work force in 1950 to 40.0 percent in 1975, while young men increased from 11.5 percent to 13.1 percent during the same period.

Problem Groups

These changes are important because, in the real world, women and young people seem to have higher "natural" rates of unemployment. If these groups have inherently greater employment problems, their increasing participation in the work force makes achievement of a full employment goal set during a time when adult males dominated the work force all that much harder to achieve.

Although the birth rate has fallen to relatively low levels in recent years, young women still tend to have more unstable employment patterns because of their role in child bearing and rearing. The overwhelming majority of women not in the labor force cite their responsibilities in the home as the reason for not seeking work.

Women returning to the job market after time devoted to the family face difficult employment problems. Isabel V. Sawhill, director of the National Commission for Manpower Policy, said there "is clear evidence that in the case of women there are a large portion of new entrants in the pool of the unemployed." In 1976 40 percent of unemployed women over age 20 were re-entrants or new entrants into the labor force, compared with only 19.5 percent of unemployed men.

Being young and new to work, young people generally have more unstable job histories than their more settled elders. "Young people come in and out of the job market more frequently," said Packer. Many are in school, looking only for part-time or summer jobs. Others, taking advantage of the natural freedom and curiosity of youth, try out different jobs. "You would expect that teenagers would experiment with jobs," said Levitan. Young people also are often the targets of layoffs, since their skills are fewer and their job seniority minimal.

Impact of Changes

Economists are divided as to the exact impact of demographic changes on the unemployment rate. Levitan, while conceding that "we ought to expect in 1978 a higher unemployment rate than we had in the 1950s," downplayed the overall impact of the demographic shifts. But Michael L. Wachter, an economics professor at the University of Pennsylvania, has estimated that the changes in the composition of the work force have increased the "non-

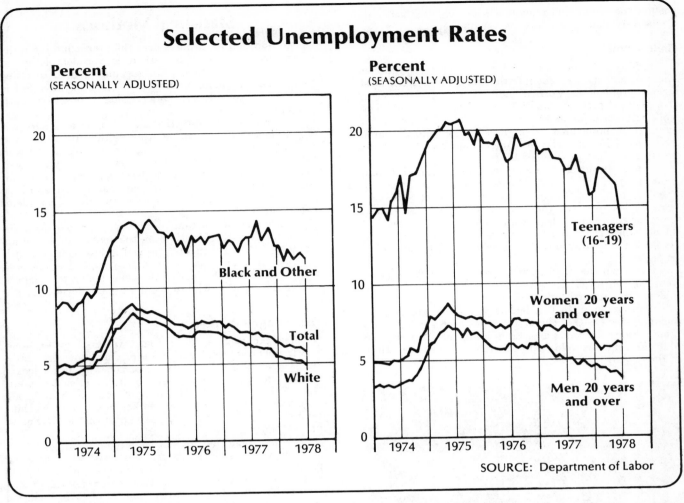

Selected Unemployment Rates

Percent
(SEASONALLY ADJUSTED)

Black and Other

Total

White

1974 1975 1976 1977 1978

Percent
(SEASONALLY ADJUSTED)

Teenagers
(16-19)

Women 20 years
and over

Men 20 years
and over

1974 1975 1976 1977 1978

SOURCE: Department of Labor

inflationary" full employment rate from 4 percent in 1957 to 5.5 percent in 1975.

One bright spot in the picture is the low birth rates experienced during the 1960s and 1970s. Once the baby boom children begin to work themselves into the mature labor force, policy makers will be faced with a much smaller group of young people starting to look for jobs every year. According to one projection, the percentage of young males in the work force could decline from 13.1 percent in 1975 to 9.4 percent in 1990.

Another argument is that, in addition to having inherently higher unemployment rates, women and youths frequently, but not always, have less urgent needs for jobs than adult males. Supporters of this idea point out that the impact on society of the joblessness of a married woman seeking to escape the boredom of home-making, or of a teenager looking for part-time work after school, is clearly not as great as that of a family breadwinner or single person.

But supporters of the Humphrey-Hawkins bill and other government jobs programs angrily reject the notion that the employment needs of women and youth are somehow less real than others. They point out that in addition to the 38 percent of women who work to support themselves, many of the working wives are married to low-income men, and seek to work out of dire economic need.

"I'm continually impressed with the number of women who have to work from necessity," said Rudy Oswald, research director of the AFL-CIO. John Carr of the Full Employment Action Council said that "the vast majority of these women are not trying to escape boredom," but to make their families' ends meet.

Full employment proponents also argue that jobs for young people yield other desirable social benefits besides just providing an income. By working, young people stay out of trouble and learn good work habits — the daily discipline of getting up and going to work that is essential for holding a steady job in later life. "The prospect of a generation of young people brought up in idleness, dependency and without skills or work habits ought to jar some of the commentators out of their complacency," said Murray H. Finley, president of the Amalgamated Clothing and Textile Workers Union.

Public Perception

The changing character of unemployment also has affected the public perception of the importance of the problem. As joblessness has become concentrated among smaller groups of the population, its central relevance to the lives of most people has declined. The escalating concern over inflation, which affects everybody, has tended to overshadow the problem of unemployment, which affects only a relatively small portion of the population.

Gallup Poll

In May 1978 the Gallup Poll found that three times as many Americans thought inflation was the nation's most serious problem as worried most about unemployment. Over half, 54 percent, cited inflation as the No. 1 problem, while 18 percent pointed to unemployment. The 18 percent naming unemployment represented a substantial drop from the 24 percent who gave unemployment as the most pressing problem in October 1977.

Concentration of unemployment among minorities and young people, and in certain communities, has helped to lower the profile of unemployment in the public consciousness. Packer observed that "if it's somebody else that is unemployed, then it's less of a problem." Oswald recalled the old adage that "you have a recession when your neighbor is unemployed; you have a depression when you are unemployed."

But when the unemployed person is a black teenager from the central city, the problem is less immediate to a middle-class suburbanite.

Another factor in the decline in public perception of unemployment is that the problem has been getting better than it was a few years ago. From a high of 9.2 percent in May 1975, the unemployment rate fell by more than a third in three years.

The unemployment rate for teenagers in June was almost three times as high as the rate for everyone aged 20 and over. The unemployment rate for minority teenagers was more than 10 times as high as the rate for adult white men.

Statistical Methods

In addition to disputes over the proper interpretation of unemployment statistics, there is considerable controversy over the validity of the techniques used to collect them. The National Commission on Unemployment Statistics has been considering major revisions in how to count the unemployed.

Unemployment statistics are collected as a survey of 55,000 households, taken monthly by the Bureau of Labor Statistics (BLS). Because of regular changes in the work force every year, the raw figures are seasonally adjusted. Persons who have worked at least an hour a week are counted as employed; those who are out of work and looking for a job are unemployed; everyone else is considered not in the work force.

Since they are a random survey, unemployment figures can differ significantly from the actual number of unemployed. Changes in the seasonal adjustments can produce an apparent change in unemployment where none really exists. But the biggest problems facing the commission lie in deciding who to count as unemployed.

Discouraged Workers

The exclusion of "discouraged workers," for example, is a frequent subject of criticism of unemployment statistics. Under BLS rules, a jobless person who hasn't looked for work recently is considered not in the labor force, and thus not unemployed, regardless of how much he or she may need a job. Discouraged workers are those who think their chances of finding a job are so poor that they've given up even trying.

Critics argue that, by not counting discouraged workers, the statistics leave out precisely those with the worst problems — thus artificially lowering the true unemployment rate. The BLS estimated that there were 842,000 discouraged workers in the second quarter of 1978. Inclusion of this group would raise the unemployment rate to about 6.7 percent in the second quarter.

Part-Time Workers

Then there are the part-time workers. BLS considers anyone who works at all to be employed. Similarly, anyone looking for part-time work is counted as unemployed.

But the situations and needs of part-time workers are different from full-timers. A worker with a 10-hours-a-week job could be near starvation, but still be counted as employed by the BLS. On the other hand, the presence of thousands of university students looking to earn a little extra pocket money through part-time work can artificially drive up the unemployment rates in some areas.

Military Personnel

Another group which the commission would have to decide whether to count is the military. Members of the armed forces have not been considered part of the labor force. But, since abolition of the draft, the armed forces now compete for workers, through pay and benefits, along with other sectors of society. Thus it is arguable that the 2.1 million military personnel should be counted as employed — a change that would lower unemployment rates, especially in areas with large military bases. ∎

CETA: A Success or Federal Subsidy?

In 1978, many members of Congress were worrying that a program originally intended to help the hard-core unemployed had become something very different — a new form of federal revenue sharing.

That issue lay at the heart of legislation that would reauthorize the 1973 Comprehensive Employment and Training Act (CETA). The Carter administration requested a four-year extension of the act, which otherwise would expire Sept. 30, 1978.

CETA programs provide on-the-job and classroom training to the unskilled, operate Job Corps and summer job programs for disadvantaged youths, and put the unemployed to work in public service jobs.

Under the public service employment system, state and local governments get federal money to hire the unemployed to perform new services to the community. First created as a small-scale effort directed towards the severely disadvantaged, it was expanded during the 1974-75 recession to fight unemployment on a broad basis.

The problem is that many cities and counties are not using the money to hire additional workers. Instead they are paying for old jobs previously funded by local taxes. Known as "substitution," this tactic improves local fiscal standing, but gives little help to the millions of unemployed.

Moreover, many governments apparently are becoming "hooked" on CETA money. Some cities have a quarter or more of their employees on the CETA payroll; the ratio is even higher for many county governments. This suggests that in practice CETA has become a disguised form of federal subsidy for local government operations.

Some studies of public service employment have estimated that CETA money pays for four old jobs for every new one created. At that rate the cost of true job creation rises to astronomical levels.

Supporters of the program have been encouraged by a Brookings Institution study which found the levels of substitution to be much lower than previously estimated. These results were based in part on the idea that communities with fiscal problems would have had to lay off workers in essential positions without CETA help. If CETA was paying for a job that would not otherwise have been available, the argument goes, then the effect was the same as the creation of a new job.

Critics also charge that CETA has failed to serve the right people with the right kind of help. Set up to assist persons whose employment future was hurt by educational deprivation and racial and sexual discrimination, its participants are mostly white, male and educated. Meant to help people in the long run get permanent, unsubsidized jobs, it places only a fraction of its participants in regular positions.

In addition, the program has been buffeted by repeated charges of misuse of funds. Since its workers are hired outside of normal government hiring procedures, CETA is a tempting plum for local politicians who want to expand their patronage powers. In some areas investigators have found that political associates and relatives of politicians have been hired for programs meant for the needy. In other areas CETA workers have been found to be doing work for political parties or officeholders.

Administration Proposals

President Carter Feb. 22, 1978, sent to Congress his proposal for an extension and revision of the CETA system. He emphasized that the plan was aimed at the "structural" employment of minorities and youth, and that its goal was to "make sure that more of our people share in the benefits of growth."

Stressing the need to help those "who have difficulty finding work even when overall economic prospects are good," the president noted that in 1977, "even while unemployment was falling to 4 percent among white males above the age of 20, it was rising — from 35 to 38 percent — among black teenagers."

The Carter administration reauthorization bill (S 2570, HR 11086) would extend CETA through Sept. 30, 1982. It would maintain public service employment at roughly 1978 levels (725,000 jobs) through fiscal 1979. After that the number of jobs would vary with the unemployment rate. Local areas with high unemployment would get 100,000 jobs regardless of the national unemployment rate. When the national rate exceeded 4.75 percent, another 100,000 jobs would be authorized, with the total rising by 100,000 for every .5 percent increase in unemployment.

To keep local government from substituting CETA workers for traditional positions, the bill would limit the time that workers could stay in public service jobs to 18 months. Salaries for participants would be held below $10,000 a year.

In response to criticisms that CETA has not served those for whom it was intended, the bill would limit eligibility to those whose income was below 70 percent of the Bureau of Labor Statistics lower living standard — a limit of about $7,000 for an urban family of four.

To increase the movement of workers from CETA programs to the private sector, the bill would establish a new program designed to increase linkage with business.

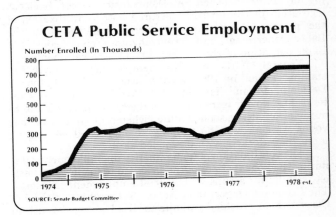

CETA Public Service Employment

Number Enrolled (In Thousands)

SOURCE: Senate Budget Committee

CETA at the Grass Roots

Howard County, Md., a growing county between Washington and Baltimore with urban, suburban and rural characteristics, offers an example of how CETA programs look when put into practice.

Part of a consortium of counties in and around Baltimore, Howard County has 120 public service employees working in government and community organizations. The county, with a population of about 120,000, received $848,000 in public service employment funds in fiscal 1978.

A large majority of public service participants are enrolled in Title VI programs. Positions range from laborers to para-administrators. Public service employees work for the county government, for example, as correctional guards, clerical workers, recreation aides, road-crew laborers and community workers. The average wage among all public service employees in the county is $4.16 an hour.

Among the community groups with CETA workers are a retarded citizens organization, the Community Action Agency, the YMCA, the Lung Association, and local colleges. About two dozen young people enrolled in experimental youth employment and training programs work in private companies and receive educational and vocational counseling.

Howard County has so far escaped charges of substituting CETA workers for regular employees. But, according to county official David White, a tight budgetary rein is needed to make sure agencies don't surreptitiously try to substitute. "Even if you don't plan to do that [substitute], the tendency among some agencies is pretty strong," he said.

Local industry training councils would be set up to plan more on-the-job training and other strategies, particularly those aimed at unemployed youth.

The bill also would begin to lay the groundwork for the administration welfare reform plan. It would fund 50,000 jobs to demonstrate the feasibility of guaranteeing jobs to heads of households in place of welfare.

Background

CETA developed out of the vast array of job and training programs spawned by Democratic "Great Society" legislation in the 1960s. It featured both centralization of the programs, concentrating overall supervision in the Labor Department, and decentralization, giving control of implementation of the programs to local governments.

Federal efforts to fight unemployment through job training began in 1962 with passage of the Manpower Development and Training Act (MDTA). Originally intended to provide retraining to workers who lost their jobs to automation, it was soon modified when it became clear that young workers with no training at all needed help much more than workers with outmoded skills.

The continuation of high minority unemployment rates during the boom periods of the 1960s led to further emphasis on training for groups with special employment problems. The Economic Opportunity Act of 1964 established the Job Corps, which provided training to disadvantaged youth in

residential centers, and the Neighborhood Youth Corps, which helped high school dropouts and poor youths needing part-time or summer jobs to stay in school.

Another program sponsored by the Johnson administration, Job Opportunities in the Business Sector (JOBS), worked through the National Alliance of Businessmen to encourage employers to hire the disadvantaged. Funds were provided to help employers bear the additional training costs of hiring unskilled workers.

Studies of these and other employment programs showed that they had a substantial effect on participants' subsequent economic performance, though their effect on overall unemployment was limited. Participants in institutional and on-the-job programs increased their earnings on the average between $1,000 and $2,000 a year. The JOBS program was successful beyond initial expectations, with many employers forgoing available government assistance for hiring.

But the programs were difficult to administer, scattered as they were through various government offices. Agencies were forced to make separate contracts with thousands of training centers, making oversight difficult.

Nixon Approach

The Nixon administration preferred a different approach. In concert with his plans for revenue sharing, President Nixon proposed that manpower funds be given directly to local governments to run their own programs.

Until enactment of CETA in 1973, Nixon and Congress engaged in a running battle over another aspect of manpower policy, public service jobs. Since the mid-1960s congressional liberals had pushed for public service jobs to put the unemployed to work. In 1970 Nixon vetoed a manpower bill providing $2.5 billion for public service employment, saying "WPA-type jobs are not the answer." But in 1971 he did consent to the Emergency Employment Act, authorizing $2.25 billion for public service jobs.

Passage of CETA in 1973 was a compromise between Nixon, who wanted to turn administration of manpower programs over to localities, and the Democratic majority in Congress, which wanted public service jobs.

Title I of the act consolidated most of the various manpower programs into a single system of block grants to local governments. Funds were provided by formula to city, country or state "prime sponsors."

Public Service Jobs

Title II established a limited program of public service jobs. It addressed problems of "structural" unemployment by providing jobs for those with long-term employment difficulties. Only persons unemployed for more than a month were allowed to participate. Assistance was provided by formula to areas with unemployment of more than 6.5 percent.

As the recession deepened in the mid-1970s, congressional leaders saw in CETA a vehicle for fighting increasing unemployment. In 1974 Congress added a new Title VI to CETA, authorizing $2.5 billion for public service jobs, allocated on the basis of unemployment rates. But in contrast to the structural emphasis of Title II, Title VI was a "countercyclical" measure attacking unemployment caused by recession.

In 1976 Congress extended and expanded the Title VI public service employment program. In addition to increasing the numbers of positions available, the extension bill contained provisions designed to limit substitution and focus programs on the poor. It required that new positions

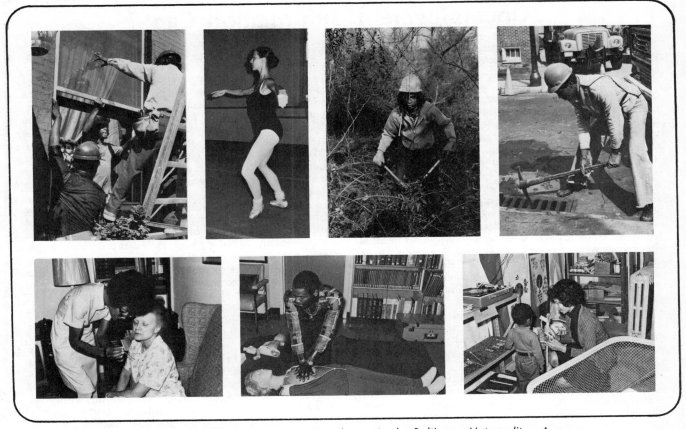

The Faces of CETA: Public Service Employees in the Baltimore Metropolitan Area

be used in community projects that could be finished within a year, and be limited to persons unemployed for more than 15 weeks who had low incomes.

In 1977 a new CETA Title VIII, designed to aid disadvantaged youth, was added. Title VIII established a Young Adult Conservation Corps and funded various experimental projects.

Also in 1977, Congress passed a simple one-year extension of CETA, authorizing the program through the end of fiscal 1978. The Carter administration requested a short-term extension in order to gain time to thoroughly study the program and propose substantive changes, as it did in 1978.

CETA in 1978

The backbone of the CETA system in 1978 were some 450 "prime sponsors" who administer employment and training programs in their areas. Cities and counties with populations over 100,000, or groups of smaller units, can qualify as prime sponsors. State governments handle the areas not covered by local prime sponsors.

Under Title I of CETA, prime sponsors in fiscal 1977 provided job training to 1,415,000 persons. Programs include classroom training, on-the-job experience, and some public service employment. Prime sponsors may contract with community groups to operate services. *(Box, p. 76)*

Public service employment under Titles II and VI reached early in 1978 the goal of 725,000 jobs set by the Carter economic stimulus plan; the total was 753,000 by the

first week of March. Jobs funded range from police and firefighting positions to park workers and arts instructors.

As originally conceived, Title II was to provide structural public service employment — for those with long-term employment problems, while Title VI was to concentrate on those out of work because of an economic downturn. But in practice the distinction between the two programs has been blurred. Shifting eligibility requirements and prime sponsor reluctance to divide up their employment programs into separate parts has made the distinction difficult to enforce.

"Prime sponsors have not heavily weighted the distinction," according to Jon Weintraub, associate director of the National Association of Counties. Statistics show that the two titles serve substantially similar target groups.

One distinction that is applied divides public service jobs into sustainment and project positions. The 1976 CETA expansion required that new Title VI funds go first to sustain the level of public service jobs already in operation. The remaining funds were to be used in projects, defined as related undertakings which could be completed within one year and would not otherwise have been started.

Impact on Cities

Whatever the type of jobs, public service funds have become a vital factor in county and municipal finance. In Buffalo, N.Y., for example, CETA workers accounted for 32.8 percent of the city government work force, while in Hartford, Conn., they made up 25.8 percent in 1978.

Unemployment: Information Gap

One problem with designing an employment and training program is that no one knows how much unemployment there really is.

Unemployment statistics are sensitive to subtle changes in techniques unrelated to real economic conditions. For example, a drop in the unemployment rate in the last months of 1977 was caused in part by a change in the way seasonal employment changes were computed in the unemployment rate formula. "A material shift in the national perception of whether unemployment is going up or down can be effected solely by a changing in methodology," said Sar A. Levitan, chairman of the National Commission on Unemployment Statistics, a study group established by Congress in 1976.

Even more difficult to determine accurately are local area statistics, which are vitally important because they decide where employment and training funds will go under CETA. In January 1978 the Bureau of Labor Statistics (BLS) began using new techniques to measure local unemployment, with a potentially sizable impact on the distribution of federal dollars.

Previous BLS procedures set local rates at a ratio, derived from the 1970 census, of larger area unemployment rates. In 11 large cities figures were computed on the basis of data from Current Population Surveys.

Under the new system local unemployment statistics will be based mainly on unemployment compensation claim data, with allowances for new entrants into the job market. The big cities argue that unemployment compensation data will significantly underrate their joblessness, since cities are more likely to have large numbers of workers outside the unemployment insurance system.

The growth of the unreported labor market in the cities illustrates the need of those computing labor data to take into account changes in social patterns. Most important, according to Eli Ginzberg, chairman of the National Commission for Manpower Policy, is the tremendous increase in the number of working women. "The BLS has been constantly underestimating the number of women who are seeking to enter the labor market — they don't recognize that there's a revolution going on."

Other changes in labor patterns complicate the situation for statisticians even more — "there's a lot of funny things going on out there in relation to employment," Ginzberg said. For example, young people are not always following the traditional pattern of entering the labor force soon after getting out of school. Men are leaving the work force earlier; Ginzberg estimated that one-quarter of men who are 55 years old have already stopped working or looking for work.

Finally, the growth of the unreported or illicit economy, especially in the cities, leaves the government ignorant of how many people are really supporting themselves. "There are very few people who don't work a little," Ginzberg said. One study of New York City estimated that a quarter of a million people supported themselves in "fringe," illicit ways. Another study estimated that the illegal and unreported sector represented 7 percent of the national economy, leaving large numbers of people outside the calculations of employment experts.

Those statistics are disturbing to regular government employees. Municipal workers feel threatened by CETA workers, according to Nanine Meiklejohn of the American Federation of State, County and Municipal Employees, because they are hired outside of normal procedures designed to protect permanent workers. Regular workers dislike the creation of special job titles for CETA workers, who are paid less than regular workers, and fear in general that the program will result in a "gradual replacement of workers and a lowering of labor standards," she said.

Substitution

In addition to providing jobs for those out of work, public service employment offers to local governments the possibility of a substantial reduction in labor costs. If the federal government is willing to pay CETA workers to do jobs that the local government would otherwise have had to pay for, then the city or county will be able to use the savings to provide other services or cut taxes.

The CETA funds can either create new jobs, or pay for old ones. But the line between created and substituted jobs is very difficult to draw. The existence of fiscal problems in many local governments blurs the distinction. For governments that for budgetary reasons have had to lay off permanent, essential workers such as police and firefighters may be reluctant to use CETA funds to pay for dance instructors.

One type of job creation, then, occurs when a local government uses CETA funds to fill a position that would have been vacant because of lack of local money. These jobs are considered created jobs because they would not have been available without CETA. Other types of job creation occur when a government begins new programs, or expands old ones, or undertakes a special project that can be completed within a year.

An obvious case of substitution occurs when a government lays off employees and then rehires them, after the minimum period of unemployment, back to their old jobs with CETA funds. Solvent governments that allow the permanent work force to decline through attrition, while hiring CETA workers to fill vacancies, are also substituting. Another type of substitution occurs when governments use CETA workers to perform tasks traditionally contracted out.

Although CETA prohibits substitution, most observers agree that some substitution is taking place. But estimates of its exact extent vary tremendously.

The first studies of substitution showed very high rates, particularly in the Public Employment Program of 1971. Estimates of substitution ranged from 39 to 90 percent. A 1977 Congressional Budget Office study found that substitution reached 100 percent after two years.

Another study, however, argued that these estimates are questionable because of the inherent limitations of the "econometric" methodology on which they are based. An analysis of past substitution studies, written by Michael Borus and Daniel Hamermesh for the National Commission for Manpower Policy, found that estimates of the same situation could be vastly different depending on the statistical assumptions on which they were based. "We can't be sure of what really is going on," observed one congressional analyst.

Brookings Study

Another study for the Manpower Commission, conducted by the Brookings Institution, used an entirely different method and came to strikingly different results. Instead of working from a mathematical model, Brookings researchers contacted a network of academics in selected areas around the country. These analysts examined public service programs in their own areas. They interviewed officials, looked at data on employment and the fiscal state of the area governments, and made independent estimates on the extent of substitution.

The Brookings study found that substitution accounted for 20 percent of all public service positions. Sustainment positions were found to be 21 percent substituted, while the newer project approach had a rate of 8 percent. Contrary to past assumptions, the study found that substitution positions did not go only to experienced workers; minority and disadvantaged participation rates were about the same as in other public service jobs.

One reason that the substitution rate was low was that the researchers found a high level (31 percent) of program maintenance, in which CETA funds were used to continue positions that otherwise would have been discontinued for fiscal reasons. Thus the low rate of substitution rested in part on the individual perceptions of researchers that the prime sponsors were in difficult financial situations. Taken together the results show that jobs formerly paid for by local government accounted for about half of all public service jobs.

'Red Herring'?

Whatever its exact extent, substitution raises serious questions as to the efficacy of public service employment. Sen. Gaylord Nelson, D-Wis., chairman of the Human Resources Employment Subcommittee, said that substitution even at the lowest estimates still involves "a very substantial amount in dollar terms." Sen. John H. Chafee, R-R.I., raised the common complaint that "CETA has become in effect a revenue sharing for the communities — even in the school systems CETA is carrying a tremendous load."

Critics of the program argue that the existence of substantial substitution raises the cost of new job creation to unacceptable levels. For example, at an 80 percent substitution rate the government would have to pay for five jobs in order to create one new one. Rep. Bill Frenzel, R-Minn., ruefully observed that this would mean that each new job would cost more than the salaries of members of Congress.

But others contend that substitution is infrequent and probably not so bad after all. Greg Wurzburg, executive director of the National Council on Employment Policy, called substitution "a red herring — a non-issue," peripheral to the real problems of municipal finance. Weintraub questioned "whether substitution is that dirty a word," because the eligibility requirement for CETA workers has had "very positive effects on affirmative action needs" of local governments. Substitution also can have local stimulative effects if CETA funds permit governments to cut taxes.

Outlays for CETA Programs

(by fiscal year, in millions)

	1974	1975	1976	1977	1978* (estimated)
Title I (training programs)	$1,136.6	$1,648.8	$1,697.5	$1,756.2	$1,891.4
Title II (public service employment)	—	519.2	544.1	496.0	970.4
Title III (special programs including summer employment)	495.1	262.2	724.4	837.1	1,572.1
Title IV (Job Corps)	164.1	170.4	180.6	201.6	274.0
Title VI (public service employment)	—	319.2	1,872.3	2,340.4	4,765.0

* Includes a requested supplemental appropriation for increased minimum wage costs.

SOURCE: Labor Department, Employment and Training Administration

Ernest Green, head of the Labor Department's Employment and Training Administration, testified Feb. 23, 1978, that the administration had already stepped up its monitoring of substitution violations, leading to the recovery of $1.4 million from prime sponsor violators. To supplement this the administration bill provides for limits on salaries and lengths of time worked. Public service employee salaries would be held below $10,000, with the recommended average wage set at $7,800. Prime sponsors would be prohibited from supplementing salaries by more than 10 percent of all public service funds received. Participants could stay in the program only up to 18 months.

Green argued that the effect of the limits would be to make "[CETA] jobs inappropriate for permanent substitution." But critics predicted that the measures would hurt participants without checking the practice. A spokesman for the Conference of Mayors said that the proposals were "totally inappropriate. The net effect impacts on workers — they're the ones that pay the price." A $10,000 limit could pose problems in some high-priced cities, where even entry-level workers often get more.

Targeting

A frequent criticism of CETA programs is that they fail to target on those who need assistance most — the economically disadvantaged and long-term unemployed. "We're not coping with the hard core," observed Sen. Thomas F. Eagleton, D-Mo. Instead of being made up mostly of the disadvantaged, argued Rep. Barber B. Conable Jr., R-N.Y., "the characteristics of CETA workers show that they are the most skilled of the unemployed."

The figures on CETA participation tend to back up Conable. Workers in public service programs are largely white, male and high school graduates. Only 15 percent come from welfare families. Critics contend that the figures show a persistent tendency by prime sponsors to "cream" the labor market — skim off the most skilled of the unemployed.

The struggle over the means for distributing CETA funds arises from the huge difference between the scope of the programs and the number of people conceivably eligible.

Role of Community Groups

Local governments are not the only entities that carry out CETA programs. Community-based organizations (CBOs) also play an important role in delivering employment and training services to the un-employed.

Prime sponsors can contract with CBOs to run job training centers. Or they can provide public service employees directly to the organizations to help run beneficial services for the community such as storefront health clinics.

There are two types of CBOs. Four national organizations — Opportunities Industrialization Centers (OIC), the National Urban League, SER-Jobs for Progress and Mainstream — are specifically named in CETA legislation. Then there are hundreds of locally based neighborhood groups, many of which sprang up in response to CETA.

CBOs have the advantage of having closer ties with poor and minority client groups than local governments. Dick Johnson of the Department of Labor said that "CBOs do a better job of getting down to the people." They also offer increased possibilities for tran-sition for their public service employees, since they typically have higher turnover of regular staff than local governments. But many prime sponsors resent what they feel is pressure from Washington to use CBOs regardless of local conditions.

The national CBOs enjoy solid support on Capitol Hill. Johnson, a former Senate committee aide, said that "there's a great deal of feeling in Congress that the CBOs have been very effective in providing services."

Under Department of Labor regulations, CBOs are supposed to receive 35 percent of job slots under the economic stimulus program of Title VI. But the most recent evidence indicates that CBOs have been getting about a quarter of the jobs, according to an Employment and Training Administration official.

Eli Ginzberg, chairman of the National Commission for Manpower Policy, estimated that as many as 22 million people could be eligible for CETA assistance — a "colossal discrepancy" with the number that could be served. "We're holding this program out to 22 million people," observed Sen. Donald W. Riegle Jr., D-Mich., "but we can only reach a minor fraction of those in need."

CETA assistance can basically be distributed in three ways — to individuals who meet income and unemployment standards, to areas on the basis of unemployment and economic hardship rates, or to special groups that Congress is especially interested in helping.

Focus on Individuals

Current individual eligibility standards are confusing and contradictory, making program coordination by prime sponsors difficult. Applicants for Title II jobs, which were originally intended for the economically disadvantaged, have no income limit — they have only to have been un-employed for 30 days. But the largest part of Title VI, meant to help those laid off by temporary changes in the economy, is now limited to persons unemployed for more than 15 weeks, with a family income below 70 percent of the lower living standard — the poor. Other programs have different criteria. This proliferation of eligibility standards, argue prime sponsors, creates administrative headaches and makes it difficult to transfer participants to appropriate programs.

The administration bill would limit participation to the economically disadvantaged — defined as those below 70 percent of the lower living standard — who had been un-employed for five or more weeks.

Prime sponsors argue that the emphasis on tightened eligibility standards reflects a suspicion that, given the chance, prime sponsors will ignore the needs of the poor — a charge they feel is not borne out by the facts. Too tight stan-dards will also exacerbate social tensions and "stigmatize" CETA workers, Wurzburg said. Opening CETA jobs only to the poorest would amount to creating "a separate kind of job for a separate kind of people," he said, further causing "too much isolation from the mainstream of the labor market."

Focus on Areas

Another way to distribute funds is to areas on the basis of local unemployment or poverty rates. Under existing law, Title I training funds are distributed to prime sponsors ac-cording to the following formula: 50 percent on the basis of the previous year's allotment, 37.5 percent on un-employment rates, and 12.5 percent on the number of poor families. Title II funds are allotted only to areas that had unemployment rates of 6.5 percent for more than three months. Half of the Title VI funds available to prime spon-sors are allotted on the basis of unemployment rates in all areas; one quarter is reserved for areas with more than 6.5 percent unemployment; the remainder is distributed on the basis of the number of unemployed in areas with over 4.5 percent unemployment.

The administration bill did not propose to change the allocation formulas. Administration representatives said that the uncertain nature of the recent changes in methods for determining local area unemployment rates made alteration of formulas problematic. But they left open the possibility of new formulas once the impact of the methodological changes could be evaluated.

Representatives of areas hard hit by unemployment argue that changes in allocation formulas are needed to give extra help to the areas that face the greatest problems. Sen. Jacob K. Javits, R-N.Y., who had introduced legislation to change the formulas, said that changes were essential to help older cities facing chronic unemployment caused by an exodus of jobs to the "sunbelt" regions. His legislation would give greater weight in the formulas to the relative severity of unemployment and poverty, diverting more funds to areas with the worst structural employment problems. Supporters of giving more weight to poverty in allocating training funds say that the change would con-centrate assistance in areas with long-term problems, rather than on areas with cyclical unemployment, where workers might not need more training.

Focus on Groups

Finally, special consideration can be given to selected groups within the eligible population. In 1978, Labor Department regulations required prime sponsors to give special consideration to veterans, welfare recipients, former manpower trainees and teachers.

But many prime sponsors dislike the imposition of special consideration. One city representative pointed out that there were hundreds of different population sub-groups that could be selected, in disregard to local conditions. "Prime sponsors don't want to be dictated to," he said. Joan Wills, director of employment programs for the National Governors' Conference, disputed the idea that special quotas help the groups that seek them. "They're such a sham for the people who need the services the most," she said, since "there's just not enough to go around" for every group that could push for special consideration.

Transition

Critics of CETA worry that the employment and training programs are failing to meet the stated ultimate goal — preparing people to take unsubsidized, permanent jobs. If participants fail to make the transition to regular jobs, it is questionable how much benefit they have obtained from a temporary, stopgap solution to their long-term problems.

Green conceded that "the current CETA program is not yet successful enough in moving workers from unsubsidized employment to the private sector." Labor Department statistics show that 39 percent of participants in Title I training programs transfer to unsubsidized jobs; 17.7 percent of Title II and 34.0 percent of Title VI public service employees make the transition. Labor Department regulations set a goal, but not a requirement, of 50 percent annual transition.

Problems

One problem with achieving high rates of transition is that it sometimes works in opposition to other desirable goals of the program. One Brookings analyst said that "it appears to me that attempts to maximize the transition rates are frequently in conflict with other goals of the program, such as minimizing displacement and reaching social targeting objectives." An urban spokesman observed that "the more placement standards you have the more creaming you get," since prime sponsors trying to meet high transition goals were likely to "recruit the folks that are more apt to find jobs."

Other reasons for the low transition rates were general economic conditions and the way the program was operated. CETA was just getting off the ground when the 1974-75 recession struck. Employers who were forced to lay off old employees were not likely to go to prime sponsors seeking new people to hire. "Anytime you have an employers' market," asked Wills, "why shouldn't the employer take the better qualified?" Furthermore, critics contend, public service jobs provide very little training to make participants more employable.

Prime sponsors and others say that many of the transition problems stem from the confusing and irritating bureaucratic aspects of the program. Private employers participating in programs must fulfill substantial record-keeping requirements — "there are too many administrative headaches and too much red tape" for the private sector to want to get involved, Wurzburg said.

Public Sector Jobs

Prime sponsors have been most successful in transferring CETA participants to permanent jobs in the public sector. This makes some people worry that training and public service programs will end up preparing workers only for the limited public sector. Chafee said that "the problem I have is that these CETA jobs are the ones that have a very

Oversight vs. Local Control

Running throughout the CETA debate is the tension between the need to give prime sponsors enough independence to run programs suited to local conditions, and the fear that they will abuse the privilege. Prime sponsor independence was a fundamental precept of the original CETA legislation. But repeated charges of corruption and misuse of funds in local programs have jeopardized that independence.

A frequent criticism has been that public service jobs are awarded on the basis of political influence or nepotism. In Chicago, jobs were reportedly handed out on the basis of recommendations from political officials. In the District of Columbia, city council members were using CETA funds to hire friends and political associates, according to newspaper reports. In Buffalo, N.Y., participants were allegedly required to do work for the local Democratic Party.

The Employment and Training Administration (ETA) in 1978 stepped up efforts to halt violations. Labor Secretary F. Ray Marshall established a special task force to track down allegations of misuse. Chicago was ordered to return nearly $1 million in CETA funds because of political favoritism and substitution. In February 1978, the ETA for the first time revoked a prime sponsorship, in East St. Louis, Ill., for violations.

Administrative Problems

Prime sponsors contend that the real problem with ETA oversight is a rigid application of national rules to local conditions. "ETA continues to apply broad-brush solutions to individual problems," said one county official. "Rather than dealing with an individual problem, they write a national regulation that decreases the flexibility of program implementation."

Hundreds of decentralized programs are more difficult to monitor than a single program run directly from Washington. The ETA has been hard-pressed to keep up with the expanding number of programs.

Prime sponsors complain that they are deluged with hundreds of ETA directives every year. "You could fill a room with the regional directives," remembered one former local program director. They also say that weekly reporting requirements impose burdensome paperwork.

The administration has cited reduction of paperwork as a major goal of its new bill. The measure would consolidate administrative functions in one title, reducing duplicative reporting requirements. Non-essential data would be cut back.

limited private sector outside requirement." He cited the example of a fireman hired under CETA — "after 18 months, that person's marketability is very limited" in the private sector.

1978 Legislative Action

House and Senate subcommittees April 26, 1978, approved bills extending the CETA programs for four years, through fiscal 1982. The bills were revised versions of the legislation requested by the administration. On May 10, the full House Education and Labor Committee approved a bill (HR 12452) aimed at quieting criticism of the program. In extending the job program for four years, the committee added a number of provisions designed to stop what critics have called a widespread pattern of corruption and misuse of funds. The Senate Human Resources Committee reported a companion CETA extension bill (S 2570 — S Rept 95-891) May 15.

Meanwhile, the Labor Department stepped up its efforts to use its existing authority to uncover fraud in CETA programs. Labor Secretary Marshall April 13, 1978, announced creation of a permanent special investigations office, charged with correcting abuses in CETA and other department programs. The office, which had been in existence on a temporary basis, began looking into problems in 11 local jobs programs.

House Floor Action

After losing a series of key votes on the House floor Aug. 9, sponsors of the CETA legislation postponed further action on the bill until September. Debate on the CETA authorization extension revealed such strongly critical sentiment among House members that leaders decided to hold off on final action, lest the legislation be crippled or totally defeated.

House Speaker Thomas P. O'Neill Jr., D-Mass., was apparently determined to complete action on the bill Aug. 9, keeping members in session until 10 p.m. But the House just scratched the surface of the many expected amendments, without considering the crucial public service employment titles.

The late-night session drew a heated reaction from Ronald V. Dellums, D-Calif., who charged that House members were "making a mockery of the legislative process." "We are tearing this legislation apart," he said, "...but many of us do not understand what is going on."

Two crucial amendments adopted by the House Aug. 9 lowered the ceiling on wages that could be paid to CETA workers and slashed authorized funding for public service employment.

The cutbacks came despite the strenuous efforts of a CETA task force of House members and intensive lobbying by unions and local government officials, many of whom are heavily dependent on the program. Lobbyists warned that the cutbacks would render the program virtually unworkable, particularly in the expensive urban areas that face the most severe unemployment problems.

The atmosphere surrounding the bill was so negative that even members who had supported CETA in the past argued that some reductions were necessary to satisfy popular complaints, and to avoid even more stringent congressional restrictions in the future.

Continuing publicity over fraud and abuse in CETA put heavy pressure on members to support some cuts. Robert J. Cornell, D-Wis., observed in an interview that many members felt that "the way to show you're against abuse is to be against the program."

Even more threatening to CETA was criticism direct-ed to more basic questions of how many public service workers to have, and how much to pay them.

An amendment offered by David R. Obey, D-Wis., to impose more stringent limits on wages paid to CETA workers was adopted by a vote of 230-175.

Cosponsored by Budget Committee Chairman Robert N. Giaimo, D-Conn., Ronald A. Sarasin, R-Conn., and others, the Obey amendment limited CETA wages paid by the federal government to $10,000 a year per employee. The committee-approved bill had set the same maximum for most areas, but had allowed wages of up to $12,000 to be paid from CETA funds in high-wage regions.

For the high-wage areas, the Obey amendment did allow local governments to supplement the CETA wages with their own funds, up to a total of an additional 20 percent of wages, or $2,000. The committee bill allowed local governments to add 25 percent of their own money to the federal amount.

In effect, the Obey amendment set a $12,000 limit for high-wage areas and a $10,000 limit for the rest of the country, compared with the $15,000 and $12,500 limits backed by the committee.

The Obey amendment also cut, to $7,000 from $7,800, the required average annual wage of all CETA workers. It allowed the average to be indexed according to the consumer price index.

The other key change made by the House Aug. 9 was an amendment that reduced funding for public service jobs. The amendment, offered by James M. Jeffords, R-Vt., was approved 221-181.

The Jeffords amendment cut about $1 billion from Title VI jobs programs by placing a $3.2 billion cap on the authorization. If unemployment exceeded 6.5 percent, however, the amendment removed the cap.

In place of the $1 billion public service cut, the Jeffords amendment substituted $500 million in extra funding for youth employment and private sector programs: $350 million for Title IV youth programs, $50 million for the Title VIII Young Adult Conservation Corps and $100 million for the administration's new Title VII private sector program. Jeffords said the amendment would still allow for about the same number of jobs, since "you get almost twice as many total jobs in the youth area for the same number of dollars."

The complex issue of the use of CETA funds for payments to local government pension funds gave members a chance to vote against supplementing local budgets with money intended for job creation. After a complicated series of amendments, the House adopted an amendment by John N. Erlenborn, R-Ill., to ban use of CETA money for payments to retirement plans after 1979. The amendment was adopted 254-148.

The closest vote of the evening came on an amendment by Andrew Maguire, D-N.J., to tighten the rules for use of CETA funds to pay outside consultants for legal or "associated" services. The amendment, adopted 200-198, allowed such payments if the work could not have been done by local government employees or the Department of Labor, and the consultant charged a reasonable fee. ∎

Carter Targets Airlines for Deregulation

Loosening economic control over the airlines was a top legislative priority for the Carter administration. Shortly after taking office, Carter chose the industry as the first target in the drive for regulatory reform he promised during the 1976 campaign.

But the issue was not greeted with enthusiasm on Capitol Hill in 1977, and Carter's prodding was not enough to dispel reservations held by several of the Senate Commerce, Science and Transportation Committee members. The legislation finally approved by the committee Oct. 27, 1977, was an amended fourth draft of an unnumbered bill that was heavily rewritten during 18 markup sessions stretched over four months. The bill would give airlines some freedom to raise and lower fares and to enter new routes without seeking approval from the Civil Aeronautics Board (CAB). Under existing law, the CAB had to approve all rates and routes. Supporters of the measure contended that relaxed regulations would lead to greater competition and reduced prices.

The Senate committee reported its version of the bill Feb. 6, 1978. But the legislation then ran into obstacles in the House. Aviation Subcommittee Chairman Glenn M. Anderson, D-Calif., linked passage of the deregulation measure — for which he had expressed only lukewarm support — to passage of a bill to provide federal subsidies to help the industry meet federal noise limits imposed by the Federal Aviation Administration (FAA). Anderson strongly supported the noise subsidy measure.

After spending six days marking up the airline deregulation legislation, the House Aviation Subcommittee at the last minute rejected the legislation and opted instead for a substitute bill lacking almost all deregulation provisions. The subcommittee was then hurriedly recessed before a vote could be taken to send the substitute bill to the full Public Works Committee.

Seven weeks of bargaining among the panel members followed. The version finally approved May 9 reinstated several deregulation provisions the substitute bill lacked, but it still was substantially weaker than the bill the subcommittee had originally considered. In the interim, the Senate on April 19 had passed its stronger version of the bill, which had the support of the White House.

Background

Despite the strong support deregulation received from the White House, getting a bill through Congress proved an arduous task.

The Senate Commerce Committee held 14 days of hearings in March and April 1977 on two proposed reform bills (S 689, S 292), but the House Public Works and Transportation Aviation Subcommittee gave only sporadic attention to deregulation, concentrating instead on a bill (HR 8729) to reduce aircraft noise. In June, Senate committee staffers unveiled a compromise deregulation bill they had drafted with the help of key committee members.

After a painful markup spanning 20 sessions, the committee reported S 2493 on Feb. 6, 1978.

Though its critics — primarily representatives of the airline industry and airline labor unions — said the bill would result in service cuts and job losses, United, Southwest, Hughes Airwest, Frontier and other smaller and regional airlines supported a deregulation measure.

At the same time, advocates of a stronger bill, including administration spokesmen, were disappointed at the number of compromises needed to win enough votes to get a bill out of committee. But they generally agreed they could support the measure as reported.

The aircraft noise bill ran into difficulty in the House Aviation Subcommittee. Though the airline industry warmly welcomed financial aid to muffle or replace noisy engines, airport operators fought provisions requiring land use planning by operators around their airports. A compromise, worked out in August 1977, encouraged rather than required land use planning.

Senate Committee Report

S 2493 was approved by a vote of 11-2 Oct. 27, 1977, and reported Feb. 6 by the Senate Commerce Committee (S Rept 95-631). Three absentees who later cast their votes made the final tally 13-3.

S 2493 attempted, according to the committee majority, "to provide the domestic air transportation industry with the same competitive incentives which face most other American industries."

In 1898, the report noted, President McKinley awarded a $50,000 federal grant to Samuel P. Langley to achieve the first manned flight by a craft that was heavier than air. Langley earlier had achieved the first unmanned flight. Instead of Langley, however, the first manned flight was made by the Wright brothers, "two unsubsidized mechanical tinkerers," in 1903.

"The lesson of Kitty Hawk" the report concluded, "is that air transportation will be more likely to expand and prosper if the heavy hand of CAB economic regulation is removed from the creative hand of carrier management."

To make the airline industry more competitive, the committee proposed a multifaceted approach, with provisions to require the Civil Aeronautics Board (CAB) to promote industry competition; speed up its decisions; permit air carriers, within limits, to change their fares and serve new routes without CAB approval; provide subsidies to protect "essential" air service to small communities; and create a new class of commuter-type air service practically free of all government regulation. The bill also authorized the Secretary of Labor to establish a fund to aid airline employees who might become unemployed by the increased industry competition resulting from enactment of the bill.

The bill, called the Air Transportation Regulatory Reform Act of 1978, was proposed as a series of amendments to the Federal Aviation Act of 1958 (PL 85-726).

Regulatory Process Study

Blaming both the White House and Congress, the Senate Governmental Affairs Committee Feb. 9, 1977, issued a report attributing the failures of the federal regulatory process to the administrators who run it.

"[T]here is something lacking in overall quality," the committee charged. "It is not a matter of venality or corruption or even stupidity; rather, it is a problem of mediocrity."

Under both Democratic and Republican administrations, the committee said, regulatory commissioners have been chosen on the basis, not of merit, but of political palatability and connections in high places. The result, it said, has been a body of regulators who are poorly informed, often incompetent, discriminatory against women and minorities and biased in favor of regulated industries and against consumers.

The report criticized Congress for acquiescing in the White House appointments process and for not exercising its oversight authority to ensure that agencies were doing their job. Members of Congress and staffs did not regularly review the performance of agencies under their jurisdiction, the committee said, often taking action only when alerted to problems by the press, constituents, interest groups or disgruntled agency employees.

To guarantee regular review, the committee endorsed the concept of a "sunset law," whereby agencies would be required to justify their existence to Congress every few years in order to be re-established.

The report was the product of an 18-month study of federal regulation conducted jointly by the Government Operations and Commerce Committees. The Government Operations report followed a similar study of regulatory agencies by the House Interstate and Foreign Commerce Committee in 1976.

To plug holes in the appointments process, the committee made 53 recommendations including requirements that the makeup of the agencies reflect the composition of society, that former commissioners be barred from doing business with their former agency for a year after leaving it, that the President set conflict-of-interest standards for appointments and that the Senate adopt general guidelines for confirming nominees.

Recommendations to strengthen congressional oversight included requiring agencies to submit legislative and budget proposals concurrently to Congress and the Office of Management and Budget, authorizing Congress to enforce in federal court subpoenas for information from agencies, and shielding agency personnel who provided information to Congress from penalization by the agency.

Major Provisions

CAB Policy. S 2493 changed the declaration of policy guiding the CAB from one of promoting and protecting the nation's air transportation system to one of increasing reliance on competition; facilitating entry into the marketplace by new air carriers; preventing anticompetitive and monopolistic industry practices; and maintaining regular air service to small and isolated communities.

Other provisions of the bill were designed to speed up CAB actions; broaden the CAB's authority to prevent potentially anticompetitive agreements, mergers and other actions; and increase the board's discretion to grant exemptions from CAB regulation.

CAB Certification. The legislation enabled the CAB to issue certificates authorizing an air carrier to serve a particular route if the service was "consistent with the public convenience and necessity." Further, the board was instructed that innovative, more efficient, less monopolistic and cheaper service all were "consistent with the public convenience and necessity."

Under current law, the CAB was authorized to certify a particular service only if it was "required" by public convenience and necessity. According to the committee report, the CAB used its discretion under the law "both to prevent any significant entry into the industry by new firms and to frustrate the expansion of existing firms." Between 1950 and 1974, the report stated, the CAB received 79 applications from new firms interested in serving domestic air routes, yet none was granted.

Dormant Authority. The CAB was required under S 2493 to approve within 90 days an application to serve a requested route if 1) only one firm currently was providing regular service on that route, 2) another carrier was authorized to regularly serve the same route, but had not done so for six of the past 12 months, and 3) the carrier's application otherwise met CAB requirements.

The legislation also permitted the CAB to restrict or revoke a carrier's authorization to serve a particular route if the carrier wasn't providing regular service on that route and if another airline applied to serve it.

Under existing law, the committee report noted, carriers routinely failed to serve some routes for which they were authorized, but which were served by another airline. These same carriers, however, routinely — and successfully — intervened before the CAB to oppose board authorization of new applicants for those same routes.

Automatic Market Entry. The legislation authorized CAB-certified air carriers, charter airlines, certain Alaskan carriers and major state-regulated (intrastate) airlines to add one additional air route in each of 1979 and 1980, and two additional ones in 1981 and every year thereafter, for a period of 18 months without formal CAB authorization. At the end of the 18-month period, the CAB would be required to permanently authorize service on the additional routes if the carriers had complied with CAB regulations.

Carriers were permitted to choose three routes annually in 1979-81, two routes in 1982 and one in 1983 which would be protected from automatic entry. Federally subsidized carriers were afforded somewhat less protection from automatic entry competition from other carriers, while commuter-type carriers were offered more protection. If the program were found to be causing "substantial public harm," the CAB was authorized to modify the automatic entry program, subject to a veto by either house of Congress.

The automatic entry provision was termed "assuredly modest" by the committee, and was needed, it said, "to provide a meaningful threat of entry to insure that carriers will not fail to provide innovative or lower priced service in those markets in which it is economically feasible."

Charters. The bill preserved the existing limit of 2 per cent of total miles flown on regularly scheduled flights on the maximum number of charter flight miles the major air carriers could fly each year. However, the limit was increased to 5 per cent for smaller carriers and to 10 per cent for regional airlines.

Under a separate provision, carriers certified by the CAB to provide regularly scheduled service were permitted, following a five-year period beginning Jan. 1, 1979, to also be certified as charter airlines and thereby have unlimited charter authority. The legislation instructed the CAB to act to increase the availability of charter flights to the public.

Small Community Service. To ensure that airline deregulation did not result in the loss of service for small communities and isolated areas, the legislation phased out over seven years the existing system of airline subsidies based on mail deliveries. This was replaced with a subsidy program designed expressly to preserve "essential air transportation" as determined by the CAB.

Local Air Transportation. The bill provided for CAB certification of a new class of service subject only to the requirement that the aircraft providing the service had no more than 36 seats and that the carrier be "fit, willing and able" to provide the service. The provision permitted commuter-type airlines — currently regulated by the states — to continue to operate in an essentially unregulated manner and still be eligible for the benefits of federal certification such as federal loan guarantees and the ability to write tickets and route baggage using the entire federally certified system.

Fares. The legislation established a zone of "reasonable and just" charges within which a carrier was free to set its fares without prior CAB approval. The zone ranged from 5 per cent above to 35 per cent below the "standard industry fare." This was defined as the fare in effect for a particular service on July 1, 1977, subject to semi-annual CAB adjustment.

Under existing law the CAB had authority to review fares, disallow "unlawful" ones and dictate "lawful" tariffs in their place. The board still could review fares, but was permitted to set only maximum and minimum fare levels in place of fares if disallowed.

Employee Protection. The bill made persons employed by an air carrier for at least four years eligible for compensation for a maximum of three years if they lost their jobs, had their wages cut or were forced to relocate due to increased airline industry competition brought on by enactment of the legislation.

Senate Passage

The Senate passed the deregulation bill April 19 by a vote of 83-9.

Senate approval provided a significant victory for the President as well as a rare opportunity for Carter administration officials and senators to credit the vote to close cooperation between the executive and legislative branches. The sole major change made in the Senate further strengthened the deregulation measure.

"This was a fantastic victory for both the Congress and the administration," commented Terrence L. Bracy, Transportation Department assistant secretary for governmental affairs, after the vote.

Sen. Edward M. Kennedy, D-Mass., a key advocate of deregulation who often had been left out of Carter administration strategy decisions in the past, also lauded the "close executive-congressional cooperation on the bill."

As passed by the Senate, major provisions of S 2493 required the CAB to 1) promote airline industry competition; 2) speed up its decisions; 3) permit air carriers, within limits, to change their fares and serve new routes without prior CAB approval; 4) provide subsidies to protect "essential" air service to small rural communities, and 5) create a new class of commuter-type air service largely free from all government regulation.

The bill also authorized the secretary of labor to establish a program to compensate airline employees who might suffer job losses or salary cuts as a result of enactment of the legislation.

During floor debate, senators beat back by large margins a number of attempts to weaken the bill's controversial automatic entry and labor protection provisions.

And the Senate accepted, by a margin of three to one, an amendment to strengthen the deregulation provisions.

"A lot of people were committed to the principles of the bill," stated Howard W. Cannon, D-Nev., chairman of the Senate Commerce Aviation Subcommittee, in noting the wide support for the bill.

The active lobbying of the airline industry against the bill may actually have worked to the bill's advantage, Cannon suggested. "I think some of the airlines were not as reasonable as they could have been," he said after the vote.

Burden of Proof

The most far-reaching amendment accepted on the Senate floor was offered by Kennedy.

Deregulation legislation introduced by Kennedy and Cannon in 1977 provided that an application for a new air transportation service should be presumed by the CAB to be "consistent with the public convenience and necessity" unless an opponent of the application could prove that it wasn't.

But during markup the committee shifted the burden to the applicant. Under S 2493 as approved by the committee, a new application was presumed not to be in the public interest unless the applicant could prove that it was.

The Kennedy amendment proposed reversing the Commerce Committee position and once more shifting the burden of proof to an application's opponents.

Supporters of the amendment argued that it would provide new applicants with a procedural advantage before the CAB, which would provide an additional spur to competition. The opponents argued that it would bring on too much competition, too quickly. The Carter administration supported the amendment.

The amendment passed, 69-23.

Other amendments adopted on the floor included:

● A Cannon amendment authorizing the secretary of labor to determine the level of compensation given airline employees harmed by airline deregulation.

● A Cannon amendment to enlarge the bill's "zone of reasonable and just" charges within which airlines could alter their fares without prior CAB approval. Under the committee bill, the zone ranged from 5 per cent above to 35 per cent below the "standard industry fare" as defined in the bill. The Cannon amendment permitted fares to drop as low as 50 per cent below the standard industry fare and still remain within the zone. The amendment was needed, Cannon said, because the CAB, under reform advocate Alfred Kahn as chairman, already was approving certain discount fares of up to 50 per cent.

Both Cannon amendments were passed by voice vote.

Automatic Entry

George McGovern, D-S.D., who said the bill, if enacted, might result in service losses rather than gains, offered two amendments he said would help preserve the existing services. Both were resoundingly defeated.

One of the amendments would have provided for a more modest program of automatic entry. Cannon argued that the result would have been to "eliminate automatic market entry from the bill and defeat the purpose of this legislation." The administration opposed the amendment, which was defeated 21-72.

A second amendment would have set minimum standards for "essential air transportation" in the event that an airline canceled an "essential" service and the CAB subsidized a second airline to provide substitute service. Cannon said the bill already authorized the CAB to preserve "essential" services, and argued that the amendment would "tie the CAB's hands." The amendment was tabled by a vote of 80-12.

A number of other amendments that were defeated would have altered the airline employee protection plan:

● An amendment by Edward Zorinsky, D-Neb., to provide that employees dislocated because of the bill be given hiring priority by other airlines, rather than compensation. Roll call, 43-48.

● An amendment offered by John C. Danforth, R-Mo., to increase the number of employees protected by the plan. Roll call, 37-54.

● An amendment by Orrin G. Hatch, R-Utah, to delete the employee protection program from the bill. Roll call, 7-85.

Another rejected amendment would have permitted the CAB to preempt state regulation of intrastate carriers as soon as they offered interstate service. The amendment was offered by H. John Heinz III, R-Pa. Roll call, 20-72.

House Action

With Senate action completed, attention switched to the House Public Works Subcommittee on Aviation, where consideration of a companion bill (HR 11145) had been stalled since March 22. At that time the panel rejected a version similar to the Senate-passed bill and chose instead to accept a substitute that lacked most of the deregulation provisions. The subcommittee was hurriedly recessed before a vote to approve the weaker legislation could be taken.

Senate and administration backers of strong airline deregulation predicted a bill would be enacted in 1978 and that the Senate's action would provide new momentum to the passage of an equally strong measure by the House.

But Rep. Elliott H. Levitas, D-Ga., author of the substitute adopted by the Aviation Subcommittee, said the Senate passage would "have no impact on the House bill other than to underline the importance of our coming out with a better bill."

Levitas, who said he personally lobbied "a number" of senators on S 2493, and who appeared briefly on the Senate floor to watch the debate, called the Senate's version "a poor bill" and vowed that the House would "improve on it."

"I don't think the senators have individually focused on the issues as much as they normally would, because they have been preoccupied with the Panama Canal de-

bate," he said in an interview after the Senate vote. "I'm convinced what they were doing was just following the leadership of the Senate [Commerce] Committee."

House Committee Action

Ending a seven-week stalemate, the House Public Works Committee May 15 approved a compromise airline deregulation bill (HR 12611) by a vote of 37-5. Committee action came rapidly after the Aviation Subcommittee had given its approval May 9. The version finally approved May 9 reinstated several deregulation provisions the substitute bill lacked, but it still was substantially weaker than the bill the subcommittee had originally considered.

"As a general rule," the House Public Works Committee stated in its report accompanying HR 12611, the policies of the Civil Aeronautics Board (CAB) before 1975 "tended to place restrictions on airline management, which gave it much less competitive freedom than management in other industries."

Since 1975, the report went on, "the board's policies have tended to favor competition and a lessening of regulatory constraints."

The board's new policies "have been accompanied by improved financial results for the industry," the report said, indicating that, "at the least, the industry's experience indicates that lower fares and better service for consumers are not necessarily incompatible with industry profits."

"While the committee has by no means concluded that total deregulation is desirable," the report said, "we are persuaded that it is time for a moderate controlled release of some regulatory fetters."

Major Provisions

As approved by the House Public Works Committee May 19, HR 12611:

● Changed the declaration of policy guiding CAB decisions by directing the board to stress competition, low-fare service, new entries into the airline industry marketplace and prevention of anti-competitive practices.

● Directed the board to approve applications for air transportation service if they were "consistent with the public convenience and necessity."

● Directed the CAB to authorize service within 15 days by the first willing and able carrier applying to serve a route on which unused authority had been granted and which no other or only one other airline actually served. Unused — or "dormant" — authority would occur when an airline was authorized to serve a route yet did not serve it. For routes served by two or more carriers on which unused authority also existed, the CAB would be permitted, within 60 days, to refuse to approve an application for additional service if it concluded the application was inconsistent with the public convenience and necessity.

● Permitted carriers to select one additional market that they wanted to serve during the first year after the legislation's enactment. The CAB would be required to authorize the new service unless it found that it would be likely to seriously harm existing air service, or unless another carrier serving that market notified the board that it wished to be protected from a new entry.

The board was directed to complete a study by June 30, 1980, evaluating the impact of the experimental market entry program and making legislative recommendations to Congress concerning the program's future.

Trying to Deregulate the Regulated — Ford to Carter

In the summer of 1975 President Gerald R. Ford unveiled a plan to wage a major war against excessive government regulation.

"In many industries — transportation, energy, communications — federal regulatory commissions have actually thwarted competition," he said at the time. "The record is clear. They have burdened the consumer with the cost of misdirected regulation.... Government regulation is not an effective substitute for vigorous American competition."

Within months, however, Ford was forced to confront an uncomfortable truth: Those groups most opposed to his regulatory reform plan turned out to be the regulated industries themselves.

Though business groups publicly praised the president for his initiative, they privately geared up to fight the deregulation moves. The nation's banks fought proposed legislation to enable Savings and Loan Associations to compete with them. Broadcasters told top Ford advisers they would work to oppose his re-election, and proposed broadcast reform legislation was relegated to the status of a study — a status that continued in 1978.

Legislation to reform the trucking industry, stalled in the Office of Management and Budget (OMB), was bitterly opposed by the American Trucking Associations and the Teamsters Union.

Of all the Ford regulatory reform efforts, including those taken over by Congress and the Carter administration, the sole major successes by mid-1978 had been the Railroad Revitalization and Regulatory Reform Act of 1976 (PL 94-210) — which permitted railroads and the Interstate Commerce Commission a measure of regulatory flexibility — and repeal of state Fair Trade laws (PL 94-145) in 1975 — which barred manufacturers and distributors from fixing retail prices for their goods.

The basis for business' opposition to reform is straightforward. Government regulators and the industries they regulate over the years have woven close relationships by which the industry agrees to follow certain rules and regulations in return for a reprieve from the rigors of the free marketplace.

In many cases, federal regulation has relieved private firms of worry over new market entry, price competition, safety standards, technological obsolescence and inefficient management. On the other hand, some firms have objected to some welfare regulations, such as those issued by the Environmental Protection Agency.

Airline Industry

The airline industry is a pertinent example. When the House Aviation Subcommittee voted March 22, 1978, to reject a strong airline deregulation bill, it did so in accordance with the wishes of most of the major airlines, which had opposed the legislation since its inception.

"I think what has happened," commented James P. Carty, director of regulatory reform and consumer affairs for the National Association of Manufacturers — which supports airline deregulation — "is that people have paid lip service to reform, but when it comes down to moving on a proposal, economic self-interest comes to the fore."

"There's a vested interest in keeping things the way they are," remarked a former congressional aide active in regulatory reform who has since gone on to work at the White House. "In 1975 everyone blamed consumers for business regulation, but in fact business has been instrumental in creating and preserving regulation."

"Actually, we're a lot farther along than we might have been had Jerry Ford stayed in office," stated James C. Miller, a former member of Ford's Domestic Council and currently director of the American Enterprise Institute's Center for the Study of Government Regulation. "I think it would have been a lot slower and harder battle with a Republican President and a Democratic Congress. But Carter has made the bill a lower priority than Ford because he has so many other irons in the fire and has a secretary of transportation [Brock Adams] who is known to be not as enthusiastic as the president on reform."

"The main problem with regulatory reform," Miller went on, "is that the ultimate beneficiaries of reform are large in number, they each have a relatively small stake in it, and they aren't organized very well. By contrast, those that benefit from regulation know their stake in it . . . and they're well organized and very efficient in presenting their views."

Carter Initiatives

Reform efforts, though weakened, were not entirely dead in the Carter administration, by any means. The president has appointed a number of strong advocates of reform to many of the regulatory agencies themselves: Alfred Kahn as chairman of the Civil Aeronautics Board, Michael Pertschuk as chairman of the Federal Trade Commission and Charles Ferris as chairman of the Federal Communications Commission.

Trucking deregulation legislation still was a possibility in 1978, according to Stanley E. Morris, OMB deputy associate director for regulatory policy. "We are in the process of getting a memo to the president." And the White House was watching communications legislation being developed by the House Commerce Subcommittee on Communications.

Legislation (S 555) to strengthen federal conflict of interest rules, require more detailed financial disclosure of federal officials and prevent former government officials from working to affect matters in which they were involved while in government service has been passed by the Senate and was being pushed by the administration in the House in mid-1978.

Finally, Carter March 23, 1978, released an executive order requiring all executive branch federal agencies to improve the quality of their regulation. The order would require, for example, that regulations be written in "plain English" and that officials responsible for the development of regulations personally approve them.

● Authorized the board to regulate intrastate carriers as soon as they began providing interstate service.

● Extended the existing mail subsidy program for 10 years and provided for a new subsidy program to assure continued air service for 10 years to all communities currently served by regularly scheduled carriers.

The CAB was required to recommend to Congress by Jan. 1, 1980, how state and local governments could be made to share the costs of the subsidy programs.

● Permitted air carriers, without prior CAB approval, to raise fares up to 5 per cent above the fare in effect for that service one year earlier, or to lower fares by up to 50 per cent of the fare in effect one year earlier. If the carrier lowered fares and wasn't satisfied with the result, it also could raise the fare back to its previous level without CAB approval.

● Authorized the CAB to approve "experimental certificates" for innovative services, and to revoke or amend them if the certificate holder failed to provide the service.

● Made commuter airlines eligible for federal subsidies; permitted commuters to enter into joint fare agreements with regularly scheduled carriers, and increased the size and weight limits for commuter aircraft that would be exempt from many CAB regulations.

● Expedited CAB actions by establishing deadlines for many types of board and administrative decisions and simplifying certain procedures.

● Limited the authority of the President to disapprove CAB decisions in awarding international routes. Under the bill, the President could reverse a CAB decision solely on national defense or foreign policy grounds, not for economic or other reasons.

● Permitted the board to withhold from public disclosure information provided it by air carriers if the information's disclosure would harm the United States' or a U.S. carrier's competitive position on international negotiations.

● Extended the federal loan guarantee program for the purchase of new aircraft for five years.

● Provided for benefits for employees harmed by the legislation's enactment.

● Provided that the CAB be terminated on Dec. 31, 1982, unless Congress acted to renew it. ▌

Difficult Hurdles for Carter Energy Bill

Jimmy Carter's crusade for a comprehensive national energy policy dominated Congress and public affairs more than any other domestic issue during his first year as President.

Both the new Democratic President and the Democratic congressional leaders made passage of a national energy policy their top legislative priority for 1977.

And yet, when the year ended, there was no comprehensive energy policy signed into law. Congress did not finish the job. Both the House and Senate passed versions of the program, but the Senate went far afield from the President's approach in two key areas—natural gas regulation and energy tax policy. Conference committees settled other issues but bogged down over gas and taxes. Conferees quit Dec. 22. *(1978 developments, p. 94)*

At his last 1977 press conference Dec. 15, Carter asserted that the inability to erect an energy policy was "the only major failure this year...." The story behind that failure tells a lot about Congress, President Carter and the formation of American public policy in 1977.

The Need. It had been painfully evident to policymakers since the Arab oil embargo of 1973-74 that America was in need of a national energy plan. That need was underscored as Jimmy Carter prepared to take the oath of office. An unprecedented cold wave caused such rapid depletion of the nation's declining natural gas supplies that many schools and factories were closed and workers went jobless. Special legislation was needed to divert supplies to gas-short areas.

Both the oil embargo and the gas crisis four years later provided vivid evidence that America no longer was producing enough fuel to power its growing economy. The difference was increasingly made up by expensive imports of foreign fuels.

With worldwide energy consumption growing faster than supply availability, the clear trend was that a devastating energy crisis loomed in the future. The Central Intelligence Agency (CIA) warned in an April 1977 study that such a crisis probably would occur by 1985 unless energy conservation measures were "greatly increased."

A month later a prestigious panel of international experts assembled by the Massachusetts Institute of Technology (MIT) warned that a worldwide shortage of oil would occur before the year 2000 and possibly as soon as 1981 unless extraordinary efforts were made to conserve energy.

Carter's Plan. Upon taking office, President Carter ordered a small team of energy planners to construct a comprehensive national energy program in 90 days; the deadline was met.

The primary goal of Carter's vaunted "National Energy Plan" was to cut America's appetite for oil and natural gas and to use energy more efficiently.

His answer was an exceedingly complex package of regulatory and tax measures. The Carter plan would have empowered the federal government: to require industries to make products meeting mandated standards of energy efficiency; to tell businesses to burn certain fuels but not others; to sponsor massive programs encouraging property owners to insulate their buildings; to levy stiff taxes against cars that guzzled too much gasoline, against businesses that burned oil or natural gas and against purchasers of domestically produced oil. The taxes were aimed at spurring energy conservation; their effect would be to drive energy prices higher.

By his own admission, Carter did not expect his program to be popular. But, he said, it was necessary.

Pushing It. Carter and the Democratic congressional leaders pushed hard to complete action on the program in 1977, before the next election year.

Carter spoke to the nation via evening television addresses only three times during his first year in Washington; each time the subject was energy. The first was a fireside chat about the natural gas crisis. The next two were to rally support for his energy program. The only speech Carter made to a joint session of Congress during his first year was also on the subject of his energy program.

When the going got tough on Capitol Hill against his plan, the President dispersed his Cabinet across the country to plug for the energy plan. Though his critics at times faulted Carter's tactics, it was clear that no other single domestic issue received so much presidential attention in 1977.

The same could be said of Congress. The first session of the 95th Congress could be said to have had two agendas: energy, and everything else. In the House, Speaker Thomas P. O'Neill Jr. (D Mass.) used all the powers he could muster to strongarm the Carter program to passage in record time, passing it as one bill (HR 8444) Aug. 5, 244-177.

Next, Senate Majority Leader Robert C. Byrd (D W.Va.) cleared all other bills from the Senate agenda to give the energy program undivided attention. It was passed as five major bills between Sept. 28 and Oct. 31.

And yet, the Carter energy program did not make it through.

ANALYSIS

There was no single, simple answer why President Carter's energy program encountered so many difficulties in Congress. But there were a number of clearly identifiable contributing factors.

Five basic problems plagued the program from the beginning:

● It was a plan tackling inherently difficult political problems that was drafted virtually in secret by nonpolitical technicians without outside consultation. That alienated not only Capitol Hill, but also interest groups and even members of the Carter administration who held relevant expertise but were not consulted.

• Its drafting was rushed and consequently the plan suffered from technical flaws, which undermined confidence in it.

• It was the object of intense and negative lobbying by a broad range of powerful special interest groups.

• It was poorly sold to Congress by Carter's lobbyists.

• It lacked a constituency.

Despite those factors, the Carter energy program managed to pass the House virtually intact Aug. 5. Then it ran into the Senate, where it was butchered. In addition to the five basic problems listed above, which continued to plague the Carter plan in the Senate, at least four other problems were thrown on the scales, tilting the balance against the President:

• There was a complete loss of momentum between House passage and Senate consideration, caused principally by two things: the August recess and the troubles of Bert Lance, then Carter's budget director.

• The two Senate committees handling the Carter energy plan were dominated by a different predisposition toward energy policy than were their two counterpart committees in the House.

• The Senate was guided by a different style of leadership than was the House, due in part to the nature of the Senate and in part to the nature of Majority Leader Byrd.

• The administration misread the Senate almost to the end, hoping it would come through somehow for the President as had the House.

The Basic Problems

Drafting

From the outset of his term, President Carter vowed to present a comprehensive national energy program to the nation by April 20, 1977, exactly 90 days after he took office.

Later Carter abandoned his early habit of forcing arbitrary deadlines for completion of complicated policy proposals. But on energy, the deadline was met.

The challenge was handed to his energy adviser, James R. Schlesinger. The Harvard-trained economist and former Nixon-Ford Cabinet member gathered around him a small, close-knit team of fewer than two dozen economists, lawyers and Washington-wise administrators.

To beat the clock, they were forced to work almost in isolation. Though the plan came to rest largely on energy tax proposals, Treasury Department tax experts later complained they had not been consulted. Though the plan would need congressional approval to become law, key members of Congress were not invited to help shape the policy and they were miffed. Likewise, experts from private industry were left out, though the plan as conceived would touch every phase of American life.

The political consequence of such a policy formation process was that many who were left out felt little or no obligation to support the final product.

Tacitly recognizing that danger, the White House attempted to present an image of openness via an innovative public relations campaign featuring "mini-conferences" with industry leaders, citizen town meetings and 450,000 letters to citizens requesting energy policy suggestions.

White House protestations to the contrary, most observers were convinced these efforts were all show. They believed the real decisions on the new energy policy were being made in isolation by Schlesinger's small band in the second floor offices of the Old Executive Office Building next door to the White House.

But the deadline was met. And with it came one of the most complex legislative packages ever devised. The Schlesinger team had strung together 113 separate interlocking provisions that together would affect virtually every facet of American society.

Technical Flaws

"The legislation itself was written at white heat, and as a result there are serious technical problems."

That observation came in early May, 1977, from Frank M. Potter, staff director of the House Commerce Subcommittee on Energy and Power. That panel held jurisdiction over most non-tax aspects of the Carter energy plan.

The "technical problems" Potter mentioned began to show up soon after administration officials began defending the plan before congressional committees. The whole program was held together by numbers—estimates of how much energy this proposal would save, how much money that proposal would cost—and with embarrassing frequency, the administration's numbers conflicted with each other.

There were repeated examples of this in May testimony before the House Ways and Means Committee. Administration witnesses from Schlesinger's team provided different answers than Treasury Department tax experts to the same queries.

Doubts about the soundness of the Carter program were magnified during the summer as four comprehensive analyses of the plan performed by non-partisan Capitol Hill research units were unveiled. In each case, the four congressional agencies—the Congressional Budget Office, the General Accounting Office, the Library of Congress and the Office of Technology Assessment—concluded that Carter's program would fall far short of attaining its energy goals.

Lobbying

When things got tough for the White House during Congress' eight-month 1977 examination of the energy plan, the President's men would scream "lobbyists."

On June 9, a House Commerce subcommittee voted to decontrol new natural gas prices, contrary to Carter's plan. The House Ways and Means Committee the same day overwhelmingly rejected the President's proposed gasoline tax, tossed out a proposed rebate for buyers of fuel-efficient cars and weakened Carter's proposed tax on "gas guzzling" autos.

The next day Jody Powell, Carter's press secretary, howled "lobbyists." Gas decontrol, he said, was a "ripoff of the American consumer.... [Y]esterday, the oil companies, the auto companies and their lobbies won significant preliminary victories," Powell said.

At a news conference June 13, the President added his voice to that theme, decrying the "inordinate influence" of the oil and auto industries on Capitol Hill.

Later, the full Commerce Committee overturned its subcommittee vote on gas deregulation and Carter's position was muscled through the House. And though his gasoline tax never resurfaced, the President got most of what he wanted from Ways and Means as well. There was no more talk from the White House about lobbies until the energy bill reached the Senate.

On Oct. 13, the White House screamed louder than ever. The Senate Finance Committee recently had rejected all of the President's key energy tax proposals. At a televised news conference, Carter suggested the nation's oil companies were preparing for "war profiteering in the impending energy crisis.... [T]he oil companies apparently want it all," Carter said.

There is no doubt that the formidable oil and gas industry lobby was working overtime against Carter's program during most of 1977. Their efforts were concentrated on natural gas regulation, but many company representatives were also working to either defeat Carter's taxes or to ensure that the proceeds from the taxes went to the oil industry instead of to consumers, as Carter preferred.

The automobile industry was well represented, especially at sessions on Carter's proposed tax on gas guzzling cars. Union lobbyists, consumer groups and environmentalists all were heavily involved. The nation's major utilities were scrambling all over, opposing Carter's proposed utility rate reforms, his tax on utility use of oil and gas and his proposal to force utilities to burn coal instead of oil and gas.

And those were just the major actors. There were scores of narrowly focused lobbies. Small oil refiners worked their own angles. One lobbyist represented shopping center associations concerned about a possible ban against master utility meters.

In short, the Capitol was crawling with lobbyists of every shape, stripe and persuasion from the day Carter sent his energy package to Congress. But blaming lobbyists alone for Congress' failure to clear the bill is too simplistic. The House, which essentially adopted Carter's program, was no less besieged by pleaders for special interests than was the Senate, which rejected much of the President's program. Lobbyists were an ever-present factor, but hardly the only one.

Selling It

From April 29, the day the White House delivered the energy program to Congress in formal legislative language, complaints were raised on both sides of the Capitol about White House salesmanship.

Key energy legislators did not receive adequate individual attention from White House liaison, they said. They felt disregarded, left out, and most importantly, in the dark.

When they did receive personal attention and briefings, it came late; too often the administration pitchmen did not know the issues sufficiently well to be of much help, members said.

And, both Senate and House members added, there were too many administration aides trying to explain the various portions of the complex package. No one White House salesman save Energy Secretary Schlesinger could make sense of the whole program, some said.

"I don't think they had anyone who could fully explain the package," said Sen. Spark M. Matsunaga (D Hawaii). "It was a truly awful mess." Matsunaga cast votes on both the Senate Energy and Finance Committees, which together ruled on every facet of Carter's energy program.

A partial exception to the criticism of the White House sales effort was President Carter himself, whose personal efforts were considered diligent and effective. He made telephone calls to round up wavering votes throughout. He held repeated White House meetings with select groups of energy legislators. His major personal slip-up was to not keep the public pressure on the Senate when it was gearing up to tackle the energy program.

No Constituency

In his speech to the nation April 18, 1977, explaining the need for his energy program, President Carter observed:

"I am sure each of you will find something you don't like about the specifics of our proposal.... We can be sure that all the special interest groups in the country will attack the part of this plan that affects them directly."

Six months later, Carter again tried to sell the public his energy program via television Nov. 8, and he noted: "I said six months ago that no one would be completely satisfied with this national energy plan. Unfortunately, that prediction has turned out to be right."

Gallup Polls throughout the year demonstrated one of the biggest obstacles Carter faced: About half the nation refused to take the energy crisis very seriously.

In mid-December, Gallup reported that 40 per cent of the nation's people believed that the U.S. energy situation was "very serious"; another 42 per cent viewed it as "fairly serious." Fifteen per cent, Gallup said, saw the problem as "not at all" serious.

Those figures had remained virtually unchanged since early April, before the President's plan was presented, Gallup said. "...[A]pproximately half of the public can be said to be relatively unconcerned about our energy problems," Gallup wrote in late June. Despite all the political fury in Washington, despite repeated presidential addresses and unceasing media attention, the American public's views on energy changed barely at all in 1977.

The absence of a strong body of public opinion behind Carter's program made it difficult to repel sophisticated lobbying campaigns against the plan waged by committed special interests. As Energy Secretary Schlesinger summed up Oct. 16 on CBS television's "Face the Nation:"

"...[T]he basic problem is that there is no constituency for an energy program. There are many constituencies opposed. But the basic constituency for the program is the future...."

Complicating Factors

As noted earlier, all those problems were present from the start, yet the House accepted the heart of the Carter plan, and the Senate did not. After House passage Aug. 5, new and critical factors came into play.

Momentum

The House, to the surprise of many—including a good number of its own members—managed to meet Speaker O'Neill's ambitious schedule and passed the Carter energy plan almost unchanged before the August recess.

Passage marked the high point of Carter's legislative year; afterwards Congress closed down for a month until Sept. 7. Carter never regained the momentum in 1977.

Having momentum, as every football coach knows, is like having an extra player on the team. The same is true in politics. Jimmy Carter still had some of the luster of political wizardry and a shiny new presidency about him going into the August recess. All that changed over the next few weeks.

Part of the explanation for the loss of momentum lies simply in the nature of the August recess. Washington tends to slow down and catch its breath. The heat is oppressive; people take their vacations while Congress is gone. Members of Congress go home, talk to people, do a little politicking. There is a collective taking of stock, looking back and looking forward. And then after Labor Day, Washington comes back and starts a new cycle.

It is hard to sustain a sense of momentum through such a break. But for Carter in August 1977 it was impossible. During that period the Carter administration had a few holes blown in its bow and was gasping for air by the time Congress returned in September.

The reason for the abrupt turn of events was the Bert Lance fiasco. The President's budget director, close friend and adviser got caught in a scandal stemming from his pre-Washington banking days. With Washington lacking in competing news during August, the Lance affair dominated the news media for weeks. In the end Lance resigned, on Sept. 21, 1977.

Lance's loss was a major blow to the young administration. Apart from the substance of the charges against him, the Lance case was also a very real power fight between the new Carter team and its established institutional opponents in Congress, the bureaucracy and the news media.

The President made it clear he did not want to yield, but in the end he was forced to. Carter looked very vulnerable once he announced Lance's resignation Sept. 21. While difficult to measure, there was no doubt that the Lance debacle contributed to a loss of influence by the Carter team that continued to weaken the President throughout 1977.

Committee Contrasts

The President's energy plan went to the House first, then to the Senate. In the House, though five committees reviewed portions of the bill, the large majority of the work fell to only two panels. Most non-tax proposals were handled by the Interstate and Foreign Commerce Committee, while all energy tax proposals went to Ways and Means.

In the Senate there were only two committees with jurisdiction. Non-tax concerns came under the new Energy and Natural Resources Committee; tax proposals went to the Finance Committee.

It was predictable that Carter's energy plan would receive a more favorable hearing before the two House panels than it did from their Senate counterparts. The House committees had compiled strong records of support for precisely the kinds of energy policies that Carter proposed. The Senate panels either had records of support for opposite kinds of policies, or no records at all.

Utility rate reform provides a good example. In 1976, House Commerce's Subcommittee on Energy and Power held eight days of thorough hearings on that complex subject. A massive record of expert testimony was compiled. The subcommittee chairman, John D. Dingell (D Mich.), sponsored a bill that year growing out of those hearings. Dingell's bill was distinctly pro-consumer.

One of the major sections of President Carter's energy plan dealt with utility rate reform, and his proposals bore a marked resemblance to Dingell's of the previous year. This was more than coincidence; one of Dingell's chief aides in drawing up his 1976 bill was committee counsel Robert Riggs Nordhaus. In early 1977, Nordhaus joined Carter's team of energy planners.

Consequently, Carter's utility rate reform proposals sailed through the Commerce Committee, and later, the House.

It was a different story in the Senate. The Energy Committee was new in 1977. Built on the old Interior Committee, its members had never examined electric rate reform before.

In 1977, the panel's Subcommittee on Energy Conservation and Regulation held two days of hearings in late July and three more in September on Carter's rate reform proposals. By the subcommittee's own admission, its members did not know enough about that exceedingly complex field to legislate responsibly.

Also working against Carter on that topic was simply the dominant value position on the subcommittee. Unlike Dingell's panel, its Senate counterpart had not built a similar record of pro-consumer positions on energy issues. It seems simply to be a more conservative forum.

Natural gas deregulation is another exemplary issue. In the House, Dingell failed narrowly to carry his subcommittee behind the Carter proposal. Carter wanted to continue federal regulation over natural gas prices.

But when the issue reached the full House Commerce Committee, its pro-consumer majority backed Carter and reversed the subcommittee.

The Senate Energy Committee was different. There was no pro-consumer majority. The issue went straight to the full committee and it deadlocked, 9-9. Later, in a major defeat for Carter, the full Senate voted 50-46 to end federal regulation over new gas sales.

The House and Senate committees handling energy taxes were distinctly different as well. The House Ways and Means Committee is large, with 37 members. Since its authoritarian chairman, Wilbur D. Mills (D Ark. 1939-77) was deposed in 1975, it had been much more democratic in its deliberations and much more responsive to the House leadership. Its approval of an ill-fated, tough energy tax bill in 1975 demonstrated that under Chairman Al Ullman (D Ore.) it had built a record of support for the kind of energy initiatives Carter proposed. And like the Energy Committee in the Senate, the Finance Committee had not.

The Senate Finance Committee was a relatively small group with only 18 members. Unlike Ullman, who worked closely with his party's leadership, Senate Finance was headed by Russell B. Long (D La.), who tended to function as a kind of supreme leader apart from either party's official leadership on tax matters. Long, far more than Ullman, was a master of both the tax code and his committee.

And on matters of energy taxes, unlike Ullman, Long's philosophical bent was very different than President Carter's.

Long represented Louisiana, heartland of the nation's oil and gas industry. He looked out for that industry's interests. From the day Carter announced his energy plan in April, Long said he thought the plan did not provide adequate incentives to the industry for production.

Long's committee was no more sympathetic to Carter's energy taxes than its chairman; arguably less so. After rejecting virtually all of Carter's energy tax proposals, the Finance Committee in October wrote its own vastly different energy tax bill. Rather than trying to induce conservation through penalty taxes, the Finance Committee bill tried to induce additional energy production primarily through tax incentives to industry.

Different Leadership

It had become a commonplace in Washington by the end of 1977 that Jimmy Carter's best ally in the capital during his first year was House Speaker O'Neill. Certainly that was true on the energy bill.

O'Neill saw to it that the Carter energy program got through the House, fast. He made it clear that he saw the energy program as a test of Congress and a test of whether the Democratic Party could govern when it controlled both the executive and legislative branches.

The House Speaker saw the Carter energy plan as the Democrats' plan, and he made it the O'Neill plan as well. He went all out to pass it.

His first move was to create a special blue-ribbon select committee to coordinate House review of the program. To it he appointed 40 hand-picked members, with a majority top-heavy with senior Democrats favorably inclined toward the Carter plan.

Next he set strict short deadlines for the regular standing committees to meet in conducting hearings and mark-ups on the complex bill. He insisted that the deadline be honored and it was; the committees finished work in six weeks and sent the bill to the select committee.

His select committee rushed the bill through in three days, proposing a handful of strengthening amendments. Then the measure was sent to the House Rules Committee, stacked with O'Neill lieutenants who obeyed his directions to protect the bill by issuing a modified closed rule, limiting floor debate and amendments.

O'Neill kept abreast of the measure's progress at every point, and when the legislation appeared in trouble on the floor, he stepped in directly to help.

Delivering a thundering oration, the Speaker appealed to party unity and congressional responsibility and helped block a move to overturn Carter's policy on natural gas.

As with so many other things, leadership on the bill was quite different in the Senate.

On April 20, after Carter outlined his energy plan to Congress, the reaction of Senate Majority Leader Byrd was noticeably cooler than was O'Neill's: "...The President cannot expect every jot and tittle to be enacted as he proposed it," Byrd warned.

Byrd's commitment to the Carter energy plan was of quite a different kind than O'Neill's. The West Virginian's deepest commitment is not to party or President, or to legislative policy, but to the Senate. Though pledged to back the plan and evidently dedicated to working with Carter as smoothly as possible, Byrd stopped short of O'Neill-like efforts.

Byrd's strongest exertions were aimed at getting the energy bill through Congress in 1977, one way or the other. His commitment was, in a phrase he repeated time and again, to "let the Senate work its will" on the program, not necessarily to force the Senate to adopt it.

But even if Byrd had wanted, he would not have been able to manipulate the Senate as O'Neill did the House. Senate rules simply do not allow a leader such power.

"I don't know that anybody today could run this Senate" as strong majority leaders have in the past, observed Sen. Lloyd Bentsen (D Texas) in an October interview.

Administration Misreading

If the Carter administration saw trouble coming in the Senate, it was slow to react.

There was little evidence that the White House was alarmed at all by initial votes against the plan in the Senate. President Carter himself conceded Oct. 13 that he

was perhaps remiss in not leaning more heavily on the Senate during August and September to pass his program.

But as late as Oct. 16 there was strong evidence that the administration still was expecting the Senate to somehow come through for the President, even though by that time the Senate had finished action on four of the five basic portions of the Carter plan and the fifth had been gutted in the Finance Committee.

On Oct. 16, in an appearance on CBS television's "Face the Nation" program, Energy Secretary Schlesinger downplayed the Senate's actions to date.

"When the original package went to the House," he recalled, "there were all these comments to the effect that the program was being gutted or riddled and so on. Then in August, when the House voted out virtually the entire package, everyone said it was a remarkable triumph. I would not be surprised if we went through the same cycle with regard to the Congress as a whole."

Conference Action

The White House and congressional leaders held out hope following completion of Senate action Oct. 31 that conference agreements on the Carter package could be reached and final action attained before the year's end.

But that was not to be. The reason, basically, was that there were such wide gulfs to be bridged between Senate and House that time simply ran out. A secondary reason was that conferees set a fairly relaxed pace in pursuing their negotiations.

Conferees took up the first of the five basic portions of the Carter energy package—general energy conservation—Oct. 18. They reached agreement on it Oct. 31, just under two weeks later. On Oct. 31, they started the second bill—coal conversion—and completed it Nov. 11, again in less than two weeks. On the third bill—utility rates—they reached their key agreement in four days, took a 10-day Thanksgiving recess and returned to finish the bill after five days more.

On each of those bills, the conferees seldom worked more than five hours a day and often took three-day weekends. Nevertheless, for such far-reaching and complex legislation, working out conference agreements between radically different bills in less than two weeks each cannot be considered unusually slow by normal standards.

It was when they reached natural gas regulation that the conference completely bogged down. That conference started Dec. 2. Battle lines on that question were rigid and there was little middle ground for compromise. Complicating negotiations immensely was the fact that Senate conferees were evenly split, 9-9, and could not agree among themselves on anything.

Completing the conference breakdown was the fact that negotiators on the complex energy tax proposals refused to do much of anything until the natural gas bill was worked out.

Because House Speaker O'Neill was insistent that the House would not vote on any conference agreement until all could be combined for a single up or down vote, none of the Carter energy plan could be sent to the floor for final congressional action until the conferees finished natural gas pricing and taxes.

Consequently, Congress adjourned Dec. 15 with three conference agreements on Carter's energy package on the shelf while two more were still caught in intense negotiations.

Genesis of Energy Crisis

The increasing energy dependence of the United States in the 1970s hit the public consciousness when the Arab oil embargo was imposed. The embargo was called Oct. 18, 1973, by the Organization of Petroleum Exporting Countries (OPEC), which was displeased with the pro-Israeli policy of the United States and certain European countries during the October Middle East war. It remained in effect until March 18, 1974.

During that period a real fear of running out of heating oil led office managers and homeowners to turn down thermostats. Consumers formed long lines to fill their gas tanks at service stations and many stations closed on Sundays, sharply curtailing weekend driving. More fundamentally, the cost of foreign oil quadrupled.

But when the embargo ended, leaving the high prices, public concern about energy seemed to fade. Moreover, partisan and regional interests came into play to complicate the efforts of the executive branch and the heavily Democratic 94th Congress to write a national energy policy. Thermostats went back up and energy consumption rose.

President Ford in January 1975 offered a plan to cut energy consumption and stimulate domestic energy production by relying on higher fuel prices. Prices would have been allowed to rise through a combination of import fees and a lifting of federal controls.

Sensitized by rising unemployment and seemingly uncontrollable inflation, Democratic leaders were wary of any plan to raise prices or cut back energy use, fearing such moves would further slow the already sluggish economy. They instead advocated a tax-based approach that involved increasing gasoline taxes to encourage conservation and providing tax incentives to spur energy production.

Congress rejected both the Ford and Democratic leadership approaches, coming up instead with the moderate "Energy Policy and Conservation Act" whose provisions fell far short of the goals implied by its title. Congressional leaders of both parties ended 1975 with a sense of frustration and weariness born of the long wrangle over energy matters.

"It is extremely difficult to write an energy bill," commented House Majority Leader Thomas P. O'Neill Jr. (D Mass.) in December. "This, perhaps, has been the most parochial issue that could ever hit the floor," he added.

"I have come to feel like the mythological Greek, Sisyphus, who was condemned to rolling the great rock up the hill in Hades, only to have it slip when he got it close to the top and roll to the bottom again where he had to start over," said Rep. Clarence J. Brown (R Ohio).

"In total candor, I must say...that what began as a thrilling and dramatic enterprise has degenerated at times into a farcical comedy of frustrations," said Jim Wright (D Texas), head of the House Democratic task force that developed the Democrats' alternative energy plan early in 1975. "Too often the Congress has been simply unwilling to make the hard decisions and take the difficult steps necessary to achieve energy sufficiency for the United States," he continued.

A year later, Wright was even more critical of Congress' record on energy: "Since the Arab oil embargo three years ago, we have tried to do a few timid things to reduce consumption, but they have not been very successful, because total domestic consumption has risen.... We have dabbled with oil and gas pricing. We have made more money

available for long-range research, for things like solar energy, that may help us 30 or 40 years from now. But as far as doing anything practical to increase the supply of energy and reduce our dependence upon foreign sources in the foreseeable future, we have done nothing."

Strong regional and political differences, compounded by the splintering of energy issues among different committees and the lack of forceful leadership, diluted the leverage the numerically strong Democrats had been expected to have in determining national energy policy.

Congress reorganized the federal energy bureaucracy, but it did not reorganize its own structure to deal with energy matters, and so one energy measure might be referred to as many as four different committees in one chamber before reaching the floor—sometimes in four different versions.

With Congress unable to write a strong energy bill, consumption rose and domestic oil production dropped. By 1976 it was down one million barrels a day from 1973—to 8.2 million barrels, despite the fact that the average wellhead price of domestic oil doubled during this same period—to $7.99 per barrel from $3.89.

By the end of 1976 the United States was not only more dependent on imported oil than in 1973; it was more dependent on expensive Arab oil. The United States was importing more than seven million barrels each day, one million more than in 1973, at a price ($13.40) quadruple that paid for each barrel in 1973 ($3.27). At the end of 1976 OPEC nations agreed again to raise their oil prices; the action seemed unlikely to affect U.S. demand.

And the percentage of U.S. oil imports coming from Arab countries doubled over this period. In 1973, almost one of every three barrels of oil imported into the United States came from Canada. Concerned about its own supply situation, however, Canada began to cut back on oil exports, announcing in 1975 that it would cease entirely to export oil to the United States by 1981. Canadian oil imports to the United States fell from 365 million barrels in 1973 to 219 million barrels in 1975, and Canada said it was reducing that amount by one-third in 1976. Meanwhile the amount imported from Saudi Arabia rose steadily, from 168.5 million barrels in 1973 to 256 million in 1975.

In March 1976, the Federal Energy Administration revised its Project Independence forecast of oil imports for the next decade. In 1974, it had projected that oil imports could be reduced to between three million and five million barrels a day by 1985 (compared to seven million barrels per day in 1976). The revised estimate projected that imports would fall only to 5.9 million barrels per day by that time.

Carter and Conservation

During his campaign, Jimmy Carter emphasized the need for conservation as the foundation of the nation's effort to move into a stronger energy posture. Critical of the failure of the nation's leaders to convince the American people of the urgency of the energy problem, he promised to institute a comprehensive conservation program to cut back on energy waste. "Americans are willing to make sacrifices," he said, "if they understand the reason for them and if they believe the sacrifices are fairly distributed." Only the future would prove, however, whether Carter could be sufficiently convincing to the American people to overcome the inertia that had frustrated earlier conservation efforts.

After he became President, one of Carter's first imperatives was to succeed where his predecessors had failed in convincing the American people that the energy crisis was indeed real, and potentially severe. An April Gallup Poll showed that a majority of Americans thought the energy crisis was something less than "very serious." On April 18, Carter delivered what he termed "an unpleasant talk" to the nation via television in an effort to change America's mind. A White House aide was quoted as calling this speech "the-sky-is-falling" message.

"With the exception of preventing war, this is the greatest challenge our country will face during our lifetimes," he said. "The energy crisis has not yet overwhelmed us, but it will if we do not act quickly...."

The energy crisis is worse now, he said, than during the 1973 Arab oil embargo, worse than during the natural gas emergency which threatened the nation the past winter.

The President recited the facts, he said, that lay behind the problem. "The oil and natural gas we rely on for 75 per cent of our energy are running out.... [D]omestic production has been dropping steadily at about 6 per cent a year. Imports have doubled in the last five years. Our nation's independence...is becoming increasingly constrained...."

Carter said America suffered from bad energy habits. "Ours is the most wasteful nation on earth," he said. "We waste more energy than we import. With about the same standards of living we use twice as much energy per person as do other countries like Germany, Japan and Sweden."

If America does not mend its ways, he said, it can look forward to a virtual doomsday nightmare as its future reality. "Unless we act, we will spend more than $550-billion for imported oil by 1985—more than $2,500 for every man, woman and child in America.... [W]e will live constantly in fear of embargoes. We could endanger our freedom...to act in foreign affairs. Within 10 years, we would not be able to import enough oil...our factories will not be able to keep our people on the job...we will not be ready to keep our transportation system running."

Carter's Program

On April 20, 1977, Carter appeared again on nationwide television, this time to outline before a joint session of Congress what he proposed to do about the energy crisis. "The time has come to draw the line," he said.

As described by Carter and outlined by administration background briefings, the President's energy program featured the following key elements:

Oil, Gas, Coal

Oil Pricing. Oil price controls would be continued indefinitely on oil under current production. Carter asked Congress to apply a tax on all domestic oil production, increasing in three annual stages, to eventually bring the price of all domestic oil to world market price levels in 1980. Net funds collected under the tax would be rebated to the public. Administration spokesmen said the tax would cause each gallon to rise seven cents, and the rebate would theoretically amount to $75 per person per year.

Natural Gas Pricing. Congress was asked to require that new natural gas be sold at federally controlled prices, whether sold interstate or in the state where it was produced. (Under the existing system, intrastate gas was not subject to federal controls.) All new gas would be priced equal to the cost of an energy equivalent amount of oil, or

approximately $1.75 per thousand cubic feet in 1978. Gas currently under production would continue under existing price controls, or under interstate market contracts. More expensive new gas would be allocated only to industrial customers; gas at old controlled cheaper prices would be reserved for residential and commercial users. The President also asked for emergency gas allocation authority for three more years.

Oil Stockpile. Carter proposed doubling the strategic oil reserve program to one billion barrels to provide enough oil to cover U.S. needs for 10 months. In addition, oil rationing contingency plans would be drafted.

Outer Continental Shelf. The administration announced its support for pending legislation to tighten leasing policies for oil and gas development on the Outer Continental Shelf.

Gasoline Decontrol. The administration said it hoped to eliminate federal price and allocation controls on gasoline by autumn 1977, reserving the right to reimpose controls if prices exceed a target level.

Coal. Carter asked for a legislative package taxing industries using oil or natural gas as boiler fuel at levels designed to encourage a switch to coal. The tax would take effect in 1979 for most industries and 1983 for utilities. A 10 per cent tax credit would apply to costs entailed in converting facilities to coal use. New industrial and utility boilers would be prohibited from being fueled by oil or gas. The administration reiterated its intent to insist on strong clean air and strip mine standards. Coal-fired plants would be required to install the best available pollution control technology. The administration also pledged to expand research on coal technologies that would reduce pollution associated with coal burning.

Transportation

Gas Guzzler Tax. Current law mandated that new car fleets must average 18 miles per gallon (mpg) in 1978, 19 mpg in 1979, 20 mpg in 1980, graduating to 27.5 mpg in 1985. Carter asked Congress to impose an excise tax beginning in model year 1978 on new cars and light trucks not meeting those standards. The tax rates would increase annually. The least efficient cars would be taxed the most.

Cars exceeding efficiency standards would earn manufacturers rebates. Total rebates would not exceed total revenue from the excise tax. Rebates for vehicles made overseas would be available after treaties or executive agreements were made. By 1985, the worst gas guzzlers would be taxed $2,488; the most efficient cars, including electric vehicles, would earn rebates of $493.

Standby Gasoline Tax. Beginning Jan. 15, 1979, if national gasoline consumption exceeded the previous year's target level, Carter asked Congress to levy a five-cent-per-gallon tax each year. The tax could total 50 cents after 10 years. Funds collected would be rebated to consumers under a mechanism not yet devised. Target consumption levels would allow limited increases in national gasoline consumption until 1980, and call for decreases thereafter, although mileage totals would increase due to improved efficiency.

Other Transportation Steps. Reduced gasoline tax revenues to states would be compensated from federal sources like the Highway Trust Fund. The Secretary of Transportation was directed to subject light trucks over 6,000 pounds to new fuel efficiency standards. Congress was asked to remove the current 10 per cent excise tax on intercity buses and to end tax breaks for general aviation, not affecting commercial airlines, and for motor boat fuel.

Chronology of Action on Carter's Energy Plan Reflects

Following is a chronology of action on President Carter's omnibus energy legislation through May 1978:

1977

● **April 18:** In a televised evening address Carter explained the energy crisis threat of the next decade.

● **April 20:** Carter outlined his energy program to a televised joint session of Congress.

● **May 2:** Carter's omnibus energy plan was introduced in the House (HR 6831).

● **June 9:** The House Ways and Means Committee rejected the Carter proposals for a standby tax on gasoline and for rebating to the people revenues from his proposed tax on gas guzzling autos.

● Contrary to Carter's plan, a House Commerce subcommittee voted to end federal price controls on newly discovered natural gas.

● **June 10:** White House Press Secretary Jody Powell denounced the House committee actions as a cave-in to big business lobbies and termed the gas deregulation vote "a ripoff" of consumers.

● **July 11:** The House Banking Committee reported a bill (HR 7893 — H Rept 95-488, Part I) on Carter's non-tax proposals for home insulation.

● **July 13:** The House Public Works Committee favorably reported Carter provisions for solar equipment in federal buildings (H Rept 95-496, Part I).

The House Government Operations Committee filed its report (HR 6831 — H Rept 95-496, Part II) approving Carter's call for a van pooling program to transport federal workers to and from work.

The House Ways and Means Committee filed its report (HR 6831 — H Rept 95-496, Part III) on the tax portions of Carter's energy plan.

● **July 19:** The House Commerce Committee filed its report (HR 6831 — H Rept 95-496, Part IV) generally approving the non-tax parts of the Carter plan.

● **July 20-22:** The House Ad Hoc Energy Committee rushed through the five-part Carter energy measure as a clean bill (HR 8444), with few amendments.

● **July 25:** The Senate Energy Committee filed its report (S 977 — S Rept 95-361) on a greatly modified version of Carter's non-tax proposals designed to force electric utilities and major industrial plants to burn coal and other fuels instead of oil and natural gas.

● **Aug. 1:** The Senate Energy Committee report (S 2057 — S Rept 95-409) was filed on a bill rolling together a broad range of generally non-controversial, non-tax portions of Carter's energy conservation plans.

● **Aug. 5:** The House passed HR 8444, 244-177, after five days of debate. As passed, the measure was very similar to the program proposed by Carter.

● **Sept. 8:** The Senate voted 74-8 to pass S 977, the modified coal conversion bill, then attached the measure to a minor House-passed bill (HR 5146).

● **Sept. 13:** The Senate voted 78-4 to pass the generally non-controversial energy conservation bill (S 2057), then attached the measure to a minor House-passed bill (HR 5037) to speed conference action.

● **Sept. 15:** The Senate Energy Committee filed its report (S 2104 — S Rept 95-436) on natural gas pricing. The committee split 9-9 on the issue and included no recommendation to the Senate.

● **Sept. 19:** The Senate Energy Committee reported a bill (S 2114 — S Rept 95-442) aimed at encouraging utilities to conserve energy but which dropped virtually all of Carter's proposed utility rate reforms.

The Senate Energy Committee voted 13-1 to urge the Finance Committee to kill Carter's proposed crude oil equalization tax, termed the program's "centerpiece" by administration spokesmen.

The Senate began debate on natural gas pricing. Sens. James Abourezk (D S.D.) and Howard M. Metzenbaum (D Ohio) launched a filibuster.

● **Oct. 3:** Senate Majority Leader Robert C. Byrd (D W.Va.), working with Vice President Walter F. Mondale, shut down the filibuster in a controversial manipulation of Senate rules.

● **Oct. 4:** The Senate voted 50-46 to pass S 2104, providing for an end to federal price regulation over natural gas sales, a major defeat for Carter. The measure was then attached to a minor House-passed bill (HR 5289).

● **Oct. 13:** Carter told a nationally televised press conference that rebuffs to his energy program smacked of "potential war profiteering in the impending energy crisis" and could lead to "the biggest ripoff in history."

● **Oct. 18:** The House-Senate conference on the non-tax portions of the five part energy bill began work on the least controversial section — the catchall measure (HR 5037) to stimulate energy conservation.

● **Oct. 21:** The Senate Finance Committee voted 13-5 to report a bill (HR 5263 — S Rept 95-529) which rolled together a mixture of tax credits for energy conservation and production but which ignored Carter's complex energy tax proposals.

● **Oct. 27:** The Senate voted 51-37 to adopt a scaled down version of Carter's proposed tax on utility and industrial use of oil and natural gas.

● **Oct. 31:** The Senate voted 52-35 to pass the energy tax bill (HR 5263), which bore little resemblance to Carter's proposals.

The non-tax conferees agreed on most of the energy conservation programs in the catchall bill (HR 5037), but did not decide what to do about Senate-passed terms banning production of certain gas-guzzling cars.

● **Nov. 7:** The State Department confirmed reports that Carter had cancelled a world tour to stay in Washington through Thanksgiving to press for enactment of his energy program.

● **Nov. 8:** Carter made a nationally televised evening address designed to pressure congressional energy conferees to reach agreement.

● **Nov. 11:** House and Senate conferees on the non-tax portions of the Carter program agreed to terms aimed at forcing utilities and industries to convert from oil and natural gas to coal and other fuels (HR 5146).

● **Nov. 17:** House and Senate tax conferees left Washington for an 11-day Thanksgiving holiday.

● **Nov. 18:** Conferees on the non-tax portions of the plan left Washington for a 10-day Thanksgiving holiday.

Slow Progress in Congress

●**Dec. 1:** House and Senate conferees on the non-tax portions reached final agreement on terms designed to foster reform of electric utility rates. The agreement was far weaker than terms proposed by Carter.

●**Dec. 2:** Non-tax conferees began deliberations on natural gas pricing.

●**Dec. 7:** Tax conferees agreed to impose a tax on certain "gas guzzling" cars, provided the other conferees abandoned terms banning production of such cars. The tax conferees then adjourned indefinitely after 11 days of meetings.

●**Dec. 22:** House and Senate conferees on the non-tax portions of the bill adjourned for Christmas.

1978

●**Jan. 6:** Energy Secretary James R. Schlesinger flew to Palm Springs, Calif., to consult with Senate Energy Chairman Henry M. Jackson (D Wash.).

●**Jan. 8:** Schlesinger announced that Jackson had pledged to try to end the impasse over gas pricing.

●**Jan. 11:** Sen. Lee Metcalf (D Mont.) died. His death altered the 9-9 split among the 18 Senate conferees on natural gas pricing, leaving a 9-8 majority favoring an end to price controls.

●**March 7:** After three months of closed door meetings, nine Senate conferees on natural gas pricing announced agreement on a compromise.

March 9: Carter told a news conference he would accept legislation providing for a phased end to federal price regulation of natural gas, reversing the position he had held since announcing his energy program

●**March 22:** House and Senate conferees on natural gas pricing held their first public meeting since Dec. 22, 1977. The meeting produced a 10-7 Senate vote for one compromise plan and a 13-12 House vote for an alternative compromise.

●**April 13:** The House voted 371-6 to protest the continued secret meetings of key conferees on natural gas pricing, demanding that the sessions be public.

●**April 21:** A group of House and Senate conferees announced, after another month of closed door sessions, that they had reached agreement on a new compromise plan to end federal regulation of natural gas sales.

●**May 4:** House and Senate conferees on gas pricing held their second public meeting of the year but did not vote on the April 21 compromise plan, apparently because its backers did not have the support of a majority of the House conferees.

●**May 9:** House Speaker Thomas P. O'Neill Jr. (D Mass.) announced for the first time that he was considering splitting the five-part energy bill.

●**May 23:** House conferees voted 13-12 in favor of the April 21 natural gas pricing agreement after adopting some amendments to it.

●**May 24:** Natural gas pricing conferees, meeting in their third public session of the year, narrowly approved the April 21 compromise agreement on gas deregulation. The vote was 10-7 among Senate conferees and 13-12 among House conferees.

Federal agencies were directed to purchase 6,000 vans for federal employees to commute in to demonstrate the economics of car-pooling. Costs would be repaid by riders.

Nuclear, Non-Conventional Power

Nuclear. The administration's indefinite deferment of programs for nuclear fuel reprocessing, use of plutonium for fuel and construction of a demonstration breeder reactor were reaffirmed.

Legislation was requested to guarantee sale of enriched uranium to countries agreeing to conditions concerning nuclear non-proliferation. Plans were announced to increase domestic uranium enrichment capacity and build a more efficient centrifuge enrichment technology plant. Safety and inspection standards for conventional nuclear power plants would be strengthened and the licensing process sped up.

Solar, Geothermal Energy. A tax credit of 40 per cent for the first $1,000 and 25 per cent for the next $6,400 would be extended for installation costs of solar equipment by homeowners. The credit would decline over time and be applicable through 1984.

Carter proposed tax deductions to stimulate geothermal drilling and increased funding for research on non-conventional energy technologies.

Buildings

Homeowners Tax Credit. Congress was asked to give homeowners a tax credit of 25 per cent of the first $800 and 15 per cent of the next $1,400 spent on approved conservation home improvements. The credit would apply for improvements from April 20, 1977, to 1985.

Utility Insulation Program. Legislation was requested mandating utilities to offer home insulation financed by loans repaid through monthly utility bills.

Federal Loans. Carter asked Congress to cut red tape to improve access to loans for home energy conservation improvements through federal mortgage programs.

Weatherization. The Carter budget would increase federal funding for low-income weatherization programs to $130-million in fiscal 1978 and $200-million in fiscal 1979 and 1980. Also the Agriculture Department was directed to implement a rural home weatherization program.

Business Tax Credit. Congress was asked to enact a 10 per cent tax credit for approved conservation improvements by business.

Schools, Hospitals. Carter requested a federal grants program be funded at up to $300-million per year for three years to help public schools and nonprofit hospitals install conservation measures.

Mandatory Standards. The Secretary of Housing and Urban Development was required to develop mandatory efficiency standards for new buildings by 1980 instead of 1981.

Other Aspects

Appliances. Congress was asked to make voluntary appliance efficiency standards mandatory for home appliances like air conditioners, furnaces and water heaters.

Industrial Conservation. Carter asked Congress to enact a five year, 10 per cent investment tax credit for industrial investment in approved equipment such as solar heaters, in addition to the current 10 per cent credit.

Cogeneration. In a new legislative proposal, Carter asked enactment of a special 10 per cent tax credit for industrial investment in cogeneration equipment, a process much used in Europe which utilizes industrial heat waste to generate energy.

Utility Rate Reform. Congress was asked to ban declining block rate structures that promote electricity consumption. Utilities would be required to offer peak use pricing rates to customers willing to pay meter costs.

Energy Information. In an administrative action, the proposed Department of Energy, once created, would take over audit and verification functions currently performed by the American Gas Association and the American Petroleum Institute. Oil and gas companies would be required to submit detailed data on their operations to the government.

1978 Developments

Six months after their first meeting, House and Senate conferees on natural gas pricing broke their deadlock by accepting a proposal for deregulation that even supporters said they didn't like.

The final votes May 24 on the compromise plan, which would remove price controls by 1985 on newly discovered natural gas, were far from dramatic as weary conferees cast their ballots just as House and Senate leaders had predicted.

But the agreement was high drama in that it removed a major obstacle to further action on President Carter's languishing energy plan. The President praised the conferees' "historic agreement" and predicted it would cost consumers "no more than they would pay if today's inadequate regulatory system were to be maintained."

The beleaguered natural gas pricing compromise appeared to be unraveling July 31 when conferees were presented with the formal, staff-drawn language embodying the principles the conferees thought they had agreed to. Several of the conferees who had agreed to the compromise refused to sign. But on Aug. 17 a majority of the House and Senate conferees signed the agreement, in part a result of a last-minute personal appeal from Carter.

Despite the conferees' accord, the agreement faced obstacles when it reached the floor of both chambers, where opponents — those who opposed deregulation and those who wanted the controls lifted immediately — promised they would try to defeat it.

In the compromise, controls on newly discovered natural gas would be lifted by 1985. But Congress could reinstate controls for an 18-month period until mid-1987. The gradual increase in the price of interstate gas that was written into the agreement was expected to bring gas prices up to $3.75 per thousand cubic feet by late 1985, just before decontrol. The existing price ceiling on interstate gas was $1.49 per thousand cubic feet.

Despite the tentative agreement on natural gas deregulation, other aspects of the energy package hung in limbo in mid-1978. The House and Senate continued to take widely different positions on the tax provisions of Carter's plan. The House backed a tax on crude oil that would bring the controlled price of domestically produced oil up to the world price by 1980. But the Senate, instead of a tax, offered industry tax credits as an incentive for increasing energy production.

In addition, although both House and Senate energy conferees wanted to discourage production of big cars that

waste gas, they could not agree on how to do it. Senate conferees wanted to ban by 1980 the production of cars getting less than 16 miles to the gallon. But the House conferees preferred Carter's proposal to tax "gas guzzling" cars. As of July 1978, no agreement had been reached.

In a setback for another feature of the administration's energy policy, the Senate June 27, 1978, voted to block the President from imposing either fees or quotas on oil imports. Carter had threatened repeatedly to impose such fees to spur energy conservation when Congress failed to act on his proposal to impose a tax on purchases of domestic crude oil. Under the administration's proposal, the tax would be phased in over three years. It was designed to gradually drive up the government-controlled price of domestically produced oil — $9.55 per average 1977 barrel — to the higher price of foreign oil. The higher prices would be designed to cut energy consumption, and thereby lower demand for foreign oil.

The Senate action came less than three weeks before the President's economic summit conference with Western allies starting July 16 in Bonn. Carter had been criticized by Western leaders for failing to cut U.S. oil imports. Carter allies feared the Senate vote would further weaken the President in dealing with foreign governments. Senate Energy Committee Chairman Henry M. Jackson (D Wash.) criticized the Senate move as "ill-timed" and said it would restrict Carter at a time of sensitive international negotiations. "To severely limit the President's options before the tax bill is complete and on the eve of his departure to the economic summit would unnecessarily damage the prospects for success at the summit and underscore our energy paralysis for the rest of the world," Jackson said.

At the July economic summit, Carter stated that a commitment to a comprehensive energy policy was necessary because "the price of oil is too cheap in our own country," and he pledged that the United States would raise the price of domestic oil to the world level by 1980 as well as promising to reduce U.S. oil imports by 2.5 million barrels a day by 1985. Nonetheless, the President was not specific about how this would be accomplished. And although Senate Majority Leader Robert C. Byrd (D W.Va.) July 16 predicted that the Senate would pass an energy bill by the end of the 1978 session, the prospects for an overall energy package remained dim.

By mid-August the Senate had passed two parts of the package — the coal conversion bill requiring some utilities and factories to switch to burning coal instead of oil and gas — by a vote of 92-6 on July 18. Urging passage of that bill (HR 5146), Byrd said, "This action comes at a very timely moment, when the President needs something to show Europeans and leaders of other countries...." He added that his own talks with foreign leaders had convinced him that they viewed Congress as "a stumbling block" to enactment of Carter's energy plan.

On Aug. 23 the Senate approved legislation giving homeowners tax credits for installing energy conservation devices. The measure would provide a tax credit — which is subtracted directly from the total taxes owed — of up to $400 for outlays for conservation devices such as storm windows and insulation. For solar, wind and geothermal energy devices, it would provide a tax credit of up to $2,200. The energy conservation provisions were attached as an amendment to a minor tax bill.

Attempts to Stem Soaring Hospital Costs

President Carter singled out hospital costs as the first target in his drive to put the brakes on skyrocketing health care costs in the United States.

Despite the opposition of much of the hospital industry and a lukewarm reception from Congress, Carter proposed legislation April 25, 1977, to limit hospital cost increases to 9 percent in fiscal 1978, with smaller increases in subsequent years until a different system for paying hospitals could be implemented.

The legislation also would set a $2.5-billion-a-year limit on new hospital building nationwide, to be allocated among the states on the basis of population. Any area with surplus hospital beds—about 80 per cent of the nation's hospital service areas—would be prohibited from adding any new ones.

In a message to Congress, Carter called for quick approval of the program so that it could go into effect Oct. 1, 1977, the start of the 1978 fiscal year.

However, by the end of 1977, only one of the four committees with jurisdiction over the plan had reported the bill—Senate Human Resources. The Senate Finance Committee appeared more interested in an alternative bill introduced by Herman E. Talmadge (D Ga.). In the House, subcommittees of the Ways and Means and Interstate and Foreign Commerce Committees had marked up bills but full committee action was put over until 1978.

Meanwhile, Health, Education and Welfare (HEW) Secretary Joseph A. Califano Jr. said, inflation in hospital costs was rising at the rate of $24-million a day, or a million dollars an hour. He did not accuse Congress of deliberate sabotage of the President's program, but he did point out: "....Not moving the legislation promptly is like throwing money away."

Yet despite these pleas, Congress had not enacted a cost control bill by mid-1978. Indeed, in July, the House Commerce Committee junked the administration's plan and voted instead to endorse a voluntary effort by hospitals to reduce their costs. On Aug. 3, the Senate Finance Committee reported a bill that mandated cost controls for Medicare and Medicaid only.

Carter April 1977 Message

Carter predicted his hospital cost containment program could save $2-billion in fiscal 1978 in federal, state, private individual and health insurance costs. Total savings would exceed $5.5-billion in fiscal 1980, he said.

"These savings will slow a devastating inflationary trend, which doubles health costs every five years," Carter said. U.S. health costs would reach $160-billion in 1977, the President said—almost 9 per cent of the gross national product. Hospital costs were the largest component of the total health care bill—about 40 per cent—and had been rising at a rate of 15 per cent a year, 2½ times the increase in the Consumer Price Index.

"For the federal budget, rising health spending has meant a tripling of health outlays over the last eight years,"

Carter noted. Without immediate action, federal payments for Medicare and Medicaid, which pay health care costs for elderly and low-income persons, would jump nearly 23 per cent in fiscal 1978, to $32-billion, he said.

"The cost of [health] care is rising so rapidly it jeopardizes our health goals and our other important social objectives," Carter said.

One of those goals, expressed by Carter often during the 1976 presidential campaign and reiterated April 25, was a national health insurance program. Carter said national health insurance could not be implemented until the runaway health care inflation had been controlled. The hospital cost containment proposal was the first step.

Background

It was only in recent years that health experts and federal officials realized that health care costs were out of control and attempted to deal with them.

According to the President's Council on Wage and Price Stability (COWPS), health care costs jumped to an estimated $140-billion in 1976 from $12-billion in 1950. This translated to 8.6 per cent of the gross national product (GNP) in 1976, compared to 4.6 per cent in 1950.

Some lowering of cost increases was accomplished during President Nixon's economic stabilization program of the early 1970s, a program which left bitter memories for many health care providers. But the increase from 1974 to 1975, following the lifting of controls, was $14.5-billion, the single biggest increase in the nation's history, according to COWPS.

President Ford in 1976 proposed limits on hospital and doctor charges paid out of pocket by elderly Medicare patients as well as reimbursement limits for hospitals and physicians. However, he coupled that proposal with a requirement that the patients pay more of their own bills for short-term care. That provision was uniformly opposed by witnesses, and the whole proposal never got beyond the hearing stage in Congress.

While Congress continued to increase federal spending on health care programs through the years, a growing number of people began to question whether all the spending had made Americans any healthier and whether the country could afford to continue paying the soaring projected costs. Some estimates indicated an uncontrolled health sector could cost $265-billion by 1981.

Arguments raged as to who was to blame for rising costs. Bureaucrats blamed doctors, doctors blamed hospitals, and hospitals claimed they were merely providing the "quality care" that Americans demanded.

Hospital Costs

Statistics released by the Department of Health, Education and Welfare (HEW) April 25 indicated that the cost of one day's stay in a hospital had risen 1,000 per cent since 1950. The cost was $175.08 a day in 1976, compared to

$15.62 in 1950, according to the Council on Wage and Price Stability.

Hospitals noted that the prices they must pay for the goods and services they buy had been increasing because of inflation in recent years—wages paid to employees, food and fuel costs, medical malpractice premiums and equipment costs. They also charged that dealing with a proliferation of overlapping federal and state regulations added to their costs.

Critics admitted that hospitals had faced rising costs, like the rest of the population, but charged that the way the system operated had led many hospitals to be inefficient, causing costs to rise unnecessarily.

"Hospitals are unlike any other segment of our economy," noted HEW Secretary Joseph A. Califano Jr. April 25. "There is absolutely no competition among them." Doctors, not the consumers, select what services are to be given, and in most cases third parties (insurers or the government) pay whatever bills are submitted, so hospitals have no incentive to control costs, he said, adding: "Hospitals have become, over the years, many of them, quite obese.... They are not trim."

Under the existing "retrospective cost reimbursement" system, hospitals were paid for the bills they submitted to insurance companies or federal or state programs such as Medicare and Medicaid. As a December 1976 COWPS study stated, "there is little provider incentive to resist higher input prices and requests for larger quantities of labor [or] supplies..." since all bills are reimbursed after the fact.

Excess Capacity. Coupled with this was the problem of excess capacity. In short, there were too many hospital beds in the United States. HEW estimated that of the nation's 947,000 hospital beds, 200,000 were unfilled at any given time and 100,000 of them were totally unnecessary.

Part of this problem was due to the hospital construction encouraged by federal funding programs such as the Hill-Burton Act of 1946. Hospitals were built with little planning as to whether or not they should be as large as they were, or even whether they were needed at all, critics charged.

Hospitals also had high capital construction costs, that must be paid over long periods of time. These costs add on to the other daily costs, such as labor and food, of a hospital bed and must be paid whether or not a bed is filled. Califano said each excess bed cost $20,000 a year to maintain; eliminating 100,000 of them thus would save $2-billion a year.

It was not until 1974 that Congress passed legislation (PL 93-641) requiring that hospitals obtain permission, called a certificate of need, from state health agencies before being allowed to build new facilities. The program was still in its infancy, however, and not yet fully functional throughout the country.

Equipment Costs. Another factor in high-cost hospital care was the tendency of hospitals to buy increasingly expensive and sophisticated equipment. No hospital wanted to have outdated equipment, to be unable to provide "quality" care.

A 1976 report by Ralph Nader's Health Research Group said that many hospital services may not be needed at all. "Because of their desire to attract or keep medical staff members and to enhance the reputation of their institution," the report said, "hospital administrations buy high-technology equipment and facilities, such as $500,000 CAT (computerized axial tomography) scanners and open-

heart surgery units which they don't need or could share with other hospitals."

Doctors' Fees

Hospital costs increases were not totally responsible for runaway health care costs, however. Physicans' fees increased almost 12 per cent in 1975—close to the 15 per cent recorded for hospitals.

Physicians, like hospitals, said they had been beset with rising costs for the goods they must purchase, the medical malpractice insurance they must buy, the extra personnel they must hire to fill out increasing numbers of government regulatory forms.

But physicians were in a unique position of authority in regard to health care in the United States. "The physician's diagnosis determines the extent to which his or her own services are required as well as the utilization of diagnostic tests, therapeutic drugs and hospitals," the COWPS study noted.

Physicians also control some of the hospital cost component, since it is their decision whether to admit a patient or not that helps determine the number of excess beds in a hospital at any given time.

A contributing factor to this problem was that many insurance policies only will cover medical care performed while the patient is in the hospital. In order to oblige the patient, who does not wish to pay for care that could be covered by the insurance company, the physician will admit him to the hospital even if the procedure could be accomplished as an outpatient.

Physicians also were practicing more "defensive" medicine, due to the rapid rise in malpractice claims—ordering more lab tests, X-rays and examinations than may be necessary in order to have protection from liability. In an American Medical Association poll published March 28, 1977, three out of four U.S. physicians said they practiced defensive medicine. The extra cost of the unnecessary tests was unknown, but some estimates said it could be billions of dollars.

Other Factors

The public, most of whom are patients at one time or another, also contributed to spiraling health care costs. Many persons abdicated much of the consumer savvy they showed in other transactions once they became patients.

Peter H. Schuck of Consumers Union told COWPS that because of their lack of knowledge of relative prices and alternative methods of care, patients tend not to question their physicians' decisions. Since they cannot judge what really produces good health, they become preoccupied with the proliferating expensive technology, he said. The result is the belief that " 'first class' care can be delivered only at 'first class' prices."

Health Insurance. Some health experts blamed soaring medical bills on the fact that an increasing number of Americans were covered by health insurance programs in which the majority of the bill was paid not by the patient, but by the third-party intermediary. More than 90 per cent of all hospital costs were paid for by someone other than the patients, according to HEW.

In addition to private insurance programs, which had been growing since the 1930s, the federal government stepped into the picture in 1966 with Medicare and Medicaid. These programs expanded the access of large numbers of elderly and low-income Americans to medical care and greatly increased the federal government's share of national health care expenditures.

Economists warned that this increase in third-party coverage, whether through private or government insurance programs, isolated the public from the reality of health care costs. Since the patient does not pay the bill directly, or only a small portion of it, he tends to overuse medical services or does not question services that are ordered for him.

Health Habits. Finally, the American life-style was blamed by some for driving health care costs up. Some health experts warned that until Americans realized that their lack of exercise, their high-fat, high-sugar diet and overuse of cigarettes and alcohol were ruining their health, they would continue to run up medical bills for unnecessary physical ailments.

Carter Proposal

With all of these problems facing the American health care industry, economists and other experts warned that the major problem was the seemingly unlimited supply of money available to health care providers. As Prof. Stuart H. Altman of the University of California, Berkeley, told the Senate Budget Committee March 11, 1977: "Only when a constraint is put on the availability of funds to providers will there be [serious] discussions about which services are really necessary."

President Carter chose to start with closing somewhat the tap of funds flowing to hospitals. The proposal was first made in Carter's Feb. 22, 1977, budget revisions. The detailed formula was released in the April 25 message to Congress.

Hospital Cost Controls

As proposed by Carter, controls would be limited to inpatient reimbursement of acute care hospitals only. There would be no cap on outpatient services; the administration said they were less costly and should be encouraged.

HEW said the plan would affect about 6,000 community hospitals. Hospitals for long-term care (mainly mental hospitals) and hospitals operated by health maintenance organizations would be exempt because they were not experiencing high cost increases, HEW said. Hospitals less than two years old and federal hospitals also were not included. Califano said the President would apply the cost controls to Veterans Administration and other federal hospitals by administrative order.

Cap Formula. HEW devised a formula that would permit any hospital included in the plan to increase its revenue from all sources, including private insurance companies, Medicare, Medicaid, and individuals paying their own bills, up to 9 per cent during the first year. In subsequent years, the formula would cut back allowable increases.

The formula was based on general price trends in the economy as a whole, plus an additional amount to cover some increase in patient services. The formula would be applied to the dollar total of the hospital's revenue from each payor for 1976, with an adjustment made for 1977, and would be applied on a per-admission basis.

Hospitals with no changes in patient load would have to hold down their charges so that their total annual revenue did not rise more than 9 per cent above their base-year earnings. The plan did provide for small changes in patient load, up to a 2 per cent increase in patient admissions or a 6 per cent decrease.

HEW said that Medicare, Medicaid and Blue Cross already had interim payment schedules in effect that would also be used in the new plan. Should hospital administrators find changes occurring in their patient load during the year, the third-party payors would be readjusting their reimbursements on a per-admission basis to ensure that hospitals stayed within the 9 per cent cap.

Penalties. At the end of the year, if total revenue received exceeded the 9 per cent limit, hospitals would be required to put the excess amount in escrow and reduce charge increases during the next year by the same amount. Failure to do so would subject the hospital to a tax equal to 150 per cent of the violation.

Exceptions. Exceptions to the total revenue limit would be allowed only for hospitals with exceptional changes in patient load or major increases in capacity, types of services or major renovation. Such exceptions would have to be approved by local and state health planning agencies and HEW. The revenue limit could also be adjusted for wage increases to non-supervisory personnel, who Califano said were earning wages about 10 per cent below the median wage for other non-agricultural workers.

Hospitals could also be exempted from the program if they were in states that had their own hospital cost containment programs in which 90 per cent of the state's hospitals were included, and other criteria were met.

Other Provisions. Other provisions would require hospitals to maintain their share of non-paying charity patients and to make public their current charge schedules and cost-reimbursement reports.

Capital Expenditures

Carter's second major proposal would limit new hospital capital expenditures to $2.5-billion nationally for the first year. The funds would be distributed to states according to population and new projects would have to obtain certificates of need from state planning agencies.

Certificates of need that would result in a net increase in beds would be denied in areas where the number of hospital beds exceeded four per 1,000 persons or the average hospital occupancy rate was less than 80 per cent. HEW said existing bed-shortage areas were mainly in the southwestern and south central parts of the United States.

Administration Defense

Carter and Califano defended the plan at a White House briefing April 25, 1977, as a necessary and workable program to control spiraling health care costs.

They said the program would not result in additional, massive bureaucracy or record-keeping, since HEW could "use essentially the information we are getting on Medicare and Medicaid forms right now."

They also said the program was intended as a transitional system until a long-term prospective reimbursement system could be devised that would not take a hospital's base cost as a given and would provide greater incentives to the most efficient hospitals. Califano said a report on such a revised program would be ready by March 1978.

Califano said the April 25 proposal was "eminently fair" and denied that it was a form of price control.

"We are permitting the hospital administrators to make all the decisions as to what they charge for, what they

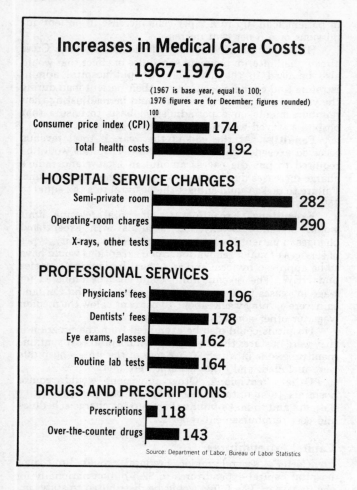

Increases in Medical Care Costs
1967-1976

(1967 is base year, equal to 100;
1976 figures are for December; figures rounded)

Consumer price index (CPI) **174**
Total health costs **192**

HOSPITAL SERVICE CHARGES

Semi-private room **282**
Operating-room charges **290**
X-rays, other tests **181**

PROFESSIONAL SERVICES

Physicians' fees **196**
Dentists' fees **178**
Eye exams, glasses **162**
Routine lab tests **164**

DRUGS AND PRESCRIPTIONS

Prescriptions **118**
Over-the-counter drugs **143**

Source: Department of Labor, Bureau of Labor Statistics

According to McMahon, hospital accounting practices would make it impossible to find out whether or not a hospital had stayed under the 9 per cent ceiling on revenues until the end of the year, when it would be too late. He also opposed the tax penalty imposed "if you guess wrong" in any given year; he said the tax would just make it more expensive to run hospitals.

The director of the Federation of American Hospitals (FAH), Michael D. Bromberg, called the Carter plan "unfair and arbitrary...nothing more than a camouflaged version of the Nixon Phase IV controls."

Bromberg said the FAH, which represented investor-owned rather than community hospitals, supported legislation sponsored by Talmadge. That bill, a revision of legislation introduced in the 94th Congress, would "provide for an incentive payment system offering economic rewards for efficiency," Bromberg said. *(Talmadge proposal, p. 103)*

The American Medical Association hit strongly at the quality-of-care theme. Its executive vice president, Dr. James Sammons, said April 22, "The medical profession is concerned about the cost of health care, but we cannot be concerned only with the cost in terms of dollars. We must also consider whether the 'lid' on spending means we can buy only second-rate care and whether some care may simply become unavailable for many people."

Califano responded to such criticism at a press conference April 27: "There is absolutely no danger of any decline in the quality of care of anyone going to a hospital."

Congressional Response, Bills, Action

Although the response from Congress was less antagonistic than from the health care sector, it was also not enthusiastic. Most congressional health care leaders supported the purpose of the legislation—controlling skyrocketing hospital costs—but were cautious about endorsing the specific provisions of the Carter plan.

The bill was introduced in both the House and Senate April 25. The House bill (HR 6575) was introduced by Paul G. Rogers (D Fla.), chairman of the House Interstate and Foreign Commerce Subcommittee on Health and the Environment, and Dan Rostenkowski (D Ill.), chairman of the Ways and Means Subcommittee on Health. The subcommittees shared jurisdiction over the legislation.

The Senate bill (S 1391) was introduced by Edward M. Kennedy (D Mass.), William D. Hathaway (D Maine) and Wendell R. Anderson (D Minn.). Kennedy's Human Resources Subcommittee on Health and Scientific Research had jurisdiction over parts of the bill. Hathaway was a member of the Senate Finance Committee, whose Subcommittee on Health had jurisdiction over the majority of it.

Most congressional observers agreed that the key person in Congress, whose action, or lack of it, would most directly affect the outcome of Carter's proposal, was Talmadge, chairman of the Finance Subcommittee on Health.

Talmadge did not cosponsor the Carter proposal and declined to be interviewed on the subject. Other congressional sources said that if Talmadge did not push the Carter proposal, House leaders would not do so either.

Talmadge introduced his own bill (S 1470) May 5, 1977. He had sponsored a similar bill in 1976.

While Talmadge claimed his bill was not competitive with the Carter plan, he did make clear that he considered it a "long-term basic structural answer to the problem of rising hospital costs" while the Carter proposal was simply a

don't charge for, and how much they charge for it," he said. There would be no item-by-item federal limitation on services, he said.

He added, however, that the program would encourage hospitals to "cut some of the fat" out of their budgets. Califano said hospitals could be more energy-efficient, for example, could share expensive equipment instead of duplicating it, and could cut out excess beds.

"There is no incentive on the hospitals in this country today to operate more efficiently," Califano said. "We hope this legislation will provide that."

Reaction

As expected, the Carter proposal was sharply criticized by members of the health care industry, who generally asserted that the quality of hospital care would suffer because of the cost cap.

J. Alexander McMahon, president of the American Hospital Association (AHA), told Congressional Quarterly, "The real victims of this bill are the sick and the injured." To McMahon the bill was "wrong in its concept and wrong in its details."

He charged that the revenue-per-admission requirement was "impossible" and would vastly increase the administrative costs of the federal government, private insurance companies and hospitals, contrary to HEW's claim that the plan would need little additional administration.

short-term solution until a permanent program could be implemented.

Talmadge said he was uncertain about the "wisdom" of an interim cap proposal and that he had not yet made up his mind about the Carter plan. He said he was concerned about four things:

● The cap could become the floor for future increases.

● The cap could prove ineffective as a ceiling because of all the exceptions in the plan.

● The cap proposal was arbitrary and penalized those who were efficient in the past while it rewarded those who were inefficient.

● A switch from the current system to a cap system for one or two years and then to a permanent program such as prospective reimbursement "may cause such chaos within the hospital field as to cancel out the dubious savings involved."

Talmadge's bill was cosponsored by a high-powered group of Finance Committee members, including the chairman, Russell B. Long (D La.), and the ranking Democrat and Republican on the Health Subcommittee, Abraham Ribicoff (Conn.) and Robert Dole (Kan.).

Dole spoke in support of the Talmadge bill May 5, calling it "a responsible alternative to the Carter cost containment plan."

Dole said the main problem with the Carter plan was the arbitrary limit it placed on hospital revenue increases without corresponding limits on the goods and services hospitals must purchase. "It is unrealistic and inequitable to expect our health care institutions to bear the entire burden of alleviating the rising health costs problem," he said. The Talmadge bill, on the other hand, would encourage what savings were possible, Dole added, "while maintaining a realistic view of changes which providers are and are not able to make."

While Kennedy introduced the Carter bill in the Senate, he said he had certain reservations about it. For example, he said he thought any cost-control system should have better incentives to encourage greater use of less expensive outpatient facilities, better methods for cutting down on overuse of services and for encouraging physicians to order fewer expensive tests.

On the House side, Rogers said he had many of the same concerns as Kennedy, adding that reimbursement systems should provide hospitals with incentives to be more efficient and to close down facilities that are not needed.

An aide to Rogers told Congressional Quarterly that Rogers was concerned about the lack of incentives in the bill and preferred incentives to punishments such as the 150 percent tax. "He prefers the carrot to the stick in regulatory legislation," the aide said.

Kennedy, Rogers and Rostenkowski all said they were interested in examining various suggestions for cost control in hearings.

Despite the administration's pleas for quick action in 1977, only one full committee, Senate Human Resources, had signed off on a revised version of S 1391 drafted by Kennedy's subcommittee. In the House, Roger's subcommittee completed work on the legislation and reported a clean bill (HR 9717).

One provision adopted by Human Resources could add to the cost of the program. It would require that wage increases for hospital nonsupervisory personnel be "passed through," in effect raising the spending ceiling.

Under the pass-through concept, wage increases for these employees would not be subject to cost controls. The rationale was that these employees had been underpaid in recent years as compared to other sectors of the economy and should not be held at their wage level because of a cost control program.

Both revised versions took a less drastic approach to hospital operating costs than the original. Both retained the wage "pass-through" provision sought by labor, but only the Senate version made it mandatory — and it included a "loophole" big enough to have earned it labor's enmity. That was a provision that exempts from the federal law those states with their own cost control agencies. The Rogers bill would exempt fewer states than the Kennedy bill.

In other changes, the Rogers bill added financial incentives to encourage hospital cost-cutting, while the Kennedy bill placed a moratorium on new capital investment by hospitals.

A third panel, the Senate Finance Subcommittee on Health, did not hold hearings on the administration plan until late in 1977, focusing its efforts instead on a rate-setting measure (S 1470) for Medicare-Medicaid reimbursements that was crafted by Talmadge.

Meanwhile, the fourth committee with jurisdiction, Rostenkowski's Ways and Means Subcommittee on Health, split 7-6 on a number of preliminary votes. As 1977 drew to a close, Rostenkowski failed repeatedly to field a quorum—partly, as one observer speculates, because "he held all the Democratic proxies and the Republicans just didn't bother to come."

In part the delay was caused by the press of other House business, notably the massive energy and Social Security bills. Progress also was hampered by factors common to all the health committees—lack of enthusiasm for the bill and annoyance at the administration's alleged lobbying deficiencies.

Substantively complex, the bill was difficult to sell. A further liability was the calibre of its opponents—the well-financed hospital industry and medical establishment. Most "supporters" were lukewarm and, in the case of organized labor, decidedly frosty.

The legislation also suffered from implications that cost controls meant service cutbacks—a theme well orchestrated by the hospitals. Most members of Congress would rather give more than less health care to their constituents.

Finally, as one lobbyist for the elderly complained, "The administration didn't do the basic educational job for members of Congress and staff." And Kennedy publicly chastised Carter for not building a public constituency for the bill. All in all, in Rostenkowski's committee, "nobody liked the bill, and they didn't like everything in it," an aide reported.

Action in 1978

Administration lobbyists, privately conceding that they were spread too thin in 1977, promised "pull-out-all-the-stops" efforts in 1978 to win congressional support for the controversial measure. But early in the year, most congressional observers were predicting that the President would have to make substantial concessions to get a cost control law on the books. As one congressional aide said of the administration, "They'll have to give up a little pride of authorship."

Attention was refocused on the year-old hospital cost bill by its prominent place in the fiscal 1979 health budget,

Key Proponents of National Health Insurance . . .

President Carter in mid-1978 found himself between a rock — his campaign promise for national health insurance — and a very hard place.

That was the off-the-record explanation at the White House and on Capitol Hill for the conspicuous lack of an administration proposal, months after the administration began promising a plan "within weeks."

The Carter-prompted 1976 Democratic platform called for "a comprehensive national health insurance system with universal and mandatory coverage." Since then, burgeoning economic problems — inflation, high health care costs, a slowing national economy — and other developments such as expensive new Social Security taxes delayed action.

Late in 1977, the President and Health, Education and Welfare (HEW) Secretary Joseph A. Califano Jr. indicated that they thought 1978 would not be a good year to introduce national health insurance legislation. But the campaign promise didn't go away.

Sen. Edward M. Kennedy, D-Mass., the AFL-CIO and the United Auto Workers (UAW) began prodding Carter to make good on the pledge in 1978.

Carter agreed to produce a statement of principles, followed by draft legislation, in time for hearings and in time to make it a 1978 campaign issue. But the timetable had slipped so much that only a general statement had emerged by August 1978.

Organized labor, beginning to feel the crunch of costly health plans at the bargaining table, wanted a concrete proposal on the record, so it could press congressional candidates for commitments.

Kennedy, long a leading congressional advocate of universal, publicly financed health care — and about the only visible one in 1978, has said that Congress must act on the issue "within two years" or wait "another generation."

The high cost of health care makes early action critical, said Kennedy spokesman Thomas P. Southwick. Also, "the momentum is there now. We think we can pass a bill in 1979," Southwick said.

Many members of Congress and many of Carter's political and economic advisers do not share the perception. That fact was a major feature of the president's difficulties with the issue. Asked where the constituency was for national health insurance, Rep. Dan Rostenkowski, D-Ill., chairman of the House Ways and Means Health Subcommittee, said, "I don't see it."

Problems in 1978

The question of how to pay the medical bills of 218 million Americans has come to dominate discussions of a federalized health system, overshadowing longstanding concerns about benefits, access to care, maldistribution of services, and quality control.

Cost has always been an issue, but several factors have pushed it to new prominence. These are the main factors credited with giving the cost issue its prominence:

● Stunning acceleration in health care spending from public and private sources. The nation's aggregate medical bill has nearly doubled in six years, quadrupled in 15 years and increased more than eleven-fold since 1950, according to a Congressional Research Service (CRS) study. The estimated $180 billion that Americans will spend in 1978 on health care divides out to roughly $860 for every man, woman and child — "more than we spend for shelter or clothing and only $155 less than we spend for food," said Paul G. Rogers, D-Fla., chairman of the House Commerce Subcommittee on Health. In 1978 health care spending was expected to constitute nearly 9 percent of the gross national product, and economists warned that the economy could not tolerate a double-digit figure.

● The fact that existing federal insurance programs for the poor and aged have turned out to be immensely more expensive than original estimates. And the fact that a substantial portion of those expenses, according to HEW, represent waste, fraud and abuse does little to enhance the image of a universal federal health system.

Both Medicare and Medicaid incorporate the traditional fee-for-service payment mechanism — in effect, an open-ended arrangement instead of a closed, budgetable system. The president's budget estimated fiscal 1979 spending for Medicare and Medicaid at $42 billion, with a 60 percent increase by 1983.

At the same time, some critics of the existing system maintain that taxpayers are paying more for less. States have been cutting back on services they're willing to provide in the cost-sharing Medicaid system. And the hospitalization deductible that Medicare beneficiaries must pay themselves by 1978 had gone to $84, compared with $40 when the program was first enacted.

● The high visibility that Carter has given the cost issue by insisting that Congress regulate hospital revenues before consideration of national health insurance begins.

● The deep resistance in Congress to enacting the Carter hospital cost bill, which most observers read as a sign of the potential strength of opposition to an all-inclusive federal health system. Rostenkowski said he warned the president that cost containment legislation would be "the best barometer" for national health insurance.

● Upward-inching inflation, which had the president "deeply and increasingly concerned," according to a White House spokeswoman. That position made it politically difficult for Carter to propose a new program potentially as expensive as national health insurance. And according to various media reports, his economic advisers, led by Charles L. Schultze, chairman of the Council of Economic Advisers, have been telling him firmly that the country could not afford the program in 1978.

● The related problems of "Proposition 13 fever" in Congress and elsewhere. The California anti-tax vote has been interpreted in many ways, but not as a mandate for more government spending. And long before the California vote, congressional leaders had been warning Carter that he was overloading them with expensive, large-scale proposals.

. . . Criticize President's Health Plan Principles

Other Problems

The growth of third-party payments (by insurance companies or the federal government), the existence of federal programs for the aged and poor and the extent of health benefits for many workers tend to dilute the urgency of demand for universal coverage, proponents concede. Only 12 percent of Americans — about 22 million people — have neither public nor private health insurance, according to CRS.

Rostenkowski suggested that national health insurance has an "intermittent constituency. People want it when they're sick, when they see the hospital bill. There's a whole education process" that must take place before political pressure builds for the program, Rostenkowski said in an interview.

Another problem is that two existing programs to establish important elements of a national health system — resource planning and quality control — have had serious problems getting off the ground.

The Case for Early Action

Those who were pushing the president to act — principally Kennedy and UAW president Douglas Fraser — turned the cost equation back to front. They argued that the only way to control costs was to control all sources of payment, through a unitary national system.

White House health analyst Joseph N. Onek suggested that embedding cost containment within a national health plan could be the only way to get congressional approval for the measure, which suffered from its lack of a constituency. "Cost containment within a benefit plan is better than cost containment naked," Onek said.

Fraser conceded that auto workers did not lack for benefits. "Our members have the best health insurance of any group — but we pay dearly for that" at the bargaining table, he said. The more health benefits cost, the less employers can afford for increased wages, pensions and other benefits.

Fraser and other labor leaders are worried also by a trend toward employer/worker cost-sharing. The March 1978 United Mineworkers agreement required "co-payment" or deductibles from workers for negotiated benefits. For the first time mineworkers were required to pay part of their medical bills before coverage began.

Proponents also argue that the relatively low percentage of persons not covered by any health insurance masks some deep gaps in coverage. Health analysts say that the "working poor" account for the greatest number of people without protection. These are persons whose salaries are too low to permit purchase of private insurance but too high to allow them to participate in Medicaid.

Many low-income persons may in fact buy insurance, but in most cases what they can buy is inadequate — perhaps $20 a day against a $100- or $125-a-day hospital room charge, according to the House Commerce Oversight and Investigations Subcommittee, which has been looking at health insurance.

For Medicaid beneficiaries there are wide variations from state to state in what benefits are available.

Rep. Toby Moffett, D-Conn., cites out-of-pocket payments by the elderly to physicians as an argument for reforming reimbursement procedures. According to Moffett, those payments amounted to $562 million in 1976, up from $126 million in 1970.

CRS figures indicate that, in recent years, private health insurance has paid for less than half of consumer spending on personal health care.

"What happens with the elderly (without supplementary coverage) who need to be in nursing homes for more than 90 days is that they pay for it themselves, until they end up medically indigent and on the Medicaid rolls," said a House Commerce Subcommittee aide.

These deficits in coverage mean that there is a real constituency for national health insurance, although it may need development, according to proponents of early action. The way to build support, they say, is to have a presidential plan on the record. "The more you debate this, the more support you'll have," said Fraser.

Carter Outlines Health Plan Principles

On July 29, 1978, the Carter administration announced the broad outlines of a national health plan that placed equal emphasis on curbing medical costs and on assuring adequate health care for all Americans. Carter's 10 principles called for "comprehensive health care coverage" as well as "quality health care" for all citizens. The principles would require that any program reduce health costs and help fight inflation in general. The plan would involve no additional federal spending until fiscal 1983, and it would be phased in gradually. Financing would come from multiple sources, including federal financing and contributions from employers and employees as well as the private insurance industry.

As outlined by HEW Secretary Califano, the plan would guarantee all Americans insurance for basic health care, including short-term hospitalization, doctors' services and X-ray and laboratory tests. The gradual approach outlined by the administration — which meant that there would be no single comprehensive health care bill — was described by Califano as "a sensible, prudent way to proceed in developing a proposal on the most complicated piece of domestic legislation this administration will propose." In agreement, Walter J. McNerney, president of the Blue Cross and Blue Shield Associations, said, "the president is wise to focus on goals and objects and to proceed on an incremental basis in implementing programs."

But others sharply criticized the administration's program. Max Fine, executive director of the Committee for National Health Insurance, said the administration was already two years behind schedule on developing a national health policy and that the new initiative represented more "procrastination." And Sen. Kennedy and AFL-CIO president George Meany assailed the program as an inadequate "piecemeal" start on a national health insurance plan.

which registered a whopping $5-billion increase in Medicare and Medicaid payments even with the proposed cost cap enacted. Without the legislation, budget calculations showed, the two federal health programs would require about $730-million additional tax dollars.

The issue was further rekindled by Rostenkowski's Feb. 1, 1978, announcement that he would like to give hospitals a 12-month reprieve, to see if they could cut their costs voluntarily.

Rostenkowski's endorsement of voluntary efforts stemmed from his Nov. 2, 1977, challenge that the industry come up with a plan — by the second session of the 95th Congress — to police its runaway costs.

By Jan. 30 the industry had announced creation of a national steering committee and a network of state "medical and hospital committees." The major goal of the "Voluntary Effort," as the program was called, was to reduce the growth rate of hospital expenditures by 2 per cent the first year and by an additional 2 per cent the second year. The program's focus on hospital spending differed from the Carter targeting of hospital income. The Voluntary Effort was organized by the American Hospital Association, the Federation of American Hospitals and the American Medical Association.

Besides pruning hospital expenditures, the voluntary program set goals of "no net increases" in hospital beds and "restraint in new hospital capital investment." Implementation was left to the state committees, which were advised to provide technical assistance and use public disclosure and a certification procedure. As defined by a Voluntary Effort policy statement, certification meant that a hospital had formally agreed to comply with its state committee plan. Public disclosure meant "hearings at which hospitals not meeting the state goals would be scrutinized by the committee to determine whether their projected revenues or expenses were justified," with committee findings published afterwards.

It was this program that Rostenkowski proposed to let run for a year. But, he told a Washington meeting of the American Hospital Association Feb. 1, "since nothing stimulates volunteers more quickly than the genuine fear of a draft," he would also push for mandatory "fallback federal controls...to assist you" if the effort failed to achieve its own goals.

Ways and Means Compromise

Concessions to the hospital industry and a lobby fight that pitted the White House against organized labor finally dislodged a compromise version of the administration's cost control plan from the Ways and Means Subcommittee on Health. On Feb. 28, 1978, the panel voted 7-6 to send to the full committee a substitute bill (HR 6575) drafted by Rostenkowski.

The committee gave hospitals about a year to trim their spending voluntarily before a mandatory federal limit on revenue increases was imposed. The goal for the voluntary phase was to cut the annual growth rate of hospital spending from the 16 per cent level to 12 per cent within two years, with a constant rate thereafter. The mandatory phase, to be activated if the voluntary program failed, permitted 9 per cent growth in the first year, although adjustments could bring that figure to 12 per cent. By 1983 the permissible rate of increase under the mandatory program would drop to 10 per cent.

The earliest the mandatory program could take effect under the subcommittee bill was Jan. 1, 1979.

The compromise bill won no ardent converts in the subcommittee, where distaste for the measure reached across party lines. Neither the hospital industry nor organized labor found the bill acceptable. The Carter administration indicated its endorsement by not objecting strenuously in markup sessions, but HEW officials said they continued to hope for immediate mandatory controls.

Representatives of the American Hospital Association and the Federation of American Hospitals privately told members of the health panel that the compromise was even less palatable than the Carter original, because it seemed more likely to pass and because it undercut the voluntary drive to prune hospital spending increases. Organized labor found itself in the difficult position of supporting the objective of the bill, but fearing its consequences for low-paid hospital workers.

The Rostenkowski bill included the administration's optional wage pass-through feature that allowed upward adjustments in a hospital's revenue limit to accommodate wage hikes for these workers. But the fact that this feature was optional and would not apply in certain states made it unacceptable, according to spokesmen for the AFL-CIO and the American Federation of State, County and Municipal Employees (AFSCME), one of several affiliates representing non-supervisory hospital workers.

The Rostenkowski bill permitted state programs meeting certain standards to replace the federal program, leaving wage adjustments to those states. Labor wanted a mandatory wage adjustment in all states, spokesmen said.

Labor officials maintained that the handful of existing state hospital cost control programs had succeeded in holding cost increases in those states below the national average by skimping on wage increases.

Commerce Committee Action

Action by the full Ways and Means Committee was put off until the House Commerce Committee acted on its version of the bill. After getting off to a troubled start and temporarily withdrawing the bill from the committee agenda, the Commerce Committee began marking up its hospital cost legislation during the week of June 5. Like the Ways and Means bill, the Commerce Committee version would let hospitals try to police their costs, with standby federal controls on revenues if the industry failed to meet a national goal. To that plan the bill's sponsor, Rogers, added financial incentives for good performance and a $3-billion national cap for major capital expenditures on hospital construction and equipment. These features were carried over from the revised administration bill reported by Rogers' panel in 1977.

In the third week of markup on the bill, the House Commerce Committee by a one-vote margin (21-20) June 21 adopted an amendment that cut deeply into the bill's projected savings in hospital costs.

Rogers said the amendment would cut the bill's estimated savings potential from $30-billion over the next five years to $24-billion. But a Rogers aide said estimates by HEW and the Congressional Budget Office showed that the effect of the amendment would be far more dramatic than that, possibly wiping out any savings at all.

The amendment, offered by Dave Stockman (R Mich.), went to the heart of a basic but largely unarticulated assumption of the administration's controversial hospital bill: controlling rising hospital costs involves holding down increases in hospital admissions. Many health economists blamed double-digit inflation in hospital bills partly on efforts by some hospitals to fill their beds, with more concern for cash flow than medical needs of the patients. Commerce Health Subcommittee Chairman Rogers told committee members, for example, that a Las Vegas hospital was offering patients a chance to win an expensive vacation if they would check in for the weekend before their scheduled surgery.

The compromise bill proposed by Rogers included a complex formula for determining the allowable rate of reimbursement for hospitals under a mandatory federal program. (The mandatory program would take effect only if hospitals failed to police their own costs effectively enough to meet stipulated national goals.)

The original formula permitted some upward adjustments in the basic reimbursement rate if a hospital's patient load increased over its patient load in the base period against which hospital performance was to be measured. But these adjustments would not fully cover the extra costs to hospitals for their enlarged patient load.

Rogers said the adjustment was adequate because the costs for the extra patients would be proportionately less. But Stockman disagreed, maintaining that the formula would unfairly penalize hospitals, and thus patients, in areas experiencing rapid population growth. Stockman also disliked a second feature of the formula that would have provided some cash incentives for hospitals whose patient loads dropped after the base year.

What Stockman's complicated amendment did was to remove the financial disincentive in the original bill for a hospital increasing its patient load after the base year. Or, as its opponents explained it, the amendment created a strong incentive for hospitals to push admissions upward. Stockman's amendment also lessened the benefits to a hospital decreasing its patient load.

In a further defeat for the administration's anti-inflation efforts, the Commerce Committee July 18 gutted the hospital cost control bill even more deeply than it had on June 21 — making the outlook for passage of a comprehensive measure in 1978 exceedingly dim. By a vote of 22-21, the panel defeated the mandatory cost control provisions from the bill. The vote came on an amendment offered by James T. Broyhill (R N.C.) that called for a voluntary effort on the part of hospitals to control their costs. The committee then voted 15-12 to approve the remaining portions of the bill, which, in addition to calling for voluntary efforts, offered federal aid to state cost-control programs and established a national commission to study the issue.

"This simply guts the administration bill," said Rogers, adding that the committee "hasn't faced this problem responsibly." HEW Secretary Califano said the vote was a "defeat for the public interest and a victory for the special hospital interests." But Dr. Robert B. Hunter, chairman of the board of the AMA, said "The AMA is pleased to learn that the efforts of the private sector, through the voluntary effort and other cost-conscious programs, has been recognized by Congress. This kind of coordinated and cooperative effort between physicians and hospitals . . . is the only responsible approach to the continued delivery of quality health care."

Talmadge Starts Action on His Own Bill

After standing back for more than a year while three congressional committees struggled with the difficult Carter administration hospital cost control bill, Sen. Talmadge in mid-1978 was ready to move with his own hospital cost measure (S 1470).

At a sparsely attended June 21 session of his Finance Subcommittee on Health, Talmadge said he hoped for quick committee and Senate approval of a complex package of changes in the way Medicare and Medicaid pay hospitals and doctors. Talmadge said he planned to attach the bill to a minor piece of legislation already passed by the House so that the Senate could request an early conference. "We've been accused of foot-dragging" on hospital cost containment legislation, he told a June 20 session of the full Finance Committee.

The Talmadge proposal aimed at replacing the fee-for-service style of paying hospitals that has been used by Medicare and Medicaid with a pre-set, fixed-fee system. The fee-for-service system has been criticized by health economists because it provides powerful financial incentives for more hospitalizations and more treatments and tests. Talmadge proposed to gradually phase in a "prospective" payment system with different rates for different types of hospitals.

The Talmadge bill also trimmed federal payments to certain hospital-based physicians, such as pathologists. And it provided for financial incentives to encourage doctors not to charge Medicare patients more than the government will pay for them.

Although President Carter strongly endorsed an earlier version of the Talmadge bill during his presidential campaign, the administration in 1978 found it too narrow. Because the bill applied only to the two federal programs, hospitals could simply shift their excessive costs to "those who pay for care themselves, or through other third-party payors," according to an administration position paper.

Also, the suggested changes for physician charges do not go to the heart of the "inflationary and complex" system of paying doctors "customary, prevailing and reasonable" fees, the paper said.

The administration planned to offer its own physician reimbursement plan in its fiscal 1980 legislative package.

Talmadge indicated that he in turn was unimpressed with Carter's plan to impose a single national limit on the rate of growth for all hospital revenue. His own proposal, which distinguished between hospitals with different levels of expenditures and patient loads, was "more practical, more realistic and more equitable," Talmadge said.

It also appeared more do-able politically, because it had the qualified support of two leading opponents of the Carter plan, the Federation of American Hospitals and the American Hospital Association.

Talmadge's plan was however, bitterly opposed by organized labor because, of all the pending alternatives, it was the least favorable to blue-collar hospital workers.

Provisions of Talmadge Bill

These were the major elements of the Talmadge proposal, according to a Finance Committee staff paper based on the 1977 bill:

Hospitals. Starting June 30, 1979, Medicare and Medicaid payments for routine hospital costs — basic bed-and-board expenses such as food, nursing and labor — would be at fixed rates. Different per-diem rates for different types of hospitals — university, rural, community — would be established by comparing routine costs of similar hospitals. The cost of the following "variables" would not be used when calculating the routine reimbursement rate: energy, malpractice insurance, education and training programs and salaries of house staff (interns and residents).

Hospitals whose costs were less than the fixed payment rate could keep part of the difference and those whose expenses exceeded their rate by up to 15 percent would be fully reimbursed. Hospitals whose costs ran over 115 percent of the reimbursement rate would have to absorb the extra expenses.

For ancillary services such as use of operating rooms, drugs, X-rays, lab tests and anesthesiology, there would be a uniform national payment rate if they rose "at excessive rates," according to the staff paper.

The routine reimbursement rates would be adjusted annually for increases in hospital costs. A hospital could seek adjustments in the routine reimbursement rate in these circumstances: if it had unusually high costs because it was new; if it had enlarged or cut services through mergers, shared-service or similar arrangements; if it had spent a lot to bring its workers' wages up to the prevailing wage rate for comparable work in its area, or if it had high "standby costs" because of where it was located — for instance, in a resort area with seasonal population changes.

In the first year of the program only, a hospital that paid workers more than others in its group could also seek an adjustment.

Hospitals subject to comparable state cost control programs would be exempt from federal controls.

Hospital reimbursements could include the costs of eliminating underused acute care beds or converting them to alternative uses.

Partial reimbursement for new capital expenditures — for major equipment or construction — would be tied directly to approval of those expenditures by the health planning system.

National Commission. The staff proposed to empower a new 15-member Health Facilities Cost Commission of "experts" to refine a fixed-rate payment system and expand it to ancillary services and to other facilities now reimbursed on a cost basis as data for cost comparisons was developed. These facilities included outpatient clinics, renal dialysis centers, nursing homes and home health care providers.

Responsibility for all cost control policy would rest with the commission, and its recommendations would be implemented unless the secretary of Health, Education and Welfare (HEW) rejected them. The commission would decide if ancillary service revenues were rising too fast and should be subject to a national ceiling until they were brought under the fixed-rate payment system.

Doctors. Doctors who agreed to accept Medicare benefits as full payment for all their Medicare claims (referred to as "participating physicians") would earn special treatment. This included speedier processing of simpler forms, plus a $1 per patient payment — referred to as an "administrative cost-saving allowance." The staff paper said the expedited handling of these claims would save the participating doctors an additional $1 per patient in paperwork and billing costs.

This arrangement was also said to help doctors charging lower fees — often rural or inner-city practitioners — because the savings would represent a larger part of their income.

Doctors could forego these savings and continue to decide on a case-by-case basis whether to accept Medicare benefits as full payment, as permitted by existing law.

To encourage doctors to practice in medically underserved areas, the bill would raise an existing limit on the fees a doctor with a new practice in these areas could

charge the federal programs. Another adjustment would lessen the wide difference between permissible fees in various parts of a state. Existing law based payments on "customary and prevailing" doctors' fees — much higher in some cities than others, or in rural areas.

New limits were proposed for services by hospital-based physicians — anesthesiologists, pathologists or radiologists — in which they were not directly involved. These limits would apply to those doctors whose income was a percentage of the revenues of the hospital services they managed. Where the work was substantially performed by a non-M.D. employee — for instance, a routine test performed by a laboratory technician — reimbursement would not be on a professional fee-for-service basis, but at a lower rate. The bill also authorized the use of relative value schedules for Medicare, Medicaid and private third-party payors. These were physician-devised lists of medical procedures and fees that have been used by private insurers to evaluate doctors' claims.

Finance Committee Rejects Carter Bill

When the House Commerce Committee in July refused to approve the administration-backed compromise bill, the White House focused its efforts on trying to resurrect the legislation in the Senate by pushing for a similar compromise bill sponsored by Sen. Gaylord Nelson, D-Wis. The administration's strategy was to attach the compromise to the Medicare-Medicaid reform bill (S 1470) that received tentative approval July 21 from the Senate Finance Committee. Under the administration proposal, a new reimbursement system would be adopted for routine "bed-and-board" hospital costs. That is, hospitals would be paid at a fixed rate for these expenses by all payors — both the federal programs and private insurers. Different rates for different types of hospitals — rural or urban, for example — would be set by comparing expenses within groups of hospitals. As introduced, S 1470 covered only the two federal programs, not other third-party payors.

But the Carter administration failed to persuade the Senate Finance Committee to endorse its hospital cost containment proposal.

By a 7-11 vote the committee Aug. 3 rejected an amendment providing for a standby cap on hospital revenues if voluntary cost-cutting efforts by the industry failed before a more sophisticated payment reform system could be put in place.

The committee then voted to report the Talmadge bill (S 1470) mandating the new payment system for Medicare and Medicaid only. The bill provided fixed rates of payment for different types of hospitals for "routine" bed-and-board costs. The federal program would pay a hospital at the average rate for its type, with extra payments for hospitals with below-average costs. Hospitals exceeding the average by up to 15 percent would be fully reimbursed, but extra expenses above 115 percent of the average would not be reimbursed.

In a major change from earlier versions of the proposal, similar controls for "ancillary" costs — drugs, X-rays, laboratory tests and other variable expenses — would not be adopted unless Congress enacted legislation requiring them. The staff draft had provided that a fixed-rate payment system for those costs would be implemented in the future by a national commission unless the secretary of health, education and welfare objected.

Nelson said he would try again to win approval of the Carter plan on the Senate floor. ∎

Concern Grows Over Dollar Problems Abroad

In economic terms, the 1970s are likely to be remembered as the period when the once "almighty" dollar fell on hard times. Its domestic purchasing power was half what it was in 1965; its value in gold was one-fifth what it was in 1972. Since the end of World War II, non-communist countries have pegged their economies to the dollar. But in the face of mounting U.S. trade deficits and spiraling inflation, the dollar's role as an international currency has been challenged as never before.

The dollar's immediate problems are related to the nation's sagging balance of trade. The U.S. State Department reported in April 1978 that America's trade deficit increased from $9 billion in 1976 to $31 billion in 1977. Imports rose by nearly $28 billion during that time, while exports increased less than $6 billion. Many economists predicted a similar deficit in 1978. And indeed, the Commerce Department reported a record $6.95 billion payments deficit in the first three months of 1978. Economists attributed these deficits to: (1) the high U.S. oil import bill — about $40 billion in 1977 — and (2) the reluctance of American businesses to seek foreign markets for their goods. Sales abroad are needed to support domestic employment, restrain trade protectionism and help bring this nation's income from abroad into balance with its foreign spending — on trade, investments, tourism, and military and foreign aid.

Another reason for the dollar's decline was the nature of the U.S. economic commitment around the world. Economist Sidney Lens wrote in the May 1978 issue of *The Progressive:* "In the last dozen years the United States has exacted from its allies a sort of reverse lend-lease. It rang up ever-increasing balance-of-payments deficits to pay — in part — for such military adventures as the Vietnam war and for a worldwide network of military bases. In the settlement of those deficits, central banks of foreign nations were flooded with dollars which — until 1971 — were redeemable for gold. But since 1971, when the dollar was divorced from gold, these gluts of U.S. currency can only be redeemed for U.S. goods. And there is no way America's trading partners can absorb enough U.S. imports to use up their accumulated dollars."

Foreign countries are stockpiling more dollars than they can spend. And as U.S. imports continue to exceed exports, the amount of dollars held abroad increases. The U.S. Treasury estimated in April 1978 dollar holdings abroad at $132.6 billion. Meeting in Mexico City that month officials of the International Monetary Fund (IMF) declared that world economic recovery was imperiled because the United States was incurring huge payment debts while a few other industrial nations — Japan and West Germany in particular — piled up big surpluses. Outgoing IMF Director H. Johannes Witteveen raised the specter of a global recession unless measures were taken to correct the growing imbalance. U.S. officials regard the trade deficit and the accompanying plight of the dollar as a consequence of America's willingness to support other national economies by buying foreign imports. But the time has come, they add,

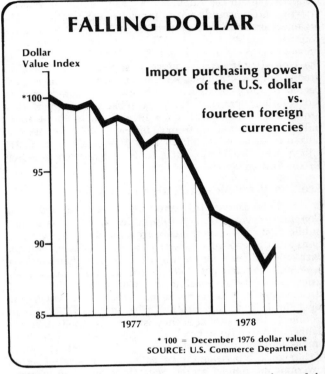

FALLING DOLLAR

Dollar Value Index

Import purchasing power of the U.S. dollar vs. fourteen foreign currencies

*100

95

90

85

1977   1978

* 100 = December 1976 dollar value
SOURCE: U.S. Commerce Department

for West Germany and Japan to carry a greater share of the deficit burden.

Uneven Growth Among Trading Partners

The most important factor in the weakening of the dollar has been the disparity between the high growth rate of the U.S. economy and the lower growth rates of America's trading partners. The fact that American imports have outpaced exports reflects a slower growth in U.S. markets abroad than at home. That difference translates into a declining exchange value for the dollar, which has fallen about 20 percent against the West German mark and Japanese yen in the period between 1976 and 1978.

IMF strategy has been to coordinate the growth of the biggest industrial countries — Japan, West Germany and the United States — to relieve the strain on the dollar and put the economies of developing nations on firmer ground. To this end, the Fund called upon Germany and Japan to expand their domestic economies by opening their markets to more imported goods. Japan announced that it would cooperate to a degree by lowering certain trade restrictions against U.S. agricultural imports. Germany, though, has been reluctant to stimulate its economy. "We will not be pushed [into expansion]," said German Finance Minister Hans Matthoefer, quoted in the May 1, 1978, *Washington Post.* "Germany wants growth," but not the sort that could cause high inflation, he added.

In April 1978, the IMF asked the United States to reduce its economic growth rate from an anticipated 4.5 percent in 1978 to 4 percent in 1979; it asked Japan to accelerate from an expected 5.7 percent in 1978 to 7.5 percent in 1979, and West Germany to increase from 3.1 to 4.5 percent.

Reaching these levels would have a positive influence on the balance of trade, the IMF predicted. However, estimates released by the Organization for Economic Cooperation and Development cast some doubt on whether growth rates would meet previous expectations. The organization said that growth for 1978 in its 25 member countries would average only 3.25 to 3.5 percent, below the previous estimate of 4 percent. The OECD's calculation for the United States was 4 percent, slightly below the IMF prediction. Growth levels for Germany and Japan were expected to fall "substantially" below what was needed to reduce their growing trade surpluses, it added. The probable German surplus for 1978 would amount to $5 billion, it estimated, up from $3 billion in 1977; Japan's surplus was expected to climb to $17 billion, up from $11 billion. The OECD forecast a continued high trade deficit for the United States.

Fears of Protectionist Trade Tendencies

H. Peter Dreyer, the European editor of the *Journal of Commerce,* wrote in a European Economic Community publication that "governments are all aware...their own actions must be coordinated with those of other countries, and with market situations going well beyond their national borders.... But against that, governments are political entities primarily responsible to their own national constituencies who will blame them...if they do not cope, or at least appear to be coping, with domestic economic troubles." International economists have warned about the dangers of imposing barriers to free trade, while labor unions and businesses, whenever they have felt the pinch of foreign competition, have called for protection. How governments manage to reconcile these opposing interests may determine the course of world economy for many years.

In its 1977 annual report, the International Monetary Fund noted that protectionist pressures were increasing in both industrialized and developing countries. A 1977 study by the General Agreement on Tariffs and Trade (GATT) concurred. It went on to argue that the trend toward trade restrictions points up a refusal by some governments to adjust to changing patterns of supply and demand, and is as much a cause as it is a consequence of the difficulties being experienced by advanced economies.

The round of GATT negotiations being held in Geneva in 1978 was seeking ways to minimize protectionism. U.S. officials have emphasized, however, that Congress probably would not ratify any agreement that did not contain provisions to guard against the use of production subsidies and duties to protect domestic markets. Treasury Under Secretary Anthony M. Solomon, quoted in the May 12, 1978, *Wall Street Journal,* said "increased discipline on subsidies should be accompanied by new guidelines on the use...of duties," specifying that they should be applied only when an import "threatens or causes injury to a domestic industry." One proposal under debate would cut existing tariffs among GATT nations by 40 percent. Another issue was whether certain allowable tariff practices could be applied selectively by country or must be applied equally to all "favored nation" trading partners, as in existing GATT requirements.

Particularly affected by more liberal trade practices would be countries like Japan and Brazil where protective barriers permit only a minimal import trade. Largely because of its tariffs, Japan in 1977 built up an $11 billion trade surplus. About half of that amount was accounted for by goods sold in the United States, which had been effectively frozen out of most Japanese markets by strict quotas and other trade restrictions.

Measures to Stabilize the Dollar

Virtually all economists agree that the dollar's problems abroad have many causes, ranging from trade setbacks to inflation. But there is no consensus among experts on what might be done to solve the dollar's problem. In 1978, the U.S. Treasury auctioned off 300,000 ounces of gold at an average price of $180.38 per ounce. The announced aim of the sale was to reduce the balance-of-trade deficit. By selling gold, Treasury officials said they hoped to drive the price down and thus strengthen the dollar. Although the gold sold for about $3 below the prevailing world price, some observers believed the amount was too small to help the dollar significantly. The International Monetary Fund has been selling 500,000 ounces of gold monthly during 1976-78, and these sales seem to have done little to hold down the world price of gold or prop up the dollar.

Concern about the condition of the dollar was heightened by bad economic news in the first quarter of 1978. The Labor Department reported that inflation in the United States climbed at an annual rate of 9.3 percent during January, February and March, a much higher figure than the 6 percent predicted by the Carter administration for the year. An 0.8 percent rise in the April Consumer Price Index (CPI) put the average yearly inflation rate at 9.6 percent. Economists are divided on how much the federal budget deficit contributed to inflation. But many think that policies to restrict the growth of the money supply would reduce the domestic demand for goods and bring the inflation rate down.

In an effort to limit the circulation of money and thus help to stabilize prices, the Federal Reserve Board in May 1978 raised the basic interest rate on loans to commercial banks to 7.5 percent, from 7. Additionally, higher interest rates were expected to raise the dollar's exchange value by attracting foreign investment in Treasury bonds and other government securities.

In terms of international trade, a lower rate of inflation anticipated as a result of the Fed's action should improve the position of American exports. According to Paul McCracken, chairman of the Council of Economic Advisers under President Nixon, the persistent undervaluation of other currencies relative to the dollar has put the United States at a "chronic" trading disadvantage by tying the dollar to an "abnormally low exchange rate."

Background

With military victory at last in prospect, finance ministers from 44 allied nations met in June 1944 at Bretton Woods, a New Hampshire resort, to draw up plans for stabilizing the world's monetary system after the war. Their chief aim was to find a way to prevent a recurrence of the financial disasters of the previous two decades.

The basic principle settled on at Bretton Woods was that foreign currencies could be exchanged for U.S. dollars at essentially fixed rates. In effect, the dollar was chosen to fulfill the same function gold had served prior to World War I. The International Monetary Fund (IMF) was established in 1946 to regulate the flow of payments between member countries. Under rules agreed to by the 26 countries that signed the Bretton Woods accord, changes in parity between the dollar and other monetary units had to be sanctioned by the IMF.

Because demands on a nation's currency may vary from time to time, a government needs monetary reserves to support the value of its money in a system of fixed exchange rates. Reserves are held both in gold and in certain foreign currencies, usually in British pounds and U.S. dollars. All countries, except the United States, are required to meet their IMF obligations by buying and selling other currencies — mostly dollars. Until Aug. 15, 1971, when President Nixon declared dollars no longer redeemable for gold, the United States met its basic commitment under IMF rules by freely buying and selling gold to foreign monetary authorities at $35 an ounce.

The 134-member IMF plays the part of "economic tutor" to member nations. But since the United States released the dollar from a fixed rate of exchange in 1971, the organization has lost a good deal of its influence over the course of the world's monetary affairs. The oil crisis of 1973 further eroded the Fund's authority. As oil-producing countries have accumulated huge surpluses, some oil-consuming countries have been forced to endure trade deficits. And the IMF, many economists believe, has been all but powerless to correct the imbalance.

Most member nations have been reluctant to cooperate with the Fund's attempts to manage their finances. Poorer countries often have resisted pressure to repair their deficit economies, while certain major industrial nations — most notably Japan and West Germany — have been unwilling to reduce their trade surpluses. The IMF was designed to exercise "firm surveillance" over its members to make sure they do not "manipulate" their exchange rates to obtain "unfair [competitive] advantage." However, that duty is often hampered by ambiguities in the IMF charter. It does not define "manipulation" or "unfair advantage."

One of the original purposes of the Fund, outlined at Bretton Woods, was to..."facilitate the expansion and balanced growth of international trade, and to contribute thereby to the promotion and maintenance of high levels of employment and real income and to the development of the productive resources of all members...." But it has been charged that the IMF often has neglected this goal — that the Fund's emphasis on public spending reductions, devaluation and free trade has undermined governments and created unemployment and political repression in many areas of the world.

While there is growing debate over the best role for the IMF, many observers say that, in the present era of trade deficits and slow economic growth, it must reassert its regulatory authority. In international lending, former Federal Reserve Board Chairman Arthur F. Burns has said, according to a May 7, 1978, *New York Times* article, the Fund should enforce "stricter terms" on its loans to borrower nations to assure that debts are paid and a banking crisis avoided.

Devaluation and 'Floating' Dollar in 1970s

At the end of the 1960s, most industrial nations experienced recurrent periods in which wages rose faster than productivity and price trends would warrant. In an effort to control the resulting tide of inflation, the United States un-

GNP Growth in Major Industrial Countries

Country	Average 1963-64 to 1973-74	1975	From previous year 1976	1977
United States	4.0%	−1.8%	6.1%	4.75%
Japan	9.4	2.4	6.3	6.0
West Germany	4.4	−3.2	5.6	2.75
France	5.4	0.1	5.2	3.0
United Kingdom	2.7	1.8	1.4	0.25
Italy	4.7	−3.5	5.6	2.0
Canada	5.4	1.1	4.9	2.25

Source: OECD

dertook a series of economic restraints. But attempts to maintain the parity of the dollar in the face of years of deteriorating competitiveness led to massive U.S. balance-of-payments deficits, an increase in the foreign demand for gold, and ultimately the breakdown of the Bretton Woods agreement.

High inflation and the declining status of the dollar abroad "came about as presidents pursued covert policies with concealed priorities," said Princeton political scientist Edward R. Tufte. Political decisions by Presidents Johnson and Nixon, he argued, inflicted heavy strains on the world economic system. From 1965 to 1968, Johnson did not finance the Vietnam War adequately through taxes. Tufte, quoted in a May 22, 1978, *Business Week* article, contended that Johnson hid the true cost of the war effort from Congress, fearing lawmakers might take funds away from Great Society programs to cover military expenses. As a result of this "guns and butter" approach to spending, military and civilian outlays rose by $22 billion between mid-1965 and mid-1966.

The Federal Reserve Board initially resisted administration pressure to add to the amount of dollars in circulation. However, in 1966 the board authorized the first of many increases in the money supply, an action that began an era of high inflation that has not yet ended. Early in 1967, Johnson did ask Congress to enact a 10 percent tax surcharge to help defray war costs. The special tax took effect in 1968, but it did not offset the easing of money restrictions. The inflation cycle continued.

The inflationary trend persisted under the stimulative monetary policies of President Nixon. Despite temporary wage-price controls put in effect in 1971, the Federal Reserve Board during the Nixon administration pumped greater and greater amounts of money into the economy. The dollar's problems both at home and abroad led to two devaluations during the Nixon presidency. In 1971, it was devalued 8.57 percent by executive proclamation. In 1973, central bankers meeting in Washington agreed to raise the price of gold from $38 per ounce to $42.22, which had the effect of an 11.1 percent devaluation of the dollar on the world market.

By far the biggest jolt to the international economic system and the condition of the U.S. dollar at home and abroad was felt in 1973-74 when the Organization of Petroleum Exporting Countries (OPEC) quadrupled the price of oil. This ushered in a new round of inflation and made more

Growth of Consumer Prices

	1974	1975	1976	1977
Total OECD	10.5%	8%	8%	7%
United States	8	5.25	5.75	5.75
Japan	11	8.25	7.25	6
West Germany	6	4.5	3.75	4
Total OECD Europe	12.5	10	10	8.75

Source: Organization for Economic
Cooperation and Development

apparent the existing faults in the world's monetary structure. In an effort to slow down the inflationary spiral, the United States and other countries hard-pressed by price increases adopted restrictive trade practices. The result was a worldwide recession. By 1974, total world production declined for the first time since the 1930s. Only massive borrowing saved many of the less developed nations from bankruptcy; even some countries in Western Europe ran up large account deficits because of the oil price rise.

Outlook for Economic Reform

The new round of troubles for the dollar, many observers believe, was directly related to the current imbalance in U.S. trade. Oil imports were the most significant contributing factor to the trade deficit. According to the American Enterprise Institute, from 1976 to 1977 oil imports from OPEC to the United States increased from $27 billion to slightly over $40 billion, while U.S. exports to OPEC nations during the same period rose from $12.6 billion to $14 billion.

In 1973, the United States was importing 6 million barrels of oil a day. In 1977, the daily average had risen to nearly 8.5 million. That steady increase in demand, some economists say, was responsible for the continued rise in oil prices from just below $3 per barrel in 1973 to well above $13 in 1978. Lester R. Brown, author of a number of books on resource economics, wrote that "the steep rises in petroleum prices reflected the decision by members of OPEC to 'administer' prices, but the strength to make their resolution stick derived from the ability of principal suppliers such as Saudi Arabia and Kuwait to restrict production and from the lack of suitable substitutes for oil." By raising its prices, Brown suggested in a Worldwatch Paper, OPEC has done "what market forces would do more gradually as oil reserves dwindle."

The oil price increase has shifted $80 billion a year in income and investments from the oil-consuming countries to the oil-producing countries, causing the rate of inflation to climb to record peacetime levels in many parts of the world. Carter administration officials have argued that a stringent U.S. energy conservation program was the only way to bring OPEC prices down. However, Carter energy legislation, which would strictly limit fuel usage, was still stalled in Congress in mid-1978. One administration proposal was a tax on domestic crude oil that would raise the fixed U.S. price to the level of OPEC prices and, officials predict, discourage consumption. *(Carter energy legislation, p. 85)*

Sanford Rose of *Fortune* magazine has argued that the oil deficit by itself does not represent a serious threat to the dollar abroad, since most dollars paid out for petroleum "are never converted into other currencies and thus do not cross the foreign exchanges to help depress the value of the dollar." However, the billions of dollars in revenues that OPEC has amassed has had a negative impact on the world economy. To the extent that this surplus is used to acquire property and other existing assets in the West, the effect is to take spending power out of the world's economic system without putting anything back in its place.

In a report to Congress in April 1978, the Energy Information Administration forecast that U.S. oil imports will climb to 11 million barrels daily by 1985 and to 14.1 million barrels by 1990. It also noted that left unchecked the consumption of energy would rise three-fourths as rapidly as the gross national product (GNP), the total amount of goods and services produced in this country. While the report pointed out that the U.S. economy between 1977 and 1985 would determine the terms on which financing would be available for energy projects, it concluded that such financing could be hampered by a shortage of credit and rising interest rates — conditions brought about by efforts to manage inflation.

Carter's Effort to Curb Inflation

The dollar's ability to recover its lost value in international trading was hampered by the surge of inflation in the United States. Although inflation varies from country to country, the overall average for the 24 OECD nations of Western Europe, Japan and North America during the second half of 1977 was 7.25, just below the 8 percent average for the last four years. "Once inflation gets going it tends to keep going," Geoffrey H. Moore of the Morgan Guaranty Bank Trust Co. observed in the bank's August 1977 newsletter. Moore and other financial experts point to rising prices for oil, steel and manufactured products as evidence that the momentum of the inflationary trend will continue.

Within countries, there is a natural motion to inflation as wages and prices race to catch up with each other. On the level of international trading, borrowing costs and the rate of return on investments are significantly affected by the relative rate of inflation among countries. If one country, such as the United States in 1978, has a comparatively high rate of inflation, its exports will cost more abroad and become less competitive; and it will pay more for its imports.

With the U.S. unemployment rate at 6 percent for April 1978, down from a 1975 peak of 9 percent, the Carter administration shifted its emphasis on expanding the economy to restraining it. This was best shown by a reduction in the administration's proposed tax cuts from $25 billion to $19 billion for fiscal year 1979 and by the creation of a voluntary anti-inflation program.

In April 1978, President Carter announced that curbing inflation was his No. 1 domestic priority. He asked Congress to impose a 5 percent ceiling on federal pay raises and called for labor and business to cooperate by holding down wages and prices. The president stopped short of requesting authority to impose wage-price controls.

Although they tended to approve the motive behind the president's effort, many international economic observers concurred in the belief that the administration's action fell short of what was needed to manage inflation to the United States and bolster the dollar in foreign trading. Arvum

Gruenwald, West German government spokesman for economic affairs, characterized Carter's anti-inflation program as "something of a disappointment" overseas. If the U.S. fails to conduct a more vigorous campaign against inflation, he said in a May 1978 speech to the National Economics Club, the world could be led into a grave monetary crisis.

The same opinion was voiced by Prime Minister Takeo Fukuda of Japan on a 1978 visit to Washington. Fukuda warned that world economy was being jeopardized by the inability of the United States to halt the climbing cost of its goods and services. By the end of May, even the White House was pessimistic about its fledgling anti-inflation drive. The success of the voluntary program was "in doubt," a spokesman said, because few business and labor leaders had shown any willingness to make the necessary sacrifices.

Replacing the Dollar as Reserve Currency

Despite its ups and downs, the dollar remains the foundation of the world's monetary system. It is the currency most widely held in reserve by foreign countries and most often accepted in payment for international debts. But the dollar's decline against the West German mark and the Japanese yen has sparked renewed demands in many quarters for worldwide monetary reform.

A growing number of economists question the wisdom of relying on the money of any single country to serve as an international currency. The existing monetary system is based on what many see as an illogical arrangement. As expressed by British journalist Frances Cairncross in the May 14, 1978, *Manchester Guardian:* "The only way the world can enjoy an increase in its main source of international money is if the U.S. runs a deficit. But if the U.S. runs a deficit, that calls into question the strength of the dollars."

The economy of the United States traditionally has been regarded as "the engine" that powers world trade. Yet fluctuations of confidence in the dollar and the effects they have had on the American economic system have led some theorists both here and abroad to suggest that the dollar be replaced by a new unit of exchange.

One proposal is that the hegemony of the dollar be divided into zones of economic influence, each clustered around the world's four strong currencies: the West German mark, the Japanese yen, the Swiss franc and the U.S. dollar. According to this plan, the strong currency countries would be required to maintain stable exchange rates among themselves and observe flexible, or floating, rates within their separate zones. The European Economic Community's consideration of a monetary union, linking the principal European currencies to the mark, would be the initial step in this direction.

Current Account Balances*

(in billions of U.S. Dollars)

	1974	1975	1976	1977
Total OECD	−33	− 6.5	−26.5	−32
United States	− 2.3	11.6	− 1.4	−17.5
Japan	− 4.7	− 0.7	3.7	10
West Germany	9.7	3.8	3.4	2.25
Netherlands	2.1	1.7	2.4	.5
Switzerland	0.2	2.6	3.5	3.25
OPEC	62	31	42	40
Non-oil developing countries	−24.5	−40	−26	−22.5

* On goods, services and private transfers

Source: Organization for Economic Cooperation and Development

Another suggestion, while not new, keeps returning to the forefront: it is that the IMF issue a new series of Special Drawing Rights (SDRs) to supplant the dollar as a form of reserve currency. The first SDRs were created by the fund in 1967. Intended to take the place of gold, they are in essence a bookkeeping device, certificates of account with the IMF that member nations use to settle international debts. In mid-1978, one SDR was worth $1.22.

In the past, similar plans have enjoyed wide backing when the dollar has been weak in trading but lost support when it regained strength. For this reason, some economists are philosophically opposed to replacing the dollar. Any other unit of account, they say, would face the same periodic problems.

The dollar has served as an international medium of exchange for more than three decades. How much longer it would fulfill that function depended largely on the ability of politicians and economists to shore up a world economic system that was threatening to fragment into regional and national entities. "Logic points inexorably to the formation of a genuine international political compact," economist Sidney Lens wrote, "one that encompasses international planning to husband dwindling world resources and divide income and wealth equitably among nations." Such a compact has long been the goal of economic planners, but it has remained elusive.

Protecting Jobs from Import Competition

In the mid 1970s, Americans were buying imported goods in greater quantities and dollar amounts than ever before. At the same time, jobs in many domestic industries were in jeopardy — or had been lost — as a result of foreign competition. Disturbed by mounting job losses in import-sensitive industries, organized labor in 1977 and 1978 launched a campaign to persuade Congress to grant legislative relief.

"Foreign trade is the guerrilla warfare of economics — and right now the United States economy is being ambushed," AFL-CIO President George Meany told the labor federation's convention in December 1977. "Free trade is a joke and a myth. And a government trade policy predicated on old ideas of free trade is worse than a joke — it is a prescription for disaster. The answer is fair trade, do unto others as they do unto us — barrier for barrier — closed door for closed door."

Support for restrictive trade legislation has increased in Congress as the number of affected industries has spread. The Congressional Steel Caucus in 1978 had more than 170 members in the House. A resolution (H Res 856) introduced by Rep. James R. Mann, D-S.C., which urged the Carter administration not to reduce textile tariffs had 248 sponsors.

Contingencies abound in any forecast of the legislative outlook, however. Pressures from labor could subside if the job picture picks up in key industries, and the substantial authority given the president in the Trade Act of 1974 gives the administration a number of weapons to deflate protectionist initiatives.

Jobs are a crucial factor in measuring organized labor's feelings about trade. An AFL-CIO report has estimated recent job losses attributable to imports at 300,000 in the textile and apparel industry, 150,000 in electronics and electrical machinery, 100,000 in steel and other primary metals, and 70,000 in shoes.

A second major contingency concerned the skill with which the Carter administration could maintain the initiative in the trade field. Activity here has focused primarily on three fronts: a plan designed to eliminate the dumping of foreign steel in U.S. markets, negotiations with Japan over the Japanese trade surplus, and the multilateral trade negotiations held in Geneva under the General Agreement on Tariffs and Trade (GATT).

These initiatives, part of the extensive authority granted to the president in the Trade Act of 1974 and earlier legislation, could serve to head off legislative activity in the trade field.

Background

The Trade Act of 1974 (PL 93-618) gave the president authority to represent the United States in both bilateral and multilateral trade negotiations. In particular, it allowed the administration to participate in the 1977-78 round of trade negotiations in Geneva.

The act also gave the president a number of weapons to deal with trade problems. When the United States has a large balance of trade deficit (estimated at close to $30 billion for calendar 1977), the president can proclaim for up to 150 days corrective action, including import surcharges of up to 15 percent and/or temporary quotas, unless he determines it is contrary to the national interest.

If the International Trade Commission finds that import competition has been a "substantial" cause of serious injury to an industry, the president has a variety of options to aid the affected industry. He can increase or impose a duty on the article causing injury; proclaim a tariff-rate quota; proclaim a modification of, or imposition of, any quantitative restriction on the import; or negotiate orderly marketing agreements with foreign countries limiting the level of imports into the United States.

The president took advantage of this provision in 1977 by negotiating orderly marketing agreements with Taiwan and Korea on shoes and Japan on color televisions.

The TV agreement with Japan, approved by the president May 20, 1977, would limit Japanese exports over the next three years to 1.56 million "complete" color television receivers and 0.19 million "incomplete" color receivers annually. The impact of the agreement has already been felt. (Box, p. 112)

The Trade Act also authorized the president to take retaliatory actions against unjustifiable or unreasonable import and tariff restrictions imposed by foreign countries against U.S. goods, services and access to supplies, including antidumping measures, countervailing duties and actions against unfair import practices.

Steel Price Plan

Granted this substantial legal authority, the Carter administration has seized the initiative on a variety of fronts.

The administration seemed to have successfully bought time with its recommendations on steel, for instance. An interagency task force headed by Under Secretary of the Treasury Anthony M. Solomon developed a series of proposals designed primarily to speed up the process of identifying instances of steel "dumping" — sales below full production costs which injure a domestic industry. The task force report, released Dec. 6, 1977, recommended developing a list of "trigger" prices for carbon and alloy steel products which would be based on estimates of the full production costs of the most efficient steel-producing nation, currently Japan.

The prices would include transportation from Japan, insurance and a profit markup, and would be set each quarter within 5 percent of the product's full cost of production. If the U.S. Customs Service found steel products being imported below the trigger price, Treasury could initiate an investigation and reach a finding within 60-90 days rather than the year or more required under the existing procedure. In the event the tentative finding was one of dumping, the importers would be required to post a bond equal to the difference between their price and the trigger price.

The Solomon task force also suggested some tax measures designed to encourage modernization of the in-

Imports of Japanese Color TV Sets

1977	Units	Value*
January	227,109	$42,856
February	114,108	23,385
March	221,350	42,086
April	154,613	29,060
May	251,766	47,372
June	220,872	40,784
July	217,822	44,363
August	160,030	32,422
September	179,082	36,632
October	116,822	23,710
November	146,145	30,614
December	116,780	25,216

* *Thousands of dollars*

SOURCE: U.S.-Japan Trade Council

dustry, reducing the guideline life for depreciation of new steel industry equipment from 18 to 15 years, reviewing environmental protection regulations in an effort to eliminate unnecessary costs, providing up to $20 million in fiscal 1978 appropriations for communities with actual or threatened unemployment due to cutbacks in steel production, and speeding up the Justice Department's antitrust evaluations of possible steel industry mergers and joint ventures.

Solomon said it was estimated that the proposals would help create from 18,000 to 35,000 jobs in the steel industry.

On Jan. 3, 1978, the Treasury Department announced its trigger prices for most imported steel mill products. The figures covered basic prices for 17 products, with extra charges added to include special processes performed on specific products.

The average trigger price for products landed on the East Coast was $330 per ton, which was 5.7 percent below the average of $350 per ton for U.S. steel products in the eastern United States. An additional 5.5 percent price hike on some products was announced by the U.S. steel industry in December 1977, but most analysts felt that so long as the price stayed within about 10 percent of the import price the domestic industry would improve its competitive position.

Congressional reaction to the proposals was generally favorable; many members felt the plan should be given enough time to prove itself before contemplating further legislation.

Talks With Japan

The negotiations between the United States and Japan over Japan's burgeoning trade surplus climaxed Jan. 13, 1978, when the two governments issued a joint communique outlining Japan's plans for reducing its surplus.

While some observers voiced skepticism about the ability of the Japanese to fulfill the commitments described in the communique, U.S. Special Trade Representative Robert S. Strauss was enthusiastic.

"We have really redefined the economic relationship between our two great nations," Strauss said.

"I don't think we have eliminated the forces of protectionism, but if we hadn't come here, those forces would have raged much stronger," he added.

Like Western Europe, Japan has been slower than the United States in rebounding from the 1974-75 recession, and the slack in the Japanese economy is chiefly responsible for its 1977-78 trade imbalance. Japan's total trade surplus for calendar 1977 was estimated at over $16 billion, and its current account surplus (total surplus minus payments for insurance, shipping and related items) was projected at about $10 billion. The United States estimated its trade deficit with Japan at $8 billion for the year.

The primary U.S. goal was elimination of the Japanese current account surplus. American negotiators were asking the Japanese to stimulate their economy and to reduce import restrictions.

The communique formally reiterated the Japanese real growth target of 7 percent for fiscal 1978 (beginning April 1). Japan's estimated growth in fiscal 1977 was about 5 percent, and several private research groups predicted that its growth in fiscal 1978 would remain in the 4 to 5 percent range.

The communique provided that both sides during the course of the multilateral trade negotiations in Geneva "would consider favorably taking deeper-than-formula tariff reductions on items of interest to each other." Japan also announced its intention "to take all appropriate steps to increase imports of manufactures," and said that in fiscal 1978 Japan's current account surplus would be "considerably reduced."

Nobuhiko Ushiba, Japan's minister of external economic affairs, said his country hoped to reduce its current account surplus to $6 billion by fiscal 1978.

Japan also agreed to:

● Reduce tariffs prior to the multilateral trade negotiations on $2 billion of imports covering more than 300 items.

● Increase high-quality beef imports from the current 1,000 tons to 10,000 tons; increase the quota for orange imports to 45,000 tons and citrus juice to 4,000 tons.

● Remove quota controls on 12 products, 11 of them agricultural.

● Conduct "a sweeping review of its foreign exchange control system."

● Provide more opportunities for foreign suppliers under Japanese government procurement arrangements.

Multilateral Negotiations

The multilateral trade negotiations in Geneva, originally launched in Tokyo in September 1973, picked up steam in the last half of 1977.

The negotiations involved a wide variety of issues, including tariff levels, subsidies and countervailing duties, government procurement practices, customs procedures, product standards, quantitative restrictions, import licensing, safeguards for domestic industries, problems in agricultural trade, treatment of tropical products, and the legal framework of international trade.

In a meeting in Washington Nov. 29, 1977, agreement was reached on a general approach to industrial tariffs: The United States agreed to accept a Swiss formula which would compress the range of duties by reducing high tariffs more than low ones, and the Europeans tentatively agreed to aim for an overall average tariff reduction of 40 percent.

Particularly tough issues included the U.S. interest in a tightening of European tax concessions and subsidies for their exports and the Europeans' unhappiness with the countervailing duties the United States has imposed against such products, and the "safeguard" clause of the GATT, which allows a country to temporarily impose quantitative limits on imports found to be injuring a domestic industry.

On July 13, 1978, trade negotiators for the United States, the Common Market nations and Japan produced a 10-page "framework of understanding," stating that broad agreement had been reached on codes covering non-tariff barriers to free trade. The statement also said that the governments had agreed to work on a resolution on steel and that a separate steel committee would be established to work on more open steel trade. The negotiators failed to make much progress on specific agricultural issues, although they said they were working on frameworks for commodity arrangements.

Five days later, meeting in Bonn, the leaders of seven major industrial nations (the United States, West Germany, Great Britain, Japan, France, Canada and Italy) issued a declaration endorsing the "framework of understanding" and calling for successful completion of the multilateral trade negotiations by Dec. 15, 1978. The emphasis of the declaration was on stimulating worldwide economic growth and reducing protectionism. President Carter restated his administration's commitment to raise U.S. oil prices to the world level by 1980, and Japanese Prime Minister Takeo Fukada pledged to reduce the Japanese trade surplus. U.S. Special Trade Representative Strauss said Japan had agreed voluntarily to put export quota limits on shipments of cars, steel and TV sets — among other products — to the United States.

Supreme Court Ruling on TV Imports

Acting in a case that had major implications for both the domestic economy and international trade, the Supreme Court June 21, 1978, unanimously ruled that Japan was not giving its manufacturers an illegal competitive advantage over U.S. companies by levying a "commodity tax" on television sets and other electronic products when sold domestically, but not when they were exported.

The ruling ended a seven-year legal battle precipitated by Zenith Radio Corp., a leading manufacturer of television sets. In April 1970 the company had petitioned the Treasury Department to offset Japanese tax remissions with countervailing duties, claiming that the remissions were a "bounty or grant" prohibited by the 1930 Tariff Act.

In 1976, Treasury ruled that "no bounty or grant is being paid or bestowed, directly or indirectly..." and argued that a countervailing duty was not required because the remission of taxes was "nonexcessive." Zenith appealed the ruling to the U.S. Customs Court in New York City, which ruled in the company's favor. However, in July 1977, the U.S. Court of Customs and Patent Appeals reversed the decision and ruled in the government's favor.

Supported by major steel companies as well as other domestic television manufacturers, Zenith appealed the decision to the Supreme Court, which ruled that the Treasury's position was a "far from unreasonable" one.

According to U.S. trade officials, the ruling headed off possible retaliatory action against the United States by Japan, members of the European Economic Community, Canada and other countries and avoided a breakdown of the international trade negotiations then under way in Geneva. Had the Supreme Court decided the other way, "it would have put an absolute freeze on everything," said Richard Rivers, general counsel for the office of the Special Trade Representative. "The trade negotiations would have come to a complete standstill, and nobody would have known where things stood for months."

The Zenith ruling also had implications for similar cases pending before the courts, among them a suit by United States Steel Corp. protesting the rebates that Western European countries allowed their exporters on value-added taxes.

Labor Issues

Smarting from jobs lost in industries hurt by import competition, organized labor put trade near the top of its legislative priorities in 1978.

"We were almost like a voice crying in the wilderness, but now we have steel as allies," said Sol Chaikin, president of the International Ladies' Garment Workers Union, reflecting the increasing unity of labor on the trade issue. In Chaikin's view additional issues like the trade deficit and the declining dollar have converged "to heighten the consciousness of Congress."

Import Quotas

Labor strategists sensed that there might be enough support in Congress for comprehensive legislation in the trade field. Their last attempt, a bill introduced in the 92nd Congress by ex-Sen. Vance Hartke, D-Ind., 1959-77, and Rep. James A. Burke, D-Mass., would have established quotas on most imports and increased the taxes on income earned by the foreign subsidiaries of U.S. corporations.

Labor was not unified on the issue of quotas, however, and it appeared that quota legislation could suffer the same fate as Burke-Hartke unless administration initiatives such as steel trigger pricing proved completely ineffective. A bill (HR 9834) sponsored by Rep. John D. Dingell, D-Mich., would impose quotas on steel imports, while a similar bill (HR 9425) introduced by Rep. Adam Benjamin Jr., D-Ind., would impose a tariff-rate quota — a 25 percent surcharge on steel imports exceeding a quota computed on an item-by-item basis. A broader bill, HR 9933, sponsored by Rep. John H. Dent, D-Pa., would limit all imports to 10 percent or less of total domestic consumption.

The United Steelworkers of America publicly preferred orderly marketing agreements over legislated quotas. The

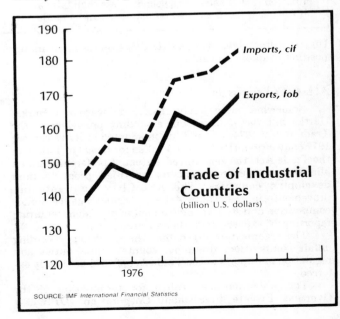

Trade of Industrial Countries
(billion U.S. dollars)

Imports, cif

Exports, fob

1976

SOURCE: IMF *International Financial Statistics*

113

Agencies With Major Trade Responsibilities

Government responsibilities in the trade area are split very roughly into three functional areas: the office of the special representative for trade negotiations, within the Executive Office of the President, deals with policy coordination and negotiations; the Treasury Department has responsibility for enforcement and administration; and the U.S. International Trade Commission (ITC) handles investigations.

The special trade representative, Robert S. Strauss, is the chief trade negotiator of the United States. The major ongoing negotiations in 1978 were the "Tokyo round" of the multilateral trade negotiations (MTN) held in Geneva and the bilateral discussions with Japan concerning the Japanese trade surplus. The trade office has also been involved in the negotiations for the renewal of the Multi-Fiber Arrangement, a multilateral textile agreement that expired at the end of 1977.

The special representative also has been charged with management of the generalized system of preferences (Title V of the Trade Act of 1974), which provides duty-free treatment for eligible articles from developing countries, and with administering Section 301 of the Trade Act, which deals with illegal and unfair trade practices. Any interested party may file a complaint with the trade representative alleging an unfair foreign trade practice, and the complaint must be reviewed.

The Treasury Department, primarily through the U.S. Customs Service, enforces the customs laws and determines sales of foreign goods at less than fair market value and the consequent assessment of dumping duties.

After receiving a dumping complaint, Treasury will initiate an investigation in which the Customs Service examines the level of home market and U.S. sales prices of the foreign exporter. Six months is usually required to reach a tentative determination. If the tentative determination is that sales have been at "less than fair value," all further imports of the merchandise can be made only if covered by a bond equal in value to the estimated antidumping duties that may become due. Within the next three months the final determination must be made; if it is affirmative, the case goes to the U.S. International Trade Commission.

The International Trade Commission (ITC) must then determine if the sales at less than fair value have caused injury to a domestic industry. If the ITC finds a domestic industry has been hurt, a dumping finding is published and antidumping duties are assessed. The entire complaint procedure takes about 13 months.

Under the new system designed to quickly identify cases of steel dumping, steel imports identified by Customs as below a minimum "trigger" price would be promptly investigated by the Treasury Department, and a tentative determination of dumping could be made within 60 to 90 days. Following the tentative determination, the case would be referred to the ITC for injury determination.

Aside from its antidumping responsibilities, the ITC receives petitions from industries, firms or groups of workers and conducts investigations on their behalf to determine whether increased quantities of an imported article are a substantial cause of serious injury to the domestic competitor. If the commission finds injury, the president may take action against the import in the form of increased duties, quantitative restrictions, or orderly marketing arrangements, and he may provide adjustment assistance for the injured workers or firms.

The ITC also may initiate investigations to determine whether "unfair methods of competition" or "unfair acts" are being committed in the importation of an article which would substantially injure a domestic industry. In a positive finding the commission can either exclude the imports or issue cease and desist orders against the unfair methods. Provision is made for the president to disallow a commission order under this section.

United Automobile Workers (UAW) also declared its opposition to quota legislation.

AFL-CIO Proposals

Somewhat more likely than a reincarnated Burke-Hartke bill was a major bill amending provisions of the Trade Act of 1974. In a resolution adopted at its December 1977 convention, the AFL-CIO called for repeal of Title V of the Trade Act, the generalized system of preferences which allows duty-free treatment for specified products from developing countries. The AFL-CIO also wants improvements in the Trade Act's provisions against unfair competition and stricter enforcement of provisions requiring reporting of exports, imports and production.

The organization urged that the provisions regarding unfair competition, dumping, countervailing duties and regulation of imports in the Trade Act of 1974 be strictly enforced.

The resolution also called for termination of the Overseas Private Investment Corporation (OPIC), a government corporation that insures U.S. investments in developing countries against the risks of expropriation, inconvertibility and war risk and provides a limited amount of development financing. The AFL-CIO said that OPIC "has been insuring huge multinational banks and firms abroad and encouraging the export of American jobs."

In 1978, however, the AFL-CIO was unsuccessful in its attempt to abolish OPIC; Congress in April cleared legislation extending OPIC operating authority through Sept. 30, 1981.

The AFL-CIO resolution also called for repeal of a tariff code provision that gives importers a credit for the value of fabricated components which are finished abroad and then returned to the United States. The importers thus pay a duty only on the value of the finishing process. Repeal of this item is a high priority of the International Ladies' Garment Workers Union, which felt that cut garments finished abroad have been an important cause of lost jobs in the domestic garment industry.

The AFL-CIO also urged repeal of a similar provision dealing with base metal articles manufactured in the

United States, processed abroad and further processed in the United States.

The Steelworkers supported a bill (HR 10039) introduced by Charles J. Carney, D-Ohio, which would remove steel from the multilateral trade negotiations in Geneva and establish separate steel sector negotiations.

The Steelworkers also favored extending the provisions of the Buy America Act in order to stimulate the domestic steel industry. Companion bills (HR 9427, S 2318) were introduced by Birch Bayh, D-Ind., in the Senate and Benjamin in the House which would extend preferences to domestic materials in state and local government purchases in projects with more than 50 percent federal financing. The bill also would establish a preference differential of not less than 15 percent and not more than 50 percent of the contract.

Carter Urban Policy: A 'Smorgasbord'

Announcing his long-awaited urban policy March 27, 1978, President Carter proposed a new series of job, tax incentive, grant, loan and public works efforts and a fundamental redirection of existing federal programs in order to reverse what he described as the "deterioration of urban life" in the United States.

The administration plan — produced by a special task force that labored for 12 months to shape a program to the president's liking — was designed to rehabilitate cities that already have suffered significant economic and physical decay, and to prevent other cities in better health from experiencing the same social and economic problems in the years ahead.

There was no "centerpiece" to the program; the task force report to the president declared that "no simplistic centerpiece policy will achieve our urban commitments. Instead a comprehensive policy approach is necessary."

As a result, the administration plan contained what one observer described as a "smorgasbord" of programs ranging from a National Development Bank to stimulate corporate investment in "distressed" areas, to tax breaks for businesses that hire hard-core unemployed or locate plants in inner-cities, to modest amounts of money for urban parks, social service programs, housing rehabilitation and urban arts. *(Major proposals, box, next page)*

Moreover, some elements of the plan appeared geared toward fighting poverty and unemployment regardless of the setting. Administration officials agreed that the concept of "distressed" areas applies in some cases to both urban and rural areas.

"Urban problems are found everywhere," said Patricia Roberts Harris, secretary of the Department of Housing and Urban Development (HUD).

Carter, who outlined the policy to a gathering of state and local officials at the White House, said he was "convinced that it is in the national interest not only to save our cities and urban communities, but also to strengthen them and make them more attractive places in which to live and work."

The president said the federal government had the "clear duty" to lead the urban revitalization effort. But, reflecting the "New Partnership" theme of his policy, Carter said that state and local governments, neighborhood and volunteer groups, and the private sector also had crucial roles to play. The urban program contains various incentives — mostly money — to stimulate involvement by each of those groups. Carter also said he planned to improve the effectiveness of existing federal programs through increased coordination.

Spending

The president proposed only limited increases in federal spending for the new programs in the urban package. Although the administration planned to ask Congress for an increase in budget authority for fiscal 1979 of $4.419 billion, it planned to increase actual spending by only $742 million.

In fiscal 1980, the administration planned to seek an increase in budget authority of $6.087 billion, with new spending of $2.933 billion. And in fiscal 1981, the administration planned to seek an increase in budget authority of $5.642 billion, with spending of $2.874 billion.

In addition, tax breaks for businesses, if approved by Congress, would cost the federal government about $1.7 billion in revenues in fiscal 1979, another $1.7 billion in fiscal 1980 and $1.5 billion in fiscal 1981.

Finally, the administration proposed loan guarantees totaling $2.2 billion in fiscal 1979, $3.8 billion in fiscal 1980 and $5 billion in fiscal 1981.

Limited Increases

The limited increases in spending proposed by the administration reflected at least three factors. Administration officials said the start-up time required for many of the new programs limited the amount of money that actually could be spent in 1979. Secondly, congressional budget leaders, who were consulted by administration officials during the preparation of the policy, predicted that Congress would not approve much more than $2 billion in additional urban spending for fiscal 1979.

Thirdly, and most important, Carter and other administration officials have emphasized repeatedly that the federal government already was pumping substantial sums of money to local governments. Estimates cited by officials placed that figure at $30 billion annually.

Indicative of that view, Carter maintained in his message to Congress that while some new spending by the federal government was required to fill "gaps," the long-term answer to saving urban areas rests with marshaling the existing resources of the federal bureaucracy to make various programs more sensitive to urban needs.

"For those who live in our urban areas, the gravest flaw in past federal policy was not that we failed to spend money. It was that too many of the programs were ineffec-

Jobs Programs, Development Bank, Fiscal Aid . . .

The "new initiatives" in the Carter administration's urban program fell into four general categories: employment and economic development; fiscal assistance; community and human development; and "coordination, streamlining and reorientation of federal, state and local activities."

Here were the major proposals:

Employment, Economic Development

● A three-year, $3 billion program of labor-intensive "soft" public works to rehabilitate and renovate public facilities. Contractors bidding for these projects would have to accept half of their workers from the ranks of the hard-core unemployed hired for public service jobs under the Comprehensive Employment and Training Act (CETA). About 180,000 jobs would be created by this proposal. *(CETA, p. 71)*

● Employment tax credits for employers who hire CETA workers between the ages of 18 and 24. Employers would receive a tax credit of $2,000 the first year and $1,000 the second per youth. The estimated revenue loss would be $1.5 billion annually.

● A National Development Bank, to be run on an inter-agency basis by a board composed of the secretaries of the Departments of Housing and Urban Development (HUD), Commerce and Treasury. The bank would guarantee loans totaling $11 billion during the next three years to businesses locating in distressed areas, both rural and urban.

The loan guarantees would be linked to a program under which companies could get grants of up to 15 percent (or a maximum of $3 million) of their capital costs for fixed assets of a project. The grants would come from HUD and the Commerce Department's Economic Devel-

opment Administration (EDA). Along with the grants, companies could obtain the loan guarantees (a maximum of $15 million per project) to cover 75 percent of the remaining capital costs. The usual interest rate would be slightly above Treasury rates (currently about 7.5 percent) although the bank in special circumstances could subsidize the interest rate down to 2.5 percent.

The grants and loan guarantees would be conditional on obtaining the balance of the financing from the private sector. EDA, through its Title IX economic adjustment assistance program, and HUD, through its urban development action grant program, would each get $275 million per year in increased funding for the grants to be used with the loan guarantees.

● Additional funding of $20 million for successful community development corporations.

● A special tax credit for companies investing in "distressed areas." Under existing law, companies can obtain a 10 percent tax break on the purchase of machinery and equipment. Carter's tax proposal calls for expanding that investment tax credit to cover new construction and rehabilitation of existing plants. The urban policy proposal calls for an additional 5 percent tax break, on top of the 10 percent, for investment in distressed areas. The program would be run on an experimental basis and would be limited to $200 million in tax credits per year. *(Tax proposals, p. 21)*

● Air quality planning grants, totaling $25 million, to accommodate economic development.

Fiscal Assistance

● A new financial aid program to replace the existing "countercyclical" revenue sharing program, which was due

tive and too many that did work had their benefits canceled out by other federal and state activities," the president declared.

Redirection

To translate that view into specific policies, the task force, formally known as the Urban and Regional Policy Group, recommended more than 160 changes in 38 existing programs to make them more urban-oriented by eliminating or changing regulations viewed as anti-urban. Some changes would require legislation, although many others would be done administratively.

Administration officials maintained that the review of existing programs was an essential part of the policy. "If we did little else than that it would have been worth going through the exercise," said Stuart Eizenstat, the president's chief domestic adviser and a major architect of the urban program.

For example, the Environmental Protection Agency (EPA) will alter guidelines for water and sewer grants to discourage large projects in developing areas, which have in the past contributed to urban sprawl. Instead, according to the administration, the focus will be on revitalization of existing facilities in cities.

Carter also said his administration intended to triple over the level of the Ford administration purchases from minority-owned businesses, which generally are located in inner cities, and require, for the first time, that all government agencies submit goals and timetables for increasing those purchases.

Although the task force cited dozens of instances where federal programs were not working, it did not recommend the elimination of any single one. Instead, the task force proposed various improvements, most of which were not spelled out in detail, to make the programs "more effective."

Also, the urban policy called for major new federal programs to be subjected to an "urban impact analysis" to determine the potential ramifications of the program on urban areas. The analysis would be conducted by the agency running the particular program and would be reviewed by the Office of Management and Budget (OMB) and the White House domestic staff.

Targeting

One theme did underly much of what the administration proposed: the concept of "targeting" programs to areas with the greatest need. Repeatedly, in documents

. . . Highlight Administration Urban Policy Proposals

to expire Sept. 30, 1978. The existing program channels about $1 billion a year to state and local governments if the national unemployment rate passes 6 percent. The new program would eliminate the state share and distribute the money to cities with high unemployment rates. Because the states would lose money under the proposal, governors and state legislators signaled their opposition to it.

● A change in the fiscal relief portion of the administration's welfare reform proposal to allow immediate financial aid to states. As initially drafted, the fiscal relief under the welfare reform measure would not become available until 1981. The administration has estimated that states would receive about $2 billion.

Community, Human Development

● An increase of $150 million above the $125 million the administration proposed to spend in fiscal 1979 for the Section 312 housing rehabilitation program in HUD. The program provides low-interest loans, at 3 percent interest, for rehabilitation of housing.

● $50 million for inner-city health clinics.

● $150 million for special social services grants under Title XX of the Social Security Act for such programs as meals for the elderly and day care.

● $1.5 million for a "cities in schools" project to assist families and students in "troubled schools."

● $40 million for an urban volunteer corps, to be run by ACTION, to create a pool of professionals such as lawyers, architects, planners and others with specialized skills available to help neighborhood renewal programs. Some of the money would also be used for small grants

for items like tools, supplies, materials and "administrative support" to carry out voluntary projects.

● $10 million for neighborhood crime prevention groups, escort services for the elderly and assistance to shopkeepers.

● $15 million for a neighborhood self-help fund for neighborhood and volunteer organizations for specific housing and revitalization projects. To ease criticism from mayors, who opposed direct aid to neighborhood groups, the administration proposed that grants for each project be approved by mayors.

● $12.4 million for "community development credit unions" to provide small loans to "high-risk" consumers in distressed areas.

● $200 million for mass transit, to be used to build new transit facilities and pedestrian transit malls, and to support joint public-private development around transportation stations.

● $15 million for planning of solid waste recovery projects.

● $20 million for a "livable cities" arts program to be run by HUD with participation by the National Endowment for the Arts.

Federal, State, Local Activities

● $200 million in incentive grants to states to encourage urban planning and redirection of state programs toward urban areas. Initially, the administration contemplated penalizing states that did not cooperate by withholding revenue sharing funds, but it backed off in the face of vigorous opposition from governors.

● Creation of an Inter-Agency Coordinating Council to smooth the handling of major urban projects considered too large and complex to be handled by one agency.

outlining the urban policy and in public statements, the administration emphasized targeting as essential if the urban policy is to have any impact.

Eizenstat and Harris took pains in briefings for reporters to note that the urban policy was based, as Harris put it, on the "targeting of need, rather than of cities."

For example, many "Sunbelt" cities of the South and West were experiencing tremendous population and economic growth, and thus could not be described as "distressed" cities. Yet these same cities — Houston and Dallas were cited by Harris as two notable examples — suffer from what she called "pockets of poverty." By targeting jobs programs to areas of high unemployment, Harris said, those cities will be eligible to share in some of the money from the urban package.

Yet, although Harris declared that "distress is not simply a Snowbelt phenomenon," most administration officials agreed that cities in the Northeast and Midwest, the Snowbelt, would probably receive the bulk of federal funds. But, they said, that was because those cities had the most acute urban problems.

Brookings Analysis

In a preliminary analysis of the president's urban plan, Brookings Institution urban specialists cited the

"heavy thematic emphasis" on targeting as a major attribute of the program. But the Brookings analysis also noted a lack of specific details on the critical components of parceling out federal money: formulas and eligibility requirements. Administration officials acknowledged the lack of specific formulas; one White House official said methods of distributing the money had been drawn up but no final decisions had been made as of mid-1978.

Some urban experts, like Brookings' Richard P. Nathan, believe the greater emphasis on targeting the better, especially given the modest amounts of new spending proposed by Carter. Otherwise, Nathan said in an interview, the funds would be spread too thin to have any substantive impact.

Nathan, like others, was anxious to see the specific formulas for distributing the money. "The name of the game in urban policy is formulas," he said.

Fiscal Aid Plan Criticized

One of the major planks in President Carter's urban program came under sharp criticism in Congress in 1978 and appeared to have little chance of passage in the form in which it was proposed. House and Senate subcommittees challenged the eligibility formula and other key features of the proposed Supplemental Fiscal Assistance Act (S 2975, HR 12293) that would provide $2 billion over a two-year period in direct federal aid to "distressed" cities and communities across the country.

Carter had urged Congress in his urban policy message to replace the existing Anti-Recession Fiscal Assistance program, which would expire Sept. 30, 1978, with a new program aimed at cities and towns suffering from long-term economic problems. The existing program, commonly known as countercyclical revenue sharing, was enacted in 1976 and extended in 1977 as a means of providing short-term financial relief to state and local governments suffering from the effects of the 1974-75 recession.

"While the fiscal condition of many state and local governments has improved dramatically over the last three years, many cities and communities are still experiencing severe problems," Carter said in his urban message. "These cities and communities require fiscal assistance from the federal government, if they are to avoid severe service cutbacks or tax increases."

Carter proposed spending $1.04 billion in fiscal 1979 and $1 billion in fiscal 1980.

The Carter proposal would make several major changes in the existing fiscal aid program.

State Exclusion. Under the plan, state governments would no longer receive the one-third share of funds they now receive under the countercyclical program. In proposing that change, the administration argued that the financial condition of state governments had improved to the point where they no longer needed countercyclical dollars.

Dual Formula. The administration proposed altering the eligibility formula in order to "target" funds to the most "distressed" cities.

The existing countercyclical program goes into action when the national unemployment rate rises above 6 percent. In order to receive money, cities must have unemployment rates above 4.5 percent.

The Carter plan proposed eliminating the 6 percent national "trigger" and leaving the 4.5 percent local unemployment rate as the main eligibility requirement.

In addition, the administration proposed an alternative formula, making it possible for governmental units also to qualify for aid if they had growth rates below the national average during the last five years in two of the following three categories: per capita income, population or employment.

In proposing the alternative formula, the administration argued that unemployment data was not reliable for small towns and rural areas. The second formula, the administration said, was designed to be "sensitive" to "distress" in those areas.

Aid Ceiling. The administration also proposed limiting the amount of money any city could receive under the program. The "cap" would be the amount of money a city received under the existing countercyclical program. Administration officials cited budget restraints and a desire not to increase dependency on the federal government in explaining the need for a ceiling.

Congressional Reaction

Members picked apart the Carter proposal during hearings before the Senate Finance Subcommittee on Revenue Sharing May 3 and the House Subcommittee on Intergovernmental Relations May 4, 5 and 9, 1978.

Much of the criticism focused on whether the legislation submitted by the administration actually would target financial aid to the most distressed cities.

During questioning, administration witnesses said the number of cities and towns eligible for aid would increase from 16,000 under the countercyclical program to about 26,000 if the new fiscal assistance proposal were approved.

That increase troubled several lawmakers, including Rep. L. H. Fountain, D-N.C., chairman of the House subcommittee, who questioned whether 26,000 cities and towns really were "distressed."

Administration witnesses maintained that despite the larger number of cities eligible under the proposal, money still would be targeted to the most needy cities.

The two eligibility formulas in the Carter bill also drew substantial criticism. Several members suggested that the minimum local unemployment rate should be raised from 4.5 percent to around 6 percent.

Some members also saw a contradiction between the administration's desire to target aid to the most distressed cities and its decision to establish a ceiling on the amount of aid any city could receive, with the "cap" set at current aid levels in the countercyclical program. ∎

Congress Approves New York Guarantees

The scheduled expiration on June 30, 1978, of a patchwork agreement that saved New York City from bankruptcy in 1975 set off an intense squeeze play in 1978 over the city's financial future. The key issue was whether federal assistance to the city should be continued.

Participants in the drama included the Carter administration, a sharply divided Congress, New York City and state government, the city's municipal employees' unions, banks, and city and state pension funds.

Most New York officials, as well as the banks and pension funds that could supply the money to keep the city solvent, argued that continued federal aid was a prerequisite for any new financial arrangement.

The Carter administration said it was inclined to agree, but Congress, which was split on the issue during the city's 1975 financial crisis, appeared even more hesitant in early 1978. Despite congressional misgivings, however, Congress once again rescued New York from municipal bankruptcy. By an unexpectedly large margin of 247 to 155, the House on June 8 approved legislation to provide the city with federal loan guarantees of up to $2 billion on city bonds. One week later, on June 15, the Senate Banking, Housing and Urban Affairs Committee approved a measure similar to the House bill by a vote of 12 to 3, despite the opposition of the panel's chairman, William Proxmire, D-Wis. On June 29, the full Senate approved the aid measure by a vote of 53-27. The Senate version was less generous than the House-passed bill. The Senate-approved bill would provide $1.5 billion in guarantees.

House-Senate conferees July 13 reached a compromise providing $1.65 billion in federal loan guarantees. The House passed the bill July 25, by a vote of 244-157, the Senate July 27, by a vote of 58-35.

Background

New York City's financial problems first became a national issue in March 1975, when the city suddenly found itself unable to raise money on the municipal bond market. Subsequent investigation showed, however, that the difficulties began long before that.

Ever since 1960, the city's revenues had been inadequate to meet its rising expenditures. It made up the shortfall through borrowing, and also by using a variety of accounting "gimmicks" that masked the true extent of the city's indebtedness until the problem had grown so large that it could no longer be concealed.

In part, the city's financial weakness resulted from problems familiar to many cities. Its tax base had steadily eroded due to the flight of businesses and affluent taxpayers to the suburbs or other parts of the country, and at the same time the portion of its population most dependent on government services — the aged and disadvantaged — had increased.

In addition, the city provided some of the most extensive public services of any American city. While some have argued that those services were unduly extensive, others have suggested that they were reasonable for a jurisdiction the size of New York.

The fiscal problem was exacerbated by the recession of 1974-1975, during which New York's economy-sensitive income and sales taxes dropped substantially even while the demand for welfare and other social services increased. The result was that the city's annual operating deficit climbed higher and higher.

In 1975, the city had borrowing needs totaling $8 billion, but it was unable to sell any bonds because investor confidence in the city had hit a new low. That raised the danger the city would default on its loans.

The 1975 Solution

Over a period of months in 1975, city, state and federal officials quilted a short-term solution to keep the city solvent.

In June 1975, the state legislature established the Municipal Assistance Corp. (MAC), a state agency authorized to borrow funds to continue essential services in the city. The MAC bonds were to be backed by city-related state tax collections and by state aid payments to the city. Part of the law setting up the new agency required that the city balance its budget in three years — with the exception of about $600 million in expenses that were being funded by the city's capital budget.

In September 1975, another state law was passed requiring the city to develop a three-year financial plan and establishing the Emergency Financial Control Board to supervise the city's financial affairs.

Still later, officials put together a special financing package, which culminated in congressional enactment of the New York City Seasonal Financing Act (PL 94-143), under which the federal government agreed to extend up to $2.3 billion a year in short-term loans to the city.

The act, which caused considerable controversy before winning congressional approval, required the secretary of the treasury to determine that the loans could be repaid during the year they were borrowed before extending them. It also required that the city pay interest on the loans one percentage point higher than the interest rate at which the treasury borrowed money for them.

Other parts of the city's financing package included a virtual freeze on wages for municipal workers; a pledge by city employee pension funds to extend $2.5 billion in loans through June 30, 1978, to meet the city's long-term financing needs; an $800 million annual advance in state aid payments to the city in each fiscal year; and a state law ordering a three-year moratorium on repayment of $2.4 billion in short-term city notes and reducing the interest rate on the notes.

The moratorium was declared unconstitutional in late 1976 by the New York State Court of Appeals, forcing MAC to issue additional bonds to raise money to pay off those loans.

Experience Since 1975

By most accounts, the city has made substantial financial improvements since the 1975 crisis. In testimony before the Senate Committee on Banking, Housing and Urban Affairs on Dec. 14, 1977, Treasury Secretary W. Michael Blumenthal praised the city for taking the following actions to correct its fiscal plight:

● Reducing its work force by more than 60,000 jobs, to a new level of 300,000.

● Negotiating the wage freeze for city workers.

● Eliminating the city's operating deficit.

● Converting $4 billion in short-term notes into long-term MAC bonds.

● Requiring for the first time that students attending city colleges pay tuition. The city also increased its mass transit fares.

● Implementing a $16 million management information and expense control system to improve the city's fiscal controls.

Blumenthal reported that the city had borrowed substantial sums under the seasonal loan program, and that it had repaid each loan with interest on time or ahead of schedule. During the city's fiscal 1976 year (July 1, 1975-June 30, 1976) it borrowed $1.26 billion. In fiscal 1977 it borrowed $2.1 billion, and in fiscal 1978 it borrowed $2 billion, the treasury secretary said.

The seasonal loans have produced a profit to the federal treasury of about $30 million.

Blumenthal told the lawmakers that the Treasury Department increased pressure on the city during the 1978 fiscal year to try to find private sources of money rather than rely on the federal loans. That pressure resulted in an attempt by the city in November 1977 to sell between $200 million and $400 million in six-month notes. The effort collapsed, however, when Moody's Investors Service gave the note issue its lowest rating. Moody's agreed that the city was likely to pay off the note issue on time, but it judged the city's financial condition to be "so precarious as not to preclude the possibility of bankruptcy in future years."

The poor rating prompted the issue's underwriters to pull out, leaving New York still shut off from the municipal bond market.

The Situation in 1978

Despite its progress, New York City in 1978 was far from being financially healthy. While the budget is balanced according to state law, considerable sums of expense money were still buried in the capital budget. In addition, the city projected that its revenue shortfall would be $457 million in fiscal 1979, $704 million in fiscal 1980, $903 million in fiscal 1981 and $954 million in fiscal 1982.

Koch's Proposal

On Jan. 20, 1978, 20 days after he took office, newly elected New York City Mayor Edward I. Koch unveiled what he called a "candid and realistic" four-year plan to restore the city to financial health.

The mayor proposed reducing the city's workforce by an additional 20,000 jobs over the four years, and he suggested a series of management improvements and purchase reductions to save $174 million in the coming fiscal year.

He said that would leave a $283 million gap to be filled by state and federal aid.

The key element in Koch's strategy included a proposal to continue the seasonal loan program, at decreasing levels, and to begin a new federal and state loan guarantee program.

He proposed that the city be allowed to borrow up to $1.2 billion under the seasonal loan program in fiscal 1979. The borrowing ceiling would drop to $800 million in fiscal 1980, to $400 million in fiscal 1981 and be phased out entirely thereafter.

Under the loan guarantee program, the federal government would guarantee 90 per cent of the value of long-term bonds up to $2.25 billion. The state of New York would guarantee 10 per cent of the value of the bonds, and it would set aside a $225 million contingency fund to back up its guarantee. Koch said the bonds would be sold to New York city and state pension systems.

Senate Opposition

Even before the new proposal was made, strong opposition to any continuation of federal aid to the city had arisen in the Senate.

In a letter to President Carter on Dec. 23, 1977, Senate Banking Committee Chairman William Proxmire, D-Wis., and the committee's ranking minority member, Edward W. Brooke, R-Mass., came out in opposition to extending aid to the city beyond June 1978.

That message was repeated in even stronger terms in a report unanimously endorsed by Proxmire's committee on Feb. 10 (S Rept 95-635).

The report suggested that the city no longer faced the danger of bankruptcy, and it said that continuing federal aid when the immediate crisis was over might encourage other cities to look for federal aid. That, in turn, would "weaken the incentive for fiscal discipline at the local level and erode the foundations of our federal system."

The committee was even more opposed to federal loan guarantees, arguing that they would "greatly increase the federal government's financial exposure, while severely limiting its ability to safeguard its investment through the types of controls that are presently available."

The committee argued in its report that the economic situation in both the city and the nation had improved since 1975. As a result, the city should be in a better position to take care of itself. Even if it was not, the impact of a city bankruptcy would be more "circumscribed" in 1978, because the municipal bond market had stabilized and other cities were in better shape, the report concluded.

The senators backed their assessment of the city's financial situation in some detail. First, they disputed Mayor Koch's contention that the city needs $5.1 billion in long-term financing over the next four years. They said that $1.6 billion of that sum, while desirable, was not essential to avoid bankruptcy, and thus need not be raised immediately.

The city's long-term financing plan called for about $800 million in new long-term bonds to be sold to replace some costly high-interest short-term bonds. The senators said that could wait.

The city plan also called for $800 million in new bonds to take the place of the annual advance payment the city was receiving from the state. The senators agreed that "bonding out" that sum would be appropriate at some point. But they argued that the advance should be continued in the short-run because it was a guaranteed source of funds for the city. Moreover, they noted that replacing the advance payment would benefit primarily the state of

New York at just the time that the state should be increasing its commitment to the city.

The Senate committee made further recommendations for how the city could raise the remaining $3.5 billion to meet its "basic capital needs" in the next four years.

The city pension systems, the report said, could supply $2.25 billion without increasing their fiscal 1978 commitment by agreeing to reinvestment of $941 million in maturing bonds and investing $1.3 billion — or 35 per cent — of new investable funds.

The pension systems in 1978 had about 35 per cent of their assets in New York City paper — almost all of it invested since the fiscal crisis began in 1975.

The committee suggested that the Municipal Assistance Corp. (MAC) could raise the remaining $1.25 billion to meet the city's long-term capital needs.

The committee further suggested that the city could reduce its needs for $1.8 billion in seasonal financing — money needed for short periods each year prior to collection of taxes and state and federal aid — by $400 million, and that the remaining sum could be acquired from financial institutions, and city and state pension funds since the risk involved in such short-term loans is relatively small.

House Response

House leaders generally were more supportive of the city than the Senate committee was. Banking Committee Chairman Henry S. Reuss, D-Wis., and the chairman of the committee's Economic Stabilization Subcommittee, William S. Moorhead, D-Pa., said that a preliminary investigation by their staff supported the city's request for more aid.

But, conceding the considerable power of Proxmire on the New York City question in the Senate, they said they would not force House members to face the political difficulties of voting on the controversial issue unless there was a good chance the Senate committee would allow a vote in that chamber.

In the meantime, Moorhead began hearings in his subcommittee to build the case that further aid was needed to prevent a city bankruptcy and to avoid disruption of urban bond markets and possibly the economy in general.

House Hearings

Lead-off witnesses at the hearing on Feb. 21, 1978, included Felix G. Rohatyn, chairman of MAC; New York Comptroller Harrison J. Goldin, and Jack Bigel, a municipal union pension consultant.

Rohatyn said the Senate committee plan was "unworkable" because financial institutions and the union pension systems would refuse to buy city bonds without continued federal credit assistance. He said the Senate plan achieved the "appearance of plausibility" by cutting the city's long-term financing requirements by $1.6 billion, but he argued that the city would be unable to re-enter capital markets as long as the lack of that money prevented it from demonstrating "capability to truly balance its budget recurringly."

Goldin and Rohatyn both warned that refusal by the federal government to assist the city could result in bankruptcy. The comptroller noted that the city had met all the "milestones" imposed by the 1975 solution, but he said the city needed long-term help to become truly solvent.

"Without continued federal credit assistance it is not possible to put together a workable financing plan," Rohatyn said. "The risk of bankruptcy in that event is obvious-ly of a very high order. . . . We have proposed a plan which avoids this risk at no cost to the federal government."

The two officials were supported by Bigel, who said that union pension systems could not afford the risk of buying more city bonds unless the bonds were guaranteed by the government. "Our veins are clogged [with city paper]," he said, adding that any pension trustee who agreed to buy city notes without a guarantee "ought to be prepared to go to jail."

The state pension system in early 1978 held no city bonds, and its trustee, Arthur Leavitt, said Feb. 22 he would not buy any without an ironclad federal guarantee.

Carter Administration Support

The Carter administration on March 2 came out in support of continued federal assistance to New York City, although it proposed less aid than the city had requested.

In testimony before the Economic Stabilization Subcommittee of the House Banking Committee, Treasury Secretary Blumenthal asked for standby authority to provide federal loan guarantees for up to $2 billion in city or MAC securities for as long as 15 years. The securities would be sold to city and state employee pension funds.

The secretary rejected New York's request for a continuation of the federal seasonal loan program, however.

As a condition to the aid program, Blumenthal said the guarantees would be secured by federal transfer payments to the city and by a New York State special reserve account or pledge of federal transfer payments. He also said he would insist that private lenders buy unguaranteed loans, that the city balance its budget by 1982 and that the state continue to monitor the city's finances.

Estimating the city's four-year capital needs to be $4.5 billion, Blumenthal said refusing federal aid wouldn't be worth the risk of bankruptcy.

"New York City in bankruptcy will prove far more expensive to this nation — both in expense and personal sacrifice — than any modest form of assistance," he said.

Legislative Action

House Passage of Aid Bill

House passage of legislation (HR 12426) allowing for federal loan guarantees for New York City by a vote of 247-155 on June 8 was in part the result of a series of interrelated developments in New York City and the New York State Legislature in Albany.

With Proxmire, Blumenthal and New York Gov. Hugh L. Carey all applying pressure, the city, its labor unions and the financial community put together several key elements of a new financial plan for preventing a city bankruptcy.

The federal loan guarantees were seen by city officials as the cornerstone of that plan. Under the bill approved by the House, the secretary of the treasury would be authorized to issue guarantees totaling $2 billion (including principal and interest) for up to 15 years on city bonds. The guaranteed bonds would be sold to city and state pension funds.

Other elements of the financial plan included:

● A pledge by banks, savings and loan institutions and insurance companies to buy $1 billion in unguaranteed long-term city bonds. That commitment has been made, subject to several conditions, including congressional approval of the guarantee bill.

● Passage by the New York State legislature of a bill expanding the borrowing authority of the state-created Municipal Assistance Corp. (MAC) to $8.8 billion from $5.8 billion. MAC has helped raise money for the city since the financial crisis of 1975. The legislature approved the bill May 26.

● Passage by the state legislature of a bill continuing the existence of the Emergency Financial Control Board, which has supervised city financial affairs. The extension, demanded by the financial institutions, Treasury Department and the House-passed bill, was approved by the state legislature along with the MAC expansion.

● Agreement on a contract involving the city and its 200,000-member coalition of municipal labor unions. After the direct intervention of Carey, an agreement was reached June 5.

None of those pieces of the financial plan were put together easily.

New York Mayor Edward I. Koch initially insisted on a labor contract that would cost the city only $610 million. In addition, he demanded that the Emergency Financial Control Board retain the power to veto labor contracts awarded by impasse panels or arbitrators, and he proposed that the panel lose many of its powers over the city's finances after seven years.

City labor unions demanded a larger contract and they strenuously objected to the veto power of the emergency fiscal board over contracts. The financial institutions, on the other hand, threatened to withdraw from the financial arrangement if the legislature weakened the control board.

The final compromises left no one entirely happy. The labor contract — which provided 4 per cent pay raises annually for two years — had a price tag of $757 million. The Emergency Financial Control Board lost its veto power over labor contracts, but the new law prevented arbitrators from granting wage increases unless they find that the city can pay for them. The law also authorized the control board to intervene in arbitration to argue against wage settlements it considers beyond the city's ability to pay.

HR 12426 had been reported by the House Banking, Finance and Urban Affairs Committee May 10 and the Ways and Means Committee May 22 (H Rept 95-1129).

Senate Hearings

Meanwhile, on June 6, the Senate Banking, Housing and Urban Affairs Committee finally opened long-delayed hearings on the issue. The hearings produced some additional encouraging signs for the city. Relaxing his opposition to continued aid a bit, committee chairman Proxmire said that he would keep an "open mind" on the matter even though he was still "leaning" against it.

Nonetheless, Proxmire questioned the financing arrangement on several grounds. He said the city could make more substantial spending reductions, called the banks' pledge to buy city bonds "pitifully inadequate," disputed whether city and state pension funds would be so "callous and indifferent" as to refuse to buy city bonds unless they were guaranteed, and — though agreeing that the city wage settlement was "modest" in view of inflation and other labor contracts — suggested that the "cruel" reality was that the city's workers would have to suffer for the city's insolvency.

The Senate Banking Committee chairman also complained that Koch had failed to win a demand that the municipal labor unions "give back" a variety of fringe benefits that have swollen labor costs, and he said that New York State government "hasn't done enough."

Proxmire also raised the possibility that, rather than provide federal loan guarantees, Congress might be wiser merely to continue the existing seasonal loan program.

In support of that suggestion, he cited a letter from former Federal Reserve Board Chairman Arthur F. Burns. Burns warned that the city would face the real danger of going bankrupt without federal aid — a risk he said was too great to take because it would "seriously interrupt" essential services in the city, set off an exodus of people and business from the city that would inflict permanent economic damage, increase interest rates on all municipal bonds, weaken public confidence in the ability of government to handle financial matters, and diminish international confidence in the United States economy.

But Burns called the loan guarantee proposal "a radical departure from the principles of fiscal federalism." He said long-term federal involvement in local affairs could eventually result in city and state governments "withering away," and he warned that the guarantee program might prompt other cities to seek similar aid.

As an alternative, Burns recommended extending the seasonal loan program for three years at diminishing levels each year. Proxmire said the idea was worthy of careful consideration, especially since it would put more pressure on the city to control its finances.

City officials bluntly warned that an extension of the seasonal loan program wouldn't solve their problems.

"Without long-term financing, the city's physical plant — its infrastructure — will continue to deteriorate, economic development will be stifled and the city will stumble from crisis to crisis with no permanent solution in sight," Koch said.

Senate Action

In what its chairman called a "remarkable turnaround," the Senate Banking Committee on June 15 approved legislation (S 2892 — S Rept 95-952) to provide up to $1.5 billion in federal loan guarantees for New York City bonds.

The 12-3 vote was a major victory for New York aid supporters, who predicted that final congressional approval and a resulting rescue of the city from bankruptcy were virtually assured.

The apparent reversal was attributed to several factors, including some last-minute lobbying by President Carter and Vice President Mondale, the decision by several uncommitted senators — most notably Richard G. Lugar, R-Ind. — to support an aid package, and a number of restrictions the committee agreed to place on the aid bill.

Under the bill approved by the committee, the secretary of the treasury would have the authority to guarantee city bonds in the following amounts: $500 million in fiscal year 1979, $500 million in 1980, $250 million in 1981 and $250 million in 1982.

The final installment would be available to the city only if it balances its budget according to generally accepted accounting principles — something the city was committed to do anyway.

Senate-House Comparison. Significant differences between the Senate committee's bill and the legislation (HR 12426) previously approved by the House included:

● The $1.5 billion ceiling on the amount of guarantees. City officials and the Carter administration had requested a $2 billion ceiling, excluding interest. The House voted to include interest in the $2 billion figure. Since the Senate committee's bill excluded interest, the actual difference between it and the House bill was about $300 million.

● A provision limiting the guarantees to long-term bonds (those maturing after one year or more). The House bill would allow guarantees on short-term or long-term bonds.

● A limitation on the last $500 million in guarantee authority to 10-year bonds. The House bill would allow 15-year guarantees, while the Senate committee voted to allow guarantees up to 15 years on only the first $1 billion.

● A provision requiring the city to use at least 15 per cent of the proceeds from any public bond sales after June 30, 1982, to retire guaranteed bonds.

● A provision allowing either the House or the Senate to veto loan guarantees for New York City in either fiscal years 1980 or 1981.

● A provision requiring the state of New York or an agency of the state to set up a special fund equal to at least 5 per cent of the amount of the bonds guaranteed as "co-insurance" to be used to pay guaranteed bond-holders in the event of default.

City Reaction. City officials were generally pleased with the committee action, although some of the amendments caused them some concern. While they planned to use only $1 billion of the guarantee authority, they said they preferred the larger amount provided by the House bill.

They also noted that the shorter life of the last $500 million in guarantees would increase interest costs, and that the possible one-house veto would substantially increase the risks associated with buying guaranteed bonds.

Senate Passage. The Senate approved the New York City aid legislation June 29 by a 53-27 vote. The lawmakers rejected four amendments before passing the bill exactly as reported by the Senate Banking Committee.

Conference Action

The House-Senate conference committee hammered out an agreement on HR 12426 on July 13, after two previous meetings had failed to produce an accord. The conference report was filed July 18 (H Rept. 95-1369).

Besides differing on the amount of loans to be guaranteed (the House wanted $2 billion, including principal and interest; the Senate wanted $1.5 billion in principal only), conferees differed over the extent to which Congress should supervise the program.

Proxmire argued that extending federal guarantees to both seasonal and long-term borrowing would in effect "give the city more" than it got in the expired seasonal financing act. He also argued that private lending institutions in New York City should be called on to make more unguaranteed loans, and he noted that there would be "very little risk" to them in making short-term loans to cover the city's seasonal borrowing needs.

House members, on the other hand, warned that putting too many restrictions on the federal aid could scare away potential investors and defeat the goal of saving the city from bankruptcy.

"We are perilously close to passing a bill that will make sure not only that New York City doesn't make it, but that you and I will have egg on our faces," Rep. Stewart B. McKinney, R-Conn., warned Proxmire.

Congressional approval of the guarantee program reflected a belief that the city had made significant strides in putting its fiscal house in order, that the original seasonal loan program was inadequate to solve the city's long-term problems, and that the guarantee program was preferable to taking the risk of allowing the economic and social disruption that might result from a New York City bankruptcy.

Still, supporters and critics of the measure were quick to assert that the new program would be the last time the federal government would come to the aid of New York City. In addition, arguing that the program caused an unfortunate federal involvement in local affairs, they said the bill would not serve as a precedent for other cities.

Partly to discourage other cities from seeking such help, Congress added to the program a number of conditions. They included requirements for annual audits of city books, a spacing out of the guarantee authority over four years coupled with a provision allowing either branch of Congress to veto guarantees in the second and third years, a provision allowing the guarantees only for bonds purchased by city and state employee pension funds, a requirement that the state of New York and private lending institutions participate in the city's financial plan, and a requirement that the state underwrite at least 5 per cent of the guaranteed bonds.

Even with those requirements, city officials hailed the bill, expressing confidence that it would enable New York City to regain its fiscal health.

Final Provisions

In its final form, HR 12426:

● Authorized the secretary of the treasury to issue federal loan guarantees totaling up to $1.65 billion for as long as 15 years on New York City bonds.

● Required the secretary to determine, as a precondition to issuing the guarantees, that the city cannot obtain enough credit from public credit markets.

● Required the secretary to determine that the city had a financial plan, involving commitments from New York State and private lenders, so that it could avoid bankruptcy if federal guarantees were provided.

● Limited the amount that could be guaranteed during fiscal year 1979 to $750 million. Of that total, guarantees up to $500 million could be extended to long-term city bonds (maturing in one year or more), and guarantees up to $325 million could be extended to seasonal loans (maturing after one year or less) to the city.

● Limited loan guarantees during fiscal year 1980 to $250 million, plus any unused or repaid amount from the sum authorized for fiscal year 1979. Only long-term bonds could be guaranteed during the year.

● Limited loan guarantees during fiscal year 1981 to $325 million, plus any unused or repaid amount from the sum authorized for fiscal years 1979 and 1980. Only long-term bonds could qualify.

● Limited loan guarantees during fiscal year 1982 to $325 million, plus any unused or repaid amount from the sum authorized for fiscal years 1979, 1980 and 1981. Only long-term bonds could quality.

● Restricted federal loan guarantees only to bonds purchased and held by New York City and state pension funds.

● Provided that either the House or the Senate could unilaterally veto proposed guarantees during fiscal years 1980 and 1981.

● Terminated the secretary's authority to issue guarantees on June 30, 1982.

• Required the city to pay an annual guarantee fee equal to 0.5 per cent of the principal amount of the bonds guaranteed.

• Required the city to balance its operating expenditures and revenues during fiscal years 1979, 1980 and 1981.

• Required the city to have a budget balanced according to generally accepted accounting principles by fiscal year 1982.

• Required the city to attempt to sell short-term bonds to the public during fiscal years 1980, 1981 and 1982, and to attempt to sell long-term bonds to the public during fiscal years 1981 and 1982, unless the secretary finds such activity against the financial interests of the city.

• Required the city to submit to annual audits of its financial affairs by an independent audit committee.

• Required the city to establish a productivity council to develop ways of making city workers more productive.

• Required New York State to maintain at least its fiscal 1979 level of financial aid to New York City. ∎

Farmers Protest Rising Costs, Falling Prices

The harsh equation of farm surpluses and plunging prices dominated farm policy in 1977 and 1978. New initiatives — such as commodities reserves to level out seesawing prices — and some old remedies in the form of subsidy payments and production limits on key crops did not stem farmer discontent.

Enactment, in 1977 of a four-year omnibus farm bill (PL 95-113) that raised federal target prices for commodities and pegged them to production costs for the first time appeared to inflame the anger of hard-pressed farmers, particularly wheat and corn producers who were hit by severely depressed prices. The $12-billion-a-year measure, which also extended domestic and foreign food aid programs, offered too little, too late, militant farmers said.

Late in 1977 the loosely organized American Agriculture Movement (AAM) called a national farm strike for Dec. 14, asking farmers not to produce or market commodities or buy farm supplies and equipment until they received federal guarantees of "100 per cent of parity" for their products.

At the end of 1977 the nation's wheat bins bulged with a two-year surplus, a buildup that many observers blamed on the full-production, free-market policy of President Carter's Republican predecessors. Nevertheless, the strikers' wrath fell heavily on former farmers Carter and Agriculture Secretary Bob Bergland, a fact that fueled political anxieties of farm-state members of Congress up for re-election in 1978.

Under the target price system begun in 1973, the government paid farmers the difference between what they could get on the market and the target price, if the market price were lower. "Deficiency" payments amounting to $1.2-billion for the 1977 crop year were mailed to farmers, the first such aid since the price support system had replaced the old parity-based system four years earlier. Payments for 1978 were expected to reach $2-billion.

But the 1977 act's $2.90 target price for wheat could not keep the nation's wheat farms—whose value often reached $250,000 or $300,000—from bankruptcy, their owners claimed. Wheat prices had hit a summer low of $1.65 a bushel, while farmers said it cost them $3 to $4 a bushel to bring the grain to market. Corn and feed-grain farmers were caught in a similar cost-price squeeze.

Under discretionary authority continued by the 1977 act, the President announced the first acreage allotments since 1973, to shrink overproduction of wheat, corn and cotton. There was some doubt that farmers would comply with the voluntary set-asides. Only by participating could farmers become eligible for 1978 loans and price supports, but some observers expected that many farmers would decide to take their chances on the market. Widespread disregard of the allotments could exacerbate the surplus situation.

For many wheat farmers, who were the leaders of the strike, the high value of their farm investments in fact represented the extent of their indebtedness for costly agricultural equipment, chemicals and land. The nation's

farm debt had doubled in four years—from $50-billion to $100-billion. Net farm income for 1977 reached just $20-billion—down from an all-time high of $33.3-billion in 1973. Economists calculated that, allowing for inflation, American farmers in 1977 earned at about the same level as during the depression year of 1936.

These economic woes were not evenly distributed across the farm population, a factor which weighed heavily against the chances for success of the strike effort. In the early days of the strike, dairy and livestock producers, who profited from the depressed grain prices, continued to move produce to markets. Nor was there any discernible drop in supplies of fresh produce, much of which was grown on large corporate farms in California.

In the last two months of the year farm prices rallied slightly, moving up 1 per cent overall each month. Bergland told Mississippi farmers in December that the higher agricultural loan levels in the 1977 bill had enabled American farmers to push corn prices up by 40 cents a bushel in just six weeks.

Farm Strike

Nevertheless, in September, the same month the President signed the new farm bill, Colorado wheat farmers organized the new protest group.

The striking farmers steered clear of the historical definition of parity, which had sought to reproduce the purchasing power farmers enjoyed during the prosperous 1910-1914 period. Instead, they sought a minimum farm price law, like the minimum wage law. Under this scheme, it would be illegal to buy or sell commodities for anything less than a price established by law that covered full production costs plus an investment return of about 8 per cent. That plan represented "parity...defined as fairness" to the strikers, as one leader said. Other demands included limiting agricultural imports to what American farmers could not produce.

Congressional sources left no doubt that, unless strike sentiment ran broader and deeper than was generally supposed, the question of higher target prices for commodities was definitely closed for 1978. The political situation was virtually impossible, said Senate Agriculture Committee Chairman Herman E. Talmadge, D-Ga., since farm interests were heavily outnumbered in Congress.

As it had historically, farm anger fell heavily on commodities dealers—"manipulators and middlemen," as farmers called them. But next to speculators, the protesting farmers blamed Carter, who was thought to have reneged on his 1976 campaign promise of "adequate price supports at a parity level which assures farmers a reasonable return." Carter's response to the farm strike was to propose improved crop insurance programs.

Farm exports, a key factor in reducing surpluses, were up for the fifth year in a row, totaling a record $24-billion for fiscal year 1977. But only late-announced Soviet wheat purchases kept exports from dipping below the previous year's total of $22.8-billion, Agriculture Department specialists said. Fiscal 1978 exports were expected to drop by $2-billion. Negotiations on an international wheat agreement to set up price-protecting reserves were underway at the end of the year. Farm imports for fiscal 1977 stood at $13.4-billion.

Food prices in 1977 rose 6.5 per cent over what they were in 1976, and they rose twice as fast as they did the previous year. Part of the rapid increase was attributed to steep hikes in coffee prices. *(Food Inflation, p. 135)*

Background

The situation facing American agriculture when Congress began shaping the 1977 farm bill was far different than it had been in 1973, when the last farm bill was passed.

Then the world was clamoring for U.S. farm products. The massive 1972 grain sales to the Soviet Union had wiped out much of the U.S. surpluses which had built up during years of overproduction under the existing, costly farm price support system. Droughts and poor harvests in other countries, as well as rising populations, resulted in a world eager for U.S. commodities. Farm prices soared.

Against that backdrop Congress in 1973 replaced the old subsidy program with the target price system.

Old Price Support System

The old system had proved costly to the government. Continued high production during the 1950s and 1960s could not be used up. The government tried various methods of control: set-asides, acreage allotments, quotas, even direct payments to farmers to not grow commodities. Still the surpluses kept building.

One problem stemmed from the government loan program, which was devised as a means of protecting farmers from the low market prices that resulted from an oversupply of grain. Farmers used their crops as collateral to obtain loans from the government. In theory, the loans were intended to allow farmers to wait until prices got better, so they would not be forced to sell at the low market prices. The loans provided them with cash in the interim to continue farming. Former Agriculture Secretary Earl L. Butz charged, however, that foreign governments waited for the U.S. price, then set their prices just under it. In Butz' words, "We then became the residual suppliers on the world market," with U.S. grain being bought only as a last resort. Farmers, unable to get a better market price, defaulted on their loans and the U.S. government ended up owning an enormous amount of grain. Storage costs alone in the 1960s were estimated at $1-million a day.

1973 Farm Bill

The situation changed in 1973, however. Republicans generally had long been interested in eliminating the old price supports and freeing farmers to take risks and grow crops for the open market.

With surpluses down and demand apparently booming, Congress revised farm policy in the Agriculture and Consumer Protection Act of 1973.

Under the new system, the government set a price for each crop, lower than existing market prices, which it called the target price. If the market price dropped below the target price for the first five months of the marketing year, the government agreed to pay the farmer the difference between the two prices. The high world prices and the probable continued demand made it appear unlikely then that farmers would have to even use the system, although the Agriculture Department warned that if huge surpluses returned and farm prices dropped, the cost of the program could skyrocket.

Farmers could still receive loans on their crops at rates below the target prices, with the option of keeping the money and giving the crops to the government if market prices did not increase within the term of the loan. The theory was that if market prices dropped because of surpluses, farmers could read the market and switch crops, planting something that was in shorter supply.

As passed in 1973, the bill set target prices of $2.05 a bushel for wheat, $1.38 a bushel for corn and 38 cents a pound for cotton. Loan levels were established at $1.37 for wheat, $1.10 for corn and 22 cents for cotton. The bill included an escalator clause to raise prices beginning in 1976 based on increases in production costs.

Cost-Price Squeeze, Growing Surpluses

But by 1975 some members of Congress were claiming that target prices and loan levels were too low to encourage farmers to keep up production. Huge increases in basic production costs such as fertilizer, energy and machinery were catching many farmers in a cost-price squeeze. Since target prices were too low to allow farmers to recoup production costs if market prices dropped precipitously, members of Congress warned, farmers were reluctant to expend their time, energy and money on all-out production. But if they reduced production, domestic prices would rise and exports—important to the U.S. balance of trade as well as to world food needs—would be curtailed.

A 1975 emergency farm bill (HR 4296) to raise target price and loan levels was vetoed by President Ford on grounds that it would cost the government too much money and would undermine the existing market-oriented farm policies of the 1973 bill.

Farmers continued to complain throughout 1975 and 1976 that production cost increases were pushing them to the wall. Yet, despite weather problems and the cost-price squeeze, farmers produced bumper crops in those two years and a different problem began to emerge.

Embargo on Exports to Russia

In August 1975 an embargo on grain exports to the Soviet Union begun by longshoremen angered farmers, who feared their all-out production would be rewarded by a surplus that could not be sold and that would drive prices down. With another huge crop in the bins by the fall of 1976, the United States was once more facing a surplus such as it had not seen since the early 1970s. The Soviet Union had an unexpectedly large harvest in 1976, as did many other grain-importing nations. Foreign markets dried up, U.S. farmers were left with grain and prices plummeted. *(Chart, next page)*

President Ford raised loan rates just before the 1976 presidential election, a move seen by many as political, to help keep farm voters on the Republican side. Whatever the reason, the higher loan rates attracted large numbers of farmers, resulting in an ominous increase in government-held grain. Wheat under loan jumped to 221 million bushels, from 31.5 million bushels during 1976, while corn went to 202 million bushels from 110 million bushels.

1977 Situation

As President Carter took office, farmers' organizations and some farm-state members of Congress were issuing dire warnings of agricultural crisis. The farm economy was as depressed as that which faced Franklin D. Roosevelt upon his inauguration in 1933, the National Farmers Union said. Many farmers, especially small family farmers, were facing bankruptcy; the entire rural economy in some areas was suffering.

Wheat farmers were particularly hard hit, as record crops and growing surpluses caused prices to continue falling.

The Agriculture Department projected that the world carryover of grain would be 167.8 million metric tons by July 1, 1977, the largest surplus since 1971. The carryover in 1976 was 111 million tons. U.S. reserves were projected at 1.1 billion bushels for wheat and 724 million bushels for corn, sharp increases over the 398 million bushels of corn and 664 million bushels of wheat carried over in 1976. These large carryovers could have provided a comfortable cushion if the 1977 winter wheat crop had been severely damaged by the bitterly cold winter weather or the spring drought. But despite the weather, 1977 wheat and corn crops reached near-record proportions, and farmers began to question the target price concept, since it was obvious target prices could not save them from financial disaster when market prices dropped.

Wheat sold for an average $5.52 a bushel in February 1974, but dropped to $2.29 by May 1977, a price far below what it costs most farmers to grow it. Prices as low as $1.95 were reported at some elevators in mid-June. The low prices caused serious financial trouble for farmers, particularly those in the major wheat states of the Great Plains, where few other crops can be grown because of the low rainfall.

The Department of Agriculture surveyed banks and the farmers who borrow from them in the wheat belt and released a report in April 1977. Of the 226,000 farmers surveyed, close to 14,000 said they could not repay their loans and some 60,000 said they would have to refinance their loans or liquidate their assets. Another 153,000 said they expected no difficulty in 1977, but if conditions did not improve by 1978 they would also be in financial trouble.

1977 Administration Proposals

In formulating his farm policy, President Carter was pulled in opposite directions by two campaign promises he had made. On the one hand, he had pledged (at the Iowa State Fair Aug. 25, 1976): "We will make sure that our support prices are at least equal to the cost of production." On the other hand, he promised to balance the federal budget by 1981.

The tugging between the two pledges continued throughout 1977, with Carter starting low and raising his farm price support offers several times to meet the outraged demands of farmers and congressional pressure.

Original Proposal. Secretary of Agriculture Bob Bergland brought the administration's long-awaited farm bill proposals to Capitol Hill in March 1977, and drew an extremely negative reaction. Farm state senators and congressmen attacked the Carter package as insufficient and even "cruel" because it did not include major increases in farm price supports. Many farmers and farm organizations charged that Carter had reneged on his campaign promises to farmers.

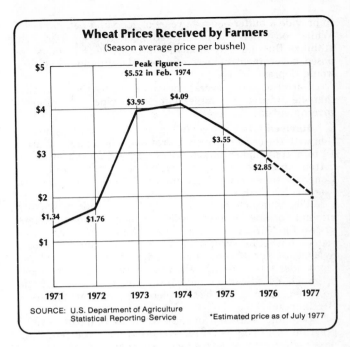

Wheat Prices Received by Farmers
(Season average price per bushel)

Peak Figure: $5.52 in Feb. 1974

$3.95 · $4.09 · $3.55 · $2.85 · $1.34 · $1.76

SOURCE: U.S. Department of Agriculture Statistical Reporting Service

*Estimated price as of July 1977

The Carter target prices were even lower than the target prices in the principal Senate committee bill (S 275)—and those levels were attacked by farmers as too low when that bill was first introduced Jan. 18.

The Carter prices were set at $2.60 a bushel for wheat, $1.75 a bushel for corn, 47.5 cents a pound for cotton and $6.75 a hundredweight for rice.

The prices in S 275 were $2.91 a bushel for wheat, $2.28 a bushel for corn and 51 cents a pound for cotton. Existing target prices were $2.47 for wheat, $1.70 for corn, 47.8 cents for cotton and $8.40 for rice.

Loan rates in the Carter proposal would be set at $2.25 a bushel for wheat, $2 for corn, $4 for soybeans, 51 cents for cotton and $6.19 a hundredweight for rice. S 275 provided for loan levels of $2.18 for wheat, $1.71 for corn and 38 cents for cotton. The existing levels were $2.25 for wheat, $1.50 for corn, 43 cents for cotton and $6.19 for rice.

Bergland, a wheat farmer himself, indicated he had recommended higher price supports to protect farmers but ran into roadblocks from administration economic and budget advisers.

Charles L. Schultze, chairman of the Council of Economic Advisers, reportedly opposed Bergland's recommendations in a meeting with Carter March 22, and his views prevailed.

Bergland conceded that he would not be making the same recommendations if he were a private citizen. But "President Carter is committed to balancing the budget by 1981 and this is part of it," he said.

At the same time, Bergland estimated that commodity program costs under the Carter proposals could go up from $500-million a year under normal weather conditions to as much as $1-billion a year more than the cost under the existing target prices.

The recommendations had been promised by March 1, but were delayed by the internal debate within the administration over the price support levels.

One campaign promise that the Carter proposal fulfilled was calling for the establishment of a grain reserve to provide a buffer between years of good and bad harvests. While consumer groups favored such a reserve to help stabilize fluctuating commodity prices, many farmers opposed government-held reserves on the grounds that they would depress prices.

Carter said on several occasions during the campaign that he wanted to implement some type of combined government-farmer reserve.

Revised Offer. Responding to widespread dissatisfaction with the earlier proposal, President Carter agreed April 18 to accept higher target prices for 1978 for wheat, corn, cotton and rice. He also warned that any attempt by Congress to exceed his recommendations would face a "serious" veto threat.

The administration's revised proposal raised its original income support levels (its new name for target prices) for 1978 by 30 cents a bushel for wheat, to $2.90; 25 cents a bushel for corn, to $2; 2½ cents a pound for cotton, to 50 cents, and 45 cents a hundredweight for rice, to $7.20.

Under the revised levels, the government could spend as much as $1-billion more over the four years of the proposed farm bill than under the original proposal, Bergland said.

Bergland warned Congress April 19 that the revised program was as far as Carter would go and that attempts to pass higher support levels faced a serious veto threat.

The Senate Agriculture Committee ignored the threat. It not only approved a 1978 wheat target price of $3.10 a bushel, 20 cents higher than Carter's revised offer, but it raised the 1977 target price as well, to $2.90, 43 cents above the existing price.

Final Carter Offer. As the Senate began debate on the farm bill May 23, the administration made a new offer.

Bergland sent a letter to Agriculture Committee Chairman Herman E. Talmadge, D-Ga., opposing the $2.90 price for 1977 on grounds that it would cost an additional $883-million. He offered a new compromise, pledging Carter to accept a $2.65 wheat level for 1977, but only on condition that the Senate adopt the administration's lower levels for the 1978 and subsequent crop years. Bergland said such a compromise would cut costs $475-million for 1977 and an average of $1.9-billion a year for the remaining years, based on favorable weather estimates.

The offer was attacked by farm-state senators, who said the cost estimates were "unrealistic," since they were based only on the good-weather scenario worked out by the Department of Agriculture.

Robert Dole, R-Kan., ranking minority member on the committee, accused Bergland of "attempting to beat down reasonable price support levels for farmers by application of cost estimates that will never materialize unless we have abnormally good weather for five years in a row."

The Senate rejected floor amendments based on the compromise proposal. It passed a bill with commodity provisions that Carter said could cost $3.9-billion a year. Carter renewed his veto threat in a news conference May 26.

In the House, Agriculture Committee Chairman Thomas S. Foley, D-Wash., had managed to keep his committee's recommendations more in line with the administration's limits. However, by the time the bill came to the floor in July there was mounting pressure to raise target prices. Another bumper crop of wheat and corn was coming in and market prices were continuing to fall. A lobbying campaign by farmers, farm organizations and farm-state representatives had paid off, and the votes obviously were

there for raising price supports to the levels in the Senate bill.

With that knowledge, the President wound down his veto threats. He kept after the conferees to accept the lowest levels in the two bills, but his acceptance of the final bill was no longer seriously in doubt.

Action in 1978

Financially squeezed between rising production costs and falling market prices, U.S. farmers looked to Congress for help in early 1978. Convinced that the target prices and loan levels of the 1977 farm bill were too low to save many farmers from bankruptcy, the American Agriculture Movement (AAM) launched a highly visible lobbying campaign to get Congress to pass a "minimum price" law for farm products — one that would guarantee farmers "100 per cent of parity," or production costs plus a reasonable profit.

The persistent lobbying campaign by disgruntled farmers came close to pushing a major agricultural aid bill through Congress in the early months of 1978. But controversy developed over the Senate-passed bill and it ran into a stunning defeat in the House.

The result was a scaled-down "emergency farm bill" (HR 6782 — PL 95-279) that mainly left it up to an unenthusiastic Carter administration to increase target prices for crops if it wished. That bill cleared Congress May 4 and was signed into law May 15.

President Carter had vowed to veto emergency farm legislation despite the pressure from financially pressed farmers for assistance. He said the four-year farm bill enacted in 1977 would improve their situation if they gave it time to work. And he insisted the emergency aid bill would raise food prices and bust the federal budget.

The bill — known as the "flexible parity" bill — ran into opposition from more than the President. A split developed within the farm community itself; critics said the measure would help some segments of agriculture (grain producers, for example) but would do nothing for or would even hurt others, such as livestock producers. Consumer groups warned of its effect on food prices, and the imprecise or frightening estimates of the bill's potential cost had their effects on inflation-conscious House members.

The plight of the American farmer, which the AAM sought to bring home to members of Congress with such a sense of urgency in January, began to seem less desperate as spring planting time rolled around, good crops were forecast and farm prices began to improve. Although angry and disappointed that the flexible parity bill failed, the visiting farmer-lobbyists were credited with increasing congressional and citizen understanding of farmers' problems and of getting far more action out of Congress than anyone predicted at the beginning of the year. AAM spokesmen said they would work to keep attention focused on farm problems by maintaining a volunteer-staffed office in Washington and by working in the fall congressional elections.

Legislative Action

The Senate responded to militant farmers' pleas for emergency farm aid by passing an unwieldy combination of programs that appeared to join two contradictory strategies for hiking farm income.

By a 67-26 vote March 21, the Senate passed the bill joining two opposing measures reported a week earlier by the Senate Agriculture Committee and adding a third alternative that had not won the panel's approval.

To a simple land diversion bill that provided direct payments to farmers who took cropland out of production, the Senate by amendment added hefty boosts in federal target price and loan levels for wheat, corn and cotton. Then it tacked on a flexible parity plan that permitted a farmer to set his own price support by deciding how much land to take out of production. Price supports tend to encourage production, while land diversion is intended to shrink price-depressing surplus production, according to agricultural economists.

The day after the Senate acted, the President's Council on Wage and Price Stability blasted the Senate bill as passed, claiming that it would add two to five percentage points to the rate of food inflation. The administration threatened to veto the bill. *(Food inflation, p. 135)*

Conference Action

In a brief March 22 meeting, the House Agriculture Committee voted 33-7 to instruct committee chairman Foley to request a conference on the emergency farm bill. Meeting April 3-5, House and Senate conferees selected the most controversial option, the "flexible parity" program, from the grab-bag farm bill passed by the Senate.

Wheat, feed grain and cotton farmers participating in the voluntary one-year program could select one of three sharply increased levels of price supports, depending on how much land they took out of production. At the top participation level a farmer would be guaranteed a 100 per cent parity target price in return for idling 50 per cent of his planted acreage (actually one-third, because of the method for calculating the acreage). The 100 per cent parity target price for wheat was $5.04 a bushel, compared with the existing $3-$3.05 level. The bill also raised commodity loan rates for these crops, an action that effectively set a floor for market prices.

Conferees dropped the Talmadge land diversion program that would have paid farmers for idling their land. That option had also included target price and loan hikes proposed by Sen. George McGovern, D-S.D.

Formal agreement came on the third day of the often confused conference deliberations, which were carried on under the watchful eyes of AAM representatives. Conferees acted without firm estimates of the bill's impact on consumer prices or on the federal budget.

Sen. Dole urged his colleagues to go ahead anyway, saying it was probably impossible to calculate the bill's true costs — a claim many economists agreed with. "Everybody who's against the bill is going to dream up the weirdest costs that they can," Dole said. Action was necessary, even though "nobody knows what it will cost consumers and nobody knows if it will help the farmer, although that's what we've been trying to do," he added.

The conferees repeatedly ignored Foley's attempts to substitute moderate raises in target prices and loans.

Foley urged his alternative because it would extend higher aid levels for the life of the 1977 four-year farm bill. Concerned with raising farmer expectations, Foley warned that there would be "absolute chaos in the countryside" if farm programs reverted to low established levels in 1979 after a brief period of high supports. Conferees informally agreed that revisions in farm programs for 1979-1981 should be attached to two pending farm credit bills (HR 11504, S 2146) reported in mid-March.

Administration Proposals

In the midst of congressional action on emergency farm legislation (HR 6782), the Carter administration March 29 announced a series of actions designed to raise farm income.

Vice President Walter F. Mondale and Agriculture Secretary Bergland said the administration would, effective immediately:

● Create two new paid land diversion programs to retire four million acres of corn land and one million acres of cotton land, in addition to existing wheat and feed grain set-asides already announced for the 1978 crop year. Payments would be figured by a yield-per-acre formula and were comparable to levels provided in the Talmadge land diversion bill, which averaged out nationally to $75 an acre. As under the Talmadge measure, payments could climb well beyond that figure — up to $200 an acre for prime wheat land, for example.

● Lift the existing ceiling on the domestic grain reserve program and waive interest charges after the first year, to encourage producers to hold grain back while market prices strengthened.

● Raise to $4.50 a bushel, from $3.50, the loan rate for soybeans. Loan rates tend to act as a floor for market prices.

● Permit farmers participating in the announced wheat set-aside program to graze livestock on their set-aside land and authorize payments of at least 50 cents a bushel (based on the expected yield on that land if the wheat were harvested).

● Purchase at market prices up to six million tons of wheat for an international emergency food reserve. Existing law authorized purchase of the wheat; the administration asked Congress for new authority to hold the wheat exclusively for world famine aid.

Bergland said the administration would also support legislation to raise wheat target prices moderately — to about $3.50 a bushel from the existing $3-$3.05 level.

The administration's adjustments to existing reserve and set-aside programs, plus some tinkering with price supports, would put an extra $3 billion to $4 billion in farmers' pockets in 1978 if they "take full advantage" of them, Mondale said. Bergland added that most of that income would come from the marketplace, as shrinking supplies drove prices up.

Bergland and Mondale claimed that the administration's "balanced" approach would bail out reasonably efficient farmers — although it would not save "Georgia farmers who grow corn at $8 a bushel" (triple the national average production costs), Bergland noted. Reliance on reserves would also shield consumers from supermarket price shocks, protect sensitive export markets by assuring dependable supplies and permit the United States to aid hungry nations in the event of a world food crisis, the administration spokesmen maintained.

Congressional leaders who had spent the last two months listening to angry farmers found the President had proposed too little too late.

Talmadge did not offer to withdraw his bill and said he was disappointed with Carter's meager farm aid plan.

Dole, the ranking Republican on the committee, had predicted earlier that Carter would mount a "half-hearted effort to delay conference on the bill, with a little sop here and there." He called the President's program a "clear signal" that Carter "doesn't care" about farmers.

Overhaul of Loan Programs

Congress in July 1978 cleared for the President a major overhaul of federal lending programs for farmers and rural communities, including a new "economic emergency" loan program for established farmers hit by shortages of credit.

The bill had moved relatively smoothly through the House and Senate, carried along with the momentum of the much more controversial emergency farm aid measure.

The new $4 billion emergency loan program was a direct response to angry lobbying by the farmers of the militant American Agriculture Movement. It was meant to bail out farmers from a prevailing low-price, no-credit situation that they said had been created by a combination of commodity surpluses, drought losses and heavy borrowing.

The House approved the conference agreement on the credit revision bill (HR 11504) July 19 by a 362-28 vote. The Senate approved it July 20 by voice vote.

Despite the farmers' demands for immediate relief, conferees took more than two months to reach a final agreement. The House originally passed the bill April 26, the Senate May 2.

Scheduling problems, plus prolonged discussions of provisions on rural housing and Indian tribal loans, held up final agreement, according to agriculture committee sources.

The bill had two main purposes: to authorize high individual loans to farm operators, and to raise loan interest rates across the board to stimulate new funding. Private sources would more readily invest in the farm lending market if the returns were higher, and Congress would be better disposed to supply funds at interest rates close to prevailing commercial rates, advocates argued. Proponents said the bill reduced interest-subsidy costs to the federal government and would actually save money, compared with existing subsidized programs. And, they argued, farmers had a good record in paying back loans.

In House debate on the conference agreement, Ed Jones, D-Tenn., said the changes were needed because agriculture, like other sectors of the economy, had experienced "a massive increase in the need for capital and financial credit." Land prices had jumped 132 per cent between 1971 and 1977, from an average value of $204 per acre to $474, Jones said. Equipment prices were similarly inflated, and, according to the Department of Agriculture, the index of prices paid by farmers increased 66 per cent from January 1972 to January 1978, he added.

Jones, chairman of the House Agriculture subcommittee with credit jurisdiction, said farmers had been saying "for a long time" that they needed expanded credit more than they needed federally subsidized interest.

Previous objections that the bill promised more than it could deliver in the new emergency loan program surfaced briefly in House debate, as did consumer-oriented objections to a beef promotion program.

An AAM organizer, Bud Bitner, rejected the administration's heavy reliance on reserves to bring prices up. Releasing reserved stocks is a classic maneuver to protect against rock-bottom prices, but it can also be used to damp swings to the upper end of the scale. "Always in the past reserves have been used to depress prices," Bitner claimed, and he pressed AAM demands for a minimum farm price law that would make it illegal to buy or sell commodities at less than 100 per cent of parity prices.

Reaction to Conference Bill

President Carter renewed his threat to veto the conference bill April 11 in an anti-inflation speech to the American Society of Newspaper Editors. He claimed the bill would raise food prices by 3 per cent and the overall cost of living by .4 per cent, "shatter confidence in the crucial export markets for America's farm products, and cripple American farm families through increased costs."

In an April 6 analysis of the bill the administration said it would take as many as 59 million acres out of production and deficiency payments could range between $3 and $9 billion — depending largely on weather. The program would cause shortages — and high prices — in commodities like soybeans that were not included in the program, analysts warned, because farmers would shift to supported crops. The administration also warned that sharp cutbacks in farm production would sabotage ongoing negotiations for international marketing agreements and disrupt local processing, marketing and farm supply industries.

AAM reaction was evident as conferees completed their work: at a mass meeting in the Capitol rotunda, leaders urged farmers to press members to vote for the measure. The group regarded the bill as a useful stopgap, but still planned to seek a permanent minimum price law that would make it illegal to buy and sell commodities at less than 100 per cent of parity.

The American Farm Bureau Federation, a powerful conservative group that has long represented farm interests in Washington, was strongly opposed to the bill, according to spokesman Donald Donnelly. "It's an administrative monstrosity and it will interfere with exports by raising grain prices too high," he said.

But the Farm Bureau found itself pitted against AAM, the National Farmers Union (NFU), which regarded the bill as the best possible legislation in 1978 but "not enough," according to a spokesman, and even some of its own Farm Bureau members. Dole said that state units in Kansas and South Carolina backed his plan.

Consumer Federation of America (CFA) director Kathleen F. O'Reilly called the bill "preposterous, because it doesn't speak to the underlying problems that have thrust farmers into the whole boom-bust cycles." Consumers also feared the bill's effect on food prices.

House Defeats Conference Bill. The Senate spent two hours April 10 rehashing themes of earlier debates — farmers' money problems, the real cost of the bill, its political liabilities — before approving the conference report 49-41. But, in a stinging defeat for militant farmer-lobbyists, the House April 12, by a 150-268 vote, emphatically rejected the emergency farm bill.

Foley told reporters after the House vote that the controversial substance of the measure and the deep split it created among farmers were probably the decisive factors in its failure. "It is very difficult to pass a bill if there is division within the agriculture community itself," Foley said.

Without united farm support, many members from rural districts reportedly shied away from the vote-trading with urban members that is the customary way to get farm legislation approved by the House.

Foley said the veto threat had also weighed heavily against the bill, and a Republican source close to one of the House sponsors, Keith G. Sebelius, R-Kan., said "it was an anti-inflation vote, pure and simple — for the Republicans anyway."

Democrats and Republicans both reported that lobbying by non-government groups was effective, although minimal when compared with the heavy AAM effort. Republican sources reported well-placed calls against the bill by the conservative American Farm Bureau Federation. Church groups, concerned with potential food shortages, and consumer groups, worried about high food prices, also opposed the measure.

Meeting again, House and Senate conferees agreed on April 26 to a scaled-down version of the defeated bill. The agreement was tailored almost exactly to stringent administration specifications, fine-tuning of grain and cotton price support programs established in 1977, except for a year 10 per cent increase in the cotton loan level.

The Senate by voice vote May 2 approved the second conference agreement, and the House followed suit May 4 by a 212-182 roll-call vote.

Provisions. As signed into law May 15, HR 6782 (PL 95-279):

● Authorized the secretary of agriculture to raise the target price for wheat, feedgrains or cotton whenever a set-aside (voluntary land diversion program) was established for these crops. The target price increase was to compensate producers for participating in the set-aside; participation costs could include fixed payments on land or equipment which a farmer had to keep up whether or not he planted. Rice would also be covered, under a provision added to the emergency farm credit bill. *(Box, p. 133)*

● Authorized the secretary to raise target prices for other commodities when he increased them for the designated crops. These increases were to be enough to ensure the effective operation of the program — that is, enough to keep farmers from switching their plantings to take advantage of designated crop payments.

● Made three technical changes in the formula for establishing the cotton loan level, and set a minimum loan level of 48 cents a pound. The existing loan level was 44 cents.

● Authorized the secretary to permit farmers to produce crops on set-aside land for the production of gasohol (an experimental fuel combining petroleum and alcohol). In years with no set-aside, the secretary could provide incentive payments to encourage production for gasohol.

● Raised the limit on the Commodity Credit Corporation's borrowing authority to $25 billion, from $14.5 billion, on Oct. 1, 1978.

● Authorized establishment of a federal marketing order for raisins that would permit certain promotional and marketing activities by a grower-producer association. ∎

Food Prices Lead Rise in Cost of Living

Food prices led this country's wave of inflation in mid-1978 and, being the most visible to the average shopper, could become troublesome politically in the fall 1978 mid-term congressional elections. The monthly Consumer Price Index released in July 1978 marked the sixth consecutive month of steady increases in food prices (see table, p. 136). They amounted to 9 percent for the first half of 1978, making food the fastest-rising segment of the nation's cost of living.

Unlike the situation with most economic goods, there is little margin for people to cut their consumption when food prices rise. And food is a big part of most family budgets. While government statistics indicate that the average household probably spends about 18 percent of its income on food, the percentage is much higher among poor families. For an urban family of four earning $12,000 a year, food costs typically absorb almost half of its income, according to the Department of Agriculture.

Just as food has been the fastest-rising element in the Consumer Price Index in 1978, the leading item involved in high food prices has been beef. Retail beef prices increased 6.6 percent in April, 2.5 percent in May and 5.6 percent in June 1978. These upturns followed steady increases in January, February and March. Since October 1977, at the beginning of this surge, these increases added up to 30.7 percent.

While the consumer is chafing, the producer is prospering — for a change. The prices that farmers and feedlot operators received for their cattle in the first few months of 1978 would, if continued, almost double by the end of the year. Agricultural economists are predicting that farm income, which fell from $33 billion in 1973 to $20 billion in 1977, may rebound to as much as $27 billion in 1978.

Although voter grievances have focused on other matters, especially taxes, food price increases provide a potential obstacle to the Carter administration and the majority Democratic Party in House and Senate elections in November 1978 — except, perhaps, in predominantly agricultural districts. A Gallup Poll conducted in July 1978 found that 60 percent of the people who were surveyed said the cost of living was the nation's top problem. This compares to 35 percent who rated it No. 1 in October 1977.

The unexpectedly high rise in food prices has forced the government to revise its cost-of-living predictions for 1978. As 1978 began, the Council on Wage and Price Stability was predicting food prices would rise 4 to 6 percent and overall inflation about 6 percent. By May, the predictions were revised upward to the 6-8 percent range for food and 6.5 percent for all items. By late July government economists were talking, but not for attribution, about food inflation reaching or exceeding 10 percent and overall inflation hitting 7.5 percent. There was a widely held belief that food prices would continue to rise for some time and that beef prices would continue to lead the climb. James Nix, a Department of Agriculture economist, predicted that "beef prospects are not particularly bright for the consumer for the next few years."

Carter's Import Action for Cheaper Beef

In an attempt to slow the rising beef prices, President Carter on June 8, 1978, used his authority under the 1964 Meat Import Act to permit an additional 200 million pounds of foreign beef to be shipped to the United States during the year. But that action was more symbolic than substantive. Since Americans may eat 27 billion pounds of beef a year — they did in 1977 — Department of Agriculture analysts say the increased imports might, at best, shave only two cents a pound off the price of hamburger and have a lesser effect on such higher-price cuts as steaks and roasts.

Not only have beef prices increased but so have prices for pork and poultry, the other main ingredients in the American meat budget. Hog prices at the producer level have advanced sharply since late in 1977, resulting in large retail boosts. Poultry prices also have risen rapidly, partly because of increased beef prices. As consumers shifted to poultry, supply could not keep up with demand.

But beef, the major item in American meat consumption, has continued to receive most of the attention. The Associated Press reported that its Marketbasket surveys showed the average price of chopped chuck at stores it checks in 13 cities had risen from $1.03 in January to $1.39 in June 1978 — a 35 percent increase. The Marketbasket bill, an index of 15 commonly purchased food and non-food items, rose 5.6 percent in the same period.

Supply Factors Determining Meat Prices

Higher beef prices are basically a result of shrinking supplies. From 1975-78, beef prices slumped and cattle raisers responded by cutting the size of their herds. Between the beginning of 1975 and 1978, the nation's cattle inventory dropped from 132 million to 116 million. Calves born in spring 1978 brought the mid-year figure to 121 million, but the increase has been considered entirely seasonal. The meat supply, being sensitive to changes in prices, is ultimately self-correcting. High prices signal production increases, and low prices warn the producer to cut back. But the response time is necessarily slow. If a rancher wants to increase his herd, it takes nearly four years before he has more cattle to send to market.

If he decides to keep a heifer (female) calf rather than sell her for slaughter, he must wait 16 to 24 months before she can be bred. Then it will take nine more months before her calf is born. The rancher will have to keep that calf on the range or in a feedlot for 12 to 16 additional months before it is large enough to be sold as a choice carcass. Hogs can breed faster, but it still takes 10 months from the time a sow is bred until her offspring are big enough to slaughter. With poultry the interval is shorter still; only three months elapse after a chick is hatched until it reaches market weight as a broiler.

Agriculture officials calculate that beef prices go through 10-year cycles, from a low point to a high point and back to low again. Nix sees the 1978 price upswing

Cost of Living Increases

1978	All CPI* Items	Food Only	1977	All CPI* Items	Food Only
June	0.9%	1.7%	July	0.4%	0.5%
May	0.9	1.8	August	0.4	0.3
April	0.9	1.8	September	0.4	0.2
March	0.8	1.3	October	0.3	0.2
February	0.6	1.2	November	0.4	0.5
January	0.8	1.2	December	0.4	0.4

*Consumer Price Index - All Urban Consumers
Source: U.S. Bureau of Labor Statistics

portending the beginning of a new cycle of beef production, although the cycle in 1978 was still downward *(see graph, p. 137)*. "Beef producers responded to favorable cattle prices during the late 1960s and early 1970s and expanded their herds," he stated in a May 1978 U.S. Department of Agriculture booklet. "The expansion continued, due to biological thrust, after prices declined to unfavorable levels for producers. . . . Then in the late 1973-74 period, grain prices rose sharply. Placements of cattle on feed dropped 17 percent below the high levels of 1971-72. This caused substantial adjustment in the cattle industry." Starting in 1975, producers began reducing ("liquidating") their herds.

In the liquidations of 1975-77, producers sent much of their breeding stock to slaughter. In 1978, to build up their herds, they will have to keep heifers off the market and breed them. *Progressive Farmer* magazine observed in the May 1978 issue: "Any move to rebuild the breeding herd by holding back heifers will trim just that many more off the slaughter total." That means further supply restrictions, and higher beef prices.

Other farm prices have followed the lead of beef, though they have not moved up as rapidly. Grain, the weak link in the economics of American agriculture in the past few years, has become costlier. Grain prices paid to farmers, as recorded on the U.S. Bureau of Labor Statistics' Producer Price Index, have shown significant increases since late in 1977, reversing a three year decline. In the following table, the figure 100 represents average 1967 prices:

April 1977	Aug. 1977	Dec. 1977	June 1978
184.4	140.5	167.3	188.1

Manipulation Charges in Beef Marketing

In addition to market conditions, there is growing concern that some factors, including criminal behavior, may affect what consumers pay for beef. The method that meat packers and supermarkets use to make purchases from ranchers and feedlot operators has come under attack and has brought forth accusations of monopoly practices. In addition, there have been scandals in meat grading by Department of Agriculture officials, leading to criminal indictments against 17 of them and against 17 companies.

According to testimony given in 1977 before the Subcommittee on Livestock and Grains of the House Agriculture Committee, prices on more than 80 percent of all beef sales are not set by open bidding but by formulae based on prices reported in the "Daily Market and News Service," the publication of a Chicago-based market reporting service, The National Provisioner. It is printed on yellow paper and known in the trade as "The Yellow Sheet." For several years cattlemen have contended that large meat-packing companies and supermarket chains can manipulate Yellow Sheet prices and thus control the large bulk of beef sales that are set by formulae. What gives the larger packers control, according to critics of Yellow Sheet pricing, is the fact that Yellow Sheet quotations are based on a very small number of sales, a "thin" market.

In a report prepared for the California Senate and entered into the record of the U.S. House Subcommittee on Livestock and Grains on August 6, 1977, James Cothern, agricultural economist at the University of California at Davis, stated that Yellow Sheet pricing is weak "because a small unknown sample of the quantity of the beef being traded is arbitrarily selected." Only verified trades are used, meaning that both the buyer and the seller in a particular trade must be identified. This "is fine in theory but the possibility for collusion is there and it does occur," he said.

According to those who challenge the formula pricing system, Yellow Sheet prices help sustain monopolies in meat packing and retail foods. Glenn L. Freie, chairman of the board of trustees of the Meat Price Investigators Association, a group of western cattlemen, told the House subcommittee that "the device of formula pricing off The Yellow Sheet must be halted before the beef producer can get a fair deal in the market." MIPA has sued the 10 largest supermarket chains and the four largest meat packers. Both suits allege that the companies used monopolistic practices to fix prices.

Food industry spokesmen deny that a monopoly situation pertains in either beef packing or retail sales. Lester Norton, president of The National Provisioner, told the House subcommittee: "Understandably livestock people don't like the low prices that resulted from their oversupplying the market. But those prices can't be changed by tampering with The Yellow Sheet any more than tampering with the thermometer will change the temperature on an uncomfortable day."

Rep. Neal Smith, D-Iowa, chairman of the House Small Business Committee, had a staff member, former FBI agent Nick Wultich, investigate formula pricing and The Yellow Sheet. Smith, whom most regard as particularly knowledgeable about meat matters, said on May 22, 1978, that Wultich's findings are "appalling, with widespread significance for the entire meat industry." Smith opened a hearing by his committee that day by saying:

We are now about as far from auction block and free market system of transaction in this industry as we can get. Chain stores have such a large share of the retail meat market that apparently they can set the terms for buying that govern the entire industry.

A significant portion buy meat based only upon Yellow Sheet prices. All concerned in the multibillion-dollar meat industry are now faced with the fact that prices are being determined non-competitively, virtually in the upstairs rooms of a Chicago trade publication building, rather than in an open, competitive process.

Investigations of Fraudulent Meat Grading

Fraudulent grading may also affect consumer beef prices. Carol Foreman, assistant secretary of agriculture for food and consumer services, said in an interview July 12, 1978, "We've had some very serious law-enforcement problems over the past few years." In 1974 and 1975, government investigators in San Diego said they discovered deliberate false relabeling of "good" carcasses as "choice," a higher standard on the Department of Agriculture's grading scale. The graders, department employees, were taking money from packers for the deception, Mrs. Foreman said. "Seventeen firms and 17 packers were indicted," she continued. "In the last couple of years we've had five serious administrative cases where people have changed grading marks or counterfeited grading stamps, that sort of thing."

It is difficult to assess the scope of this practice, but it appears widespread. "No one area of the country seems to be free of it," Mrs. Foreman said. "The [grading] process is such that we are probably only getting the tip of the iceberg. If a grader can just upgrade those carcasses that come past him that are borderline between good and choice — say every tenth carcass — he could increase the income of the packer by $2,400 a day. And that is just the borderline situation. There are places where they are doing substantially more than that. There is a major midwestern firm that was recently discovered putting choice labels on boxed beef that wasn't choice."

Another problem that appears to be widespread is the practice of advertising ungraded "house" beef so that it appears to be USDA (U.S. Department of Agriculture) "choice." Some supermarkets display their meat in such a way that consumers think they are buying choice meat when in fact they are buying ungraded meat.

In light of these problems, Mrs. Foreman has proposed changes in department regulations to require: (1) carcasses not graded by department inspectors to be stamped "USDA ungraded"; and (2) new ways of handling, opening and inspecting meat carcasses to make grading less subjective and supervision easier. Beef packers and suppliers have objected, saying that consumers will not buy meat marked "USDA ungraded." Matt Georges of the Georges Meat Co. in Harling, Texas, said in the June 1978 issue of *Progressive Farmer*: "We won't even try to merchandise U.S. ungraded beef." There are also objections that proposed grading methods would be costly and difficult to administer.

'Middlemen's' Share of Total Food Costs

In other years, soaring food prices were accompanied by cries of consumer outrage against the "middlemen" involved in getting food products from the farm and to the grocery shelf. In 1966, 1972 and again in 1974, food price increases resulted in consumer boycotts of some supermarkets in various cities and certain foods. One such boycott was a national campaign in 1974 to stop buying beef. To the surprise of many, such a movement has not occurred in the 1978 surge of food inflation. "I think the president's action on imports may have had something to do with that," Mrs. Foreman said. "Some cattle producers have told me that his action may have kept the consumers from organizing a boycott."

Despite the lack of organized protests, the matter of middlemen remains important in questions of food inflation. As long ago as 1966, a government study by the National Commission of Food Marketing reported that retailers had a significant role in pushing prices for food up through questionable pricing practices and the rise of the supermarket. Circumstances since then have made the

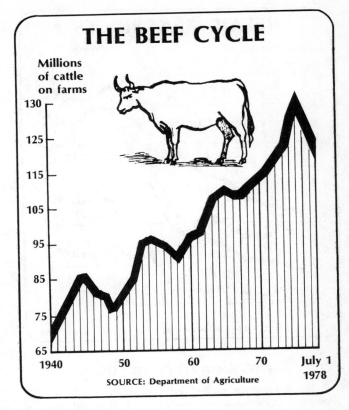

THE BEEF CYCLE

Millions of cattle on farms

SOURCE: Department of Agriculture
July 1 1978

wholesaler, transporter, processor and retailer even more important in the final price of food.

In 1959, farm costs represented half of the consumer's food bill. But by 1977, according to Department of Agriculture figures, the farm share had dropped almost to one-third. Middlemen were getting 63 cents of the consumer's food dollar, and farmers 37 cents. Of the 63 cents, processors and manufacturers claimed 20 cents, transporters 6 cents, wholesalers 11 cents, and retailers 26 cents. Even before the higher farm prices started being felt in 1978, agriculture officials were predicting that food prices for 1978 would rise 6 percent — due to increased costs for middlemen.

A major factor in the growth of these costs has been fuel and labor. Both have risen faster than farm prices in recent years. In 1977, the labor costs involved in food marketing exceeded the farm value of food for the first time. Another contributing factor to the increase in food prices, according to some who have studied the food industry, is the growth of monopoly practices in processing and retailing. Carol Foreman — when she was executive director of the Consumer Federation of America — singled out growing economic concentration in food as the major factor in rising food prices. "The real problem is a disturbing trend in our food system: greater and greater concentration in both processing and retailing; less and less competition; higher and higher profits and returns on investment," she said in 1975.

Food retailers have consistently answered that in terms of sales their profit margins are quite low, around 1 percent, a figure substantially below those of other industries, and a claim substantiated by several government studies. But the return on investment, about 12 percent, is above average, according to Cothern's report.

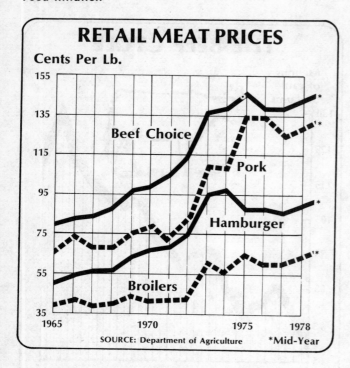

RETAIL MEAT PRICES

Cents Per Lb.

Beef Choice

Pork

Hamburger

Broilers

155
135
115
95
75
55
35

1965   1970   1975   1978

SOURCE: Department of Agriculture   *Mid-Year

Formation of Farm Policy

American farm policy today is descended from the 1920s and the changes in government policy and practice that emerged from those years. To understand the current policies and institutions requires an understanding of the events that led up to them. Agriculture entered the depression well ahead of other segments of the economy. Economic busts were not unusual in American agriculture. The panics of 1819, 1837, 1857, 1873 and 1893 had all taken heavy tolls. But the 1920s represented something more fundamental for farming, not just another swing in the economic pendulum. Historian Gilbert Fite diagnosed the problem in *George N. Peek and the Fight for Farm Parity*, published in 1954. He wrote, "Agriculture was a sick industry, with a sickness resulting from its position in a society that was becoming predominantly industrial."

Farm prices began declining in June and July 1920 and continued downward for nearly two years. They finally began to rise again, but they never reached pre-depression levels until World War II. Wheat, bringing $2.94 a bushel in Minneapolis in early July 1920, dropped to $1.72 by December and 12 months later had fallen to 92 cents.

It was clear to many that a government solution was required. But no clear policy was emerging from the sea of proposals inundating Washington. President Harding's Secretary of Agriculture, Henry C. Wallace, labeled all the plans "visionary." One of the agricultural visionaries was a successful and tough-minded businessman named George N. Peek, who had established himself in the John Deere Co. and later became president of the Moline Plow Co., rescuing it from financial ruin. When the farm depression hit, Peek approached the American Farm Bureau Federation with a plan for agricultural recovery, embodying a concept he called "agricultural equality," but which later came to be called "parity."

Peek's proposals became embodied in a series of bills, the McNary-Haugen farm bills, named for Sen. Charles L.

McNary, R-Ore., (1917-44), and Rep. Gilbert N. Haugen, R-Iowa, (1899-1933), which would establish a government corporation to buy and dispose of surplus commodities — supporting the market. The government would pay a price for the commodities that would equal "parity," the pre-war (1910-1914) price-cost ratio. McNary-Haugen never became law, ultimately falling victim to two vetoes by President Coolidge. But the proposal won acceptance in New Deal agricultural policies.

New Deal Plans to Relieve Farm Poverty

Agricultural recovery received high priority from President Roosevelt when he took office in March 1933. Many of the nation's farmers, like their urban brethren, had been impoverished by the nation's economic ills. Congress quickly passed the Agricultural Adjustment Act of 1933, which embodied many of Peek's ideas. In addition, the 1933 act included mechanisms for restricting the acreage that farmers could plant to certain crops. Acreage restrictions would be a continuing feature of farm programs for the next 40 years. The restrictions, administered through crop allotments, were the brainchild of Secretary of Agriculture Henry A. Wallace, the son of Henry C. Wallace. Peek, who had been rumored to be the leading candidate for the job Wallace got, was opposed to production restrictions. But Wallace had persuaded Congress and President Roosevelt that overproduction was the major cause of continued low prices for agricultural goods.

Upon passage of the 1933 law, the Agricultural Adjustment Administration was formed to implement it. The first administrator was George Peek. Peek stayed for seven months, but left when it was clear that production restrictions, rather than parity pricing, were to be the Wallace way of helping agriculture.

The Supreme Court declared the act unconstitutional in 1936, but most of its features reappeared in subsequent New Deal agricultural programs. Those programs were frankly eclectic and experimental. Farm economist Don Paarlberg in *American Farm Policy* (1964) wrote of the New Deal farm programs: "Despite the errors of diagnosis and prescription, certain benefits flowed from governmental intervention in the pricing and production of farm crops during the Great Depression. For one thing, farmers became convinced that government was concerned about their difficulties. This was vital if our governmental and indeed our economic institutions were to survive."

Under Henry A. Wallace, the department became a vital and busy organization, rather than the bureaucratic backwater it had been in previous administrations. It became an agency where social experimentation and attempts at social engineering flourished, and where some of the brightest talent in Washington were gathered during the 1930s. The AAA's chief counsel, for example, was Jerome N. Frank, a leading liberal legal scholar. He gathered around him a coterie of urban liberals that included, among others, Alger Hiss. The results in agriculture were mixed. While the psychological effects of the New Deal farm policies were clear and salutary, only after America's entry into World War II did the economic circumstances of American agriculture improve significantly.

Fight Over Price Supports, Free Market

Understandably, farm income was high during the war years. There was an enormous demand for food products by America's armies and allies. In the war years came the first stirrings of the technological revolution in farming, characterized by heavy use of machinery, fertilizer and pesticide, great specialization in crops, and concentration of production into large farms. Wartime government policies called for high and rigid price supports and all-out production.

On the whole, farm prices and income remained high during the first eight years of the postwar period. The farm economy was stimulated by the rebuilding of Europe and by demand for farm goods during the Korean War (1950-53). Price supports for farm commodities continued high and production boomed. Serious farm policy problems developed by the mid-1950s. Farm technology boosted production beyond the ability of the market to consume it.

To prevent a price collapse, the government made enormous purchases of commodities, which it stored. The costs to the taxpayer of high supports and enormous surpluses stimulated Congress in 1961 to pass a bill encouraging voluntary cutbacks in production. The 1961 program proved to be costly; farmers took some land out of production but managed to get bigger yields than ever from the remaining acreage.

When the 1973 Agriculture and Consumer Protection Act was passed, Secretary of Agriculture Earl L. Butz proclaimed it as a historic turning point in U.S. farm policy — the return to "a market-based philosophy." The act eliminated parity as a goal. Target prices and loan rates were geared to follow the world market — with consideration for the costs of production — and Butz was given authority to eliminate acreage controls if the market warranted that action. The name of the act also served notice that there was a new element in farm programs — the consumer.

While most agricultural economists think that Butz' claim was overstated, the 1973 act was created in an economic atmosphere entirely different from the farm programs of the 1960s. Because of world food shortages, demand exceeded supply and farm prices were rising rapidly. The market carried prices far above the loan and target levels set by the new law. Butz used his authority to suspend acreage controls and advised grain farmers to plant their fields "fence row to fence row."

Wheat prices in 1973 rose above $5 a bushel, more than farmers had ever received before or have earned since then. The next year retail meat prices climbed to their highest levels in decades — touching off a nationwide consumer boycott. The farm economy was healthy and farmers, their bank accounts fat with crop receipts, bought new equipment and committed themselves to additional acreage on an enormous scale.

Consumerism in Agriculture Department

The farm prosperity of the Butz years was short-lived. Good harvests abroad contributed to price declines for meat and grain at home. Also contributing to the declines were enormous crops produced by farmers who heeded Butz and started planting more than ever. By 1976 farm policy had, once again, become a political issue. Democratic presidential candidate Jimmy Carter promised a retreat from the Butz policies. The 1977 Food and Agriculture Act did not signal a retreat, however. Congress, which had been more responsible than Butz for the shape of the 1973 legislation, had no intention of radically reshaping agricultural policy. *(1977 Act, p. 127)*

Some Carter administration policy innovations have come administratively. The administration has tried to re-

solve the longstanding ambiguity over the role of the Department of Agriculture. For some years there has been a question whether it is supposed to represent only the needs of the farmers, or consumers as well. Under Butz, despite the title of the 1973 farm legislation, most observers regarded the department as the agency of large, wealthy farmers and agribusiness corporations. Carter, a farmer, appointed another farmer, Rep. Bob Bergland, D-Minn., Secretary of Agriculture; Bergland has moved to make the agency much more responsive to non-farm groups and interests.

Bergland quickly appointed Carol Foreman to the newly created position of assistant secretary for food and nutrition. Both her title and background suggested a new consumer orientation in the department. Another key appointee was Rupert Cutler, a Washington environmentalist who had been a critic of the department's environmental policies. Cutler was named assistant secretary for conservation, research and education. The degree to which this new openness to non-farm voices has gone was evidenced by the reaction of Butz, who in *The Washington Post*, July 4, 1978, blasted the agency for "rampant consumerism and environmentalism."

American Agriculture Movement Activism

One of the ironies of the food pricing situation is that farmers in mid-1978 finally found themselves in the midst of good — or at least hopeful — times. That was a marked contrast with the situation of just four months previously, when wheat and grain farmers were leading tractor brigades on Washington seeking relief from their problems. The rapid turnaround suggests the volatility of American agriculture. It appeared that the American Agriculture Movement, which arose spontaneously in the fall and winter of 1977 and helped bring about Senate passage of the Emergency Farm Act of 1978, was a product of unusual circumstances. The troubles that set off that round of activism, it seems, were not shared by farmers in general.

Drought hurt 1977 crops in many places but, according to a March 1978 study by the Congressional Research Service, good growing conditions prevailed in enough of the nation to keep production up — and prices down. The hardest hit were grain growers, particularly western wheat farmers. But livestock markets improved somewhat, benefiting from abundant supplies of cheap grain. "It was a picture of an industry coming off a five-year economic roller coaster with participants trying to hold onto gains in assets as their incomes tended downward," the study added. "For those with real estate to use as collateral, getting additional credit posed few problems. For renters, however, the declining income was a serious threat to continued farm operations."

The AAM came to Washington demanding 100 percent of parity. Its members said they would plant no crops unless Congress and the president met their demands. Congress had passed a new Food and Agriculture Act in the fall of 1977, renewing most of the provisions of the 1973 Agriculture and Consumer Protection Act. The 1977 act was not enough to satisfy the troubled farmers who invaded Washington in the winter of 1977-78. Through diligent and effective lobbying, they persuaded the Senate to pass on March 25, 1978, a sweeping revision of the 1977 act. The Carter administration persuaded the House to pass a bill that would be much less costly to the government, and on May 15 compromise legislation was signed into law, giving the secretary of agriculture power to raise target prices on wheat, feed grains and cotton.

Wheat target price for the 1978 crop year was immediately raised to $3.40 a bushel, up from $3, assuring wheat farmers a much better return. In order to be eligible for new loan rates and target prices, farmers had to agree to take up to 20 percent of their land out of production. Activity on the wheat futures market suggested that wheat prices could rise above the target price for the 1978 crop. Wheat futures at the Chicago Board of Trade in the last week in July 1978 reached $3.39 a bushel for March delivery contracts. While futures are highly speculative and not necessarily indicative of what farmers will receive for their crop, many analysts feel they are significant predictors of the general direction the market will take. Thus a big jump in wheat futures, particularly at a time when wheat prices usually fall — the period between late June and August — is significant.

Even if wheat prices go well above the target price, they would probably not have a great effect on consumers. A May 1978 Department of Agriculture study observed: "The average retail price for a 1-pound loaf of white pan bread in March was 36.2 cents, up 1.2 cents from January and the highest since May 1975. Three-fourths of the increase took place at the retail level with baking-wholesaling accounting for most of the remainder. The farm share for wheat in the loaf (8 percent) remained at the lowest level since 1932. These developments again demonstrate that retail bread prices are only modestly affected by the price farmers receive for their wheat."

U.S. and World Agriculture

Between 1972 and 1978, U.S. agriculture entered world trade in a bolder way than ever before. Until about 1972, when the United States made the first in a series of massive grain sales to Russia, American food exports were rather modest. Most were either gifts of food to needy countries under the Food for Peace program or the result of export subsidies paid by the government to American farmers to make them competitive abroad. The problem was that U.S. price support levels were so high U.S. farmers could not otherwise afford to sell in the world market.

By the early 1970s that picture began to change, and America's expanded role in world trade is one of the most significant recent developments in U.S. agriculture. According to the Department of Agriculture's Economic Research Service, agriculture netted this country in 1970 $1.4 billion in its international trade accounts; by 1975 the figure was $12.5 billion. Farm exports are one of the few

bright spots in the country's trade picture, helping to offset some of the enormous cost of buying foreign oil.

According to figures from the office of White House Counselor Robert S. Strauss, chief U.S. trade negotiator at the 1978 international trade talks in Geneva, agriculture accounted for about $24 billion of this country's $120 billion in exports in 1977, making it the largest single export category. Food imports ran to about $12 billion, leaving a balance of about the same amount. Wheat and soybeans are the big farm items for export. Strauss's figures show that about 25 to 30 percent of all U.S. farm products are sold to foreign markets; about 30 percent of the wheat and 60 percent of the soybeans go abroad.

Agriculture was a key element in the 1978 Geneva negotiations. Sources in Strauss's office indicated that the United States had made progress in getting the European Economic Community (Common Market) and such other food importers as Japan to agree to increase their purchases of American farm goods. The likely effect on U.S. retail food prices from such added purchases, again according to Strauss's office, would be negligible unless the world demand were to increase enormously, pushing prices up to where they were in 1974.

World Food Supply and Price Questions

During the last period of world food shortages, in 1974, U.S. agriculture prospered on foreign sales but retail prices soared. Despite good harvests in much of the world in recent years, international food agencies clearly are troubled about the future. In April 1978, John A. Hannah, executive director of the World Food Council, told the United Nations Committee on Food Aid Policies and Programs: "The basic solution to the world's food problem is to increase food production. . . . This is universally recognized. . . . There is little positive to report."

According to U.N. statistics, the average increase in food production during the 1970-1977 period in the developing countries was only 2.8 percent, well below the U.N.'s target of 4 percent. It was even less than the 2.9 percent average growth rate of the 1960s. The food growth rate was by far the lowest in Africa (1.3 percent), the area most in danger of famine. These low figures mean that even slight weather disruptions over a broad area could result in famine.

Probably no other aspect of an economy touches people as directly and immediately as food. In much of the world, when food prices rise governments tremble and sometimes fall. In the United States, food has not assumed the life and death proportions it has in some other countries. But food inflation clearly is as unwelcome to the nation's political leaders as it is to the food shoppers. ∎

Appendix

CQ

Economic Policy, 1973-1977

The nation endured severe economic jolts in 1973-74, as the deepest recession since the 1930s followed the worst price inflation since the years after World War II. Those intertwined traumas, along with critical energy supply trends, shook confidence in the nation's future prosperity.

The economy's erratic course also cast doubt upon the federal government's ability to guide the nation's giant productive machinery back into steady, sustainable growth. Republican Presidents and a strongly Democratic Congress fought all four years to a virtual economic policy stand-off that left the country with no consistent, coordinated corrective measures for either inflation or unemployment. Partly as a result, recovery was slow and uncertain; and inflation was stubbornly persistent.

At the same time, the government was only beginning to consider the increasingly complex web of international commercial and financial ties that made most nations' economies more dependent on stability in other parts of the world. The 1973 oil export embargo, followed by a more than fourfold increase in crude oil prices set by a producing nations' cartel, was the most dramatic evidence of the U.S. economy's growing vulnerability to economic and political forces beyond the government's direct control. *(Energy Policy, p. 85)*

Inflation-Recession Cycle

In a broader context, the U.S. economic troubles were but a major part of a widely swinging cycle of inflationary and recessionary pressures that swept through industrialized nations. Although the United States remained one of the strongest economic powers, along with West Germany and Japan, the international turbulence was perhaps more difficult for a U.S. population that had grown to expect a steady diet of prosperity. *(International developments, box p. 146)*

At home, the statistical toll was dismaying. Consumer prices rose by 12.2 per cent during 1974, and the unemployment rate reached 9 per cent in 1975. The economic collapse that had started in the first months of 1974 neared its nadir during the first three months of 1975, when total actual output dropped nearly 10 per cent. Before the 15-month recession had run its course, the real gross national product had fallen by $79.8-billion.

Recovery was halting. After picking up strongly in the last half of 1975 and early 1976, economic activity slowed markedly. With labor force growth outpacing the expansion, unemployment crept back up to 8 per cent late in 1976. Inflation moderated as demand pressures were reduced, but the underlying rate still held in the range of 5 per cent.

Confronted with the unprecedented combination of a steep economic downturn and continued inflation, the Democratic Congress and Republican administrations responded in accordance with traditional concerns, constituencies and philosophies of government.

President Nixon abandoned the wage and price controls he experimented with in 1971-72, resorting to restrictive budget policies to gradually curb the inflationary forces that broke loose thereafter. President Ford tried to continue those policies after Nixon resigned in 1974, promising a steadier fiscal course to bolster business and consumer confidence.

But Ford's efforts to consolidate congressional support behind the anti-inflation drive were quickly overtaken by an economic downturn that far exceeded the warnings that administration critics had been voicing most of 1974. The President shifted course by proposing one-time tax rebates to stimulate recovery—while still demanding fiscal restraints against inflation—but congressional Democrats began an all-out push for much greater stimulative measures to counter unemployment.

Congress deepened the tax cuts and eventually kept them in effect into 1977. House and Senate Democrats, their majorities bolstered by 1974 congressional election sweeps, proposed substantial federal spending increases on job-creating programs and other recession-fighting initiatives. Ford resisted with vetoes, although some were overridden.

Budget Battles

Inconclusive battling over federal fiscal policy and budget priorities went on throughout the four-year period. Re-elected by a landslide in 1972, Nixon launched a campaign to dismantle Democratic-inspired spending programs with his 1973 budget proposals. Congress fought back by refusing proposed cutbacks and challenging Nixon's impoundments of funds that it had previously appropriated. The initiative shifted with Nixon's resignation in 1974. Using the new budget procedures the House and Senate had devised in response to Nixon's policies, Congress in 1975-76 refashioned the cautious budget policies proposed by Ford, an unelected president.

In addition to establishing firmer budget limits, Congress by revamping its budget-handling methods tried to reclaim control over federal spending priorities. That effort was a political response by congressional Democrats to President Nixon's continued effort to constrict the share of federal resources directed to the domestic programs that previous Democratic administrations and Congress had constructed. Congress resisted most spending reductions, countering with legislation to curtail the presidential impoundment powers that Nixon claimed.

The federal budget swung deeply into deficit in response to rising unemployment-related spending and to

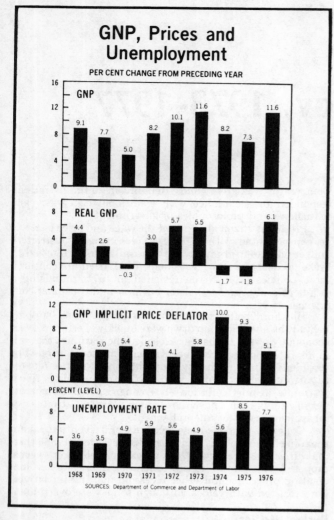

GNP, Prices and Unemployment

PER CENT CHANGE FROM PRECEDING YEAR

GNP

9.1, 7.7, 5.0, 8.2, 10.1, 11.6, 8.2, 7.3, 11.6

REAL GNP

4.4, 2.6, -0.3, 3.0, 5.7, 5.5, -1.7, -1.8, 6.1

GNP IMPLICIT PRICE DEFLATOR

4.5, 5.0, 5.4, 5.1, 4.1, 5.8, 10.0, 9.3, 5.1

PERCENT (LEVEL)

UNEMPLOYMENT RATE

3.6, 3.5, 4.9, 5.9, 5.6, 4.9, 5.6, 8.5, 7.7

1968 1969 1970 1971 1972 1973 1974 1975 1976

SOURCES: Department of Commerce and Department of Labor

falling government revenues. The deficits reached $45.1-billion, $66.5-billion and an estimated $57.2-billion in fiscal 1975-77, by far the largest since World War II years. Built-in stabilizing mechanisms, along with tax cuts and some spending initiatives, helped cushion the downturn and encourage recovery. But the pace of the upturn was disappointing, and the long-term consequences of the resulting federal borrowing for prices and private financial markets was a subject for debate.

Other Economic Issues

The Federal Reserve Board meanwhile kept a tight check on money supply expansion for most of the period, aiming at cooling inflationary pressures. Interest rates shot upward during 1974 in response to monetary constraints and expectations of continued rapid price inflation. Congressional criticism of tight monetary policies grew as economic recovery lagged, with influential members charging that money supply restraints negated the stimulative budget policies that Congress approved. But the Federal Reserve Board and its Nixon-appointed chairman, Arthur F. Burns, fended off most serious congressional challenges to its independent monetary policy administration.

Congress began looking at structural problems in the economy, notably in financial markets. A measure en-

couraging an overhaul of U.S. securities markets was enacted in 1975. Under ambitious new chairmen who took over in 1975, the House and Senate banking panels undertook a comprehensive overhaul of the federal bank and thrift institution regulatory system, but those efforts foundered in 1976.

Congress continued to back federal fiscal assistance to state and local governments, continuing through 1980 the general revenue sharing program started in 1972. Over Ford's veto, the House and Senate also enacted a package of public works and countercyclical assistance grants to tide state and local governments through recovery from recession. Congress continued a host of existing federal regional, small business and other development programs, resisting administration proposals to transform their funding and functions into block grant assistance with fewer federal stipulations.

On international economic matters, Congress generally deferred to the administration's judgment, with one notable exception. In 1974, it gave the President most of the trade negotiating authorities that Nixon had requested, while effectively vetoing a 1972 trade agreement with the Soviet Union by conditioning U.S. preferences upon relaxation of that nation's restrictive policies on emigration by Soviet Jews.

1973

Safely re-elected to a second term, President Nixon in 1973 abruptly abandoned economic policy initiatives he had taken in mid-1971 to speed economic growth. Nixon Jan. 11 lifted most of the wage and price controls that had been used to slow inflation, then submitted a restrictive $268.7-billion fiscal 1974 budget featuring wholesale spending cuts in federal domestic programs.

Nixon's return to the fundamentalist economic policy stance of the first years of his administration proved to be ill-timed. The largely voluntary Phase III wage and price controls system he adopted was overwhelmed by a burst of inflationary pressures that had been building up in a booming economy throughout 1972. Reinforced by growing worldwide demand—and compounded by food and critical materials shortages and industrial capacity bottlenecks—the resulting price spiral forced the administration to reimpose a 60-day freeze and then undertake more gradual decontrol.

In February, underlying economic problems forced the administration to negotiate the second dollar devaluation in two years. The 10 per cent devaluation, later confirmed by Congress, attempted to correct an overvaluation of the dollar's official value against other currencies that discouraged U.S. exports and contributed to persistent trade and international payments deficits that had grown worse in 1972. Nixon followed up by asking for authority to negotiate trade barrier reductions. The House complied, but politically touchy disputes over Soviet trade preferences stalled final action until the following year.

Federal fiscal policy turned less stimulative during 1973, although Congress resisted most of Nixon's program reductions. Concerned by the administration's budget assault, the House and Senate both passed legislation to curb presidential impoundment powers, then shelved that measure to concentrate on updating their own budget-making procedures.

Federal Reserve monetary policy, accommodative during 1972, also turned more restrictive. The narrowly defined money supply, which includes currency plus demand deposits, increased by 6 per cent from December 1972 to December 1973, down from 9.2 per cent in 1972. The more broadly defined money supply, also including bank time deposits, increased by 8.8 per cent, down from 11.4 per cent in 1972.

For the year as a whole, real gross national product grew by 5.5 per cent. Unemployment fell to 4.6 per cent in October before rising again. After devaluation, the dollar gained strength against other currencies, now floating against each other on international monetary markets; and the U.S. trade and payments positions recovered strongly to record slight surpluses.

But those figures disguised the trouble for which the economy was heading. The boom in output that carried over from 1972 spent itself in a frantic first quarter, and actual growth slowed drastically during the rest of the year. Inflation festered: the consumer price index rose 8.8 per cent and the wholesale price index a disturbing 15.4 per cent for the year despite the freeze and subsequent slower decontrol. Interest rates jumped; stock prices fell throughout most of the year; unemployment started back up; and shortages developed.

By the end of 1973, those troubles were being compounded by energy shortages that were severely amplified by the October Arab oil embargo. Led by fuel oil and gasoline, energy prices began accelerating in response; the embargo resulted in widespread shortages of gasoline and other petroleum products by early 1974. The higher crude oil prices brought a massive flow of wealth from industrialized and developing energy-consuming nations to the petroleum-producing nations that were members of the Organization of Petroleum Exporting Countries (OPEC). That development severely strained international monetary mechanisms, leaving consuming nations with large balance of payments deficits because the Arab producing nations' economies could not return the flow of wealth by increasing imports or investments in other economies. Energy price increases raised inflation rates throughout the world and made industrial and agricultural processes requiring intensive energy use uneconomic.

At the same time, mounting worldwide demand for food contributed to a 20 per cent increase in U.S. consumer food prices. Poor 1972 harvests in many countries, along with continued rising international demand, prompted a rapid growth in U.S. exports. The dollar devaluation made U.S. farm products cheaper overseas, moreover. Although farm products were exempt, U.S. price controls contributed to domestic shortages.

1974

The forces that had gathered during 1973 came together in the following year to send the U.S. economy reeling into its worst recession since World War II brought the nation out of the Great Depression of the 1930s. Although output fell throughout the year, it took a fourth-quarter collapse to make clear how drastic the downturn would be.

For most of the year, attention focused on inflation, which reached double-digit rates before slackening as demand deteriorated late in the fall. Severe petroleum shortages, resulting in long lines at gasoline filling stations and curtailed production and consumption that undercut first-

quarter activity, perhaps helped disguise the general weakness that was spreading throughout the economy.

In the meantime, the federal government floundered in a fruitless search for policies to correct those dismal economic trends. Preoccupied with the Watergate revelations that finally forced him from office in August, Nixon let the economy take its course while stressing fiscal and monetary restraints on inflationary pressures. The Federal Reserve Board bore most of the burden of fighting inflation through efforts to hold down monetary growth, and its restrictive policies sent interest rates to record levels before being eased late in the year.

Wage and price controls were abandoned, except for oil price restrictions, when Congress refused Nixon's request for continued limited controls and for inflation-monitoring powers. Fiscal policy remained restrictive, and the fiscal 1974 budget wound up with a slight $4.7-billion deficit.

After replacing Nixon, President Ford continued the restrictive stance against inflation but moved to bolster confidence in the economy. Congress quickly granted his request for renewed inflation-monitoring authority—but no controls—and the President tried to enlist congressional and public support for an expanded anti-inflation program through a series of domestic summit conferences on the economy.

But Ford's Oct. 8 economic program that resulted from those deliberations was made irrelevant by the economy's accelerating plunge. The President tried a down-the-middle approach, balancing tax and spending assistance to hard-pressed industries and individuals with anti-inflationary fiscal restraints built around a 5 per cent tax surcharge on 1975 federal taxes.

Congress ignored the program, but neither did it act on most economic policy proposals that House and Senate Democrats drew up during the year as alternatives to administration strategies. With Ford's support, Congress rushed through a public service jobs program in its post-election session; but the House Ways and Means Committee failed after two years of trying to produce comprehensive legislation to toughen petroleum taxes, relieve hard-pressed taxpayers and make revenue-raising tax revisions.

Some significant economic measures were given final approval, however. Congress approved new House and Senate budget procedures devised to strengthen its control over fiscal policy and budget priorities. After lengthy delay caused by Soviet trade issues, Congress also granted presidential authority for international trade negotiations.

While government policy remained ineffective, economic performance deteriorated. The first-quarter decline in output moderated slightly during the spring and summer months, but spread into a general collapse in the final three months of the year. Real gross national product fell at a 7.5 per cent annual rate during the final quarter, ending the year 1.7 per cent below its 1973 level. Personal consumption fell sharply in the October-December quarters. Automobile sales collapsed due to 1975 model price increases, energy problems and general uncertainty; and the industry began large-scale lay-offs of workers. Business fixed investments fell off; a coal mine strike undercut activity; and purchases by the federal, state and local governments held steady, providing no countercyclical stimulus to demand. Real disposable income fell for the first time since 1947 as price increases outpaced wage and salary gains. The unintended workings of the federal tax system helped undercut consumer purchasing power as inflation

Unsettled International Economic System . . .

An unsettled international economic system contributed to U.S. problems in 1973-77 and complicated government policies to deal with them.

Throughout the non-Communist nations, rapid inflation rates and steep recession paralleled and reinforced the extreme U.S. economic cycle. Counteracting government fiscal and monetary policies, along with adjustments to massive oil price increases and crop failures, strained new international trade and financial arrangements that came into use following severe currency exchange disruptions in early 1973.

A series of extraordinary economic shocks—including grain harvest shortfalls, critical commodity shortages and petroleum price increases dictated by a producing nations' cartel—helped set off a worldwide round of inflation in 1972-73. Their effects were boosted by simultaneous stimulative actions by all the major trading nations that fed a short-lived boom in early 1973. The ravages of the resulting rising prices, along with concurrent deflationary efforts by governments, then helped bring on a cumulative 1974-75 recession. An uneven recovery followed, led by the United States, Japan and West Germany, but the pace faltered in mid-1976 even in those relatively strong economies. Recovery lagged behind in other nations, notably Great Britain and Italy, where inflation persisted at higher levels that forced governments to tighten restraints on demand.

Oil Price Increases

All the western industrialized nations, and most less developed countries as well, spent 1973-77 making painful adjustments to skyrocketing energy costs. The most deeply felt international economic development of the period was the four-fold crude oil price increase that the Organization of Petroleum Exporting Countries (OPEC) cartel imposed in stages. The OPEC nations' determination to multiply their earnings from production of their vital petroleum reserves—and willingness to use oil as a political weapon as demonstrated by the 1973 export embargo imposed after war broke out with Israel—produced severe energy shortages and inflationary reverberations that contributed heavily to recession. Even as other raw material producing nations considered similar cartel tactics, the petroleum crisis made the industrialized nations all too aware of their disturbing dependence on dwindling supplies of critical materials that often were beyond their direct control.

Rising oil import bills created severe imbalances in the flow of goods, services and capital among nations. Energy-consuming nations ran up heavy trade and international payments deficits as oil payments flowed to the OPEC nations.

In 1974 alone, OPEC countries accumulated $70.5-billion in payments surpluses. Because the producing nations could absorb relatively few imports, and had not begun to reinvest oil earnings in other countries, that wealth was not returned to reverse flows back to the industrialized economies.

The resulting payments drain eased in 1975, when recession curtailed energy demand in industrialized nations and when OPEC countries stepped up imports and foreign investments. But the trend was expected to reverse with economic recovery and additional oil price increases. And the financing of continued oil deficits threatened to exhaust the ability of some nations, such as Great Britain, to borrow foreign funds to cover rising government debt and domestic consumption. The resulting financial problems were forcing retrenchment in domestic economic goals in some countries, while rising oil prices fueled inflation in all nations and discouraged needed investment in industries requiring intensive energy use.

International Monetary Structure

Those painful adjustments were thrust upon an improved international monetary system that began evolving from the ruins of the post-World War II structure. That previous system, negotiated at the 1944 Bretton Woods, N.H., conference and centered on a strong U.S. dollar, fell apart in 1971-73 in long-delayed recognition of new world economic realities.

The Bretton Woods system, which assigned each nation's currency a fixed value pegged to the dollar and through it to gold, began unraveling during the 1960s when the United States encountered chronic outflows in its balance of payments with other nations.

The turning point came in 1971, when President Nixon suspended the long-standing U.S. commitment to exchange its gold reserve assets for unwanted dollars accumulated by other nations, in effect allowing the dollar to float. He then negotiated a general currency exchange rate realignment that devalued the official value of the dollar to a level that more realistically reflected international assessment of the U.S. economy's strength.

boosted taxpayers into higher brackets and Social Security tax wage base increases continued payroll tax deductions from workers' paychecks later into the fall.

Unemployment jumped as a result, reaching 7.2 per cent in December after a steep rise from 5 per cent in May. Civilian employment started falling in August, and steady reductions in available jobs left more than 6.6 million workers out of work by December.

While the severe lag in demand brought some fourth-quarter relief, prices continued rising throughout the year at annual rates of more than 10 per cent. The most comprehen-

sive measure, the gross national product (GNP) price deflator, rose 10 per cent above its 1973 level; the consumer price index increased 12.2 per cent for the year and the wholesale price index by a whopping 20.9 per cent.

The cost of borrowing money reached the highest levels ever recorded in the United States in response to money supply constrictions and to expectations for continued high inflation. The prime rate that commercial banks charged their best corporate customers reached 12 per cent by mid-year before declining in the fall. Demand for business credit rose during the year as industries found themselves short of

. . . Contributed to U.S. Problems in 1973-77

The 1971 currency realignment failed to end international payments problems, however, and a wave of speculation against the dollar forced another 10 per cent devaluation in February 1973. Shortly thereafter, inflationary pressures and volatile flows of capital among nations led governments to give up all attempts to maintain fixed exchange rates through market intervention. The Bretton Woods structure was replaced by a *de facto* system of floating exchange rates, in which supply and demand forces on international exchanges were left free to determine the relative values of currencies. The International Monetary Fund (IMF) nations meanwhile continued negotiations on devising a new monetary system to replace the Bretton Woods arrangements.

Floating Exchange Rates

In theory, the floating exchange rate system was expected to help correct international payments imbalances through largely automatic adjustments. Market judgments would cause the currency of a country with a weak economy, high inflation and persistent payment outflows to float downward in value against other currencies. With the currency costing less in terms of other currencies, and the country's products therefore cheaper in other nations, demand for its exports would strengthen, more costly imports from other countries would decline, its domestic output would strengthen and its payments balance would swing back toward equilibrium. A country with a payments surplus, on the other hand, could expect its currency to appreciate, cutting back foreign demand for its exports while making imports more attractively priced.

In practice, the system worked less smoothly. Despite large currency fluctuations in response to inflation rate differentials, countries such as Great Britain and Italy whose currencies had depreciated were unable to maintain their export market shares as world trade began expanding with recovery from the recession. Germany and Japan, with much stronger currencies, on the other hand increased their exports, perhaps because their lower inflation rates and amicable management-labor relations promised better performance in fulfilling contracts. Critics contended that exchange rate fluctuations worsened price pressures in inflation-plagued nations as depreciation made imports more costly; defenders of the system argued that exchange rates could be held steady only if a government took adequate measures to curb underlying inflation pressures at home.

Regardless of such problems, the floating rate system weathered the fluctuating worldwide economic fortunes without disastrous strains. Along with special arrangements by the IMF for directing OPEC surpluses to deficit nations, the system was beginning to accommodate to the redistribution of economic power and assets resulting from oil price increases.

Following a 1975 understanding between France and the United States, the IMF drew up revised international monetary agreements that in effect confirmed the floating system. Congress in 1976 approved U.S. ratification of the agreement, under which IMF nations agreed to avoid exchange rate manipulation except to counter disorderly conditions, provided for possible reinstitution of fixed rates in the future, replaced gold with IMF special drawing rights (SDRs or paper gold) as the medium of settlement in IMF transactions, and authorized sale of part of IMF gold reserves to finance a trust fund to help poor nations adjust to higher oil import costs.

Trade Negotiations

The major industrial nations in the meantime were engaged in wide-ranging trade negotiations aimed at further reductions in tariffs and other barriers to international commerce. Congress in 1974 authorized U.S. participation by giving the President authority to negotiate and implement some trade barrier reductions, ignoring organized labor support for strong protectionist measures to curb competition from foreign imports. Despite the unemployment that accompanied the recession, the industrialized nations for the most part resisted drastic trade curbs designed to bolster domestic production.

Less-Developed Nations

The United States and other industrialized nations were still weighing responses to demands by less-developed countries for new international arrangements to relieve them of their heavy debt burdens, provide additional development assistance and assure stable export earnings indexing the price of the raw materials they produced to the prices of industrial products. The Ford administration was divided on the proper response, with the Treasury Department taking a hard stance against such proposals and the State Department more willing to negotiate.

cash to finance capacity expansion and inventory accumulation. Profits rose substantially but for the most part reflected huge inventory value adjustments due to inflation that did not provide additional internal funds for reinvestment. Equity investment fell as stock prices continued their general plunge.

The combination of monetary stringency and business loan demand severely squeezed credit markets, and high interest rates drew funds away from the thrift institutions that provide most mortgage financing; residential construction fell 27 per cent, its worst decline since World War II.

Before shifting policy late in the year to ease monetary growth to counteract the recession, the Federal Reserve kept the clamps on the money supply. The narrowly defined money supply grew only 4.7 per cent for the year, with the broader supply increasing 7.2 per cent.

The U.S. trade and payments balances swung back into deficit, partly in response to oil import price increases and to a worldwide recession that cut demand for U.S. exports. The pattern of inflation and recession was repeated in other nations, reinforcing U.S. economic troubles. *(International developments, box above)*

Gross National Product

Billions of Dollars (Seasonally Adjusted Annual Rates)

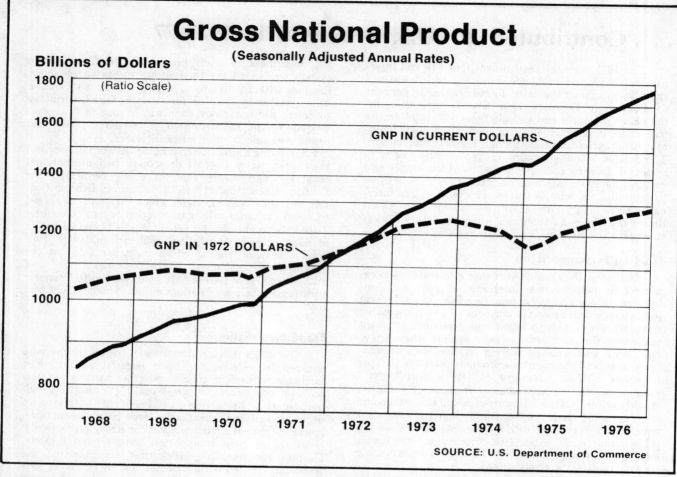

SOURCE: U.S. Department of Commerce

1975

The downturn carried over into 1975, climaxing with a 9.9 per cent first-quarter drop in actual output, before the slide ended in April. Prodded by stimulative tax cuts, the economy recovered through the rest of the year, although the pace began slowing in the final three months.

The surge of unemployment reached 9 per cent in May before starting to gradually decline. Inflation fell to roughly half its 1974 pace, still high by any other standards. The recovery responded in part to automatic cyclical developments, notably the massive sell-off of unwanted business inventories that had accumulated because of lagging sales. Federal fiscal measures spurred the recovery, both through the emergency tax cuts and through built-in budget stabilizing mechanisms that boosted transfer payments to individuals and families and curtailed federal tax collections.

Still divided over basic fiscal strategies, Congress and the President agreed on a tax reduction package to bolster consumer and business spending power. Ford asked for a one-shot rebate of 1974 tax payments, but Congress deepened the impact by combining rebates with 1975 tax withholding reductions. While approving business tax relief as well, Congress tied curbs on the controversial oil and gas depletion allowance to the measure. It also tacked on $50 bonus payments to federal benefit recipients as a further stimulative measure. The administration and Congress

thereafter resumed their battle over budget policy. The House and Senate ignored Ford's pleas to restrain existing program spending to reduce the risk of renewed inflation. And Ford opposed and sometimes vetoed additional stimulative spending programs that the heavy Democratic House and Senate majorities devised. Congress strengthened its case for more assertive budget measures by implementing its new budget procedures a year ahead of schedule. At year's end, the tax cuts were extended into 1976 after a brief veto impasse over budget restraints.

Fiscal policy turned decisively stimulative. The fiscal 1975 budget wound up with a $45.1-billion deficit as strong growth in transfer payments through Social Security, unemployment and other programs replenished personal income. The emergency tax measure went into effect in April, pumping $8.1-billion back into the economy through rebates and another $1.8-billion through bonus benefits. Lower tax withholding rates, put into effect on May 1, reduced tax collections by $7.8-billion through the rest of the year. Working through its new budget procedures, Congress aimed at increasing Ford's estimated $51.9-billion fiscal 1976 deficit to a record $74.1-billion.

The Federal Reserve Board continued to go its own way in guiding monetary growth, generally sticking to a restrictive stance against inflation despite congressional pressure to accelerate money supply expansion to accommodate a faster recovery. The House backed away from proposals by Rep. Henry S. Reuss (D Wis.), the activist new chairman of its Banking, Currency and Housing Committee, to dictate money supply goals.

Federal Reserve Board Chairman Burns made one concession by agreeing to disclose monetary growth target ranges in periodic House and Senate testimony. As outlined by Burns, those goals aimed at narrowly defined money supply expansion to levels between 5 per cent and 7 per cent above year-earlier levels.

By the end of the year, however, the narrow money supply had grown only 4.1 per cent and the broader supply 8.5 per cent. The money supply had accelerated sharply in the second quarter as the Treasury paid out tax rebates and bonus payments, but the pace slowed markedly during the second half of the year.

After bottoming in April, output began recovering at a 5.6 per cent annual rate in the second quarter of the year. Inventory liquidations that had started in the first quarter continued at high levels, and the Federal Reserve Board's industrial production index started climbing again after falling 12.5 per cent below its September 1974 level. Recovery quickened in the summer months, and actual GNP grew at a boom-like 11.4 per cent rate in the July-September quarter. That pace was not sustained, however, as personal consumption slowed, government purchases moderated and business fixed investment continued to lag. In the fourth quarter, actual output rose by only 3.3 per cent.

Unemployment declined from its 9 per cent May peak but stayed well above 8 per cent. After several months of slow decline, the rate stood at 8.3 per cent in December, with 7.7 million workers out of jobs.

The slow rebuilding of demand allowed inflation to continue abating, although the GNP deflator still hung at 9.3 per cent. The consumer price index increased by 7 per cent for the year, while the wholesale price index rose a more moderate 4.2 per cent.

Despite general monetary stringency, interest rates continued the decline that had begun late in 1974 through most of 1975. After rebounding upward during the summer following the business turnaround, short-term interest rates resumed their decline as private credit demand remained weak. As competing interest rates fell—and personal savings rates remained higher than normal—funds flowed into thrift institutions. With mortgage funds more plentiful, the housing industry recovered.

Stock prices climbed steadily during the first half of the year, then fluctuated well below pre-recession levels. Early in the year, Congress completed action on legislation to encourage securities industry competition and modernization.

The U.S. recovery was followed by economic improvement in other nations. Still, the volume of world trade fell significantly for the first time in 30 years, and the worldwide recovery was uncertain as consuming nations continued adjusting to energy price increases. The U.S. trade and payments balances recorded strong surpluses, partly because imports fell off more drastically than exports to other nations. Agricultural exports remained strong, although the government temporarily embargoed Soviet grain sales that threatened to push food prices upward.

1976

The economic recovery sputtered in 1976. After growing at a 9.2 per cent annual rate in the first three months, actual output slowed progressively during the rest of the year. In the final quarter, actual GNP grew only 2.6 per cent, below the rate of expansion considered sufficient to provide jobs for a growing work force. After falling to 7.3 per cent in May, unemployment in fact edged back up to 8 per cent in November before settling down to 7.8 per cent in December.

Ford and the Democratic Congress continued their fiscal policy struggles through the year. Pressures for stimulus to reduce the politically sensitive unemployment rate were heightened by the approach of the Nov. 2 presidential and congressional elections, and Ford's narrow defeat by Democratic candidate Jimmy Carter was partly due to continued economic sluggishness. The Federal Reserve Board maintained its cautious monetary policy course despite continued grumbling in Congress.

Despite Ford's opposition to stimulative measures that risked long-term inflation, Congress finally was able to enact increased fiscal assistance through public works and countercyclical aid to state and local governments. The tax cuts again were extended, and Congress enacted a long-promised tax revision measure. But actual federal outlays fell inexplicably short of intended levels at critical junctures during the year, perhaps contributing to the recovery's slowdown, and the incoming Carter administration made stepped up stimulus to speed the recovery one of its 1977 priorities.

By any measure, federal fiscal policy was stimulative in 1976, which covered the last six months of fiscal 1976, a three-month July-October transition quarter preceding a switch to a new Oct. 1 beginning date for the fiscal year, and the first three months of fiscal 1977. The fiscal 1976 budget wound up with a $66.5-billion deficit, less than the $74.1-billion projected by Congress but more stimulative than $51.9-billion that Ford had proposed in 1975. The transition quarter deficit was less than $13-billion, well below the congressional target, as spending was considerably less than projections. The spending shortfalls were concentrated in the middle months of the year and resulted in a sharp temporary reduction in the government's deficit, thus curtailing fiscal stimulus while the economy still was struggling upward.

The Federal Reserve Board maintained its monetary expansion goals for the upcoming year in the 4.5 per cent to 7 per cent range for the narrowly defined money supply, after lowering the upper target to 6.5 per cent. That signaled continued caution about price pressures, and Burns suggested that the underlying inflation rate remained at 6 per cent to 7 per cent. During 1976, the narrowly defined money supply grew at quarterly annual rates that fluctuated above and below 5 per cent; while broader money supply growth held at around 9.5 per cent for most of the year before accelerating to 10.9 per cent in the final quarter.

For the year, real GNP grew by 6.1 per cent, despite the slowdown of expansion in the last nine months. Unemployment, after rising through the late summer and fall, came down again in December and fell once more in January 1977, although that improvement may have been temporary. Interest rates fell steadily throughout 1976, with short-term rates reaching their lowest levels since 1972, but were starting to climb again in early 1977. Corporate profits improved, and business fixed investment showed some signs of reviving after lagging behind the levels needed to help lead a stronger recovery.

Price increases generally were moderate, but the GNP deflator still measured at 5.1 per cent for the year. By the fourth quarter, the consumer price index had risen by 5 per cent from its 1975 fourth-quarter level, and the wholesale price index had gone up by 4.1 per cent over the same period. All three measures reached their highest rates of increase during the second half of the year, however.

With inflation moderating, real wages rose by 2 per cent in 1976 after declining in the two previous years. After rapid first-quarter starts, real disposable income and personal consumption slowed through the middle of the year before reviving in the final three months. Strong Christmas season activity helped boost retail sales in the final quarter. Housing starts and residential investment held up well during the year and accelerated significantly in the fourth quarter of 1976.

The U.S. trade and international payments balances swung back into deficit as rising domestic demand brought in more imports. Most of the import volume increase was due to rising fuel imports as the nation's energy use increased about 3.5 per cent after falling for two years.

1977

The nation's economy continued on an uncertain course in 1977.

As in 1976, the economy grew rapidly in the first half of the year but slowed in the second, and 1977 ended as it began — with calls for new economic stimulus to maintain the recovery from the 1974-75 recession.

President Carter was widely criticized for his handling of economic issues in 1977. Critics faulted the administration for failing to weigh individual programs within the framework of an overall economic policy. They said Carter's failure to pursue consistent policies had created a damaging crisis of confidence in the business community.

By year's end, Carter had committed himself to development of a comprehensive economic program. And he postponed his long-awaited tax package until 1978 so that it could reflect the impact of pending Social Security and energy legislation, as well as the need for stimulus tax cuts.

Meanwhile, skepticism grew about Carter's pledge to balance the budget by fiscal 1981, and administration officials started hedging. There had been doubts right along that the President could redeem all his promises for welfare reform, health insurance, aid to the cities and other costly programs without increasing expenditures faster than revenues would rise.

In addition, the pace of economic growth fell behind the administration's expectations, and independent analysts doubted that the economy would expand vigorously enough to provide the revenues needed to balance the budget, even if spending could be held down. Tax cuts to stimulate the economy would put a balanced budget even further beyond reach, it was contended.

Administration officials qualified the budget-balancing pledge. They specified that the administration intended to balance the budget in a high-employment economy. That is, if economic growth and employment fell below targets, budget deficits would continue.

Mixed Performance

As it did in 1976, the economy spurted dramatically during the first quarter of 1977. The "real" gross national product (GNP), adjusted for seasonal variations and inflation, increased at a 7.5 per cent annual rate, up from 1.2 per cent in the last quarter of 1976. The GNP tapered off later in the year, though not so sharply as in 1976.

Consumer spending, which makes up roughly two-thirds of the GNP, continued to climb steadily. Business investment in plants and equipment posted smaller gains than some observers felt was necessary.

Inflation, as measured by the GNP price deflator, increased at 7.1 per cent annual rate in the second quarter but abated later in the year.

Consumer prices rose faster than in 1976, when the increase in the consumer price index was 4.8 per cent. The average worker's take-home pay increased faster than prices through most of 1977, maintaining moderate gains in purchasing power.

Although the growth rate during the first three quarters stayed above the 4 per cent level economists believe is necessary to prevent unemployment from rising, the unemployment rate hovered around 7 per cent during most of 1977, after dropping from 7.8 per cent in December 1976.

Business confidence in the economy was a matter of concern during 1977. There were complaints that inflation was eroding true profits and that uncertainties about taxes and government policies made business commitments too risky. Industries produced at a relatively low 82 to 83 per cent of plant capacity during much of the year, according to the Federal Reserve Board.

Bucking some other business trends, the housing industry recorded its best year since 1973. New housing starts increased from 1.5 million units in 1976 to about 2 million units, despite the fact that the median new home price exceeded $49,000, according to the National Association of Home Builders.

Uncertainty over government policies, concern about rising interest rates and recession fears were blamed for sharp delines in the stock market. Administration officials remained moderately optimistic about the economic outlook, and said the gloom on Wall Street was exaggerated. They tried to bolster business confidence and promised programs for 1978, including tax measures to encourage investment, to promote strong economic growth.

Carter on the Issues

President Carter's first major policy initiative in 1977 was a two-year, $31.6-billion package of tax cuts and job-creation programs aimed at stimulating the sagging economy.

Carter's handling of the proposals proved characteristic. Officials unveiled the stimulus package in stages over a two-month period, meanwhile continuing to tinker with the details. Then, while Congress was debating the package, Carter abruptly withdrew its keystone—a controversial proposal to provide $50 tax rebates or payments to individuals, as well as proposed tax credits for business. Carter insisted that improved economic conditions led to his decision, but the rebates had won only narrow approval in the House and faced possible defeat in the Senate.

Carter's surprise policy reversal angered Democratic congressional leaders who had backed the new President on the issue. "It was a little less than fair to those of us who supported it against our better judgment and worked hard to get it passed," said Rep. Al Ullman (D Ore.), chairman of the House Ways and Means Committee. Senate Budget Committee Chairman Edmund S. Muskie (D Maine), who had pushed through revisions of the fiscal 1977 budget to accommodate the payments, also deplored Carter's action. "If economic conditions in April justify this abandonment of the course we set two months ago, Congress has a right to know why those conditions were misjudged in February when the program was proposed," Muskie said.

Tax Reform. President Carter also gave mixed signals on the issue of tax reform, to which he was committed by a 1976 campaign pledge. Carter's tax package, originally scheduled for submission to Congress in September, ultimately was put off until 1978.

Both the timing and the shape of the eventual package remained in doubt. Carter originally contemplated a comprehensive revision of the nation's tax structure. By late 1977, however, the emphasis had switched to tax cuts, and on Dec. 3, the President told a news conference: "In 1978, there will be substantial tax reductions and combined with that will be an adequate proposal for a tax reform." Carter conceded that "some of the more controversial items on tax reform that have been proposed to me...might be delayed until later on."

Accommodations With Labor. Organized labor, which had provided crucial backing for candidate Carter in 1976, found the President's 1977 stimulus package inadequate. It thought Carter too cautious in other areas as well.

Labor and civil rights groups were dismayed by Carter's original proposal for a modest 20-cent increase in the hourly minimum wage. Months of behind-the-scenes negotiations were required before Carter and labor finally reached agreement on a compromise minimum wage hike, as well as an understanding on collective bargaining legislation pressed by the AFL-CIO.

It took even longer to convince Carter to get behind the Humphrey-Hawkins full employment bill. A revised version of the legislation endorsed by Carter Nov. 14 sought to reduce the overall unemployment level to 4 per cent — and the rate for workers aged 20 and over to 3 per cent — in five years. The revised version did not spell out specific government job-creation steps, however, and it gave the President a chance to revise the goals themselves at a later date.

Reflecting concern over a resurgence of inflation in 1978, the revised bill included anti-inflation provisions sought by the administration. Earlier in the year, a voluntary anti-inflation program announced by Carter sank without a trace.

Labor also figured in administration attempts to devise some form of import relief for the ailing U.S. steel industry. While labor backed a steel aid plan announced by the White House Dec. 6, the AFL-CIO served notice that it would press in 1978 for legislation that would give U.S. workers broader protection from foreign competition.

Carter and the Cities. Although cities benefited from the economic stimulus program — which included money for public service jobs, public works projects and countercyclical aid targeted to hardship cities — the urban employment picture remained bleak, especially for minority teenagers.

Under pressure from black leaders, President Carter in late summer stepped up plans for development of a national urban policy. The program, expected to focus on creating jobs through incentives to business, was to be announced in 1978.

Meanwhile, Carter proposed and Congress enacted a $12.5-billion urban aid bill that channeled new funds to the aging cities of the Northeast and industrial Midwest. The bill also included a one-year extension of major government housing programs.

Monetary Policy. The Federal Reserve came under increasing criticism from some members of Congress and Carter administration officials as short-term interest rates rose. Federal Reserve Chairman Arthur F. Burns fought back, resisting pressure for "easier" monetary policies.

President Carter, worried about losing the confidence of conservative business leaders, tried to avoid a clash with the Fed. He kept business and financial leaders guessing about whether he would reappoint Burns as chairman when his term expired early in 1978.

The Federal Reserve raised short-term interest rates steadily from the spring until early autumn in an effort to restrain growth of the money supply, which it feared would aggravate inflation. But then the Fed halted its rate-raising moves, at least temporarily. The money managers apparently shared the administration's fears that substantially higher rates might damage the economy seriously. They also hoped that they had raised rates high enough to get growth of the money supply back on a safe track, without the need to squeeze credit still harder ▮

Selected Bibliography on Economic Policy

Books and Reports

Aaron, Henry, ed. *Inflation and the Income Tax*. Washington, D.C.: Brookings Institution, 1976.

American Assembly. *Capital for Productivity and Jobs*. Englewood Cliffs, N.J.: Prentice-Hall, 1977.

American Enterprise Institute for Public Policy Research. *Does the Government Profit From Inflation?: A Round Table Discussion held on May 25, 1977*. Washington, D.C., 1977.

————. *The Future of the Social Security System*. Washington, D.C.: 1978.

Ball, Robert M. *Social Security Today and Tomorrow*. New York: Columbia University Press, 1978.

Brandon, Robert and Rowe, Jonathan. *Tax Politics: How They Make You Pay and What You Can Do About It*. New York: Pantheon, 1976.

Brannon, Gerard M. *Energy Taxes and Subsidies*. Cambridge, Mass.: Ballinger, 1974.

Break, George F. and Pechman, Joseph A. *Federal Tax Reform: The Impossible Dream?* Washington, D.C.: Brookings Institution, 1975.

Brookings Papers on Economic Activities. Washington, D.C.: Brookings Institution, 1970-.

Brown, J. Douglas. *Essays on Social Security*. Princeton, N.J.: Princeton University, 1977.

Campbell, Collin D. *Income Redistribution*. Washington, D.C.: American Enterprise Institute for Public Policy Research, 1977.

Chiswick, Barry R., and O'Neill, June A., eds. *Human Resources and Income Distribution: Issues and Policies*. New York: W. W. Norton, 1977.

The City in Transition: Prospects and Policies for New York; the Final Report of the Temporary Commission on City Finance. New York: Arno Press, 1978.

Cline, William R. *Trade Negotiations in the Tokyo Round*. Washington, D.C.: Brookings Institution, 1978.

Committee for Economic Development. *Fighting Inflation and Promoting Growth*. New York: 1976.

Commoner, Barry. *The Poverty of Power: Energy and the Economic Crisis*. New York: Bantam Books, 1977.

Cose, Ellis. *Energy and the Urban Crisis*. Washington, D.C.: Joint Center for Political Studies, 1978.

———— and Morris, Milton, eds. *Energy Policy and the Poor*. Washington, D.C.: Joint Center for Political Studies, 1977.

David, Martin. *Alternative Approaches to Capital Gains Taxation*. Washington, D.C.: Brookings Institution, 1968.

Davis, Karen. *National Health Insurance: Benefits, Costs, and Consequences*. Washington, D.C.: Brookings Institution, 1975.

Douglas, George W. *Economic Regulation of Domestic Air Transport: Theory and Practice*. Washington, D.C.: Brookings Institution, 1974.

Frank, Charles R. Jr. *Foreign Trade and Domestic Aid*. Washington, D.C.: Brookings Institution, 1977.

Friedman, Milton. *Dollars and Deficits: Inflation, Monetary Policy and the Balance of Payments*. Englewood Cliffs, N.J.: Prentice-Hall, 1968.

Garms, Walter L., et al. *School Finance: The Economics and Politics of Public Education*. Englewood Cliffs, N.J.: Prentice-Hall, 1978.

Goodwin, John W. *Agricultural Economics*. Reston, Va.: Reston Publishing Co., 1977.

Haberler, Gottfried. *Incomes Policies and Inflation*. Washington, D.C.: American Enterprise Institute for Public Policy Research, 1971.

Harberger, Arnold C. and Bailey, Martin J., eds. *The Taxation of Income from Capital Gains*. Washington, D.C.: Brookings Institution, 1969.

Kaplan, Robert S. *The Financial Crisis in the Social Security System*. Washington, D.C.: American Enterprise Institute for Public Policy Research, 1976.

Kenen, Peter B., ed. *International Trade and Finance: Frontiers for Research*. Cambridge, Mass.: Cambridge University Press, 1975.

Krueger, Anne O. *Growth, Distortions, and Patterns of Trade Among Many Countries*. Princeton, N.J.: Princeton University, 1977.

Lecht, Leonard A., ed. *Employment and Unemployment: Priorities for the Next Five Years*. New York: Conference Board, Report no. 718, 1977.

McAdam, Terry W. and Slutsky, Lorie. *The New York City Fiscal Situation*. New York: Citizens Union Research Council, 1977.

Mermelstein, David and Alcaly, Roger. *The Fiscal Crisis of American Cities: Essays on the Political Economy of Urban America with Special Reference to New York City*. New York: Random House, 1977.

Munnell, Alicia H. *The Future of Social Security*. Washington, D.C.: Brookings Institution, 1977.

O'Rourke, A. Desmond. *The Changing Dimensions of U.S. Agricultural Policy*. Englewood Cliffs, N.J.: Prentice-Hall, 1978.

Ott, Attiat F. *New York City's Financial Crisis: Can the Trend be Reversed?* Washington, D.C.: American Enterprise Institute for Public Policy Research, 1975.

Ott, David J. and Ott, Attiat F. *Federal Budget Policy*. Washington, D.C.: Brookings Institution, 1977.

Parker, Richard. *The Myth of the Middle Class: Notes on Affluence and Equality*. New York: Harper Colophon Books, 1974.

Pechman, Joseph A. ed. *Comprehensive Income Taxation*. Washington, D.C.: Brookings Institution, 1977.

————. *Federal Tax Policy*. Washington, D.C.: Brookings Institution, 1977.

————, ed. *Setting National Priorities: The 1978 Budget*. Washington, D.C.: Brookings Institution, 1977.

————, ed. *Setting National Priorities: The 1979 Budget*. Washington, D.C.: Brookings Institution, 1978.

————, and Okner, Benjamin A. *Who Bears the Tax Burden?* Washington, D.C.: Brookings Institution, 1974.

Perry, George L. "Stabilization Policy and Inflation." In *Setting National Priorities: The Next Ten Years*, pp. 271-321. Edited by Henry Owen and Charles L. Schultze. Washington, D.C.: Brookings Institution, 1978.

Richardson, Harry W. *Economic Aspects of the Energy Crisis*. Lexington, Mass.: Lexington Books, 1975.

Ritson, Christopher. *Agricultural Economics: Principles and Policy*. New York: St. Martin, 1977.

Schurr, Sam H. and Netschert, Bruce. *Energy in the American Economy, 1850-1975*. Washington, D.C.: Resources for the Future, 1960.

Sharkansky, Ira. *The Politics of Taxing and Spending*. Indianapolis, Ind.: Bobbs-Merrill, 1969.

Solkoff, Joel. *You Reap What You Sow: How the Government Regulates Agriculture*. Washington, D.C.: New Republic Books, 1978.

Surrey, Stanley S. *Pathways to Tax Reform: The Concepts of Tax Expenditures*. Cambridge, Mass.: Harvard University Press, 1973.

Vincent, Phillip E. *School Finance Reforms and Big City Fiscal Problems*. Cambridge, Mass.: United States Committee on Taxation, Resources and Economic Development Conference, 1977.

Wares, William A. *The Theory of Dumping and American Commercial Policy*. Lexington, Mass: Lexington Books, 1977.

Weidenbaum, Murray L. and Harnish, Reno. *Government Credit Subsidies for Energy Development*. Washington, D.C.:

American Enterprise Institute for Public Policy Research, 1976.

————, et al. *Matching Needs with Resources: Reforming the Federal Budget.* Washington, D.C.: American Enterprise Institute for Public Policy Research, 1973.

Wiegand, G. Carl, ed. *The Menace of Inflation: A Symposium.* Old Greenwich, Conn: Devin-Adair, 1977.

Articles

Auster, Richard D., and Gordon, Josephine G. "Incentives in a Government-Controlled Health Sector?" *Policy Studies Journal,* Spring 1977, pp. 295-300.

Balz, Daniel J. "When Better Farm Policy is Made, Who Will Make It?" *Working Papers for a New Society,* Spring 1977, pp. 62-67.

Beebe, W. T. "Deregulation and the Airlines." *Finance,* November 1977, pp. 3-5.

Brinner, Roger and Munnell, Alicia. "Taxation of Capital Gains: Inflation and Other Problems." *New England Economic Review,* September/October 1974, pp. 3-21.

Buffett, Warren E. "How Inflation Swindles the Equity Investor." *Fortune,* May 1977, pp. 250-254.

Campbell, Colin and Reese, Thomas. "The Energy Crisis and Tax Policy in Canada and the United States: Federal-Provincial Diplomacy v. Congressional Lawmaking." *Social Science Journal,* January 1977, pp. 17-32.

Cohen, Richard E. "Airline Deregulation is Not Yet Cleared for Take-Off." *National Journal,* July 30, 1977, pp. 1193-1195.

"Controversy Over Proposed Airline Deregulation-Pros & Cons." *Congressional Digest,* June-July, 1978.

Corcoran, Patrick J. "Inflation, Taxes, and Corporate Investment Incentives." *Federal Reserve New York,* Autumn 1977, pp. 1-10.

Corrigan, Richard. "The Energy Tax Bill's Long Road From the Senate to Conference." *National Journal,* November 5, 1977, pp. 1716-1719.

Duncan, Marvin and Harshbarger, C. Edward. "A Primer on Agricultural Policy." *Federal Reserve Kansas City,* September/October 1977, pp. 3-10.

"Economic Revival: Can New York City Help Itself?" *City Almanac,* April 1977, pp. 1-15.

Eisner, Robert. "A Direct Attack On Unemployment and Inflation." *Challenge,* July/August 1978, pp. 49-51.

Feldstein, Martin. "The High Cost of Hospitals: and What To Do About It." *Public Interest,* Summer 1977, pp. 40-54.

Gans, Herbert J. "Jobs and Services: Toward a Labor-Intensive Economy." *Challenge,* July/August 1977, pp. 41-45.

Gray, Robert T. "The Taxpayer Fights Back." *Nation's Business,* April 1978, pp. 25-28.

Habicht, Ernst R., Jr. "America's Hidden Energy Policy: Federal Regulation and Taxation," *Current History,* May/June 1978, pp. 219-221; 224.

Harshbarger, C. Edward and Duncan, Marvin. "Solving the Farm Income Dilemma: the New Farm Program and the Outlook for 1978." *Federal Reserve Kansas City,* December 1977, pp. 3-12.

Helleiner, G. K. "Transnational Enterprises and the New Political Economy of U.S. Trade Policy." *Oxford Economic Papers,* March 1977, pp. 102-116.

Iglehart, John K. "And Now It's Carter's Turn to Try To Control Health Costs." *National Journal,* April 9, 1977, pp. 551-556.

Kahn, Alfred E. "Airline Deregulation: Getting From Here to There." *Policy Review,* Winter 1978, pp. 55-60.

Kennedy, Edward M. "The Case for Airline Deregulation." *Enterprise Journal of the National Association of Manufacturers,* November 1977, pp. 16-17.

Kroger, William. "Why the Farmers Are Angry." *Nation's Business,* January 1978, pp. 74-78.

Leahy, William H. "An Economic Perspective of Public Employment Programs." *Social Economy,* October 1976, pp. 189-200.

Lee, L. Douglas. "Carter's Inflation: How Hard Is He Trying?" *The Journal of the Institute of Socioeconomic Studies,* Summer 1977, pp. 20-26.

Lekachman, Robert. "Carter's Economics As Usual." *New Leader,* January 31, 1977, pp. 5-7.

Lens, Sidney. "The Sinking Dollar and the Gathering Storm." *Progressive,* May 1978, pp. 22-24.

Loving, Rush. "The Pros and Cons of Airline Deregulation." *Fortune,* August 1977, pp. 208-212.

Luttrell, Clifton B. "Farm Price Supports at Cost of Production." *Federal Reserve St. Louis,* December 1977, pp. 2-7.

McDonald, Stephen L. "Energy Policy, the Price System, and the Future of the Energy Economy." *Nebraska Journal of Economics and Business,* Winter 1978, pp. 23-36.

McNamara, William, "The Tax Credit Debate." *Change,* March 1978, pp. 44-45; 60.

Martin, Philip L. "Public Service Employment and Rural America." *American Journal of Agricultural Economics,* May 1977, pp. 275-282.

Meyer, Jane A. "Job Protection and Free Trade." *Editorial Research Reports,* December 16, 1977, pp. 955-972.

Moynihan, Daniel P. "Government and the Ruin of Private Education: Tuition Tax Credits." *Harper's,* April 1978, pp. 28-38.

Munnell, Alicia H. "The Carter Proposals for Social Security." *Challenge,* September/October 1977, pp. 57-58.

————. "Federalizing Welfare: The Fiscal Impact of the Supplemental Security Income Program." *New England Economic Review,* September/October 1977, pp. 3-28.

Nesbitt, Tom E. "How to Curb Medical Costs-Without Surrendering Free Choice." *Enterprise Journal of the National Association of Manufacturers,* July 1978, pp. 10-12.

Norman, Colin. "The Staggering Challenge of Global Unemployment." *The Futurist,* August 1978, pp. 223-228.

Orr, Daniel. "Toward Necessary Reform of Social Security." *Policy Review,* Fall 1977, pp. 7-30.

Oswald, Rudy. "Trade: The New Realities." *The AFL-CIO American Federationist,* July 1978, pp. 12-14.

Pfister, Richard L. "The Carter Tax Package." *Business Horizons,* June 1978, pp. 17-22.

Piore, Michael J. "Unemployment and Inflation: An Alternative View." *Challenge,* May/June 1978, pp. 24-32.

Quantius, Frances W. "A Questionable Aspect of Proposed Financing in the Energy Program." *Bulletin of Business Research,* September 1977, pp. 1-3.

Samuelson, Robert J. "Carter's Early Economic Choices: It's As Simple as 2+2=5." *National Journal,* January 8, 1977, pp. 59-65.

Schroeder, Richard C. "Farm Policy and Food Needs." *Editorial Research Reports,* October 28, 1977, pp. 807-824.

Schultze, Charles L. "Carter's Economic Policy." *Business Horizons,* June 1978, pp. 5-10.

————. "Inflation and Unemployment: The Dilemma of the Humphrey-Hawkins Jobs Bill." *Wage Price Law and Economic Review,* no. 1, 1976, pp. 65-70.

Seidman, L. William. "The Health of the Economy, Governmental Involvement and Capital Spending." *Journal of the Institute of Socioeconomic Studies,* Spring 1977, pp. 63-70.

Sennholz, Hans F. "Unemployment is Rising." *Freeman,* July 1977, pp. 387-396.

Shefter, Martin. "New York City's Fiscal Crisis." *Public Interest,* Summer 1977, pp. 98-127.

Slater, Courtenay and Lee, L. Douglas. "Economical Growth and Social Promises: Are They Compatible?" *The Journal of the Institute of Socioeconomic Studies,* Winter 1977, pp. 21-29.

Smith, Dan Throop. "Taxation of Capital in a Political Economy." *Tax Review,* July 1977, pp. 25-28.

"Social Security: There is a Better Way." *Citibank Monthly Economic Letter,* July 1977, pp. 9-12.

Sommers, Albert T. "The Package and the Recovery." *Across the Board,* March 1977, pp. 59-63.

Steffens, Dorothy R. "Employment by Mandate: The Promise of Humphrey-Hawkins." *The Nation,* January 21, 1978, pp. 50-52.

Stein, Rona B., "New York City's Economy: A Perspective On Its Problems," *Federal Reserve New York*, Summer 1977, pp. 49-59.

Tatom, John A. and Turley, James E. "Inflation and Taxes: Disincentives for Capital Formation." *Federal Reserve St. Louis*, January 1978, pp. 2-8.

Teal, Roger and Altshuler, Alan. "Economic Regulation: The Case of Aviation." *Policy Studies Journal*, Autumn 1977, pp. 50-62.

Underwood, John M. "U.S. International Transactions in a Recovering Economy." *Federal Reserve Bulletin*, April 1977, pp. 311-322.

Wachtel, Howard M. and Adelsheim, Peter D. "How Recession Feeds Inflation." *Challenge*, September/October 1977, pp. 6-13.

Weinstein, Bernard L. "The Demographics and Politics of Economic Decline in New York City." *Annals of Regional Science*, July 1977, pp. 65-73.

West, E. G. "Tuition Tax Credit Proposals: An Economic Analysis of the 1978 Packwood/Moynihan Bill." *Policy Review*, Winter 1978, pp. 61-76.

Young, John H. "Toward a Consensus on Inflation?" *Finance and Development*, March 1977, pp. 12-14.

Government Publications

Advisory Commission on Intergovernmental Relations. *Changing Public Attitudes on Governments and Taxes*. Washington, D.C.: 1978.

The Budget of the United States. Washington, D.C.: Government Printing Office, 5 vols., 1978.

Economic Report of the President. Washington, D.C.: Government Printing Office, 1978.

International Economic Report of the President. Washington, D.C.: Government Printing Office, 1978.

U.S. Congress. Congressional Budget Office. *An Analysis of the President's Budgetary Proposals for Fiscal Year, 1979*. Washington, D.C.: Government Printing Office, 1978.

U.S. Congress. Congressional Budget Office. An Analysis of the President's Budgetary Proposals for Fiscal Year, 1979. Washington, D.C.: Government Printing Office, 1978.

U.S. Congress. Congressional Budget Office. *Catastrophic Health Insurance, January 1977*. Washington, D.C.: Government Printing Office, 1977.

U.S. Congress. Congressional Budget Office. *Employment Subsidies and Employment Tax Credits, April 1977*. Washington, D.C.: Government Printing Office, 1977.

U.S. Congress. Congressional Budget Office. *Expenditures for Health Care: Federal Programs and Their Effects, August 1977*. Washington, D.C.: Government Printing Office, 1977.

U.S. Congress. Congressional Budget Office. *Federal Aid to Postsecondary Students: Tax Allowances and Alternative Subsidies, January 1978*. Washington, D.C.: Government Printing Office, 1978.

U.S. Congress. Congressional Budget Office. *Federal Assistance for Postsecondary Education: Options for FY 79, May 1978*. Washington, D.C.: Government Printing Office, 1978.

U.S. Congress. Congressional Budget Office. *Financing Social Security: Issues for the Short and Long Term, July 1977*. Washington, D.C.: Government Printing Office, 1977.

U.S. Congress. Congressional Budget Office. *Five-Year Budget Projections: FY 79-83*. Washington, D.C.: Government Printing Office, December 1977.

U.S. Congress. Congressional Budget Office. *President Carter's Energy Proposals: A Perspective*. Washington, D.C.: Government Printing Office, June 1977.

U.S. Congress. Congressional Budget Office. *Overview of the 1978 Budget: An Analysis of President Carter's Revisions, March 1977*. Washington, D.C.: Government Printing Office, 1977.

U.S. Congress. Congressional Budget Office. *President's FY 1978 Tax Expenditure Proposals, April 1977*. Washington, D.C.: Government Printing Office, 1977.

U.S. Congress. Congressional Budget Office. *Public Employment and Training Assistance, February 1977*. Washington, D.C. Government Printing Office, 1977.

U.S. Congress. Congressional Budget Office. *Recovery With Inflation*. Washington, D.C.: Government Printing Office, July 1977.

U.S. Congress. Congressional Budget Office. *The U.S. Balance of International Payments and the U.S. Economy, February 1978*. Washington, D.C.: Government Printing Office, 1978.

U.S. Congress. Congressional Budget Office. *U.S. Food and Agricultural Policy in the World Economy, April 26, 1976*. Washington, D.C.: Government Printing Office, 1976.

U.S. Congress. House Committee on Agriculture. *General Farm Bill: Hearings, Parts 1-2, February 17-March 4, 1977*. Washington, D.C.: Government Printing Office, 1977.

U.S. Congress. House Committee on the Budget. *College Tuition Tax Credits, April 28, May 12, 1977*. Washington, D.C.: Government Printing Office, 1977.

U.S. Congress. House Committee on the Budget. *Economic and Budget Impact of the President's Energy Proposals Hearing, June 29, 1977*. Washington, D.C.: Government Printing Office, 1977.

U.S. Congress. House Committee on the Budget. *Economic Aspects of Federal Regulation on the Transportation Industry: Hearings, July 13, 14, 18, 19, 1977*. Washington, D.C.: Government Printing Office, 1978.

U.S. Congress. House Committee on the Budget. *Economy and Economic Stimulus Proposals, January 24-25, 27, 1977*. Washington, D.C.: Government Printing Office, 1977.

U.S. Congress. House Committee on the Budget. *Report on College Tuition Tax Credits*. Washington, D.C.: Government Printing Office, November 1977.

U.S. Congress. House Committee on the Budget. *Rising Energy Prices and Alternative Energy Policies*. Washington, D.C.: Government Printing Office, November 1977.

U.S. Congress. House Committee on the Budget. *Task Force on Distributive Impacts of Budget and Economic Policies: Hearings, June 14-27, 1977*. Washington, D.C.: Government Printing Office, 1977.

U.S. Congress. House Committee on Education and Labor. Subcommittee on Employment Opportunities. *The Full Employment and Balanced Growth Act of 1977, February 8-10*. Washington, D.C.: Government Printing Office, 1977.

U.S. Congress. House Committee on Interstate and Foreign Commerce. *Energy and the Economy: Economic Impact of Alternative Energy Assumptions*. Washington, D.C.: Government Printing Office, 1978.

U.S. Congress. House Committee on Ways and Means. *Causes and Consequences of the U.S. Trade Deficit and Developing Problems in U.S. Exports: Hearings, November 3, 4, 1977*. Washington, D.C.: Government Printing Office, 1978.

U.S. Congress. House Committee on Ways and Means. *President's 1978 Tax Message: Prepared Statements of Administration Witnesses, January 30, 31; February 1, 1978*. Washington, D.C.: Government Printing Office, 1978.

U.S. Congress. House Committee on Ways and Means. Subcommittee on Social Security. *Long-Term Financing of the Social Security Trust Funds*. Washington, D.C.: Government Printing Office, 1977.

U.S. Congress. House Committee on Ways and Means. Subcommittee on Social Security. *President Carter's Social Security Proposals: Hearings: Parts 1-2, May 10-July 27, 1977*. Washington, D.C.: Government Printing Office, 1977.

U.S. Congress. House Committee on Ways and Means. Subcommittee on Social Security. *Short-Term Financing of the Social Security Trust Funds*. Washington, D.C.: Government Printing Office, 1977.

U.S. Congress, House Committee on Ways and Means. *Summary of the President's 1978 Tax Reduction and Reform Proposals, January 27, 1978*. Washington, D.C.: Government Printing Office, 1978.

U.S. Congress. House Committee on Ways and Means. *Tax Aspects of President Carter's Economic Stimulus Program: Hear-

ings: February 2-9, 1977. Washington, D.C.: Government Printing Office, 1977.

U.S. Congress. House Committee on Ways and Means. *Tax Treatment of Tuition Expenses: Hearings, February 14-17, 21, 1978.* Washington, D.C.: Government Printing Office, 1978.

U.S. Congress. House Committee On Ways and Means. *Taxation and National Energy Policy.* Washington, D.C.: Government Printing Office, 1976.

U.S. Congress. House Committee on Ways and Means. Subcommittee on Social Security. *Social Security Benefits.* Washington, D.C.: Government Printing Office, 1977.

U.S. Congress. House. *President's Hospital Cost Containment Proposal: Joint Hearings: Parts 1-2, May 11-13, 1977.* Washington, D.C.: Government Printing Office, 1977.

U.S. Congress. Joint Committee on Taxation. *Estimates of Federal Tax Expenditures, March 14, 1978.* Washington, D.C.: Government Printing Office, 1978.

U.S. Congress. Joint Committee on Taxation. *Tax Reduction and Reform Proposals.* Washington, D.C.: Government Printing Office, 1978.

U.S. Congress. Joint Economic Committee. *JEC Staff Analysis: Projected Taxes and Revenues Under President Carter's Energy Package.* Washington, D.C.: Government Printing Office, 1977.

U.S. Congress. Joint Economic Committee. *Joint Economic Report.* Washington, D.C.: Government Printing Office, 1978.

U.S. Congress. Joint Economic Committee. *The Social Security System: Hearings, May 26-27, 1976.* Washington, D.C.: Government Printing Office, 1977.

U.S. Congress. Joint Economic Committee. *Some Questions and Brief Answers About the Eurodollar Market, February 7, 1978.* Washington, D.C.: Government Printing Office, 1978.

U.S. Congress. Joint Economic Committee. *U.S. Economic Growth From 1976 to 1986: Prospects, Problems, and Patterns.* Washington, D.C.: Government Printing Office, 1977.

U.S. Congress. Joint Economic Committee. *U.S. Long-Term Economic Growth Prospects: Entering New Era, January 25, 1978.* Washington, D.C.: Government Printing Office, 1978.

U.S. Congress. Office of Technology Assessment. *Analysis of the Proposed National Energy Plan.* Washington, D.C.: Government Printing Office, 1977.

U.S. Congress. Senate Committee on Agriculture, Nutrition and Forestry. *Agriculture in the U.S.: Constraints and Opportunities, March 24, 1978.* Washington, D.C.: Government Printing Office, 1978.

U.S. Congress. Senate Committee on Agriculture, Nutrition and Forestry. *General Farm and Food Legislation: Hearings: Books 1 and 2, February 22-April 7, 1977.* Washington, D.C.: Government Printing Office, 1977.

U.S. Congress. Senate Committee on Banking, Housing and Urban Affairs. *Oversight on New York City Loan Program: Hearings, December 20-21, 1976.* Washington, D.C.: Government Printing Office, 1977.

U.S. Congress. Senate Committee on Commerce, Science and Transportation, Subcommittee on Aviation. *Regulatory Reform in Air Transportation: Hearings, March 21-24, 1977.* Washington, D.C.: Government Printing Office, 1977.

U.S. Congress. Senate Committee on Energy and Natural Resources. *Economic Impact of President Carter's Energy Programs: Hearings, May 3, 1977.* Washington, D.C.: Government Printing Office, 1977.

U.S. Congress. Senate Committee on Energy and Natural Resources. *Natural Gas Pricing Proposals: A Comparative Analysis, September 1977.* Washington, D.C.: Government Printing Office, 1977.

U.S. Congress. Senate Committee on Finance. Subcommittee on Administration of the Internal Revenue Code. *Recycling Energy Tax Revenues: Hearings, June 6-27, 1977.* Washington, D.C.: Government Printing Office, 1977.

U.S. Congress. Senate Committee on Finance. Subcommittee on Taxation and Debt Management. *Description of Bills Relating to Tuition Credits and Deductions: Hearings, January 17, 1978.* Washington, D.C.: Government Printing Office, 1978.

U.S. Congress. Senate Committee on Human Resources. Subcommittee on Health and Science Research. *The Hospital Cost Containment Act of 1977: An Analysis of the Administration's Proposal.* Washington, D.C.: Government Printing Office, 1977.

U.S. Department of the Treasury. *The President's 1978 Tax Program, January 30, 1978.* Washington, D.C.: Government Printing Office, 1978.

Index